THE RUNNER'S WORLD

BIG

BOOK

OF

RUNNING

FOR

BEGINNERS

LOSE WEIGHT, GET FIT, AND HAVE FUN!

THE RUNNER'S WORLD®

BIG BOOK OF RUNNING FOR BEGINNERS

JENNIFER VAN ALLEN, BART YASSO, AND AMBY BURFOOT

with Pamela Nisevich Bede, RD, CSSD

RODALE.

© 2014 by Rodale Inc.

Photographs © 2014 by Rodale Inc.

Printed in the United States of America
Rodale Inc. makes every effort to use acid-free ♾, recycled paper ♻.

Photographs by Mitch Mandel/Rodale Images

Book design by Elizabeth Neal

Library of Congress Cataloging-in-Publication Data is on file with the publisher.

ISBN 978–1–62336–475–5

2 4 6 8 10 9 7 5 3 1 Direct mail hardcover

We inspire and enable people to improve their lives and the world around them.
For more of our products, visit rodalestore.com or call 800–848–4735.

Dedicated to all the readers who have yet to take
their first steps but will soon be a part of the running community

CONTENTS

Part I
Getting Started

Part 2
Nutrition and Weight Loss

Part 3
Staying Healthy and Managing Injuries

Part 4
Appendix

FOREWORD

BY AMBY BURFOOT

The old Chinese proverb got it right: "The journey of a thousand miles begins with a single step." Rarely is this more true than when you start a beginning-running program.

The journey might be long and it might be arduous. So many things depend on your starting point, particularly your age, your fitness, and your weight. There's no reason to claim that this will be easy as pie, an instant makeover, or a 10-minute miracle. It probably won't.

But here's the big payoff: Nearly everyone who sticks with the program eventually reaches their goal. I won't go so far as to say "Your success is guaranteed," but I'll say it's about 99 percent guaranteed. That's an important point to remember when the going gets tough. Don't give up! Because if you stick with the plan, you'll reach the journey's end—your finish line.

It will take more than 1,000 steps. In fact, if you're counting, your step total will likely reach 100,000. That may seem an impossibly big number, but it's not—not when you break it down into small chunks. Not when you do a little at a time, and a lit-

tle more, and then a little more. A step at a time, day by day.

At any rate, you'll get there. Trust me. You won't have to call yourself a "beginning runner" anymore. You'll be a full-fledged runner, capable of reaching whatever goals you choose next. You could easily run a few 5-K races, for example. Or you could aim higher and choose to tackle a half-marathon, the incredibly popular race distance that has become a national sensation. You could even—yes, you could, with enough preparation—decide to enter a marathon, all 26 miles, 385 yards of it.

You are the captain of your own ship, and you get to choose what course you want to follow.

Or you could remain content running 2 or 3 miles several times a week, alone or with friends, as your personal, lifetime fitness program. Millions of runners do the same. They rarely enter races. They're happy for the stress-relieving, health-enhancing benefits of a consistent running program.

At last count, medical experts had proven more than 30 ways that fitness running can improve your health. These range from long-established truths like the increased heart health and longevity enjoyed by consistent runners to newer and exciting exercise-health links. Sure, the high-calorie burn of running will help you achieve and maintain a healthy weight. You can buck the rising tide of obesity and diabetes that is threatening the public health in sedentary societies worldwide.

Amazingly, you might also be able to ward off dementia and Alzheimer's. A few decades ago, we runners never imagined that our happy activity would stimulate the brain as much as it does the heart and the legs. Now such discoveries seem almost obvious. Exercise pushes fresh, vibrant blood to all parts of the body, the brain included, so why shouldn't all parts benefit?

Once runners worried that their "pounding" on the roads and trails might lead to broken bones and knee replacements. But today we realize that a modest pounding builds strong bones, while sitting (or swimming or riding on a bicycle seat) allows the bones to deteriorate. It turns out that bones are meant to support our weight, and that they grow weak and brittle when not utilized. In other words, bones are actu-

ally quite a bit like muscle. When you use them, they thrive. When you stop using them, they wither.

Similarly, while some runners develop knee arthritis, studies have shown that arthritis rates are as high or even higher among sedentary nonrunners. The knee joint and the muscles around the knee prefer activity to lack of activity. They also appreciate it when you don't force them to carry excess weight around all day long. Most runners do a good job of controlling their body weight, and this helps them avoid knee arthritis.

But I linger too long on the physical side of running. The mental story is even more powerful and much more important. While research has shown that runners generally have low rates of depression, it's the flip side of the coin that I find more impressive: Running gives you more energy and self-confidence. Running teaches you that you can accomplish more than you ever imagined possible.

It's been said a million times, but never more forcefully than by Oprah Winfrey after she completed the Marine Corps Marathon in 1994. "Running is the greatest metaphor for life, because you get out of it what you put into it," she said. In other words, you succeed in running when you put all your determination and self-discipline into it, and the exact same qualities will help you succeed at anything else you pursue: education, work, art, family, community, and more.

Some potential runners never make the big leap. They suffer from a crisis of confidence and an excess of excuses. These usually include: I don't have long legs, I'm too heavy, I'm too old, I was never a good runner in grammar school, I was never even good at baseball/ basketball/football/tennis/swimming, etc.

This perspective suffers from false logic. It assumes that you need certain physical traits or skills to be a runner. Nothing could be further from the truth (unless you're trying to win the Olympics, which I doubt you are).

To succeed in running, you need only one thing: a strong mind. Yes, your legs carry you across the ground, but only after your brain tells them to. The legs are merely an appendage, and besides, they've been supporting you for many years, so you know they are up to the physical task.

It's the mental task that is sometimes difficult and always crucially important. If you have the drive and determination to become a runner, you will succeed. You don't need a big heart, a thin waist, or long legs.

You only need the will to put your body in motion and to follow a sensible plan.

This book is full of sensible plans and much more time-proven advice. It will answer all the questions that come up in your early running, everything from your shoe questions to your diet questions to the one all runners encounter at some point: What should I do when it's too hot (or cold) to run outdoors? The answers are in the pages that follow.

But those pages can't give you the most important factor of all: willpower. That's where you come in. Only you can hitch your mind to a beginning-running plan and resolve to get going. And not to stop until you reach your goal.

I hope you'll begin today. You'll never find a better time. Good luck. Be sure to enjoy every step of the journey.

INTRODUCTION

BY JENNIFER VAN ALLEN

I don't think anyone ever forgets a first run. And not usually because it's such an awesome experience.

Mine took place in Indiana back in the 1980s. Up until that point, I had been utterly unathletic. The only practice I did occurred on a piano bench. Most of my free time was spent watching reruns of *One Day at a Time* while consuming large quantities of leftover mac and cheese. Like so many others, I was last to get picked for teams in gym class; I found anything even remotely physical thoroughly mortifying. My body was this thing from which I felt alienated, and yet also this bloated vessel in which I felt trapped.

I can't even remember what prompted me to go outside. Perhaps the cable went out.

What I do remember is how gripped with fear I felt, standing there in my driveway, trying to muster the courage to take the first step.

I wasn't scared of cars, rabid dogs, or even the discomfort of pushing my body farther than it had gone.

I was petrified that someone would see me. And laugh.

"Look at that girl trying to work out," I imagined they'd say. *"She looks so stupid!"*

They would find it hilarious that someone who clearly never intentionally sweats would be making an effort to do so.

To drown out those fears, I put on headphones, fired up my Wham! cassette, and started on a route away from the busiest roads. It felt so awkward at first, my flabby thighs rubbing, my Tretorns scraping the concrete, the sweat soaking through my cutoff cotton sweatpants. But somewhere along the way, the self-consciousness fell away. I got lost in how beautiful the clouds were, how fresh the breeze smelled, and how energizing the beat of "Wake Me Up Before You Go-Go!" felt blasting in my ears. There's a fairly good chance I was swinging my hips.

And then my worst fears materialized. A classmate drove by. The next day, loud enough for the crowd to hear, she commented on how silly I looked, without a clear destination, grinning for no apparent reason.

"You looked like a *total idiot!*" she said. "What were you *doing?*"

It took me a while to venture out again. When I did, I convinced a friend to come along. The walk became less about exercise and more about just hanging-out. So we went again, and again and again, until it just became our after-school routine.

In college, in a vain effort to fend off the freshman 15, I'd rise before dawn to walk and jog along the country roads, hours before any other students woke up. I found a peace that seemed thoroughly inaccessible at any other waking moment. I could take in the world without having to worry about what I looked like, being asked a question I couldn't answer, or encountering an awkward social situation I didn't know how to handle. I was free to dream. I could breathe.

Today, those are the same reasons that get me out the door each morning. On the empty, dark roads, I get to watch the sun rise and witness the world waking up, one little bird chirp and bunny hop at a time. I can glimpse the sights and sounds of my outer and inner worlds that are, at every other hour, muffled by the grime and clamor of everyday hustle and bustle. I feel ventilated.

No matter how bad I feel before the first step, my runs always renew me and unleash in me a sense of gratitude and hope. And

when I finish, all day long I ride the confidence boost I get from knowing that I had the courage to get out there and just do it.

It's a miracle that I took those first steps and kept going even after that first humiliating try. But it is a gift for which I am forever grateful. Running has brought me friends and adventures that I wouldn't have otherwise had. But most important, it has given me the patience, tenderness, and clarity to live my fullest life and to be the best version of myself for my family, my friends, and my work.

In this book, we hope you find everything you need to take *your* first steps.

We have compiled all the tools you need to get going, stick with it, and develop a love of running that lasts for life. You'll find all the information you need on walking, running, motivation, weight loss, nutrition, injury prevention, and strength training plus some of the best articles that have appeared in *Runner's World* on the subject. Additionally, you'll find the inspirational stories of people just like you who had the guts to get up, who found the determination to keep going and were rewarded beyond what they ever imagined for doing so.

You'll read about people like Andy Aubin, who overcame the intimidation of walking into a gym at 328 pounds and fell off the treadmill on his first try. He got up and went on to lose 133 pounds and finish half-marathons. And that's to say nothing of the transformation that came on the inside.

"It's empowering to be able to do something you never thought was possible. And that shifted everything," says Aubin. "Now I don't view anything as undoable. Nothing is off the table. That doesn't make it easy. But now I have the confidence to know that if I'm willing to put in the work, there's nothing that can't be done. That carries over into work and relationships and everything else."

For so many people, running is a way to rise up from the rock-bottom moments of life. John Golden, overcome after his wife's sudden death, woke up the next day and "couldn't stay still," he says. "I had to find a way to escape the grief, and the only thing I knew to do was grab a pair of shoes and run." Christine Casady started running after an agonizing, 2-year battle with infertility. "I needed to start a new chapter," she says. "I needed something to help pull me out of the hole that I had been in for so long." Jamie Kontos became a runner after she broke off her engagement. "It was about taking control of my life during a time when I felt completely helpless," says Kontos. Running helped Brian Robertson shed his "why me?" sense of resignation after being diagnosed with multiple sclerosis at the age of 25, just a few weeks before his daughter was born.

"I felt broken and sorry for myself," says Robertson, who went on to shed 145 pounds from his 310-pound frame. "Running helped me leave all that behind me."

Inspired as they are, most people find that the first days are never easy. The muscles cry. The cheeks flush with embarrassment. The shins feel like they're being stabbed, and the sweating and jostling just feel so uncomfortable.

"It took me a long time to realize that the runner's high wasn't total crap," says Jodi Edwards, who started running after she, too, was diagnosed with MS. "But every day I was able to go out a little bit longer or feel a little bit better afterward. So I'd talk myself down from the fear. And there was a sense of freedom, even when it was hard, because I could make my legs work like that. I was so thrilled that I was able to do it."

Indeed, step by step, for so many people running becomes a way to make themselves over from the inside out. It's a way to piece together a shattered self-confidence, renew tattered hope, and rebuild a sense of self that got trampled somewhere along the way.

"After a run, I feel like I can accomplish any goal I set my mind to," says Kontos. "I cannot control what happens at work or school, but I can control how I take care of myself. I feel more confident at work, school, and among my friends and family. Since I started running, I've become more outgoing and started tackling issues head-on."

ACKNOWLEDGMENTS

I'd like to thank the many great running teachers I've had through the years, all of whom willingly shared their passion, experiences, failures, and unrelenting drive for excellence. These particularly include John J. Kelley; Hal Higdon; Bill Rodgers; Dave Costill, PhD; and Jack Daniels, PhD.

Just as important: the thousands of beginning runners who persisted through the difficult early weeks of their new sport to eventually reach 2 miles, 5-K, and far greater achievements. Their successes often amazed me almost as much as they amazed themselves. Running is the perfect outlet for those who believe in the old saying "Where there's a will, there's a way." Every beginning runner inspires me and countless others by reproving the influence of determination and willpower.

—*Amby Burfoot*

I'd like to thank all of the experts who so generously shared their knowledge and their time for this book and for all the work we do at *Runner's World*. I am so indebted to my coauthors, Amby and Bart, for always making the time in their jam-packed schedules to share their knowledge with me and any other runner who needs it. I feel so blessed to be able to count them, my mentors, as my friends and colleagues. Many thanks go to Pamela Nisevich Bede, who, while juggling motherhood and a full-time job of her own, took so much time to be a part of this book and to help so many *Runner's World* readers with their nutrition and weight-loss questions. I am very grateful to coach and exercise physiologist Janet Hamilton, who designed The Starting Line plans and has been a tremendous mentor to me over the years. Many thanks to all the experts who contributed to this book, including Susan Paul, Adam St. Pierre, Christy Barth, Douglas Casa, Jeff Gaudette, Reed Ferber, Clint Verran, Bruce Wilk, and Heather and Kevin Vincent. Thank you to David Willey, John Atwood, Mark Weinstein, and Warren Greene for believing in this project and giving me the opportunity to make it happen. I am grateful to so many members of the *Runner's World* staff who contributed to this book in ways big and small, including Scott Douglas, Lindsay Bender, Barb Webb, Lori Adams, Chris Kraft, Kimberly Draves, Robert Reese, Hannah McGoldrick, Kevin Knabe, Mark Remy, Caitlin Giddings, Ted Spiker, Charlie Butler,

Caleb Daniloff, Marc Parent, and Carly Long. I am so appreciative of all the contributors to *Runner's World*, for graciously allowing us to excerpt many of the fine articles they did for the magazine for this book. Thank you to all of you beginners who found the courage to get going and stick with it, and to all of you who so bravely shared your stories with us. Above all, thank you to Peter, Noah, Kate, and Phoebe: for supporting my every cockamamy plan and for being the greatest gifts that a person could ask for in this very good life.

—*Jennifer Van Allen*

I want to thank the entire running community. Whether you're the first finisher or the last one to cross the line, the courage that you show to put yourself out there every day inspires me to do what I do. I often meet people who claim, "I'm not a *real* runner." But if you run, I assure you, you're a runner. You're demonstrating what's possible to so many others who are trying to get up the courage to start. And you're inspiring them to get going. Always remember, it's not about how far you go but how far you've come and what you've overcome to arrive where you are today. Don't ever stop. And never limit where running can take you.

—*Bart Yasso*

ABOUT THE STARTING LINE

The Starting Line is just that: a place to start running. It doesn't matter who you are, what you look like, or how much (or how little) you've exercised in the past. *Runner's World* launched The Starting Line as a digital destination to get the beginners the help, guidance, and encouragement they need to get going. The program includes:

- **FREE** beginner-friendly articles on weight loss, nutrition, walking and running, and more

- **FREE** e-mail access to our panel of experts on working out, weight loss, injuries, motivation, and nutrition

- **A FREE** private online community full of other beginners just like you. Our mission is to get you moving and help you reach your goals—whatever that means for you.

- **A FREE** Start Walking plan designed for people who are just starting to exercise. This 7-week plan will help you get into the habit of exercising on a regular basis and develop a foundation of fitness to begin your running life.

- **TRAINING** plans to help you Start Running, Run Nonstop (up to 30 minutes), Run Longer (up to 60 minutes), and Run Faster

Where Do I Begin?

The Starting Line is designed to accommodate people of all levels of fitness and ability. The best way to start running and get fit—without getting hurt—is to start where you are; not where you were in high school or where you hope to be 1 year from now.

The Starting Line training system was designed by exercise physiologist and coach Janet Hamilton, owner of Atlanta-based Running Strong, in partnership with the experts at *Runner's World.* Below find more details about each stage. Consider what kind of exercise you've been doing on a regular basis—three to five times a week—for the last 3 months and decide where it's best for you to start. Then go to runnersworld.com/the-starting-line to get going.

- **START WALKING:** For those who are not working out on a regular basis, the Start Walking stage will help you develop the fitness—and the habit—to start walking 30 minutes a day, four to five times a week.

- **START RUNNING:** If you're already exercising and want to start running, the Start Running stage will help you to add short bouts of running to your regular walks.

- **RUN NONSTOP:** If you're already exercising and want to reduce or eliminate walk breaks, the Run Nonstop stage will help you run for 30 minutes.

- **RUN LONGER:** If you're already running 30 minutes nonstop, the Run Longer stage will help you develop the endurance to extend your runs to 60 minutes.

- **RUN FASTER:** The Run Faster stage will guide you through your first speed workouts and help you develop the cardiovascular and muscular fitness you need to get faster.

For more information, visit the Web site **runnersworld.com/the-starting-line**.

PART I

GETTING STARTED

You've probably heard it said that "exercise is medicine," and Wylde Parnelle is living proof of that.

He had a heart attack at the age of 47, packed 210 pounds on his 5'4" frame, and had a resting heart rate of 90 beats per minute, blood pressure of 210/115, and was on large doses of blood pressure and cholesterol medication.

"I used to joke that I was in shape—and that round was a shape—but it was no longer a laughing matter," he says. "It took the heart attack to make me see the damage I had done to my body and decide it was time to change. I want to live a long, happy life. And I can't do that if I am overweight. Or dead."

Less than 4 years later, he's more than 65 pounds lighter and down to the smallest doses of cholesterol and blood pressure medications. He's run more than 4,300 miles and has finished 15 half-marathons and a full marathon. Now his resting heart rate is 55 beats per minute. His average blood pressure is 115/75.

"Running has changed me in ways I never imagined," he says, "and I will never stop."

Indeed, exercise *is* medicine. A raft of scientific evidence proves that a regular workout routine (150 minutes per week, which is about 30 minutes five times per week)—and running in particular—has health benefits that extend well beyond any pill a doctor could prescribe.

Studies have shown that running can help prevent obesity, type 2 diabetes, heart disease, high blood pressure, stroke, some cancers, and a host of other unpleasant conditions.[1] It will lower cholesterol, increase energy, and improve depression and anxiety.[2] If you're older, being fit will lower your risk of falling, mitigate age-related cognitive decline, and improve your quality of life. If you're overweight, it will help you shed pounds. If you already lost weight, exercise will help you keep it off better than diet alone. What's more, scientists have shown that running also vastly improves the quality of your emotional and mental life and even helps you live longer.

In the next section, you'll find all the tools you need to get started on an exercise routine, stick with it, and get fitter. Step by step, we'll walk you from where you are now—even if that's the couch—to your first 5-K and 10-K. Most important, we'll show you how to enjoy it. Along the way, you'll hear stories of people like Parnelle who reached their breaking points, drummed up the courage to take their first steps, and just kept going, despite embarrassment, fear, setbacks, injuries, and their own deepest doubts about whether they could do it. We hope that all the tools in this chapter—and these moving stories—will give you the inspiration and the know-how to take this journey yourself.

CHAPTER 1

THE BASICS

Running is simple. You just put on your shoes, step outside and go. Right?

Well, if you've ever tried it, you know it's not that simple. Or quite that easy.

Just ask Jeremy Oliver. Five years ago, tipping the scale at 400 pounds, he desperately wanted to start exercising and lose weight. He knew he had no choice if he wanted to be around to see his infant son grow up.

"I had the drive," says Oliver, 31, a banker from Columbia, Mississippi, "but never got to the point where I was successful."

Figuring that running was the simplest and most convenient way to start, he bought some minimalist shoes "that looked cool," put on a cotton sweatshirt, and headed for the track. He made it 200 meters huffing, puffing, and nearly fainting from the stabbing pains in his shins. "I thought my legs would explode," says Oliver. "I just figured I was the type of person who had no business running."

Like Oliver, most people have their fair share of false starts. But running doesn't have to be painful. Or embarrassing. Or leave you so discouraged that you want to throw your running shoes out of the window.

In this chapter, you'll find all the basic training tools you need to get started, from what to wear and where to run to how to get perfect running form and how to handle your first group run.

Check with the Doctor

Before you start any exercise program, it's best to get a checkup, especially if you're contending with injuries or you have a family history of heart attack, diabetes, or other chronic illnesses. If you're over 40 or your doctor recommends it, get a stress test. Answer the following questions from the American College of Sports Medicine to decide if you should make an appointment.[3]

- Has your doctor ever said that you have a heart condition and that you should only do physical activity recommended by a doctor?

- Do you feel pain in your chest when you do physical activity?

HOW REGULAR EXERCISE DOES A BODY GOOD

If you've been working out regularly, you've already discovered it: No matter how good or bad you feel at any given moment, exercise will make you feel better. But what you may not realize is exactly *how* working out improves your quality of life. Here's a guide.

1 IT WILL MAKE YOU HAPPIER. It goes beyond just the "runner's high"—that biochemical rush of feel-good hormones known as *endocannabinoid*s. Researchers have found that even a single bout of exercise—30 minutes of walking on a treadmill—can instantly lift the mood of someone suffering from a major depressive disorder.[4] And even on those days when you have to force yourself out the door, exercise still protects you against anxiety and depression, researchers have found.[5] Other studies suggest that exercise helps you cope with anxiety and stress even after you're done working out.[6] Yet more research has shown that just 30 minutes of running for 3 weeks boosted sleep quality, mood, and concentration during the day.[7]

2 IT WILL MAKE YOU THINNER. So you know that exercise burns calories while you're working out, but the sounds-too-good-to-be-true news is that the burn continues even after you stop. Studies have shown that regular exercise boosts "afterburn"—that is, the number of calories you burn after exercise.[8] (Scientists call this EPOC, which stands for *excess post-exercise oxygen consumption*.) That's kind of like getting a paycheck even after you retire. And you don't have to be sprinting at lightning speed to get this benefit. This happens when you're exercising at an intensity that's about 70 percent of max VO_2. (That's a little faster than your easy pace.)

3 IT WILL STRENGTHEN YOUR KNEES (AND YOUR OTHER JOINTS AND BONES, TOO). It's long been known that running increases bone mass and even helps stem age-related bone loss.[9] But chances are, you've had family, friends, and strangers warn you that

- In the past month, have you had chest pain when you were not doing physical activity?

- Do you lose your balance because of dizziness or do you ever lose consciousness?

- Do you have a bone or joint problem (for example, back, knee, or hip) that could be made worse by a change in your physical activity?

- Is your doctor currently prescribing drugs (for example, water pills) for your blood pressure or heart condition?

- Do you know of any other reason why you should not do physical activity?

If you answered yes to one or more of these questions, see your doctor before you start becoming much more physically active or before you have a fitness appraisal.

"running is bad for your knees." Well, science has proven that it's not. In fact, studies show that running actually improves knee health.[10]

4 IT WILL KEEP YOU SHARPER AS YOU AGE. Worried about "losing it" as you get older? Working out regularly will help you stay "with it." A 2013 study published in *Psychonomic Bulletin & Review* concluded that the evidence is "insurmountable" that regular exercise helps defeat age-related mental decline.[11] Studies consistently found that fitter older adults scored better in mental tests than their unfit peers.

5 IT WILL HELP FEND OFF CANCER. Maybe exercise doesn't cure cancer, but there's plenty of proof that it helps prevent it. A vast review of 170 studies in the *Journal of Nutrition* showed that regular exercise is associated with a lower risk of certain cancers.[12] To name a few:

- **COLON CANCER:** risk reduced by 40 to 70 percent
- **BREAST CANCER:** risk reduced by 30 to 40 percent
- **PROSTATE CANCER:** risk reduced by 10 to 30 percent
- **ENDOMETRIAL CANCER:** risk reduced by 30 to 40 percent
- **LUNG CANCER:** risk reduced by 30 to 40 percent

6 IT ADDS YEARS TO YOUR LIFE. Even if you just meet the minimum amount of physical activity—(30 minutes of exercise per day, 5 days a week), you'll live longer. Studies show that when different types of people started exercising, they lived longer. It even helped smokers and people suffering from conditions like heart disease.[13]

How Running Changed My Life

Brian Robertson became a runner, lost half his body weight, and gained control over multiple sclerosis

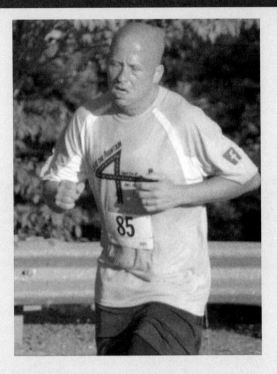

In 2012, Brian Robertson hit rock bottom. A decade earlier, at the age of 25, just 2 months before the birth of his first child, he'd been diagnosed with multiple sclerosis, a chronic, often disabling disease that attacks the central nervous system. By 2012, he weighed 330 pounds. He had high blood pressure and high cholesterol, and his doctors told him that he was way too young to be taking medication to treat these conditions. *There's a better way to solve these issues*, one doctor said. *Push back from the table and get some exercise*, another said.

So Robertson started walking. A lot. He'd rack up 15 to 20 miles a day, walking for 2 to 3 hours in the morning after dropping his daughters off at the bus stop, and 2 to 3 more hours after lunch.

It's unknown how the MS will progress and impact him in the future. For now, his vision is impaired—most of the time he has blurred vision; sometimes he has double vision. So on the road, he uses his other senses to listen for oncoming cars and barking dogs and does his best to stay out of the way of both. He gets periodic muscle spasms in his hands and feet.

He gets flulike symptoms from the injections he takes to slow the progression of the disease.

But Robertson hasn't let the symptoms—or questions about how the disease will progress—stop him. If anything, he says, having the disease has motivated him to work out harder and get healthier.

"I feel like the MS is something I have to overcome," he says. "When I was first diagnosed, I felt broken and sorry for myself. I have left all that behind me, and running helped me do that."

AGE: 35

HOMETOWN: Union Mills, North Carolina

What's your regular workout routine? I run 5 days a week.

What was the biggest hurdle, and how did you get over it? Getting past the mental wall that I created myself. I had myself believing that I couldn't do this because of my disease. A few years ago, I took my daughters to an amusement park. My older daughter wanted to ride a ride. We stood in line for almost an hour. Our time came to get on the ride, and the bar that holds us in would not fit over my belly. We had to leave, and she didn't get to ride. I felt so bad. On all those days I thought about not running, I thought of my girls and that day at the amusement park. That gets me out the door.

What kinds of changes did you make to your diet? I had a horrible diet before. I ate fast food, fried food, mostly processed foods, and very few vegetables and fruits. I never paid attention to portion sizes or nutritional information. Then in May of 2012, I started juicing and changed everything. I still drink a gallon of green juice a day. We do not have sodas in our home. When I do eat meat, it is turkey, chicken, or shrimp. I eat Greek yogurt a few times a week.

What is the biggest reward of your running life? Running has given me a sense of confidence. I am not the fastest, but it is fun and I am improving, and that is great. The biggest reward came at a 5-K. Someone said to my older daughter, "Look at him go; he sure is fast!" She turned and said, "Yeah, he is my Daddy." I can't express how it made me feel to make her proud of me. Running did this for us, and I plan to run as long as I can.

What advice would you give to a beginner? It is better to run smart than run fast. Read about running. Seek advice from other runners. Take your time in training and don't log too many miles.

Favorite motivational quote: "There will be haters. There will be doubters. There will be nonbelievers, and there will be you proving them wrong."

What's your long-term goal? One day, I want to run the Asheville City Marathon and the Outer Banks Marathon. I want to become a certified personal trainer to help others reach their weight-loss goals.

What advice would you have for others who have MS? Just get out and do what you can. Don't be afraid to push yourself. You only fail by not trying. Don't listen to those who try to define you by your illness. After you start an exercise program, listen to your body and rest as needed.

What Should I Wear?

When you first start, it's tempting to dust off whatever sports gear is already in your closet. But it's not a good idea, regardless of what kind of fashion statement you do or do not care about making. A few pieces of running apparel and some good-quality shoes can make a huge difference in the quality of your exercise life and how enjoyable your workout is. After all, it's hard to have any sort of fun when you're wearing a sweat-soaked cotton T-shirt that chafes your skin into a bloody-raw state. Major advances in apparel and shoe technology have created a wide array of products that will help keep you cool, cozy, and unscathed. You don't have to splurge on an extensive running wardrobe, but you won't regret investing in a few well-made basics. Some high-quality items will ensure that you're comfortable, no matter how far or fast you go. Here are the bare essentials that you need to get going.

TECHNICAL SHIRTS AND SHORTS: Avoid cotton apparel. Instead choose socks, shirts, pants, and shorts made of "technical" materials, which pull sweat and moisture away from your skin. They're lightweight, and they prevent irritating and painful chafing that nontechnical fabrics may cause. In the summer, they help you stay cooler. In the winter, you'll be warmer. Look for materials like nylon, wool, Lycra, Coolmax, and Merino wool.

HAT: For the summer, get a cap or visor that will keep the sun out of your eyes. For the winter, get a warm hat that covers your ears.

UNDERWEAR: Here, too, stay away from cotton; it absorbs sweat, which can keep you cold and lead to chafing. If you're wearing shorts, it's okay to rely on the liner and go underwear free—it's a personal choice. If your shorts or pants don't have a liner, wool or synthetic underwear will offer the insulation and support you need.

SPORTS BRA: Every female runner needs the right sports bra—one that fits well, offers adequate support, and wicks away sweat. Try on a variety of brands and styles to find the perfect bra for you. To get the perfect fit, grab three sizes to try on—the cup size you normally wear, one that's smaller, and one that's larger. Straps shouldn't gape, dig into skin, or move around. You should be able to slide two fingers under each strap. The base band should feel snug and lie flat. If the bra's material wrinkles or gathers anywhere, it's too big. If your skin bulges out in spots or if the bra's edges cut into you, it's too small. Once you've found a bra that fits well, run in place for 15 seconds. The bra shouldn't twist or ride up when you move.[14]

REFLECTIVE GEAR: If you run before sunrise or after sunset, it's critical to wear gear that helps you see and be seen. Your best bet is a handheld light or a headlamp. Drivers will see the light, but they'll also see the movement and figure out that you're a runner. At the very least, wear a reflective vest or a blinking red light.

A WATCH: At first, all you'll need to know is how long you've been running. Any watch will do. As you progress, you might invest in a heart rate monitor or a GPS watch, which can tell you how fast and how far you're going, as well as your pace and heart rate. There are dozens of gadgets out there, from the simple to the elaborate. Some runners swear by these devices; others do fine without them. There certainly are some benefits: These devices provide feedback on how hard you're working, which can help you keep from working out too hard (which can lead to injury) or too easy (which may cause your fitness to plateau).

Get Good Running Shoes

Spending more than $100 on a pair of running shoes might seem indulgent. But shoes that offer the support and fit your feet need are actually the cheapest form of health insurance you'll find. Worn-out or ill-fitting shoes are a leading cause of injury. "There's no magical shoe that makes running easier, but a bad shoe will ruin your running," says Bruce Wilk, a Miami-based physical therapist, coach, and owner of The Runner's High specialty shop. Follow these tips to make sure you get the pair that you need.

Don't skimp. Making a beeline for the On Sale rack is not a good idea. Don't shop by price. Get the pair that fits you best.

Consider this: Whatever your new shoes cost, it is likely less than the money and time you'd spend seeing the doctor because you got hurt.

See the experts. It's best to go to a specialty running shop (not a big-box or department store) where a salesperson can watch you run and help you select the right pair for you. Our store finder at runnersworld.com /store-finder can help you find a specialty running store near you.

Size yourself up. You may think you know your size, but it's best to get your feet measured each time you buy new shoes. Your feet change over time, and one model's fit can be different from another's.

Bring what you've been wearing. When you go shopping, take along the shoes, socks, and any inserts that you've been using. That way you can make a realistic evaluation of how well the new shoe will fit your feet.

Make some space. Many people end up getting a running shoe that's a half size larger than their street shoes. The extra room allows your foot to flex and your toes to move forward with each stride. When you're standing with both shoes on, make sure you have at least a thumbnail's space between the tip of the shoe and the end of your longest toe. Try shoes on both feet and take them for a test run around the shop, on a treadmill, or on the sidewalk.

Don't be a trendsetter. There is a dizzying array of shoes to choose from, and many people are wooed by shoes that "look fast" or a promise to cure an injury. But there is no one best shoe for everyone. Only one shoe offers your feet the unique support and fit you need. Try on as many different models and pairs as possible. And what about those minimalist shoes designed to mimic barefoot running? There's no scientific evidence that forgoing shoes decreases injury risk for everyone. When you're just starting out, stick with traditional running shoes.

Keep up the rotation. Shoes should be replaced every 300 to 500 miles. Keep track of the date that you bought them in your training log, and record your mileage daily so you know when it's time for a new pair.

Where to Work Out

Running builds bone and muscle strength. To prevent injury—and burnout—it's a good idea to map out a few safe, scenic, and traffic-free routes that you feel comfortable on in various weather conditions and at different times of day. But what's best—the road? Treadmill? The trails? Or the track? Here's a guide to the trade-offs you'll need to make with any kind of surface.[15]

Asphalt Roads

Sidewalks are your best option. But in many areas, they just don't exist. If you have to hit the asphalt, be sure to pick safe, flat, low-traffic stretches that have plenty of space on the shoulder so that you can step to the side to avoid oncoming vehicles. Always run facing traffic—it's easier to see oncoming cars, and cars will see you; wear bright or reflective attire (especially at night or at dusk); and avoid using iPods or wearing headphones (better to hear approaching vehicles). If you are going to run with headphones, run with only one earbud in; you want to make sure that you can still hear outside noises, such as the sound of an approaching vehicle. Assume that drivers do not see you; be sure to wave to them as they come toward you, and give a wave of thanks if they let you pass. Allow at least 3 feet between you and the passing vehicle. If you're running with someone else on the road, go single file when cars need to pass. Run with proper ID and carry a cell phone with emergency contacts taped to its back.

Trails

This softer surface can be great if you've struggled with overuse injuries like runner's knee, iliotibial band syndrome (also called IT band syndrome), or shin splints. Just be wary of "technical" trails with lots of roots, rocks, and uneven ground that cause your feet to land at an angle. Avoid trails if you've ever had an ankle sprain. It increases your risk of a repeat sprain, which is more likely to occur on soft, uneven surfaces. For

ESSAY

Starting to Run? Abandon All Reason

By Marc Parent, author of "The Newbie Chronicles" column, *Runner's World*

Here is what I call the abandon-all-reason-and-do-it-now approach to your first run ever. Explained simply, what you have to do is this: Abandon all reason and do it now. Put down whatever you are holding, tell anyone in the immediate vicinity to hang on a second, walk calmly through the nearest exit, and when you hear the door close behind you, take off. Three rules: Go only about as fast as a 2-year-old at top speed; stop when you feel tired, no matter how short the distance; and then walk back.

It's okay if you want to wave and point ahead like you need to catch a bus to disguise the rather personal fact that you are running for no other reason than to begin the long, slow journey to a healthier mind and a happier body. I know how embarrassing it is to suddenly care about your health when it looks as though you've ignored it for so long. I've been there. So put a few bills in one hand and, if anyone looks at you suspiciously, wave them over your head and shout, "Pizza guy—forgot your tip!"

The abandon-all-reason run is good not only for the first run ever but also for the first run in years or the first run after a potentially run-ending hiatus, or really any run when you just don't feel like running. The point is to not think too deeply about it. You can either put this off until you get the perfect shoes/weather/outfit/opportunity, or you can start calling me names and head out the door now.

Okay, then!

Now that you're a runner (and yes, you may call yourself a runner after just one brief, slow trot), how do you get out again tomorrow, next week, next month, next year? You know why you should stick with it, but if you don't know how to stick to it, you might as well build a wall of happy ignorance around yourself and eat a whole bowl of cashews. There's nothing worse than knowing why you should do something without knowing how. Any dope can tell you why you should stop eating the cashews, but try to find the genius who can tell you how.

Despite a litany of fits and starts, I somehow survived the long, excruciating run-hating period and made it to the other side with an ability to tolerate and even (on good days) enjoy successive sweat-soaked miles. Discipline played only a minor role in my transformation. I relied on a hodgepodge of tricks, cheap thrills, and occasional deep thoughts laid out here in no order of importance—they were all important. I made plenty of mistakes when I started running 5 years ago, but I'm still in, so I must have done something right. If only one of these points keeps you from quitting, then, as they say, this will all have been worth it.

Keep it comfortable. *Easy* may never be the first word that comes to mind when you think about running, but it should be more tips for going off road, see "Your First Trail Run" below.

Sand

It's best to stay away from sand unless it's hard-packed. It's unstable and can twist the knee, ankle, and hip. If you do run on sand, keep it short. Avoid sand altogether if you have a history of ankle sprains or Achilles tendinitis.

Grass

Grass is a great alternative if you're just getting back into walking or running following an injury. On grass, the bulk of th[e] from your footfall goes into the [g] instead of reverberating back up you[r] you're prone to plantar fasciitis, tread fully. You're more likely to overpronat[e] this soft, uneven surface.

Track

While tracks may bring up bad memories of grade-school gym class, they can be an ideal place to start running outside. They're flat and traffic free, and the distance is measured. You don't have to worry

(continued on page 14)

YOUR FIRST TRAIL RUN

Trails offer a change of scenery that can refresh your routine, give your bones and joints a break from the impact of pounding on pavement, and even give your fitness a boost. Here are some tips to help.

LOOK FOR THE RIGHT TRAIL. Before you get started, it's best to start with trails that are flat, dirt-packed, asphalt, bridle path or fitness trails, macadam, or even paved Rails-to-Trails routes. Avoid technical terrain, stay away from doubletrack trails, which often have gravel, and singletrack trails, which are often narrow dirt paths and strewn with rocks and roots that can make footing challenging.

FORGET ABOUT PACE. It's best to focus on level of effort—not how fast you're going—when you hit the trails. With uneven footing and an unfamiliar route, it's only natural that your pace will slow. Take it as easy as you need to avoid falling. You'll still get a great workout.

EXPECT SOME SORENESS. With the uneven surface, your muscles, joints, and ligaments will be worked in ways that they aren't when you're pounding pavement. So you may feel a little soreness in the 2 days after the workout, particularly in your ankles, calf muscles, or shins.

MIND YOUR MANNERS. If someone is coming toward you, stay to the right. If you see another runner or a hiker or cyclist ahead of you, call out "On your left" before you pass.

in the beginning. If you suddenly realize your gut has reached the edge of your desk and you hit the road in a panic to try to erase the problem with a desperate, blistering run, you may go out a few more times, but at some point shortly thereafter, you'll quit. On the other hand, if you go out and stop the moment you grow uncomfortable, you'll think running is easy because it actually will be. Your long-term chances of continuing a brief, easy habit are much greater than they are for a desperate, punishing one.

Don't worry about speed. Go as slow as your pride allows—as slow as the people you ridiculed before you tried this yourself. If you run alone on desolate country roads like I do, you're at an advantage. And you can always speed up when the rare car passes. The person in the car doesn't care how fast or slow you're going, by the way.

Tell someone. Walk up to your most unsupportive acquaintance and inform him you've started running. This is preferably a person who is as lazy as you were just before the first run; someone who will chuckle or even make fun of you. Ridicule is a strong motivator.

Get new shoes. I had a hard time with this one because there were decent shoes lying all over the house. Not running shoes, but I didn't want to spend $100 on something I wouldn't use in a month. Which is exactly why you should buy them. Get the expensive ones that will shame you, from the closet floor all the way across the room, into a run.

Find a running partner. It doesn't matter if he is faster, slower, or right on pace. You have to have one. I see my partner, Gerry, once a week or so. He's an affable tyrant. I need an affable tyrant. Every new runner does.

Put on blinders. Believe you're the only person in the world who runs this well. There is only one road: the one you're on. There is only one body: yours.

Keep the cashews. If you give them up at the same time you start running, you'll grow to resent the running. One battle at a time. If you do everything at once, you'll do them all badly.

Put off thinking. Draw no sweeping conclusions about running while making your way up a large hill, if it's hotter than 80 degrees, during or following a cramp, on the scale, or before the ibuprofen kicks in. While you're at it, make no conclusions about spouses, children, friends, or pets at these times either.

Race. Don't wait until you can actually "race." What you need more than a race is to see people cheering for you. You need to run with a mob of strangers and then eat bananas and bagels with them—the best, you'll swear, you've ever tasted.

If you're still sitting comfortably with your feet up, reread the dangerous third paragraph. The first run is the shortest, slowest, craziest one you'll ever do. If you've been a bad runner for a long time, you can turn the train around in less than 5 minutes. It might feel like a silly little exercise that means nothing, but that's only true if you never do it again.[16]

about dodging roots, curbs, or aggressive motorists. Many schools open their tracks to the public when they're not in use. Call ahead to ask. (For more, see "Track 101" below.)

The Pool

Aqua jogging is a great low-impact workout that can boost your fitness A flotation belt allows you to "run" in deep water, so you can use the same stride as you do on solid ground. And if you're injured, aqua jogging can help you stay fit while you rehab. Here

are some tips from Jeff Galloway, *Runner's World*'s "Starting Line" columnist, on how to make the most of your time in the water.[17]

- **EASE INTO IT.** Using a flotation belt, start running at a depth at which your feet lightly touch the bottom; this helps you establish an upright body alignment. Then move into deeper water, maintaining your stride. Run 5 minutes, then rest 5 minutes. Repeat two to four times. Each session, increase the length of the run seg-

TRACK 101

The track isn't just for speedsters. In fact it can be the perfect place for new runners. Here are the basics you need to know the first time you hit the oval.[18]

FOLLOW THE RULES. Many schools open their tracks to the public during times when school isn't in session. Plan your workout around open hours, and make sure you don't interfere with special events.

GO COUNTERCLOCKWISE. Most runners travel counterclockwise on the track. To avoid collisions, you should, too.

LEAVE THE HEADPHONES AT HOME. When you are close to fatigued runners in a confined space trying to hit top speed, you'll want to tune in to what's going on around you.

CLEAR LANE ONE. The innermost lane of the track is typically the place for the fastest runners. If you're warming up, cooling down, or

running slower, move to an outer lane. (*Note:* Schools sometimes bar the public from using multiple inside lanes—for example, lanes one through three—to preserve them for their athletes.)

KNOW THE NUMBERS. Most tracks are 400 meters around, as measured in lane one; that's just a bit less than $\frac{1}{4}$ mile. Here are some other helpful measurements.

- **200 METERS:** the length of the straightaways
- **800 METERS:** roughly $\frac{1}{2}$ mile or two laps around the track
- **1600 METERS:** roughly 1 mile or four laps around the track

ment and decrease the rest until you can run for 30 minutes continuously.

- **TURN UP THE INTENSITY.** At first, keep your effort level easy. No huffing and puffing. Once you get comfortable in the pool, gradually speed up the turnover of your legs so you're breathing at a rate that's the same as you would during a moderately paced run.

- **SWIM SOME LAPS.** Swim a lap or two during your rest periods or alternate pool runs with a lap workout: Swim one lap easy, rest for 20 to 30 seconds, then swim a slightly faster lap. Rest 1 minute, then swim two easy laps. Rest 1 minute, then swim two to four fast laps, resting as much as you wish after each.

- **MIMIC ROAD WORKOUTS.** For a long run, simply run in water for the same duration of time you would run on land. For speed workouts, shorten your stride and quicken your turnover, moving your legs faster, and keep the duration of your effort and recovery the same. During rest periods, move your legs slowly and gently.

TRACK TERMS

Here are some key terms that you might hear at the track. For a complete dictionary of running terms, see "A Guide to Common Running Terms" on page 229.

INTERVALS: Technically, *intervals* refers to the time you spend recovering between speed segments. But people generally use it to refer to track workouts in general, or workouts where you alternate between fast and easy bouts of running.

RECOVERY: Walking or easy jogging between faster-paced segments. Recovery lets your heart rate return to the point where you're ready to run fast again and helps you regain the energy you'll need for the next burst of speed.

REPEATS: The fast segments of running that are repeated during a workout, with recovery in between. If you're training for a marathon, you might run 800-meter (or $1/2$-mile) "repeats" four times, resting for 400 meters (or $1/4$ mile) in between.

SPLIT: The time it takes to complete any defined distance. If you're running 1 mile, or four laps around the track, you might check your "split" after you have covered four laps.

Treadmill

Not ready to step outside? Treadmills offer a safe, convenient way to get your workouts even when it's dark, snowy, or dangerously hot. And the music, the TVs, and the company of other people can make the miles roll by much easier. The belt's cushioned surface reduces stress to your back, hips, knees, and feet. And it's clear of obstacles, like uneven terrain, rocks, and traffic. It's also warm and dry, no matter what the weather. Find a gym nearby with treadmills and hours that fit your schedule. Before you sign up, find out when the prime times are so you can steer clear and be sure to get an open treadmill.

TREADMILL TRAINING

The treadmill can be a lifesaver when the weather is bad, or you're homebound caring for kids. And while studies have shown that the stress your body sees running on the treadmill is very similar to running outside,[19] there are some unique injury risks you face when logging monster miles on the 'mill—even beyond the risk of falling off the back of the machine.

Jay Dicharry, director of REP Biomechanics Lab at Rebound Physical Therapy in Bend, Oregon, has conducted research showing that the torque of the ankle and hip joints is similar on the treadmill as it is running on the ground outside. "People might have that preconception (that there's a difference between running on a treadmill versus outside) but it's not actually been shown," he says.

But factors like the uniformity of the treadmill surface, and the tendency to let form fall apart and to overstride, can set you up for injury if you're not careful.

Plus, because the treadmill surface is so uniform, if you don't vary your pace, change the treadmill grade, or do some of your runs outside, you risk turning smaller aches and pains into full-blown injuries, just as you would if you ran all of your miles on the exact same track or stretch of road.

"It's important to remember that you run the treadmill," says Dicharry, author of *Anatomy for Runners*. "Don't let the treadmill run you."

Here are some steps to make your time indoors as easy as possible.

PROBLEM: You can run faster on the treadmill than you can on the road. Because the treadmill keeps moving even as you tire, you overstride to keep up with the moving treadmill and ultimately strain a hamstring. "Some people allow themselves to cheat more on form when they're running fast, whether they're on a treadmill or running outside," says Dicharry. "But if you're on a track or on the road and you're tired, you'll slow down. A treadmill doesn't let you do that. You have to press a button to slow down."

Solution: Try to match the stride rate you have when you're running on the road, says Dicharry. If your stride rate—the number of steps you take per minute—is much slower on the treadmill than it is outside, that's a sign that you're struggling to catch up with the treadmill belt and likely risking injury, and you need to slow down. To find your stride rate, count the number of steps one foot takes in 20 seconds. Multiply that times three. Then double it. That's your stride rate.

PROBLEM: Treadmills bore you to tears, so you cut all your workouts short or skip them altogether.

Solution: A structured workout may help the miles roll by more easily than slogging through easy miles at the same pace. You might try this tempo workout which you can do as you watch a sitcom:[20] After 10 minutes of easy running to warm up, ramp up to your tempo pace when your show begins. Jog for recovery during the commercials, then return to tempo pace during the show segments. Cool down with 5 minutes of easy running. (Find more boredom-busting workouts at runnersworld.com

EASE INTO IT

Logging all your miles on the treadmill? Step outside gradually with this 6-week plan suggested by Adam St. Pierre, coach and exercise physiologist from the Boulder Center for Sports Medicine. If you're doing some outside running year-round, you can make a quicker transition. As always, listen to your body, and stay particularly alert for aches and pains in your hamstrings, calves, and hip flexors.

WEEKS 1–2: 75 percent of miles on treadmill; 25 percent outside
WEEKS 3–4: 50 percent of miles on treadmill; 50 percent outside
WEEKS 5–6: 25 percent of miles on treadmill; 75 percent outside

/treadmill-training.) And you don't just have to slug it out solo on the treadmill. Hit the gym and run alongside a friend you wouldn't ordinarily get to outside because you run different paces. Or reserve your favorite books, podcasts, or movies for your treadmill time. After all, on the treadmill, you don't have to worry about the danger of being plugged in and not hearing traffic, as you would when running outside. Or make a new playlist. Studies have shown that music

MAINTAINING GOOD FORM ON THE TREADMILL

To avoid injury, aim to run as relaxed on the treadmill as you do outside, experts say. Here's how.

- **JUST LET GO.** Holding on to the handrails causes excess rotation in the lower body. "Your arms are critical in terms of maintaining forward velocity," says Reed Ferber, director of the Running Injury Clinic at the University of Calgary. If you're holding the handrails—just as when you're pushing a jogging stroller—the upper body rotates less, which means the lower body has to rotate extra to compensate. That can lead to pain in the knees, shins, Achilles, and IT band, says Adam St. Pierre, coach and exercise physiologist from the Boulder Center for Sports Medicine.

- **LOOK STRAIGHT AHEAD.** Keep your gaze forward and level. If you're staring at a TV screen that's slightly to the side, you're going to end up craning—and straining—your neck, says Jay Dicharry, director of REP Biomechanics Lab at Rebound Physical Therapy. And by the same token, be careful not to stare down at a number on the treadmill display that might be below you, causing you to hunch over. "Whatever you're looking at should be in front of you."

- **KEEP YOUR TOES UNDER YOUR NOSE.** Have a leg swing as close to your body as possible, says Dicharry. Avoid overstriding, which can lead to hamstring strain.

- **DON'T RUN WITH A NARROW STANCE.** St. Pierre says he sees people who run with too narrow a stance on the treadmill, possibly because they're worried about stepping off the moving belt. So pick a belt that's as wide as possible. Your feet should not completely cross over the center line of your body. As you run, imagine a line dropping straight down from your belly button. The inside edge of each shoe should just barely touch the edge of the line, or at most one-third of the shoe should cross over. Excessive crossover puts more stress on the inner ankle, shin, IT band, and hip, says St. Pierre.

- **DO THE BODY SCAN.** Periodically check in with yourself, St. Pierre suggests. Ask yourself, How does this pace feel? What's my heart rate? What's my stride rate? If your treadmill is in front of a mirror, focus on running symmetrically, he says. Your hands should approach, but not cross, the center line of the body. You should see your hands coming up to your nipples with each stride. Make sure your feet aren't crossing over the center line. If you notice your knees collapsing in, you may add some glute-strengthening work with exercises like hockey kicks. Pay attention to whether your trunk shifts side to side. It's normal to lean a little to the right when you are landing on your right leg and a little to the left when landing on your left leg, but if you're leaning excessively, you may have some weakness in the glutes, he says.

lowers perceived effort, so you feel less tired than you would without music, and fast-tempo music in particular can pump you up before a hard effort. (Check out runnersworld.com/running-playlists for ideas.)

PROBLEM: You do all your training on the treadmill, but your race is outside. The whole purpose of training is to prepare your body for the rigors you will face on race day. If you're constantly running on a flat belt, without having to contend with factors like wind resistance or weather, the challenge will be greater on race day.

In addition, because running on a treadmill is so redundant, doing all your runs inside can worsen issues, like it would if you did all your running on the exact same stretch of track or road every day. "Because your foot is striking every single time the same way, if you've got little niggling issues, they can become magnified on a treadmill because there's no variability," says Dicharry. "Anything that's more variable is going to work your body more evenly."

Solution: Do some workouts, like long runs, outside so you get experience dealing with headwinds, elevation changes, and running in rain, snow, heat, or any other weather you might face. And on the treadmill, vary your pace and your incline as much as possible to mimic—or just resemble—the changes you'll encounter outside. Technology can assist with that: Most treadmills have preset programs that provide variation in elevation and speed. "You want to train your body for unexpected events. The more you can vary the conditions, the better," says Reed Ferber, director of the Running Injury Clinic at the University of Calgary. And as you're transitioning to outside running, start off running by effort, not pace, as you get accustomed to contending with wind resistance, warns Adam St. Pierre, coach and exercise physiologist from the Boulder Center for Sports Medicine. "At first, you may have to slow your pace significantly outdoors."

RUNS OF THE MILL

Training on a treadmill doesn't have to be torture. Doing a structured workout can help the time pass faster. And it can help you get fitter. Try one of these workouts assembled by *Runner's World* contributing editor Lisa Jhung, next time you have to take your workout inside.

IF YOUR GOAL IS TO: Introduce your legs to the treadmill.[21]
Try this: Start at an easy pace. After 5 minutes, crank up the speed by 0.5 mph for 1 minute, then back down to your easy pace for 2 minutes. Crank up the incline by 0.5 percent for 1 minute, then back down for 2 minutes. Continue alternating, experimenting with pace and incline.

IF YOUR GOAL IS TO: Return from injury or illness.
Try this: Alternate jogging and walking— 2 minutes jogging, 2 minutes walking—for a total of 20 to 30 minutes. If your injury or illness doesn't flare up, increase the run interval during subsequent workouts to 3 minutes, then 4, then 5 (and so on), and bring the walking segment down to 1 minute in between.

IF YOUR GOAL IS TO: Make the most of 15 minutes.
Try this: This workout is recommended by Starting Line columnist Jeff Galloway. Warm up with 3 minutes of easy running. Gradually increase to a faster pace for 2 minutes. Then walk for 30 seconds. Repeat that cycle. Then run for 3 minutes fast and walk for 30 seconds. Repeat that cycle. Cool down by walking for the remaining time.[22]

IF YOUR GOAL IS TO: Make the most of 20 minutes.
Try this: Warm up at a slow to moderate pace for 5 minutes, then increase the speed to your fastest sustainable pace and hold it for 10 minutes for a hard tempo. Cool down for 5 minutes.

IF YOUR GOAL IS TO: Beat boredom.
Try this: Watch TV. During the show, run at an easy-moderate pace, then punch up the speed to run hard for the duration of the commercial. Return to your moderate pace when the show resumes. If no TV is available, listen to music, varying your pace or effort by song.

IF YOUR GOAL IS TO: Improve speed at any distance.
Try this: Set the treadmill to a 2 percent incline. After warming up, match speedy segments with equal recovery (e.g., 1 minute hard, 1 minute recovery) for 1-2-3-2-1-1-2-3-2-1 minutes, then cool down.

IF YOUR GOAL IS TO: Get a long workout in with a run/walk pattern.
Try this: This long workout, from "Starting Line" columnist Jeff Galloway, will allow you to build endurance. Start with 3 minutes of easy jogging. Then do a 2:1 run/walk ratio and repeat that three times. Then do a 3:1 run/walk ratio and repeat that three times. Finish the workout with a 2:1 run/walk, followed by a 1:1 run/walk.[23]

building your fitness. It's best to begin any of these classes at a time when your running mileage is low. Once you're familiar with the class, try to fit it in on your recovery day or the day after an easy run. Don't feel pressure to keep up with the class; if you're feeling sore or worn-out from your runs, it's fine to modify the moves to suit yourself.

Ease into it. If you're going to a class, start with a beginners' class, or find an instructor who offers modified poses or exercises. Tell your instructor that you're new, and whether you have any chronic injuries, so that he or she can show you how to ease into the exercises without getting hurt.

Listen to your body. If something starts to hurt, back off or take a break; if it keeps hurting, stop and seek help from a trainer. It may take time for your muscles to adapt to something new, so be patient.

Get the balance right. Cross-training, while very beneficial, can fatigue athletes, warns running coach and exercise physiologist Susan Paul. Remember that the purpose of cross-training is to improve your running. So limit cross-training sessions to two times a week, 1 hour or less, and at a moderate intensity level. This means it's okay to skip some of the jumps in a spin class, or lighten the tension on the bike, or cut the kick segment short in your swim class. Cross-training should enhance your running, not detract from it.

Popular Ways to Cross-Train

There are an unlimited number of ways to keep up your fitness when you're not running. Below you'll find a guide to some popular options at the gym.[24]

ELLIPTICAL: It's easy to adjust these machines to mimic the range of motion you use while running. The activity will stimulate your neuromuscular system to maintain the adaptations your muscles have made to training, while giving the bones and tendons a break from the pounding of running.

ROWING MACHINE (ERGOMETER): Rowing can offer a great cardiovascular workout and strengthen your core, upper body, and glutes. Because it requires a lot of upper-body strength, which most people lack, even a short workout is going to feel tough. So be prepared for a hard workout. Start with 15 minutes of rowing and build gradually from there. It's especially important to consult a trainer before getting on an ergo to get pointers on proper technique, as it's easy to hurt your back if you don't.

CYCLING: Whether you're riding your bike on the road, boarding a stationary bike at the gym, or heading into a spin class, it's critical to work with an expert before you start so that you adjust the seat and the handlebars to the position that fits your body best. If, say, the seat is too low, you could end up putting excessive stress on the joints and putting yourself at risk of injury. Focus on cycling at a high cadence—at least

85 revolutions per minute—and in a low gear. This will develop the quick leg turnover that will help you when you're running.

Cross-Training Workouts

The following routines, recommended by *Runner's World* expert Jeff Galloway, allow you to mimic the running workouts that you'd do on the road.

- **EASY**—Do the following on a single machine or on a combination of machines: Warm up, then "run" on the elliptical, spin, or row at a very easy pace or resistance for 2 minutes. Increase the intensity or resistance for 2 minutes. Repeat the sequence three or four times, then cool down.

- **MODERATE**—Complete one sequence of the easy workout (above) and also walk for 10 minutes. Then do this: "Run," spin, or row easy for 3 minutes, followed by 3 minutes of increased intensity or resistance. Repeat the sequence three or four times, then cool down.

- **HARD**—Complete one easy workout, walk for 5 minutes, complete one moderate workout, walk for 5 minutes. Then do the following: "Run," spin, or row easy for 1 minute, then do 2 minutes at a moderate pace, then 1 minute hard. Repeat four times, then cool down.

Hills

Hills build leg and lung power and help you build stamina and muscle you'll need to run faster down the road. You won't feel fast going up hills, but you'll feel strong. Hills do put extra stress on your muscles, tendons, and bones, especially the knees and Achilles tendons, so if you have an injury, talk to your doctor before you do any audacious climbs.

Get some variety. It's easy to fall into a rut of doing the same route, day after day. If

HILL REPEATS

Learning to run well both uphill and downhill builds muscle, tendon, and bone strength, says coach and exercise physiologist Janet Hamilton, founder of Running Strong in Atlanta. Uphill climbs build strength the hips, hamstrings, quads, and calves, while downhill running builds quad strength. And a hill repeat workout is a great way to get those benefits. Start by incorporating hills that take 60 seconds to climb. Run down the hill to recover, with the same level of effort you had going up, then climb it again. Repeat this cycle four or five times. Learn to take advantage of the free gift of gravity without losing control or braking with your feet. Find the fine line between those two extremes and you'll get enough recovery for the next hill repeat. And you'll be much better off in the long run!

you do, after a while, the hills won't feel as challenging. So incorporate a variety of short, steep climbs and long, gradual inclines. Running the shorter climbs at higher intensity will give you a quick cardiovascular boost and help improve your aerobic capacity. Running the longer climbs at an easier effort will help build your endurance as well as strength.

Exercise some cruise control. When you're going downhill, it's easy to fly and enjoy feeling gravity's pull. But steep descents can tax your muscles even more than big climbs: They pound your muscles more. Running downhill requires the muscles to lengthen and make eccentric contractions, which can generate more force (and soreness) than running up hill or on level ground. It's easy to go fast and let the feet slap the pavement or try to "brake" with your legs. See page 62 for tips on good running form. To reduce risk of injury, start by running on a gentler surface, such as grass, before moving to the road. Sometimes it helps to think "go with the flow" or "don't ride the brakes."

First, forget about pace. When you first run uphill, it's going to take more time and effort. Don't worry about your pace. Just try to maintain an even effort, says coach and exercise physiologist Janet Hamilton, founder of Running Strong in Atlanta. You don't want to feel completely spent by the time you get to the top. Your goal is to have enough energy at the top to carry your momentum forward. If you fade and need to "recover" at the top, then you need to work on running with an even effort! Focus on letting the road rise to meet you. Push up and off the hill. Once you master that, then try to work on maintaining the same pace on the way up the hill as you do on flat ground. Obviously, this is going to feel harder. But the same rules apply: Try to carry your momentum up and over the top of the hill.

AMBY'S ADVICE

Find an exercise partner or a group of them. For most runners, the biggest challenge we face is motivation. And the best way to stay motivated is to have a training partner or training group who is waiting for you at a specified time and place. It's important to make sure your training partners run at about the same level as you, and that they are socially compatible with you. Fortunately, there are so many runners today, and so many ways of being in touch with them with tools like Facebook, that anyone who wants a training partner should be able to find one or many. Even if you run with a partner just once a week, it will keep you motivated on other days, because you'll want to keep in shape for the workout you do together.

Running with Others

At first, Jeremy Oliver never even ran with his "training partners." He and some buddies from work each started training for a local 5-K and would just report back to one another about how their workouts were going, new gear that they were trying out, and other ideas on how they could get better. He admits he was a little nervous about it at first.

"I hesitated a little bit because I was concerned how they would perceive me," he says.

But over time, he felt the benefits. "It keeps you accountable and motivated," he says. "If I do not meet my goal, they're the first guys who will tell me I'll get it next time," he says. "Sharing my running with others has become one of my largest long-term assets."

Sports psychologists have long known that athletes perform better in groups than alone. You can definitely benefit from buddying up. The miles roll by quicker when you're chitchatting away. It's harder to hit snooze on the 5 a.m. alarm when you know that you've got someone waiting for you. And having company with whom you can commiserate about your setbacks and celebrate your successes can help you stay on track.

"I wanted partners, so that those 5:30 a.m. wake-up calls weren't as scary when I was starting, and it was still dark," says new runner Tara Cuslidge-Staiano (see page 196). "When I'm accountable to other people, I usually have more incentive to get up and get going. Plus, it's nice to have someone there to talk you into 'just a few more minutes' when you want to stop." Here are a few key principles to keep in mind when working out with others.

Be choosy. Though it seems like runners are everywhere, finding someone you want to work out with again and again can be tricky. Be prepared to ask direct questions about schedules, needs, and goals.

Find matching paces. It's important to find a person or group of others with a compatible pace. Even if you're just running for fitness and your partner has a marathon on a bucket list, that's okay, as long as you can and want to comfortably run the same pace for your workouts. If you're running faster than you feel ready to, you'll eventually get injured. And if you're slowing down uncomfortably—and unhappily—to run with the other person, it will be difficult to sustain the running relationship.

Check your calendars. Next to pace, possibly the most important factor is being able to meet at a mutually convenient time and place, even if that's side-by-side treadmills at the gym. If you have to shoehorn the workout into a packed schedule that's not *really* convenient for you, and you're stressing and speeding to meet up with your buddy or rushing home afterward to pick up the kids, the partnership isn't likely to last. Before your first run, discuss your schedules. Your answers don't have to match perfectly, but this information will help you plan workouts to benefit you both.

Encourage, don't compete. Keep your eyes on the prize. Your goal is to improve your fitness and your health and become a runner. If it gets to the point where you're just focused on getting faster than the other person, at the cost of listening to your own body and progressing at a pace that works for you, you risk injury. Only run with someone who can genuinely cheer on your success and help you improve. And you want to be that same cheerleader for that other person. If you sense the vibe getting too competitive, then it might be time to go your separate ways.

Determine compatibility. Ask potential partners (and yourself): On a scale of 1 to 5, how competitive are you? It's also wise to discuss how each of you will react if the other has to cancel a workout or arrives late. "I believe it's chemistry," says Cuslidge-Staiano. "You want to enjoy yourself on a run, even when you're pushing. So you want to be able to relate and laugh."

Go for some test runs. In the euphoria of meeting someone who might be a good running mate, it's easy to, in your excitement, commit to a long-term rela-tionship. But it's a good idea to go for a few test runs before you commit to more. "You can go on a 'first date' with a person without committing to a marriage with it," says Cuslidge-Staiano. "Some people just don't make good running teams. You'll know if something is working for you. You'll also know if it's not."

Keep it honest. If schedule conflicts, injuries, or differing rates of improvement add stress to the relationship, be honest and move on. You don't want to let personality conflicts throw you off track and get in the way of accomplishing your big-picture personal goals for health and fitness. If the other person is gunning for a pace that is too fast or slow for you, let that person go ahead and leave the hard feelings behind.

Maintain your independence. If your partner gets derailed because of injury, scheduling conflicts, or something else, don't shut down your own running goals. "Just because your running buddy gets sick doesn't mean you're free to veg out on the couch," says Cuslidge-Staiano. "As much as you depend on another person or people, you still need to maintain your own goals." She's seen many groups on a training program, and when the training ends, the people who were once so active stop being active altogether without the support of the structured workouts.

Group Dynamics

When Christine Casady went to her first group run, she had the same fears that most people do: being the last person in the group, holding others back, and being someone that everyone else has to wait for. In addition, the class called for a distance on the outer limits of her ability, on trails that were new to her.

"Going to a new place and a new class and not knowing anyone was nerve-wracking enough," she says. "But going to a class that I didn't have the training or endurance for, I felt even more nervous."

Nevertheless, she got up the courage to go, figuring "the fear of feeling the disappointment of not trying was greater than the fear of trying," she says.

Even though she was unfamiliar with the trails, took a wrong turn, got lost, and they had to send out someone to find her, it wasn't as horrifying as she feared. "There was so much support and camaraderie that those fears never had a chance to materialize," she says. "The moment I rejoined the group, it was like it never happened."

Not only that, but she found everyone superfriendly and welcoming. "There were all levels, ages, and genders," she says. "The first person I introduced myself to turned out to be one of the fastest runners of the group and also one of the most welcoming."

She completed the class and now calls that small step of going to the first one the "turning point" of her life.

"I drew strength from the encouragement and camaraderie I got from others; I found happiness completing the class successfully, and I felt invigorated by the intensity of the workout," she says. "It was a stepping-stone for future increased miles, races, relationships, and friendships. I found hope, love, recovery, and life in running. In so many ways, it changed my life forever."

Indeed, for many people, group runs can be a great way to mix social life and fitness. Most running shops have regular workouts, and you can find groups near you through local chapters of the Road Runners Club of America (RRCA.org) or sites like dailymile.com. But there's no doubt about it; it's downright scary to walk up to a group of runners you don't know and start running.

These tips can make your first outing a little easier.

Reach out ahead of time. Before you go out for your first run, contact someone in the group to find out about the typical pace, distance, and types of runners for each event. Try to find people who run at your pace or slower.

Introduce yourself. Remember: Most people join group runs so they can relax and socialize. So go ahead and introduce yourself just as you would at any other gathering where you are new. Chances are, when regulars spot an unfamiliar face, they'll reach out to welcome you. Everyone has been the new guy at one point.

Get familiar with the route. To avoid getting lost, find out about the course the group will take when you join them. Drive it beforehand if possible, so you don't get lost.

Decide on the vibe. Some groups are serious about speed; others are more social and welcome runners with a wide range of abilities. Chances are, you'll tune in to it right away when you show up for a run. If it's not for you, keep shopping around for another group.

RUNNING WITH YOUR DOG

Incorporating your canine companion into your exercise regime can be a great way to stay consistent and get some quality together time. In fact, a 2013 study in the *Journal of Physical Activity and Health* showed that dog owners were more likely to meet recommended physical activity requirements than people without dogs.[25] Here are some tips from Maui-based dog trainer and runner Jt Clough to keep in mind to ensure health and happiness for you and your pup.

START SLOW. If you're just starting to run, chances are your dog is, too. Keep in mind that the dog's muscles, bones, and joints may need just as much time to adapt to your new routine as you do. Start with short distances and build gradually, just as you do to avoid injuries of your own.

WATCH THE HEAT. If it's hot, particularly if it's humid, the dog isn't going to be able to go as far as you can. Dogs have sweat glands only in their paw pads, noses, and tongues, so they're more prone to heat exhaustion than humans. Check the heat index before you go out, and leave the dog in if it's above 55.

DON'T OVERDO THE DRINKING. If you're going for 30 minutes or less, your dog likely won't need water during the run; just be sure to offer it before you go and after you

return. "If you have them drink a whole bunch, the dog will get an upset stomach, just like you would," Clough says.

BE PATIENT. It can take time to teach a dog that you're going to run, not just walk. Don't be surprised if the first few times, the dog wants to spend the entire time stopping, going to the bathroom, and exploring every smell. Remember, this is the dog's normal walking routine. It's going to take time for him to get used to running. Slowing up when the dog stops gives the dog the cue that it's okay to slow down. So when the dog wants to slow down, keep moving. "The dog isn't aware that you're training for the 5-K," says Clough. "It's your job to lead the dog." She adds, "It's not that your dog doesn't like running. He [or she] just doesn't know the new protocol."

Remember, everyone was the new guy once. Every runner started out going solo and remembers vividly how nerve-wracking that can be. "Give the group at least one chance," says Casady. "If it's not for you, you haven't harmed anything in trying. If you don't try, you'll never know what you might be missing."

FREQUENTLY ASKED QUESTIONS ABOUT TRAINING

Every day, letters come into *Runner's World*'s "For Beginners Only" column from beginners of all levels of fitness and experience, all over the world. Exercise physiologist and coach Susan Paul, of Orlando Track Shack Foundation, answers many of them. Here are a few of the most common questions we get, and Paul's expert answers.

I'm just starting to run. Do I have to take walk breaks?

For most folks, it can be a good idea. The idea behind walk breaks is that they stave off muscle fatigue and delay exhaustion of glycogen stores, therefore allowing a runner to go longer and finish stronger. They can be a great technique to use when increasing the distance of a long run. Walk breaks also break up the distance mentally. For example, instead of thinking, "I'm running 30 minutes today," which can be very intimidating, you can think in terms of running for 1 or 10 minutes and then walking. When a large goal is broken down into smaller increments, it suddenly becomes very doable! While initially walk breaks may feel like a disruption to your normal rhythm, the body adapts fairly quickly and soon they become your new rhythm.

That does not mean you have to use walk breaks on every workout. It's okay to mix up your training and do some runs with them and some runs without them. Think of walk breaks as simply another tool in your toolbox; they can come in quite handy on some runs, and on other runs you won't need them. Routine can be very grounding, but it can be easy to become set in your ways, so using different run routes, running at different times of the day, running continuously, and also running with walk breaks and running with groups are great ways to change things.[26]

Is it okay to run every day?

Creating a solid base can take up to 6 months for a brand-new runner. At first, it's a good idea to work out for 3 to 5 days a week. Adding more run days primarily depends upon your goals, so define your goals first before increasing mileage unnecessarily. We tend to think that if a little is good, then more is better, but that's not always the case.

If you're new, and especially if you're over 40, it's very important to give your body plenty of time to recover so it can adapt to the training. The body responds in different ways and in different time frames to the applied stress of running. Running stimulates the body to expand its aerobic capacity by building new blood capillaries, which is somewhat similar to building new highways, so more oxygen and nutrients can be delivered quickly and efficiently to working muscles. Slow-twitch oxidative muscle fibers are developed, blood volume increases, and glycogen stores expand. More mitochondria and enzymes, necessary for greater energy production, are created. Bone cells are stimulated and make stronger bones; connective tissue, muscles, tendons, and ligaments are strengthened, and on and on. We don't realize all of this internal work is going on because we can't see it; however, it becomes evident when overuse injuries, like tendinitis, stress fractures, muscle strains, or shin splints appear.

Overuse injuries are the result of demanding too much too soon. This is even more important for masters runners, because research has shown us that the body's processes slow with age. Adaptation time and recovery between workouts simply take longer for those who are over 40 than they do for younger runners.

That said, there are some options if you feel like you are ready to ramp it up a bit. Three-days-a-week training schedules usually have a speed day, a strength day, and a long run day. For a speed workout, after a warmup, push the pace for 2 minutes, then back off and recover for 3. Repeat this for the rest of the run. On your strength day, strive to gradually increase the distance of this run by 10 percent each week. After increasing mileage for 2 or 3 weeks, drop your mileage back down for 1 week to give yourself more recovery time.

Three-days-a-week training programs also typically call for 2 additional days of aerobic cross-training, like swimming, spinning, or rowing. Preferably, cross-training is an aerobic activity that differs from running enough that it allows your running muscles a break but still stimulates your aerobic system for a training response. This allows you to increase your aerobic base while not fatiguing your running muscles. Cross-training is intended to enhance your running, not detract from it. It is best done at a moderate intensity level for 45 to 60 minutes, twice a week. (For more information, see "Cross-Training" on page 29.)

If cross-training does not fit into your weekly schedule, then you can add 1 additional run day per week. Think of it as a recovery run and keep the run short and the effort easy. Listen to your body as you train and you will learn what is best for you. All runners can benefit from weight training, so consider adding weights into your training plan twice a week, too.

Increasing muscle strength can improve performance and may even reduce the risk of injury![27]

I have been running for 6 months and have hit a plateau. I feel stuck, like I am not getting more fit. What do I do?

When we begin running, we experience dramatic physical improvements. Within a relatively short period of time, we are able to run faster and longer, lose weight, and feel great. Success comes easily. We follow a training plan, run several days a week, same pace, same time, same place. But then one day, all of a sudden, it doesn't seem to work anymore. Improvements flatten out. We don't get faster, we can't run longer, a few pounds creep back on, and our enthusiasm dwindles. Welcome to the dreaded training plateau!

When fitness gains level out, it's simply an indication that the existing routine is no longer challenging enough to stimulate further physical changes. Congratulations! Your body has met the bar that you set. But if you wish to continue improving, it means you need to change your routine and up the ante.

Understanding the training process helps one appreciate the plateau. The physical exertion of running triggers a cascade of physiological responses at the cellular level, affecting all of the body's systems. Once stimulated, the adaptation process to meet the demands of this new stress begins

and continues until the demand is met. Some of these adaptations take 4 to 6 weeks, while others may take 4 to 6 months. As adaptations occur, the body is better equipped to handle training, and running becomes easier.

Training increases are applied in gradual increments. As training physically stresses the body, it responds by becoming stronger. The amount of applied overload must be just right; too much and we break down, not enough and no physical response is elicited. It's a bit like our feet developing calluses or blisters. Too much overload, and we develop blisters or an injury; the right amount of overload, and we develop calluses or strength.

Naturally, once the body has adapted to the training load, we reach a plateau. If improvement is still desired, a training plan designed to stimulate the body at this new fitness level is required, and we begin adapting again to achieve an even higher level of fitness.

If you have reached a plateau, review the three fitness components and begin by manipulating one variable at a time.

Increase frequency. Are you ready to add another day or two of running? Then consider increasing the frequency component by adding another run day. Don't increase your mileage more than 10 to 20 percent of your weekly volume to avoid too much overload too quickly.

Increase intensity. This is a great option if you don't have more time to invest in your training, if you enjoy racing, or if you tend to train at the same pace most of the time. Increase intensity by adding a speed day or a hill run into your weekly routine. Hills naturally increase the intensity of a run.

Increase duration. If you prefer longer runs, increase the duration component by adding some miles to your weekly long run; just how long depends upon your running goals. For example, when training for 5-Ks and 10-Ks, gradually build up to 10 miles for a long run.

Keep a log to track your training and the changes you make so you can continue adjusting and fine-tuning your training as needed.

Next time you hit a plateau, remember to congratulate yourself rather than berate yourself. Take stock of your training plan and redefine your goals. Figure out where you wish to go from here, and that will help you decide which components to change.[28]

How can I run farther without getting injured?

Consider alternating your run days rather than running consecutive days. In other words, try running 3 days a week rather than 5 days a week for 8 to 12 weeks. Why 3 days a week? Because recovery is an essential part of training, too. The body needs time to adapt to the new physical demands being placed upon it, and research has shown that it takes a minimum of 4 to 6 weeks for adaptation to occur from the training stimulus.

My difficulty in increasing your distance may come from a lack of recovery time.

After 12 weeks, assess your progress, and if you feel ready for more running days, add 1 day of running. Adapt to 4 days a week over the next 4- to 6-week period and then, if you feel ready, add another day of running. It's always better to start conservatively and build gradually. Sometimes less is more!

Also, vary the distance you run every workout. Avoid running the same distance, or the same route, day after day. Keep it fun and interesting! Plan a different route and a different distance for each run. Next, designate 1 day of the week as your long run day. This is your longest run of the week. Use the long run day to increase your mileage to your desired distance. Your other 2 run days of the week will be of shorter distance than your long run day. For example: run one: 3.5 miles; run two: 3 miles; run three: 5 miles (long run day).

Increase total weekly mileage by 10 percent each week. That gives your body time to adapt to the new distance and get stronger and reduce your risk of injury or burnout. Running 3 days a week also gives you freedom to cross-train. You can swim, spin, lift weights, do yoga, or take Pilates two or three times a week to complement your running. Cross-training benefits your running by building muscle strength and flexibility.

Focus on the distance, not the pace, for now. Keep it comfortable and at a conversational intensity level, especially when increasing your mileage. If you need to take walk breaks, use them to catch your breath and recover. Breathe deeply, exhale forcefully, and relax your shoulders. If necessary, you can opt to walk more frequently to cover a given distance and, very often, knowing you have the next day off from running helps motivate you to do the distance that day![29]

I'm training for my first 5-K. How much time off should I take to recover afterward?

The downtime of recovery is when the body heals, repairs, and strengthens from the rigors of training and racing, which results in improved fitness.

A 5-K recovery plan would include 3 easy days after the race. Give yourself 1 day completely off after the race to sleep in and enjoy your accomplishment as a nice reward. This also gives you time to see how you fared and notice any postrace aches or pains. Follow your day off with 2 easy days. Days 2 and 3 postrace can feature cross-training at an easy intensity

level or short runs done at an easy pace. By day 4, you should feel able to resume your usual training routine. Most important, learn to listen to your body! If you feel you need additional days off or more easy days, take them.

One great training tool for monitoring your training and recovery is measuring your resting heart rate (RHR) daily. It's easy to do, free, and provides you with valuable objective information on the status of your body. If you don't feel like getting up to run one morning, do you ever wonder if you are really fatigued or if you are just being "lazy"? Sometimes, it's hard to tell whether we are lacking motivation or if we really need a rest day. Monitoring your RHR can give you that objective data and let you know if you need to sleep in, change a hard run to an easy one, or if you just need to suck it up.

Measure your RHR first thing in the morning, after awaking but before hitting the caffeine, and record that number in your training log. Repeat this process at the same time each day. After recording it for several days, you will establish your baseline measurement for your normal RHR. Find your pulse by placing your first two fingers on the underside of your wrist, at the base of your thumb. Once you locate your pulse, count the number of beats for 1 minute, or count the beats for 30 seconds and multiply by 2. Your RHR stays much the same each day, give or take a few beats, so when your RHR is elevated, it's a red flag. When your RHR is elevated by as much as 5 beats, take notice and go easy. If it is elevated by 10 beats or more, it's a real warning, and it may be best to take the day off. Our RHR can be elevated for a variety of reasons—stress, lack of sleep, not recovered from a previous workout, an illness, overtraining, etc. While you may not be able to pinpoint the exact reason your heart rate is elevated, simply knowing that it is elevated provides you with valuable information. Armed with this knowledge, you can decide your next step and choose to sleep in, shorten a run, or skip the speedwork. And if you just don't feel like getting up, but your RHR is normal, suck it up and hit the road! This information allows you to stop second-guessing your decisions. Keep your runs easy until your heart rate returns to its normal level and then resume your regular training.[30]

Running Etiquette 101

By Mark Remy, author of *The Runner's Rule Book*

When I first starting running, I had no idea what "PR" meant. I was too embarrassed—or was it too proud?—to ask anybody. So I blundered my way through conversations with other runners, desperately hoping no one would ask about my "PR," whatever that was.

Eventually I learned that PR stands for "personal record"—the fastest time you've ever clocked over a certain race distance (also known, mostly in the UK, as PB or personal best). I learned lots more stuff, too, of course. But it came in dribs and drabs, from a multitude of sources—or, worse, through trial and error. *Which side of the road do I run on? Where do I line up during a race? Is it okay to spit?* Looking back, I wish I'd had some sort of cheat sheet.

Well, beginners, guess what? Here is just such a cheat sheet. To compile it, I asked my running friends:

> What are some of the "running etiquette"–type questions you remember having, back when you first started? Stuff so super-basic you may have been embarrassed to ask about it.

See below for their questions and my answers. No doubt this list is incomplete, so if you have a question not answered here, leave a comment or reach out to the *Runner's World* experts at thestartingline@runnersworld.com and we'll do our best to address it. And by the way, for a glossary of common running terms—like "PR"!—see page 227.

Q: Sometimes when I'm running, I pass people wearing earbuds who clearly don't hear my warning. How do you let a person who can't hear you know that you're there?

A: This is precisely why I encourage everyone not to run with earbuds or headphones—or, if you must, to leave one ear free and the volume low. Be aware of your surroundings! That said, it sounds like you're already doing everything right. Whenever you're about to overtake another runner (or walker), you should try to make your presence known. Often the other person will hear your footsteps, and glance back before you pass. If not, you can try coughing, shuffling your feet as you approach, or even saying "hello" or "passing on your left." The idea is to avoid startling somebody.

If that somebody is wearing earbuds and can't hear you? Well, what can I say? Swing as wide as you can and hope for the best.

Q: When overtaking a slower runner, do I pass on the right or left? Does it matter?

A: Doesn't matter. Let circumstances, and common sense, be your guide. Above all, safety should be your prime consideration.

Q: How do I pass a group of walkers without seeming rude?

A: There's nothing inherently rude about passing others, whether they're jogging or walking or whatever. Simply alert them to your presence (see the answer on the opposite page) and give them some room as you pass. Also, a friendly "hello" or "good morning" never hurts.

Q: After I finish a race, is it okay to blow by someone in the chute?

A: First, some context for those who need it: At most larger races, runners cross a finish line and then find themselves in a "chute" that moves them along to keep the actual finish line clear. The chute is lined with volunteers who offer space blankets, bottles of water, finisher's medals, and so on.

It's fine to pass other runners in the chute. (Though I can't imagine needing to "blow by" someone there—at that point, the race is over.) Just be courteous. In fact, try a pat on the back and a "nice job!" It'll make you both feel good.

Q: Will anyone make fun of me if I run with water?

A: No. In fact, this question is really a larger one, being a variation on a theme, i.e., "Will anyone make fun of me if I _____?" (Carry water? Use a Fuel Belt? Take walk breaks? Run really slow?") The answer is always no.

It's natural, when you're just starting anything new, to feel as if everyone is watching you and judging your every move. Runners are especially vulnerable to this, given how we put ourselves "out there" in plain view, whether we're

in a race or just running through our neighborhood. The truth is, no one is judging. In fact, most other runners are barely even watching! They're too focused on their own runs to care about your water, or your clothing, or your pace. So try not to worry what others think. You're out there, and you're moving forward, and that's all that matters.

Q: Race number: on front or back?

A: Bib numbers should be pinned on the front of your shirt. This makes it easier for race officials to see that you belong on the course. It also ensures that official photographers can identify you in their shots and later e-mail you a link to view your race photos online.

Note: Be careful not to fold, twist, or crumple your number. Increasingly, you'll find an electronic timing strip glued to the back. (See B-Tag on page 48.)

Q: How do I put a timing chip on my shoe?

A: When it comes to race timing devices, actual chips are becoming rare. Today you're more likely to find a thin strip on the back of your bib or a "D-Tag" meant to loop through your shoelaces. All of these use radio-frequency identification technology to record your crossing the starting and finish lines of a race and sometimes points in between. This is why we're able to see such detailed race results so quickly after races.

Here's an overview of the most common kinds of timing devices.

- **CHIP:** A small, usually round plastic disc usually worn on the shoe. Curved slots on each side can accommodate shoelaces or special Velcro straps to keep the chip in place. Chips are collected at the end of a race, usually by volunteers in the chute.

- **B-TAG:** A thin plastic strip attached to the back of a race bib. Do not remove it!

- **D-TAG:** A smaller plastic strip with an adhesive tab on one end. Thread it through your shoe's laces, form a D-shaped loop, and stick the ends together.

Detailed instructions should be included with your chip or tag.

Q: What do I do at stoplights? Wait, jog in place, etc.?

A: In my book *The Runner's Rule Book*, this is Rule 1.46: "For Pete's Sake, Stand Still at Red Lights" ("Sharks die when they stop moving. Runners do not."). That's tongue in cheek, of course. But honestly, no, there's no need to jog in place or otherwise bounce around while waiting for a light.

Q: In a race, should I just drop my empty cup, gel packet, banana peel, etc.? Or carry it until I find a trash can?

A: If you're in or around an aid station, it's always nice to chuck your cups, wrappers, etc., into a trash can. Or at least *toward* one. If it's too crowded or chaotic to manage that, it's fine to just toss them onto the road. Volunteers are there to clean up (often with rakes, to manage the volume of trash).

If you're far from an aid station, however, I'd urge you to carry your trash until you see some-place suitable to throw it away. Not everyone follows this advice. But races would be more pleasant—and runners would enjoy a better reputation—if they did.

Q: Can I wear shorts over running tights?

A: Can you? Of course. Should you? That's a matter of personal taste. (Personally, I think that if you find tights immodest, the solution isn't to put shorts over them; the solution is not to wear tights. Opt for looser-fitting running pants instead.)

Q: Is it okay to run side by side with a buddy in a race?

A: Sure—but only if doing so doesn't create hassles or hazards for other runners. If it's very crowded, for instance, running two or more abreast can be very irritating for anyone trying to pass you. In that case, better to run single file until the pack thins out.

Again, there's a larger (and therefore more useful) guideline here: When you're running, and especially when you're racing, be aware of your surroundings and be courteous to those around you.

Q: Are you supposed to make eye contact when you pass other runners? Smile? Or pretend to be superfocused and just look straight ahead?

A: Based on feedback I've gotten, and on my own experience, the running community is split on this. Which baffles me. When it comes to passing other runners, I've always been a wave-and/or-smile sort of guy—or at least a subtle-nod sort of guy. Acknowledging the existence of fellow runners just seems natural to me. And, well, nice.

Ultimately, how—or whether—you respond to other runners is up to you. I'd encourage you to do something, though. The world could use a little more "nice," I think, and a little less "looking straight ahead."

Q: How should I deal with people who heckle or make fun of me?

A: People like that are bullies, pure and simple. So you deal with them the same way you deal with any sort of bully: Ignore them.

Q: Is it okay to take walk breaks during a race?

A: Sure. Just follow some commonsense guidelines: Take your walk breaks on the side of the road, not in the middle. If you're with a friend (or friends), don't walk two (or more) abreast if there are runners behind you. And don't slow or stop abruptly; glance around you first to be sure you won't cause a collision. Or some swearing. Or both.

Q: May I use a high school track during school hours, assuming it's empty?

A: The easiest way to find out is also the most logical: Call the school and ask. Rules vary, but most schools allow the public to use their track during off hours. Simply helping yourself, however, is never a great idea. (Even if you feel, as many folks understandably do, that as a taxpayer you have a "right" to use it.) Be

courteous. Learn the rules for your local track, then follow them.

Q: Does it matter which direction I run on a track?

A: Almost always, you go counterclockwise on a running track.

Q: Is there a polite way to clear my nose while I'm running?

A: Yes! Even if the names for the technique in question—the "farmer's blow" or "snot rocket"—don't sound too polite.

Here's how to do it:

1 Take a deep breath.

2 Press an index finger firmly against one nostril.

3 Purse your lips.

4 Cock your head in the direction of the open nostril, and exhale forcefully through your nose.

5 Repeat with the other nostril, if needed. *Note:* As always, use common courtesy. Before you attempt this, glance around you to be sure the coast is clear.

Q: Should I run with traffic or against it?

A: Almost always, you should run against traffic.

Q: Is it okay to run in bike lanes?

A: I wouldn't recommend it, unless there's no safe alternative. Bike lanes are for bikes. Using them for walking, jogging, or running can be hazardous—for everyone.

Q: Undies or no undies?

A: This is a matter of personal choice. Some runners swear by "going commando," pointing out that running shorts have built-in liners. Others can't imagine going without underwear when they run. Try it both ways and see what works for you.

Q: Is stopping my watch at stoplights considered "cheating"?

A: I don't think so. But if it feels like "cheating" to you, don't do it!

Q: Where should I line up at the start of a race?

A: Where you belong.

Race starts work best when the very fastest runners are at the very front, the next-fastest are just behind them, and so on until we reach the slowest runners bringing up the rear. Most races—especially smaller ones—rely on the honor system for this. Runners are expected to line themselves up based on their goals and honest assessments of their fitness levels. That's the ideal.

The reality, of course, is that everyone wants to start ahead of most everyone else—regardless of their fitness levels. So the race director counts down, the air horn blasts, and chaos ensues.

Especially as a newbie, try to avoid this. You'll have a much happier experience if you err on the side of starting too far back.

Q: What do I do when I come to a water stop?

A: Water stops, or aid stations, can be tricky, especially for mid- to back-of-the-packers who have to deal with the worst crowds. But don't freak out! Here are some tips to help you navigate them.

- Plan ahead. This means studying the course map and knowing when and where you'll find aid stations and what they'll offer (water, sports drink, gels, etc.).

- Skip the first table. Everyone around you will make a beeline for the very first table or group of volunteers, resulting in a huge, sweaty traffic jam. Bypass them and aim to grab a cup from a table or volunteer down the road, where it's less crowded.

- Make eye contact. Single out a volunteer and look directly at him or her. Reach out toward the cup that he or she is extending.

- Look around. Before you make your move, be sure you have a clear path. Lots of collisions and near misses occur around aid stations as runners veer and dart, trying to grab a cup.

- Take your cup, pinch the top to form a spout, and drink up. If you want to walk or stop to drink, again: Move to the side, and look behind you first!

Q: **What's the etiquette on wearing (or not) the official race shirt in the race?**

A: Many experienced runners consider this a faux pas, but an exceedingly minor one. I liken it to wearing a concert T-shirt at the concert.

Q: **Who has the right-of-way on a trail—an uphill runner or a downhill runner?**

A: Runners going uphill generally have the right-of-way over runners heading downhill.

Q: **Can I run on any road I want?**

A: Well, no. But most roads that are legally off-limits aren't very attractive to runners anyway—interstates, for instance. Otherwise, most public streets and roads are perfectly fine to run on. For safety's sake, of course, try to avoid roads with little or no shoulder and roads with especially heavy traffic.

Q: **How tight do I tie my shoes?**

A: Think Goldilocks: not too loose, not too tight. Rule of thumb: If you can remove your shoes without untying them, your laces are too loose; if the tops of your feet hurt, your laces are too tight.

Q: **Are running clubs just for superfast runners?**

A: No way! While it's true that some clubs attract faster runners than others—especially in large metro areas that can support several clubs—I can't imagine a running club anywhere that would make a newbie feel unwelcome. And joining a running club is a fantastic way to stay motivated, meet other runners (including other beginners), and learn the ropes. Ask around about the clubs in your area. I'm sure you'll find one you love.

CHAPTER 2

BECOME A RUNNER IN FIVE EASY STEPS

False starts and frustration are common when you're starting out. But with a systematic approach and a little patience, they don't have to be.

Being big was always a part of who Andy Aubin was. Growing up, his nickname was "Big Andy." "I was okay with it," he says. He had made half-hearted attempts at dieting and exercise, but "I'd always lose interest and end up back where I started."

He tried a popular 5-K plan a half-dozen times, "but I was in such poor condition that I could never keep up with the first workout of the first week. I would just repeat it over and over and get frustrated and quit."

It took the birth of his daughter—and realizing that he couldn't get up a flight of stairs without catching his breath—to get him moving for good. He found a plan that let him build up to covering 1 mile in 4 weeks, working out three times per week.

"It eased me into running a mile, got me used to being active, and showed me that I can do it," he says. "I finally experienced some success, which gave me the confidence to try the 5-K plan."

Indeed, Aubin learned the hard way what so many other runners do.

"You definitely have to start where you are, not with where you think you should be or ultimately want to be," says exercise physiologist and running coach Janet Hamilton, founder of Running Strong in Atlanta. "If you go farther or faster than you're ready to go, your body can't adapt and you'll get injured, and that will interrupt your momentum."

That's why we've developed a five-part program that can take you from your first steps to your first 10-K even if you've never exercised before, or it's been so long that your body feels like it has forgotten how.

In this system, you'll find everything you need to know to make exercise into a regular part of your everyday life; how to get over some of the most daunting obstacles right out of the gate; and how to plow through the inevitable discomforts at the start, not to mention the overwhelming temptation to sleep in, sit down, or give in to your own crippling fears that someone will laugh at you or that you'll get hurt.

And beyond these pages, you can continue your journey online with *Runner's World*'s beginner's program, The Starting Line at **runnersworld.com/the-starting-line.** It includes five different training plans—which you can customize to meet your goals and needs—along with a private online community where you can connect with both *Runner's World* experts on training, nutrition, and injury prevention and other runners from all over the world who are making their first steps just like you. To find out more, see "About The Starting Line" on page xx or go to **runnersworld.com /the-starting-line.**

WHY FOLLOW A TRAINING PLAN?

Sure, you can free-form your running life, adding more miles and picking up the pace as soon as you feel ready. But many beginners make the mistake of doing too much too fast and too soon—resulting in injury or burnout. Or both.

Developing a sustainable exercise routine is a balancing act. The trick is to push your legs, lungs, and willpower farther than ever . . . but not so far that you get hurt and end up sidelined for weeks.

A training plan helps you strike that balance. With 4 or 5 days of exercise each week, plenty of time for rest, and a gentle, gradual buildup of mileage and speed, you'll get in shape without getting hurt, one step at a time.

Use the plan as a guide, but let your body and your life be the boss. You can move the workouts around so you can fit them into your busy lifestyle. You can repeat each week as many times as you'd like if you don't feel ready to advance. You can get the plan as a printable, downloadable pdf or load it onto our online training log, the *Runner's World* Personal Trainer, which lets you track your fitness, record your workouts, and more. To find *Runner's World*'s training plans for beginners, go to runnersworld.com/starting-line-training-plans.

So pick the training plan that best fits your background and level of fitness. **Have questions? Write to us at thestartingline@ runnersworld.com.**

STEP ONE
START WALKING

The best way to start running is to just get up and go, right? Not so fast. If you haven't been exercising on a regular basis—30 minutes a day, five times a week for at least 6 weeks—walking at a moderate intensity is the best first step you can take.

"If you haven't been exercising for a while, I wouldn't recommend starting with running," says Steven N. Blair, PED, FACSM, professor of exercise science and epidemiology and biostatistics at the Arnold School of Public Health, University of South Carolina. "First you have to get into the regular habit of exercising."

This will help you develop the fitness you need to start running comfortably—and get your bones, muscles, and tendons the foundation they need to become a runner without getting hurt.

Many aspiring runners dismiss "walk" as a four-letter word, as if it's cheating, quitting, or not really exercising. But walking is actually the ideal form of exercise for most people who are starting out. It's free, and you can do it anytime in any place; no special skill, pricey membership, or equipment (except good shoes!) is required. It is the best way to build strong bones, muscles, and tendons without getting hurt.

Walking puts the body through the same range of motion as running—but with less impact on the hips, knees, and ankles. Because you're not moving as fast, you're not landing with as much force.

"Walking builds a good infrastructure for running," says Hamilton, "so you'll get fitter without risking injury."

Try to rush that process, and you could end up sidelined—not to mention demoralized—right out of the gates.

And contrary to what you might think, it's the walk breaks that are going to allow you to exercise for longer and boost your calorie burn.

"Taking a walk break might make the difference between being able to work out for 20 minutes and exercising for 60 minutes," says Jeff Gaudette, who is the founder of RunnersConnect, an online training service, "and the cardiovascular benefits and all the things people get into running for, that's huge."

Plus, it's the easiest way to develop the fitness you need to run down the road. Here's more on the power of walking.

It makes you stronger. Running strengthens muscles and bones that support your feet, hips, and knees. And because you will have the endurance to go longer, it will help you build your overall fitness and endurance.

It gets you in the habit and helps you keep a routine. Plus, it gives you an opportunity to explore convenient, safe, traffic-free routes, which will become superimportant as you get into a routine.

It keeps you healthy and injury free. When you're running, at some point both feet come off the ground at the same time, and when you land, the impact can be up to two to three times your body weight, says Hamilton. But when you're walking, one foot is on the ground at all times. That drastically reduces the impact on your bones and joints compared with running.

The Start Walking Plan

This Start Walking plan, developed by Janet Hamilton, can get you in the habit of regular exercise and lay the foundation for your running life. With this 7-week plan, you can build up to 150 minutes per week (about 30 minutes five times a week)—the amount that the American College of Sports Medicine says will stave off diabetes, heart disease, and stroke; lower blood pressure and cholesterol; increase energy; and improve depression and anxiety. This should be a brisk walk ("not a race walk, but not a window-shopping walk either," says Blair). You can substitute time on a stationary bike or an elliptical trainer, but walking is the best foundation for running. "It's about what

*If you have a BMI of at least 25, are 60 years or older, or if you'd like to take a more gradual approach, you can repeat any week, or every week, and stretch this out to an 8-, 10-, or 12-week plan.

works for you," says Blair. "The best exercise is the one you will do consistently and the one you can fit into your life."

PLAN LENGTH: 7 weeks*
WORKOUTS PER WEEK: 4
FIRST WORKOUT: 15 minutes
GOAL WORKOUT: 60 minutes
ROOM TO MANEUVER: Got no time for a long workout? Split the longest workout of the week in half; you'll get the same health benefits.

Keys to Success

Be flexible. Don't feel like you have to do these workouts on the days specified here. Do the workouts on whatever day gives you enough time to do the workout and clean up without feeling rushed. "If you start to equate it with stress, you're not going to do it," says Charles Duhigg, author of *The Power of Habit.*

Sneak small activities in. Augment your exercise routine with small bouts of activity in your everyday life. Take 15 minutes of your lunch break to walk the office halls, park at the back of the lot, take the stairs instead of an elevator, and set a timer to chime every hour to remind you to get up and walk around, says Hamilton. This will help build your overall level of fitness. Even standing rather than sitting at your desk is a step in the right direction. A study published in the *Journal of Physical Activity* showed that

START WALKING PLAN

WEEK	MON	TUE	WED	THURS	FRI	SAT	SUN	TOTAL MINUTES (ESTIMATED MILEAGE)***
1	15 minutes	25 minutes	Rest or optional 15-minute walk	25 minutes	Rest	35 minutes	Rest	100–115 minutes (5–7.7 miles)
2	15 minutes	28 minutes	Rest or optional 15-minute walk	28 minutes	Rest	38 minutes	Rest	109–124 minutes (5.4–8.3 miles)
3	20 minutes	30 minutes	Rest or optional 15-minute walk	30 minutes	Rest	40 minutes	Rest	120–135 minutes (6–9 miles)
4	20 minutes	35 minutes	Rest or optional 15-minute rest walk	35 minutes	Rest	45 minutes	Rest	135–150 minutes (6.7–10 miles)
5	20 minutes	40 minutes	Rest or optional 20-minute walk	40 minutes	Rest	50 minutes	Rest	150–170 minutes (7.5–11.3 miles)
6	20 minutes	40 minutes	Rest or optional 20-minute walk	40 minutes	Rest	55 minutes	Rest	155–175 minutes (7.8–11.7 miles)
7	20 minutes	45 minutes	Rest or optional 20-minute walk	40 minutes	Rest	60 minutes	Rest	165–185 minutes (8.25–12.3 miles)

***The range here is based on the lowest mileage for a person who walks four times per week at a 20-minute mile (or 3 miles per hour); the highest end of the range would be the person who walks five times per week at a 15-minute pace (or 4 miles per hour).

You can get a downloadable pdf of this plan at runnersworld.com/the-starting-line, or refer to pages 224–225.

standing at your desk during an 8-hour workday will burn 163 more calories than if you were sitting.[31] A study published in the June 2011 issue of the *International Journal of Behavioral Nutrition and Physical Activity* found that taking a 5-, 10-, or 15-minute walk break once an hour for an 8-hour day would burn 24, 59, or 132 calories per day. And over time, that's enough to influence weight loss.[32]

Hit the hills, the stairs, and the trails. As with running, the more varied your walking route, the better workout you'll get. Hills can help you build leg and lung strength. If weather permits, walk a

AMBY'S ADVICE

Runners have ignored walking for far too long, but new research shows that 20 minutes of walking is just as good—just as health enhancing—as 10 minutes of running, so don't disdain walking as exercise.

few hills (or walk the same hill a few times) or do several repeats of stairs at stadiums, campuses, or parks or even in your own office building. Go to a park where you can get some varied terrain.

Watch your form. Most walkers find an upright posture to be the most natural and comfortable. Take short steps to avoid overstriding, which can cause aches and pains in your legs, feet, and hips. Keep your feet low to the ground and step lightly.

Make the time. Establish a workout routine that blends well into the rhythm of your daily life. Figure out what times of day are most convenient to work out and find a variety of safe, traffic-free routes that you can take on a regular basis. Find the time of day when running is a nonnegotiable. For many people, that's first thing in the morning, when no meetings are scheduled and the kids are still in bed. And make sure that

you have cleared enough time to work out so that it doesn't jam up your day. If a morning run means you're speeding to work and stressed about being late, the workout will start to feel like punishment, says Duhigg. (See "Make Your Workout Happen Any Time of Day" on page 91.)

Build your own support system. Enlist a buddy for your first outing to the gym or trail or try a group workout or a class. Research shows that connecting with others—whether it's a person, an online forum, or a workout group— increases your chances of sticking with an exercise routine. And remember that everyone feels self-conscious at first. "We get so caught up in the anxiety and fear of being negatively evaluated by others," says Christy Greenleaf, a professor of kinesiology at the University of Wisconsin. "But the reality is that most of the time, other people are way more concerned about themselves."

Stick to a plan. While you may not feel like you need a schedule for working out, having a training plan will help keep you on track to meet your goals and ensure that you build up your workout time gradually enough that you don't get injured. Plus, crossing off each workout as you complete it will give you a sense of accomplishment and confidence.

START RUNNING PLAN: SAMPLE WEEK

WEEK 3	MON	TUE	WED	THURS	FRI	SAT	SUN	TOTAL MINUTES (ESTIMATED MILEAGE)
1:4 ratio of run/ walk	TIME: 20 Walk 5 minutes, then run 1 minute/ walk 4 minutes for 15 minutes (1.3 miles**)	TIME: 35 Walk 5 minutes, then run 1 minute/ walk 4 minutes for 25 minutes; walk 5 minutes to cool down (2 miles)	Rest or optional 20-minute walk (no running segments)	TIME: 35 Walk 5 minutes, then run 1 minute/ walk 4 minutes for 25 minutes; walk 5 minutes to cool down (2 miles)	Rest	TIME: 50 Walk 5 minutes, then run 1 minute/ walk 4 minutes for 40 minutes; walk 5 minutes to cool down (3.2 miles)	Rest	140–160 minutes (8.5–10 miles)

**Miles are approximations, based on a 15- to 20-minute-per-mile walking pace and an 11.4-minute-per-mile running pace.
For the full plan, go to runnersworld.com/the-starting-line, or refer to pages 226–227.

STEP TWO
START RUNNING

If you're already in the habit of regularly working out, then you're ready to start running and move into a run/walk routine. And here's the good news: Because you'll be moving faster, you'll be able to cover longer distances without adding any more workout time to your schedule. After 7 weeks, you'll be able to complete 175 minutes of workouts per week, running for about twice the amount of time that you spend walking. You

*If you have a BMI of at least 25, are 60 years or older, or if you'd like to take a more gradual approach, you can repeat any week, or every week, and stretch this plan out as long as you'd like. Ideally, you'd complete the plan in 14 weeks.

can buy the plan sampled below at the Web site runners world.com/the-starting-line. Or you can use the 8-week plan on page 231.

Are you ready? If you have spent at least 2 weeks walking or doing some other form of exercise (like using a stationary bike or an elliptical trainer) for at least 150 minutes per week (roughly 30 minutes, 5 days per week), you're ready.

PLAN LENGTH: 7 weeks*

WORKOUTS PER WEEK: 4–5

FIRST WORKOUT: 20-minute workout with run/walk ratio of 1:4

GOAL WORKOUT: 1-hour workout with run/walk ratio of 2:1

ROOM TO MANEUVER: Want more of a challenge? Work out for the same amount of time, but build up to a run/walk ratio of 4:2 then 6:3.

Keys to Success

Start with run/walks. While it's tempting to just go out and run as fast as you can for as long as you can, you'll ultimately run longer, feel stronger, and stay injury free if you start by adding short bouts of running to your regular walks and gradually increasing the amount of time that you spend running. Our Start Running plan will help you safely add running to your routine and build up to a 1-hour workout with a run/walk ratio of 2:1.

You'll start by adding 1 minute of running for every 4 minutes of walking and gradually increase your running time so that eventually you'll be running for twice the amount of time that you spend walking.

Beware of the terrible toos. Your main goal is to get fit without getting hurt. Going too far too fast before your body is ready is one of the most common causes of injuries like shin splints, IT band syndrome, and runner's knee, which sideline many people. You can stay injury free by gradually building up the time you spend walking and running, increasing the time by no more than 10 percent from week to week. By following our Start Running plan, you'll get week-to-week guidance on exactly how much running to add so you stay healthy. (To read more about injuries, see page 212.)

Let the body be the boss. Some muscle aches and soreness—especially in the quadriceps and calves—are to be expected anytime you are pushing your body farther or faster than it's accustomed to going. But there are some pains that you shouldn't ignore. Any sharp pains or pains that persist or worsen as you walk, run, or go about your daily activities are signals to rest for at least 3 days and see a doctor. Also beware of any pains that are on one side of the body but not the other. You may need to start with your general practitioner, but it's best to see a sports medicine doctor or orthopedist if it persists. (For more, see "Should I Run or See the Doctor?" on page 215.)

Practice patience. Many of the positive changes that are happening when you start exercising won't be visible in the mirror or on the scale. "Everyone expects to lose the weight in an instant and go longer and faster right away," says Paul. "The weight loss will come if you're consistent, but it takes time to condition your muscles, ligaments, and tendons so you can run faster and further." The body makes more capillaries (tiny blood vessels that transfer oxygen and waste products into and out of cells), more mitochondria (the energy-producing structures in cells), and more enzymes that help the body use fat as fuel, Paul explains. Plus, every time the foot strikes the ground, it stimulates bone growth, so your bones get stronger and denser. "When you're not patient," says

Paul, "you make all the mistakes of doing too much too soon and too fast and getting overuse injuries and thinking, 'Oh, running is bad for you.'"

Log your miles. It can be as simple as a notebook and a pencil or as state-of-the-art as a GPS that delivers morale boosts at timed intervals. Any way you log your miles, you'll draw confidence from watching the miles pile up; the next day's workout won't seem so daunting when you see how far you've already come. There are many affordable GPS watches on the market, including devices like the Gymboss (gymboss.com) that you can program to beep through your different intervals or the Garmin Forerunner 10 ($129), which includes a run/walk timer that alternates between two segments of a preset duration, so you can program running stints and walk breaks.

Train your brain. After a few weeks, you'll begin to believe that the whole idea of an exercise high is not a myth. But it can be hard to get out the door at first. And relying on willpower alone just won't work. Make a plan. Listen to certain music, choose the most convenient time to work out, and pick some rewards that will motivate you to just get up and go. Write out a plan and place it where you can see it, like the bathroom mirror. If the best time to run is in the morning, make sure you've got an energizing music mix to listen to and a relaxing hot shower to look forward to after you're done. Create a

prerun routine to cue your body and mind that it's time to go, and repeat it every time you go. Try to get out at the same time of day. Put your workout clothes next to your bed. Play the same workout music before you go out. Right after your workout, treat yourself to something you genuinely enjoy—like a hot shower or a smoothie—so your brain associates exercise with an immediate reward. (See "Making Exercise a Habit" on page 87.)

Relax and run tall. You don't have to worry too much about form at this point, but a few adjustments can make the running feel more comfortable, says running coach and exercise physiologist Janet Hamilton. Take short strides. Keep your elbows flexed at about 90 degrees and keep your hands relaxed, as if you were holding a piece of paper between your thumb and pointer finger. Envision yourself walking tall, looking straight ahead at the horizon; avoid looking down at your feet. For more see "Proper Running Form" on page 62.

Take breaks before you need to. Once you're running, you may feel comfortable enough to skip the walk breaks. But it's important to take walk breaks before you feel like you need them. This will help fend off fatigue and prevent you from doing too much too soon. By taking walk breaks at the regular intervals that are scheduled for the day, you can ensure that you'll finish each workout feeling strong.

PROPER RUNNING FORM

Your running mechanics are determined by the strength and flexibility of certain muscles and how your body is built. Here are a few basics to help you maintain proper running form on any terrain from exercise physiologist Adam St. Pierre and Christy Barth, a physical therapist and strength and conditioning specialist, both of the Boulder Center for Sports Medicine:

- **MAINTAIN A SHORT, QUICK STRIDE.** Do not try to lengthen your stride; avoid reaching forward with your foot, which can lead to overstriding and will set you up for injury.

- **KEEP YOUR KNEE IN LINE.** Make sure your foot strikes under your knee, not in front of it, which can lead to injury. It doesn't matter whether the heel or forefoot hits the ground first, as long as your foot is not in front of your knee. This is especially important when running downhill.

- **PUSH UP AND OFF.** Focus on pushing up and off the ground behind you.

- **WATCH YOUR ELBOWS.** Keep your elbows bent at 90 degrees or less.

- **RELAX YOUR HANDS.** Keep hands loose and below your chest. Make sure your hands don't cross your midline and your hands don't punch forward, both of which can throw off your gait. Pay careful attention to this when you're carrying something like a music player or a dog leash. Switch hands halfway through the workout if possible.

- **WORK YOUR CORE.** When starting a running program, it is critical to work on the strength of your glutes and abdominal muscles. A strong core makes it easier to stay upright—even when you're tired—and avoid leaning too far forward from your hip, which can lead to injury.

STEP THREE
RUN NONSTOP!

Want to build up the endurance to run more and reduce or eliminate those walk breaks? You're ready if you've been doing some combination of running and walking for at least 150 minutes per week. Over a period of 7 weeks you can build from walking 1 minute for every 2 minutes of running up to continuous running with no scheduled walk breaks. You'll still be running up to 180 minutes per week. Each run should be done at a conversational pace; that means you're running comfortably enough to hold a conversation. If you're huffing and puffing, you're running too fast.

Are you ready? To begin this plan, you should have spent at least 6 weeks doing some running and walking for a cumulative total of at least 150 minutes per week (roughly 30 minutes, 5 days per week) and running for at least twice the amount of time that you spend walking. The sample below is for the first week; if you wish to purchase the full 7-week plan, go to runnersworld.com/the-starting-line.

PLAN LENGTH: 7 weeks*

WORKOUTS PER WEEK: 4–5

FIRST WORKOUT: 25-minute workout with run/walk ratio of 3:2 (about 1.8 miles)

GOAL WORKOUT: Run 3.1 miles (the distance of a 5-K) without taking walk breaks.

ROOM TO MANEUVER: There is flexibility within this plan; if it's too easy for you, you can skip ahead to the next week. If

*If you have a BMI of at least 25, are 60 years or older, or if you'd like to take a more gradual approach, you can repeat any week, or every week, and stretch this plan out as long as you'd like. Ideally, you'd complete the plan in 14 weeks.

it is moving too fast for you, you may spend 2 weeks or more at each week. You can stretch this plan out for as long as you'd like, although ideally you'd complete it within 14 weeks.

Keys to Success

Find your happy pace. When you first start running, the trick is to be consistent enough that you're building strength and endurance and slow enough that you don't get hurt. To do that, you're going to need to do all of your training at an easy pace. Get into a rhythm that feels like you could maintain it forever and lock into it. "A lot of runners try to run too fast, because they see other people and feel like 'I'm not a runner unless I'm going *X* pace,'" says running

RUN NONSTOP PLAN: SAMPLE WEEK

WEEK 1	MON	TUE	WED	THURS	FRI	SAT	SUN	TOTAL MINUTES (ESTIMATED MILEAGE)
1:4 ratio of run/walk	TIME: 25 Walk 3 minutes, then run 3 minutes/walk 2 minutes for 20 minutes; walk 2 minutes to cool down (1.8 miles**)	TIME: 40 Walk 5 minutes, then run 3 minutes/walk 2 minutes for 30 minutes; walk 5 minutes to cool down (2.9 miles)	Rest or optional 20-minute walk (no running segments)	TIME: 40 Walk 5 minutes, then run 3 minutes/walk 2 minutes for 30 minutes; walk 5 minutes to cool down (2.9 miles)	Rest	TIME: 55 Walk 5 minutes, then run 3 minutes/walk 2 minutes for 45 minutes; walk 5 minutes to cool down (4 miles)	Rest	160–180 minutes depending on pace (11.6–12.9 miles)

Miles are approximations, based on a 16-minute walking pace and 11.30-minute running pace.
To get the full plan, go to runnersworld.com/the-starting-line, or refer to pages 228–229.

coach Jeff Gaudette. "No matter what your pace, it needs to be comfortable, even if that means throwing in walk breaks. If you run faster than you should, it's going to hurt all the time and you'll never get to a point where you can do it for 20 to 30 minutes." Develop the endurance; speed will come later.

Find your place. Map out a few safe, scenic, flat, and traffic-free routes that you can cover in various weather conditions and times of day. Or try a track at a local school, where the terrain is flat and free of cars and the distance is measured. Many schools open their tracks to the public when they're not in use. Not ready to venture outside? Find a gym nearby with treadmills and hours that fit your schedule. Before you sign up, find out when the prime times are so you can steer clear and be sure to get an open treadmill (for more, see "Treadmill Training" on page 16).

Stay flexible. Use the training plan as a guide, but don't hesitate to swap workouts around to fit them into your busy schedule. Make time to work out—and take care of yourself—first thing in the morning, before meetings and family responsibilities can interfere. Set your clothes out in a brightly lit room so you can get dressed without waking up everyone else in the house. Make a date with a buddy so you'll be less likely to hit the snooze button. Midday, block out the time on your calendar and treat it like a meeting that you can't miss. If you have to switch around your workouts from the

morning to the evening, or vice versa, don't be surprised if it takes a while to adjust. You may have a sluggish, jet-lagged feeling at first. That should go away within 2 weeks. (For more, see "Make Your Workout Happen Any Time of Day" on page 91.)

Take it in small doses, if needed. While longer sessions are ideal, if you'd like to split up the workouts into two or three sessions at first, that's okay. Studies have shown that, say, three 10-minute sessions of exercise deliver the same health benefits as a single 30-minute workout, says Steven N. Blair, professor of exercise science at the University of South Carolina. "The evidence we have shows that the benefits are comparable," he says. Indeed, a study published in December 2012 showed that short bouts of activity are as effective for delivering health benefits as a single longer workout.[33]

Get distracted. Tuning out—not in—can help you get through those tough first workouts, says Christy Greenleaf, a professor kinesiology at the University of Wisconsin. Recruit a friend to walk the neighborhood with you; watch your favorite sitcom while you're on the treadmill; put together a workout mix with tunes that evoke happy memories. "Any way that you can focus your attention on something other than how your body feels will help," says Greenleaf.

Fuel up for your workouts. It's okay to head out for a workout on an empty stomach, but you may have more energy if you have a wholesome snack and some fluids beforehand. Drink 8 to 16 ounces before you go; water is best. (No need for sports drinks on any workout that's less than 75 minutes.) Have a 200-calorie snack that's low in fat and low in fiber (less than 2 grams of fiber per serving) before you head out. Eat at least 30 minutes before your workout. Each individual is unique in terms of digestion time, so you may need to eat closer to your workout or a few hours earlier than what's prescribed here.

Here are some great ideas for preworkout fueling:

- 1 cup low-fiber cereal with ½ cup fat-free milk
- 2 fig cookies
- 1 cup of berries with ½ cup low-fat cottage cheese
- 3 graham cracker squares with 1 teaspoon honey
- 1 orange
- Applesauce (without added sugar)

For more, check out your best prerun meals and snacks on page 129.

STEP FOUR
RUN LONGER
(Up to 60 Minutes)

If you're able to run 2 to 3 miles without walk breaks, or finish a 5-K, you're ready to start extending your runs up to 1 hour. At this stage, you'll develop the endurance to run 6 miles without walk breaks and build the strength to race a 5-K (3.1 miles) or finish a 10-K (6.2 miles). The plan includes some hills and loosely structured speedwork (fartlek) to help build your strength. Start by running 1 to 2 miles on your weekly runs, with one long run on the weekend that is 3 miles. You'll gradually add distance so that by the end of the plan you'll be able to cover 6 miles without stopping and without getting hurt.

Are you ready? To begin this plan to build endurance so that you can go longer distances, you should have spent at least 6 weeks running for at least 150 minutes per week (30 minutes, five days per week). You should be able to complete a 3-mile run

RUN LONGER PLAN: SAMPLE WEEK

WEEK 1	MON	TUE	WED	THURS	FRI	SAT	SUN	TOTAL
	1-mile run**	2-mile run	Rest or optional 1-mile run or walk	2-mile run	Rest	3-mile run	Rest	8–9 miles

Before you start each workout and after you finish, add a 3- to 5-minute warmup and cooldown.
For the full plan, go to runnersworld.com/the-starting-line, or refer to pages 230–231.

without walking. To buy the full 7-week plan, go to runnersworld.com/the-starting-line.

PLAN LENGTH: 7 weeks*

WORKOUTS PER WEEK: 5

FIRST WORKOUT: 1-mile run

GOAL WORKOUT: Run 6 to 7 miles continuously so you can either race a 5-K or finish a 10-K race.

ROOM TO MANEUVER: If you feel ready for a greater challenge, skip ahead a week. But don't rush it. It's better to build gradually so your body gets used to the extra load. On the other hand, if you feel the plan is moving too fast for you, you can repeat any week for as long as you'd like. Ideally, you would complete this plan in 14 weeks.

Keys to Success

Think big. It's tough to log a personal record every day. At a certain point, the huge gains in fitness are going to naturally level off, and that can be a letdown. "At first, every run you do is going to be longer and faster than it was before, but at some point those wins are going to be harder to come by," says Boston-based running coach Jeff Gaudette of RunnersConnect. This is a good time to make some long-term goals to work toward, says Gaudette. That way, even the

*If you have a BMI of at least 25, are 60 years or older, or if you'd like to take a more gradual approach, you can repeat any week, or every week, and stretch this plan out as long as you'd like. Ideally, you'd complete the plan in 14 weeks.

short, easy runs that aren't PRs for speed or distance are steps toward achieving the larger goal ahead.

Stick with the plan. At this stage, it may start to take more discipline to hold back than to push harder. If you push beyond what the plan calls for, you risk getting hurt or tiring out before your time for the day is finished. "People get too excited and push it without thinking about accumulation of fatigue," says Gaudette.

Stay on high alert. Watch out for any aches or pains that persist or worsen as you run or prompt you to change your gait. Each person has a unique orthopedic threshold for how many miles they can log and how fast they can go before getting injured. That's determined by a person's unique genetics, anatomy, biomechanics, and history of injury. (See "Should I Run or See the Doctor?" on page 215.)

Take it easy. As you're training your body to go longer, it's important to run relaxed. Don't worry about your pace; you should be running at a pace that feels comfortable and conversational—like you could maintain it forever if you had to. Just focus on covering the distance for the day feeling strong and exhilarated, with enough energy and desire that you're psyched about getting out for your next workout. Lots of people make the mistake of going out too fast; that's a surefire recipe for injury and burnout. And what's more, if you finish your workout feeling demolished and demoralized, it's going to be that much more difficult to get out for your next run.

Fill up your tank. Before heading out on any run that nears an hour, make sure you're hydrated and well fueled. Stay well hydrated throughout the day. Aim to consume at least half the amount of fluids of your body weight, in ounces. So if you weigh 150 pounds, you'd try to consume 75 ounces of water per day. If you weigh 200 pounds, you'd aim for 100 ounces. Stick with water or other calorie-free drinks; you don't need sports drinks unless you're going for longer. Try to eat 30 to 60 minutes before you go out. Stick with a snack or meal that's low in fat and fiber and that will provide you with carbs you need for fast energy. Have a piece of fruit and pair it with cottage cheese. Other options: fig cookies, half a bagel with nut butter and jam, or a cereal with less than 2 grams of fiber per serving with $\frac{1}{2}$ cup of fat-free milk.

Avoid eating back the calories. Many people are surprised to find that when they start exercising, the pounds don't just magically and immediately melt off. And that can be frustrating. Indeed, whether you're ravenous when you return from your run or you just feel entitled to treats, it's easy to go overboard. It's easy to eat back your calories after pushing your body and your mind farther than you've taken them before. To avoid that, track your calorie intake with one of the many Web sites or apps that offer this service; it will force you to pause and think before you taste, and exercise portion control. Also, schedule nonfood rewards when you reach certain milestones: some new running duds, a new book or some new music, a day at the spa, or a night out with friends.

Press reset. No matter how good your intentions are, inevitably you're going to get busy, become too sick to run, or find yourself caught up in something that gets in the way of your exercise routine. And it may feel tough to start over. Don't let one missed workout totally derail you. Just get going again and press the reset button, says Gaudette. "Let go of the past and focus on what you can control today," he says. "Ask yourself, 'Can I run today?'" Your fitness will return. "People are always so surprised at how quickly they can get back on track," says Susan Paul, of Track Shack of Orlando. "Even if they took 2 weeks off, they haven't lost as much fitness as they think." (For more, see "Get Over Mental Roadblocks on the Run" on page 92.)

Stick with the plan. At this stage, it may start to take more discipline to hold back than to push harder. If you push beyond what the Run Longer plan calls for, you risk getting hurt or tiring out before your time for the day is finished. "People get too excited and push it without thinking about accumulation of fatigue," says Gaudette.

RUN FASTER PLAN: SAMPLE WEEK

	MON	TUE	WED	THURS	FRI	SAT	SUN	TOTAL
Week 1	2-mile run	4-mile run	2-mile run	4-mile run	Rest	6-mile run	Rest	18 miles
Week 2	2-mile run	4-mile run with hills	2-mile run	TRACK 1 mile easy warmup 4 x 100 meters @ 10-K pace w/100 jog recovery 4 x 200 meters @ 10-K pace w/200 jog recovery 2 x 400 meters @ 10-K pace w/400 jog recovery 1 mile cooldown (4.5 miles)	Rest	7-mile run	Rest	19.5 miles

For the full plan, go to runnersworld.com/the-starting-line, or refer to pages 232–235.

STEP FIVE
RUN FASTER

Want to run faster? If you can complete up to 5 or 6 miles, you're ready to boost your speed and your cardiovascular fitness.

Our Run Faster plan will ease you into track workouts to boost your leg and lung power—and your finishing time at the next 5-K or 10-K race. You'll also develop a

sense of "pace awareness"; that is, how your legs and lungs feel when you're pushing the pace, which will help you avoid the most common racing mistake: going out too fast.

Are you ready? This plan is for an "advanced beginner." You should be able to run 18 miles per week and should be able to complete a long run of 5 to 6 miles before you start this plan. The first 2 weeks are sampled above. To buy the complete 8-week plan, go to runnersworld.com/the-starting-line.

PLAN LENGTH: 8 weeks*
WORKOUTS PER WEEK: 5
FIRST WORKOUT: 2 miles easy

*If you have a BMI of at least 25, are 60 years or older, or if you'd like to take a more gradual approach, you can repeat any week, or every week, and stretch this plan out as long as you'd like. Ideally, you'd complete the plan in 14 weeks.

GOAL WORKOUT: 9-mile long run; 4 × 800 @ 5-K pace

ROOM TO MANEUVER: Only have 4 days per week to run? That's okay. Just skip the shortest easy run of the week. Most runners do long runs on the weekends, but you can move it to a different day if your schedule permits.

Keys to Success

Get a baseline. Even if you're young and healthy, getting your vital fitness stats can pay off. Get weighed and get your body fat measured so you have some baseline that allows you to track your progress, says running coach Mindy Solkin, founder of The Running Center in New York. "It's tangible evidence of your success," she says. "Seeing those improvements is a big achievement and really helps get over the emotional hurdle when you may not otherwise notice results."

Don't make up for lost time. Lots of people get hung up on running a certain number of miles per week, and if they miss a day or two, they end up cramming in extra miles, so they go from nothing to a lot in short order. That's a recipe for disaster, experts say. "People will miss a day or two, then try to make up their missed miles and run 3 days in a row, and that's when they get injured," says Solkin.

Don't discount your life stress. While exercise is a proven stress reliever, if you start your workout frazzled or drained for reasons that have nothing to do with your running—say you're getting over a cold, sleep deprived, anxious about work, or had one too many late nights partying—the workout is going to feel harder. A 2012 study in *Medicine & Science in Sports & Exercise* showed that muscles take longer to recover when you're stressed out.[34] Other studies have shown that for people who were stressed out, workouts felt harder than they did for those who weren't, even when they were working at the same level.

Why Do Speedwork?

When you're first getting moving, it's important to just focus on getting into the exercise habit: making your run or walk a regular part of each day, finding times and places to exercise that feel convenient and comfortable, and finding a way to enjoy it so you keep it up for the long term.

But over time, you will inevitably start to wonder, how can I get fitter and faster? You can simply add time to your workout as you get stronger or increase the distance you cover. Another approach is to add some structured speed workouts to your routine. These workouts, which involve running specific intervals or times or distances at a specific pace, can help you develop endurance, speed, and stronger legs and lungs. But most important, they can keep your exercise regime from getting stale, says coach

(continued on page 72)

How Running Changed My Life

Running helped John Golden endure and heal from the most painful time of his life

On July 14, 2009, John Golden's wife of 20 years died suddenly. It was a complete shock.

The next morning, he woke up and couldn't stay still. He didn't know what to do. "I had to find a way to escape the grief; I couldn't stay where I was," he says. "The only thing I knew to do was grab a pair of shoes and run." So he took off and started running through the mountains.

"I can remember looking up at the sky and being really angry about the whole situation," he says. But then something shifted. "I started focusing on the running: my breathing, my stride, my pace, how I was striking my foot and swinging my arms. There was tightness in my chest, and my quads were sore. Physically it felt bad, but it was so much better than the emotional pain I was feeling."

The next morning, he got up and wanted to go right back out and do it again. And so he did.

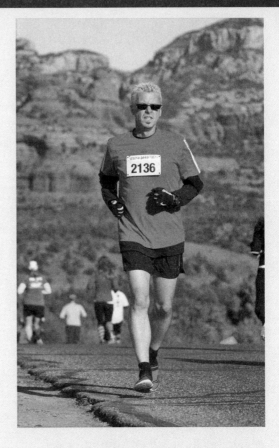

"Now I don't have to run just to emotionally cope," he says. "This is something I love to do, and I'm not going to stop."

AGE: 48

HOMETOWN: New Orleans

OCCUPATION: Drummer

What's your regular workout routine? I get up daily unless I feel overtired or hurt and run through the streets of New Orleans. I regularly run a 5-K and a 10-K on alternating days and then one long run without watches or anything once a week.

What was the biggest hurdle, and how did you get over it? When I stopped just running and started "thinking" about running, I felt I had to compete with every runner I saw. I stopped and asked questions and received a lot of good advice from experienced runners to utilize the tools to improve but never forget that you run for the love of it and you should feel that when you're out there. It shouldn't be all about PRs.

What kinds of changes did you make to your diet? I'm a vegan, so if I stay away from chips and junk I'm okay, but my success is I love to run all of the time, so a little indulgence isn't a big deal for me.

What advice would you give to a beginner? Buy good shoes, start out slow, and build. When I decided I needed to get serious, I stopped running all-out with no goal. I wanted to run long distances without the strain, so I started running 2 minutes and walking 1 minute for an hour. Then every week, I knocked 10 seconds off the walk until I was continuously running for an hour. After that, I just increased my running time by 2 minutes a week.

Naturally, there's going to be pain when you're doing anything that you're not used to. But if you can just push through it, it does get easier. Take it slow and understand that it does take a while. As lousy as I felt, I never thought I'd be someone who was a runner just for the sheer love of doing it. Now I don't miss a day.

Favorite motivational quote: I use the lyrics to Muse's song "Survival," Iron Maiden's "Loneliness of the Long Distance Runner," and Rush's "Marathon" for inspiration.

and exercise physiologist Susan Paul. "If you just go out for 30 minutes over and over every day, it can be very boring," she says. With structured workouts, "the time goes by much quicker. They engage your mind, and the body goes along with it."

And by breaking up the distance into smaller intervals, you can cover more distance overall. It can help you even if you don't have any racing ambitions. "Even if you don't want to race, it will help you make fitness improvements a lot faster," says running coach Jeff Gaudette of Boston-based RunnersConnect. "You'll lose weight, breathe easier, and progress faster toward whatever your goals are." Here's why.

You'll burn more calories. Running a mile burns about 100 calories, but the faster you cover the distance, the sooner you'll burn those calories.[35] Plus, high-intensity training keeps your metabolism revved even after the workout is over. "You get more bang for your buck," says Gaudette. What's more, research seems to suggest that the afterburn—the number of calories your body burns after your workout, when your metabolism is revved—lasts longer when you run faster.

You'll build stronger muscles. Speedwork gets fast-twitch muscle fibers firing and recruits different muscles than slow runs do. Speedwork strengthens the bones, ligaments, and joints, so they can absorb the easy runs better, says Gaudette. It's similar to weight training. For instance, consider lifting a dumbbell into a biceps curl. The heavier the weight, the stronger your biceps will get, because the muscle is having to resist more weight. With speedwork, the more you push the leg muscles to move faster, the more total muscle fibers you activate and the more explosively you contract them. This results in greater strength and injury resistance. So on days when you're running slower, your stronger musculoskeletal system won't have to work so hard.

You'll boost your heart health. Speed sessions help maximize your aerobic capacity. When you hit a fast pace, you force the heart to pump oxygen through the body at a quicker rate. Over time, that makes your heart stronger, so it can deliver more oxygen to the muscles, and your muscles can use that oxygen more efficiently. Just as it is with pushing the biceps to lift a 10-pound weight, it's easier to lift a 5-pound weight. So when you push the heart more during speedwork and make it stronger, it takes less effort for the heart to pump blood throughout your body to power everyday daily activities, where you're not working as hard.

You'll develop faster footwork. One of the easiest and simplest ways to stay injury free is to increase your stride rate. (Overstriding is a common cause of hamstring, knee, and hip issues, as well as shin splits and IT band syndrome.) And speedwork will help you increase your stride rate and shorten your stride, so you don't get hurt. When you're holding a swift pace, your feet turn over at a more rapid rate. So with enough practice, this quicker cadence becomes more natural, which means you'll need less effort to move faster on any run. Ideally, runners have a cadence of 170 to 180 steps per minute (see "How to Increase Your Stride Rate" on page 212 for guidance on how to do that).

You'll see progress. One of the biggest challenges when you just start out is to stay motivated. And one of the easiest ways to do this is to see progress, says Gaudette. "Running an easy pace is going to feel the same every day, and you're generally not going to feel like you're making any progress," he says. "Every few weeks, when you go to repeat an effort and you find that you're running faster, or with less effort, you're going to feel like you're getting fitter. Even if you don't have a race goal, all that motivation will keep you going when you don't want to get out the door or the weather gets bad."

You'll glimpse your potential. Everyone feels like they're slow at first, no matter how fast they're going. Doing speedwork, in which you're running faster for short bouts of time, can give you a big confidence boost. "It allows you to see what your abilities are," says Gaudette. "You'll see that a certain pace—that you might have thought was out of reach—is possible. Even if you're only holding that pace for a minute at a time, it changes your belief in yourself."

Your easy runs will get easier. After a while, even easy runs can feel tough. But if you've done a faster workout, that easy run will feel easier by comparison. Knowing that you have run faster in the past will make the easy run feel less daunting.

Below are workouts that Paul and Gaudette recommend, whether you're just getting moving, starting to run, or returning to running after taking time off. Some of these workouts are best done on a track. Find out everything you need before hitting the track on page 14. If you don't have access to a track or a treadmill, any flat, traffic-free stretch of road will work.

Try one of the workouts below each week. When you're ready, increase the time or distance of each of these workouts by 10 to 20 percent. Stay alert for aches and pains (beyond typical muscle soreness) that persist during your run and after you're done. Find out more about when to run and when to see the doctor on page 215. Be sure that you've been regularly running for at least 4 weeks before doing any of these workouts.

YOUR FIRST FARTLEK: Start with 10 minutes of walking or easy running to warm up. Then run 1 minute hard and 3 minutes easy to recover. Repeat that cycle four more times. Cool down with 10 minutes of walking or easy running. The hard pace should be difficult, but you shouldn't feel like you're going to pass out. At the end, you should feel like you could go farther if you had to. But you wouldn't want to.

What it does: For your first workout, Gaudette suggests a loosely structured fartlek session rather than going to a track. Running one loop around the track—or 400 meters—can be overwhelming at first, he explains. A fartlek session run on the road, where you're alternating between bouts of fast and slow running, "allows you to just chip away at your fear of running harder," he says. "And it helps you learn what it feels like to run hard."

STRAIGHTS AND CURVES: Walk for 5 minutes to warm up. Then run the straight stretches of the track and walk the curves. Repeat that cycle twice. Leave water at a spot that you can drink after you finish each loop. On the run segment, get into a rhythm that feels comfortable, says Paul. "Don't sprint." As your fitness improves, you can start to pick up the pace. On the road, use different landmarks to mark your walking and running intervals. You might run to a tree, mailbox, telephone pole, or stop sign. Then walk. Once you catch your breath, pick another landmark to run to. Then walk to recover. Repeat the cycle two or three times.

What it does: This helps you get your body and mind accustomed to picking up the pace and running faster for short periods of time. The short intervals make the bouts of hard work seem doable. With each walk break, you have a chance to recover enough for your next bout of hard work.

GEAR SHIFTER: In this workout, alternate between your easy, medium, and fast paces. Warm up with 3 to 5 minutes of walking. Then ramp up to your easy pace (see below) and hold it for 2 to 3 minutes. Then shift into your medium pace and sustain it for 1 minute. Then shift into the fast pace for 30 seconds. Repeat the cycle two or three times. Walk for 5 minutes to cool down. Use this guide to find each gear:

- **EASY:** Conversational pace—a pace where you could chat with a friend running alongside you. This is a rhythm that feels like you could maintain it all day long if you had to.

- **MEDIUM:** This should be faster than your easy pace, but you shouldn't feel like you're speeding. You would prefer not to hold a full conversation, but if someone asked you a question, you could answer in two- or three-word sentences.

- **FAST:** Quicker than your medium pace. In this gear, you should be able to say one or two words, but if someone asked you a question, it would make you mad because you wouldn't want to expend the energy to answer them. Don't sprint all-out or push to the point of pain, or where you feel like you're going to pull something. You should feel like "I'm okay, I just don't want to do this for very long."

What it does: This workout will elevate your heart rate, boost your fitness and calorie burn, and keep you from falling into a rut with the same easy pace. "It makes running fun, ups the intensity, and recruits different muscle fibers," says Paul. "It's like adding spice to a recipe." By getting used to what different paces feel like, you can get more benefits out of all your workouts going forward, whether you're doing a recovery run or racing in your first 5-K. Why is that important? "If you're aware of your running pace, you can control your effort based on the distance or the purpose of the workout or in the race," says Paul. What's more, it can help you stay injury free. If you run the same pace all the time, you recruit the same muscle fibers in the exact same way over and over. That, says Paul, sets the stage for many common overuse injuries, like runner's knee and IT band syndrome. "If you mix up your paces, you recruit different muscle fibers and some different muscles," says Paul. "You get more balanced out."

THE EVEN STEVEN: Walk to warm up, then run three laps around the track. Try to run each loop at the same pace, within 5 seconds faster or slower than the previous loop.

What it does: This workout builds endurance and teaches you to maintain a steady, consistent effort, which is what you'll want to do in your first race. "Runners of all abilities tend to just start running as fast as they can, until they tire out and have to quit," says Paul. Knowing that you have three loops to do, you'll learn to start your first loop slower and get into a rhythm that you can maintain for all three loops.

THE LONG RUN: Want to stretch out your workout for longer? Take walk breaks before you need to at even intervals. That may mean running for just 20 seconds at first, says Paul. You should be running at a pace that's easy enough to hold a conversation, she says. "If you can't, slow down." On the other hand, if you're running so easy you can sing, pick up the pace, she adds.

What it does: This helps you build endurance without getting injured or discouraged. Taking walk breaks will help you sustain a higher level of energy over a longer period of time for a longer distance.

DESTINATION RUN: Covering the same old route can get downright old. Run or walk to someplace nearby that you usually drive to and that involves going farther than you usually do. Go to the grocery store; meet a friend at the gym and arrange to get a ride home.

What it does: This builds endurance, and it's fun. "It feels like you're on an adventure," says Paul. And it really changes your perspective! Never noticed that hill before? You will now!

Reasons to Race

Even if you don't have a competitive bone in your body, it's a good idea to sign up for a 5-K. Most areas have casual 5-K events each weekend. (To find one near you, use our race finder at runnersworld.com/race-finder.) Here's why it pays to race.

1 Track your progress. Racing on a regular basis helps you measure improvement. Even if your only goal is to get fitter—not faster—this is a concrete way to track your progress. Run a 5-K each month to see your improvements.

2 Find your other training paces. It helps you figure out your easy pace. If you finish a 5-K as fast as you can, the pace of

your easy runs should be 2.5 to 3 minutes slower, says running coach Jeff Gaudette of Boston-based RunnersConnect. If you try to run all your easy runs at your 5-K pace, you're going to get injured and burned out. That's a very common cause of injury.

3 Get some company—without the pressure. If your work and family life requires you do to all your workouts on your own, that can get lonely after a while, not to mention boring. When you enter a race, you can enjoy the company of others without worrying about whether you're running too slow and holding someone else back, or what to talk about, or planning out a route. You can socialize with others as much or as little as you would like.

4 Get some perspective. At a race, you'll see people of all ages, abilities, shapes, and sizes. You're sure to see people who look more or less fit than you, and you'll likely be surprised at how they'll finish. You may be amazed to see how fast some people who seem less fit are able to go. And this may lift the limitations you envision on your own potential. Likewise, you may be able to pass people who look fitter than you and gain confidence from that. And seeing people who seem older or who seem to have more obstacles finish a race might help you get out the door when you're struggling to get motivated.

Bart Says . . .

In my mind, these are the keys to success for your first race.

1. Set smart goals. Start with the goal to finish the race feeling good and wanting to do it again. Don't put the pressure of some lofty time goal on yourself.

2. Don't start too fast. Your first mile should feel so easy that you think you're going too slow. In the final mile, you'll pass everyone who passed you.

3. Celebrate your accomplishment. Don't take it lightly. Be proud of it. It's too easy to dwell on the negative. Savor the positive.

5 **Find new routes.** It's easy to get into a rut of covering the same distance over and over, when it's measured. If you run a 5-K nearby, you'll get to see new routes and runnable roads that might mix up your routine on other days.

6 **Feel like a runner.** It's easy for us all to write ourselves off as not real runners. But when you pin on the race bib, then cross that finish line, it helps you see yourself more like a runner and reinforces that feeling that you're a runner.

7 **Boost your confidence.** Even if you're not competitive, there's a good chance you'll feel a shot of adrenaline when you pin on the race bib, when the starting gun fires, when you hear the cheers and applause from spectators, or when the finish line comes in sight. That may help you cover the mileage faster than you ever have before. In that way, racing can give you a glimpse of your own potential.

Your Prerace Checklist

Even for seasoned runners, the days before a race can be stressful. With all the hard work that you've invested in your goal event, you want to arrive at the starting line feeling calm, healthy, and ready to run your best. Here are a few reminders to keep you on track in the critical days and hours before the starting gun fires and to help you recover after you cross the finish line.

The Days Before the Race

Stop stressing. 5-Ks and 10-Ks are typically very positive community events. You get to spend a morning with strangers cheering you on, feeding you, and offering water; and you're celebrating doing something healthy for yourself. Everyone fears that they'll be last, but don't worry. In all likelihood, you won't be. People with a very wide range of abilities and levels of fitness do 5-Ks, and many people just go to walk them from start to finish.

Cover the route beforehand. If you can, work out on the route where the race will take place so you can get familiar with where you'll need to push and where you can cruise. Finding the race start beforehand will prevent you from getting lost on race morning.

Eat what works for you. Your best bet is to eat whatever has worked best for you—that's given you a boost without upsetting your stomach—during your regular weekday runs. Don't eat anything heavy within 2 hours of the race. A smoothie containing fruit and yogurt is always a good choice

FUELING UP FOR YOUR FIRST 5-K

What should you eat and drink before your first 5-K? The proper prerace fueling will help you stay energized for the race, without leaving you with an upset stomach. Follow these tips from nutritionist Pamela Nisevich Bede.

STAY HYDRATED WELL AHEAD OF RACE DAY. It's best to sip on water throughout the days before the race. Avoid pounding the fluids right before the starting gun; this could you leave you feeling sick to your stomach or needing to take a break from the race to hit the bathroom.

NO NEED TO CARB-LOAD. The practice of carb-loading (increasing your intake of carbohydrate-heavy foods while cutting back on protein and fat in the days before a race) is geared for events of 90 minutes or longer. More than likely, you'll be done with your 5-K long before that! For a 5-K, you probably have enough fuel in your muscles—and from a healthy prerace meal—to race your best without risking running out of energy. If you attempted to carb-load before a 5-K, you'll end up with lots of extra calories and feeling bloated, nauseous, and like you have heavy legs by the time the starting gun fires.

FOR A MORNING RACE, EAT A LIGHT PRERACE BREAKFAST. Plan to consume a 200- to 300-calorie meal 1 to 2 hours before the race. The majority of the calories should come from wholesome carbs. Keep the meal low in fiber and fat; both take a long time to digest. Aim for less than 10 grams of fiber per serving, or less if you have a sensitive stomach, and 5 to 10 grams of fat. It's also a good idea to stay away from the spicy stuff, which could upset your stomach.

You don't need too much food to fuel you across 3.1 miles. A bakery bagel along with a small apple is a great option; wash it down with 8 ounces of sports drink. Or you might try an English muffin topped with 2 tablespoons of jam and some fruit. Others swear by a bowl of oatmeal topped with some raisins and brown sugar. Your goal is to have a carb-rich meal that's easy to digest and not too big. Experiment with different foods before your training runs so you know what works for your system—and what doesn't—so there will be no surprises on race day.

FOR A LATE-DAY RACE, EAT LIGHT AND HEALTHY ALL DAY LONG. If your race is in the late afternoon or early evening, what you eat at breakfast and lunch will have a big impact on how you feel for the event. For breakfast,

because it gives you a good balance of carbs and protein but not too much fiber (which could cause GI distress).

Don't do anything new. Race week isn't the time to try new shoes, new food or drinks, new gear, or anything else you haven't used on several workouts. Stick with the routine that works for you.

Get off your feet. In the days before your race, try to stay off your feet as much focus on carbs with some lean protein. You might try oatmeal with fruit, low-fat yogurt topped with fruit and granola, or a bagel topped with a scrambled egg and some fruit. Cereal is a great bet, but avoid high-fiber cereals (those with more than 5 grams of fiber per serving).

At lunch, avoid high-fat and high-protein items since they take longer to digest. You might have a cup of pasta tossed with some marinara sauce with a cup of skim milk. (Skip the cheese and buttery garlic bread). Or you might try a turkey sandwich (hold the mayo and go easy on the veggie toppings) with a side of pretzels and a bottle of water. Avoid eating until you're stuffed. You don't want to arrive at the starting line still feeling full.

DON'T FORGET THE FLUIDS. Be sure to wash down your prerace meal with plenty of fluids. Aim to consume 17 to 20 ounces of fluids 2 to 3 hours before the race, and another 7 to 10 ounces 10 to 20 minutes before the race begins. It's okay to have coffee, tea, or a sports drink if you regularly drink those fluids before your runs and they don't upset your stomach.

HAVE A PRERACE SNACK IF YOU'RE HUNGRY. If you feel hungry on the way to the race, have a small snack of 150 to 250 calories that quiets your hunger without filling you up. You might grab a small banana or a handful of animal crackers. Another option: Have some energy chews or even an energy bar, which provides quick fuel that's easy to digest. Choose one that is high in carbohydrates and has less than 10 grams total of protein and fat. Be sure to wash it down with 7 to 10 ounces of water or sports drink.

MAKE TIME FOR A PIT STOP. Plan to arrive at the race with enough time to hit the bathrooms without feeling rushed before the race begins. Arriving at least 1 hour before the starting gun fires should give you plenty of time.

DON'T DO ANYTHING NEW. Whatever you consume, make it something that's worked for you during your regular training runs. It should be something that energizes you but doesn't leave you with an upset stomach. Avoid anything new; you don't want your first 5-K to be derailed by a pit stop.

as possible. Relax and leave the lawn mowing or shopping or sightseeing for after the race.

Gather your gear. The night before the race, lay out your clothes, and if you have your bib, fasten it on. That's the one thing you need at the starting line. Don't show up without it! Get as much sleep as possible—aim for 8 hours.

Race Day

Limit your sipping. Yes, you need to stay hydrated, but no major drinking 30 minutes before the gun; sip if your mouth is dry or it's particularly hot out. Your best bet is to stay hydrated throughout the day every day. Aim for half your body weight in ounces. So for instance, if you weigh 200 pounds, aim for 100 ounces of calorie-free fluids like water each day. If you weigh 160 pounds, aim for 80 ounces per day.

Arrive early. Get to the race at least 1 hour before the start so you'll have time to pick up your number (if you don't already have it), use the porta potty, and warm up. You don't want to be running to the starting line.

Identify yourself. Put your name, address, cell phone number, bib number, and e-mail address clearly on your race bib, or better yet, use a RoadID, which you can wear on your wrist or shoe.

Bring extra tissue. The only thing worse than waiting in a long porta potty line is getting to the front and realizing that there's nothing to wipe with.

Don't overdress. It's likely to be cool at the start, but don't wear more clothing than you need. Dress for 20 degrees warmer than it is outside. To stay warm at the start, you may want to bring (expendable) clothes that you can throw off after you warm up.

Set at least two goals. If it's your first time covering the distance, just focus on finishing. Set one goal for a perfect race and another as a backup in case it's hot, it's windy, or it's just not your day. If something makes your first goal impossible halfway through the race, you'll need another goal to motivate you to finish strong. And it's best to set a third goal that has nothing to do with your finishing time. This performance goal could be something like finishing, running up the hills rather than walking them, or eating the right foods at the right time and successfully avoiding GI distress!

Fix it sooner, not later. If your shoelace is getting untied or you start to chafe early in the race, take care of it before it becomes a real problem later in the race.

Start slow and stay even. Run the first 10 percent of the race slower than you normally would, with the idea that you'll finish strong. Don't try to "bank" time by going out faster than your goal pace. If you do that, you risk burning out early. Try to keep an even pace throughout the race and save your extra energy for the final stretch to the finish.

After the Race

Keep moving. After you cross the finish line, keep walking for at least 5 to 10 minutes to fend off stiffness and gradually bring your heart rate back to its resting state. Be sure to do some postrace recovery stretches (see page 194) to loosen up your legs, back, and hips.

Refuel. There are usually snacks at the finish line, but what the race provides may not sit well with you. To recover quickly, bring a snack with a combination of protein to rebuild muscles and healthy carbs to restock your energy stores. Consume it within 30 minutes of finishing the race. You might try a sports recovery drink, energy bar, or other packaged food that won't spoil, spill, or get ruined in transit.

Get warm. Change out of the clothes you ran in and get into dry clothes as soon as possible. After you cross the finish line, your core temperature will start to drop fast, and keeping sweaty clothes on will make you cold.

The next day, get going. As sore as you might feel the day after the race, it's important to do some sort of nonimpact activity like swimming, cycling, or working out on the elliptical trainer. The movement will increase circulation to your sore muscles and help you bounce back sooner. Just keep the effort level easy.

AID STATIONS

Most races provide some aid stations on the race course with bathrooms, water, and food. This is great if they do, because you don't have to bring your own. However, aid stations can be tricky to negotiate when you've got lots of runners all trying to get through at once. Here are some tips to get through them smoothly.

FIND OUT WHAT THEY'RE SERVING BEFOREHAND. Check the race Web site before the big day to find out whether they're serving water or sports drink at the race. Try the brand and flavor that they're serving before the big day so that you can make sure it sits well with you. If it doesn't, you can bring your own.

DON'T STOP SHORT. As you're approaching an aid station, you'll see a lot of people piling up right in front to get their drinks. Run past the pileup and target the end of the aid station.

LOOK BEFORE YOU SIP. Look for one of the last volunteers—make eye contact—and hold your hand out to reach for it. Make sure to ask "water or sports drink?" before you take it.

STEP AWAY. Once you get your cup, step away from the aid station, so no one collides into you from behind.

PINCH AND SIP. Pinch the cup at the top so that it forms a spout, and sip. *Remember: Pinch and sip.*

TAKE YOUR TIME. Don't worry about losing time here. It's worth the few extra seconds it takes to slow down to make sure you're getting the fluids down and staying hydrated. If you try to drink while you continue to run, there's a good chance you'll end up with the drink up your nose, or all over your clothes, and that can make the rest of the race pretty uncomfortable.

How Running Changed My Life

By Bart Yasso, chief running officer, *Runner's World*

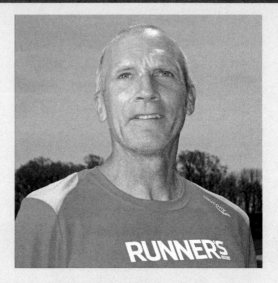

Starting at age 14, I got drunk every day. I refused to acknowledge it at the time, but I was an alcoholic and a dopehead. Then I got busted when I drove a friend to buy marijuana from a guy who turned out to be an undercover narcotics agent. If relations between my father and me were difficult before, they grew far worse after my arrest. He refused to have anything to do with me. Being arrested scared the crap out of me. I knew if I ever got charged with a drug-related offense again, I'd end up in jail. I never wanted that address, so I stopped smoking pot. To compensate, I drank more. Much more.

Four years later, I stopped binge drinking, and a dog called Brandy, ironically, was my savior. Brandy was my girlfriend's dog, a rambunctious collie that needed a lot of exercise. I started taking her for walks through the woods, and when we arrived in a clearing, she'd take off like a rocket. I envied the sense of freedom and joy she got from bounding through the grass. One day, I decided to try it myself. I ran a half mile to a local bar before collapsing on a stool. I downed two beers to celebrate, then walked home. I considered the jaunt a success and marveled at my willpower to leave before closing hour.

I continued to walk Brandy after work each night and run on my own. One morning as I was driving to the grocery for milk and a newspaper, I spotted an old friend from grade school running in the rain at 5 a.m. *Now that's dedication*, I thought. I started following this regimen, rising early every morning to log 3 miles before work. I struggled at first. My lungs burned from smoking two packs of cigarettes a day, and my legs felt like cinder blocks. But gradually it got easier, and I began to relish the peace and stillness of dawn. These runs became a form of therapy, a time to sweat and breathe and disconnect from the distractions of life.

At first, I didn't think about racing. I would just get out there and enjoy the freedom I felt. I would try to challenge myself, starting to run certain distances. It was fun to see that it would take me 20 minutes to cover 2 miles, then see that I could do it faster. It took time. But it was amazing to me. The improvement was way easier than I thought it would be. Running gave me confidence. It gave me belief in myself, which is what I needed the most. Running gave me focus. And it gave me guidance. I started each day with a run, and knowing that I had run set the tone for the rest of the day.

Running changed every aspect of my life. I was a better person and a better worker. Once I started running, I really cut back on the alcohol. There were no more drinking binges; I just would drink socially. About 2 years after I started running, I completely gave up drinking. I just realized I was much better off without it.

Quitting drinking was easy because of running. I don't think I would have been able to quit without the running. Running just gave me focus. I started to think, *Some day I'll try to run 6 miles. Some day I'll try to run 10 miles.* I read everything about running that I could get my hands on. I read *Runner's World.* I bought Jim Fixx's book *The Complete Book of Running*, and I read that three times. I read everything George Sheehan wrote.

Running really did save my life. If I'd kept up all the drinking and drugs I was doing at age 14, there's no way I'd be here today. All the people I hung out with from those days are either dead or institutionalized, and I would be, too, if I had stayed on that track. I always say "never limit where running can take you," and I mean that in a geographical sense. But more important, I mean that in an emotional sense. And I mean that in a mental sense. This sport is powerful. And it can change your life.

CHAPTER 3

MOTIVATION: GETTING GOING AND STICKING WITH IT

Like a lot of people, B.J. Keeton will never forget the breaking point that got him moving.

When he boarded a roller coaster in the summer of 2010 with his wife, the attendant could barely click the safety harness over his gut—even though he was sitting in the plus-size seat. The harness only clicked once; everyone else's clicked three times.

"I thought I was going to fall out of the seat and die," says Keeton, who was 310 pounds at the time. "At that moment, I knew my life had to change. I couldn't let my weight—which I had never cared about that much before—hold me back from living my life. I was 27 years old and a newlywed. I had my whole life in front of me. I needed to be able to enjoy it."

Indeed, for most of us, our call to action strikes like a bolt of lightning. Maybe we've been haunted for years by the awareness that we *should* be doing some exercise but were always seduced by the many very good reasons not to—we are too busy, too tired, too stressed, too cash strapped, too sick, too embarrassed, too haunted by bad memories of grade-school gym class, or just too scared. The inertia just feels too leaden to overcome.

For sure, the mental challenges are more difficult to overcome than anything our legs and lungs will have to endure. But if you've exercised even a little, you know—if you can get over those obstacles and get out the door, you will be rewarded handsomely in the form of confidence, weight loss, optimism, improved health, and too many other benefits to name. Just ask Keeton. He started walking, then running, made over his diet, and lost 146 pounds. Now he's training for his first half-marathon.

"It gets better. Really. I promise," he says. "The hurting stops. The exhaustion goes away. The cramps and blisters and all of that is temporary. It doesn't seem that way at first, but it eventually becomes one of the best things in the world. But you have to stick with it. Oh, and those first 2 miles? They always suck. Always. For everyone."

In this chapter, you'll find all the tools you need to get going and stick with it. You'll learn how to get over the mental obstacles to getting out the door, and the ones that you inevitably face when you're on the road. Most important, you'll learn how to develop a love of running that will last for life.

Getting Over Obstacles to Getting Out the Door

Here's how to clear some common mental roadblocks that can keep you from getting going.

THE OBSTACLE: I missed working out for a week because of my job (or I was hurt, sick, or insert excuse here), and it feels like too much work to start over. I might as well give up.

Get over it: Press the reset button and start over, like you would on a video game, says running coach Jeff Gaudette of Boston-

based RunnersConnect. Just focus on moving forward.

THE OBSTACLE: I'm worried everyone will laugh!

Get over it: Enlist a buddy for your first outing to the gym, the trail, or even a group run. Or connect online with other newbies who are venturing out for their first runs at sites like runnersworld.com/the-starting -line. Studies have shown that buddying up— whether it's a person, a running group, or an online group—increases your chances of sticking with an exercise routine.[36] Everyone feels self-conscious at first. Susan Monk, training coordinator for the Atlanta Track Club, says she often hears from people who came to the first day of training but felt too daunted to get out of their cars. Recruit a support crew of non-runners to support your efforts, whether it's your spouse, parents, roommate, boss, or coworkers, says coach Mindy Solkin of The Running Center, which is based in New York. "When someone who isn't in the running world knows that you used to be on the couch, they can appreciate what a big deal it is that you just ran 2 miles," she says. "It's a big deal."

THE OBSTACLE: I'm too busy!

Get over it: Find the time of day when running is a nonnegotiable, says coach and exercise physiologist Susan Paul of the Track Shack Foundation in Orlando. For most people, that's the morning, when no meetings are scheduled and the kids are still in bed. "If you do it first thing, you don't have time to think up an excuse," she says.

And make sure that you have cleared enough time to work out so that it doesn't jam up your day. If a morning run means you're speeding to work and stressed about being late, the workout will start to feel like punishment, says Charles Duhigg, author of *The Power of Habit*. "The brain starts relating to the workout in a negative way," he says, "and it will be hard to make it into a habit."

Making Exercise a Habit

When Tom Cattell resolved to start running, he didn't want to give up. After all, he was 278 pounds with high blood pressure, high cholesterol, and prediabetes. He had tried exercising in the past, running three or four times a week at different times of day, but it never stuck.

He started working out 6 days a week and walking on the seventh day. He started working out every day after work and first thing on weekends, no matter what time it was and no matter what the weather conditions were.

"It's sort of like brushing your teeth," says Cattell, 50, a father of five from Birmingham, Alabama. "I never forget to brush because I do it at the same time every day. Now it is the same for running."

Indeed, Cattell discovered firsthand what experts have found to be true. If you take steps to make exercise into a habit, you'll find it easier to stay on track and reach your fitness goals.

"Once exercise becomes a habit, it just feels easier," says Duhigg, who trained for the 2012 New York City Marathon. "So when you don't feel like doing it, it doesn't take as much willpower."

After a few weeks of running, you begin to believe that the whole concept of a "runner's high" is not a myth. Feel-good brain chemicals—like dopamine and endocannabinoids—will be released while you're on the road, and you'll feel so proud of what you accomplished that it will take more discipline to rest than to run.

But until that happens, it can be hard to force yourself out the door. And relying on willpower just won't work, experts say. "We tell ourselves we will 'make ourselves do it,' but that puts a lot of strain on your willpower resources, and everyone's willpower is a limited resource," says Heidi Grant Halvorson, associate director of the Motivation Science Center at the Columbia University Business School. Once your resolve gets weak—when you're tired, stressed, and so many things seem more appealing than running—willpower breaks down.

Indeed, Cattell is the first to admit that "running isn't fun all the time.

"Sometimes it's a great run; sometimes it's difficult," he says. "But once running became a habit, it didn't matter if yesterday was a good run or not. It was just habit."

And his healthy habit has paid off. Not only has he lost nearly 100 pounds, but most important, getting out the door feels second nature. "The great thing is I do it without

(continued on page 90)

How Running Changed My Life

Running helped Jamie Kontos heal from a painful breakup and gain control over unhealthy eating habits

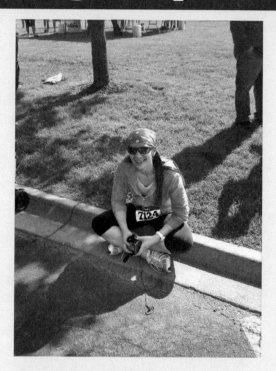

Jamie Kontos desperately needed a stress reliever. Just 2 weeks after breaking up with her fiancé, she was starting an internship as a mental health professional. She knew that she wouldn't be able to help her clients if she couldn't help herself first.

She also wanted to shed some weight. So she joined a gym and started working out, alternating between 1 minute of running and 1 or more minutes of walking.

"Running helped me escape from painful emotions and provided me with a way to manage stress while simultaneously building my fitness," she says. Rather than eat her emotions or become a couch potato, she used her pent-up emotions on the treadmill or bike path.

"Running was the time I gave to myself to sort through any emotion I felt, whether it was anger, sadness, or loneliness," she says.

Now, though she's a full-time graduate student working three jobs, 4 days a week, Kontos wakes up at 5 a.m. and runs and strength trains. And it's paid off. She is 45 pounds lighter and feels more confident.

"Running makes me feel empowered," she says. "Running has given me a renewed sense of confidence that I have not received anywhere else. After a run, I feel like I can accomplish any goal I set my mind to."

AGE: 24

HOMETOWN: New Lenox, Illinois

OCCUPATION: Mental health professional/full-time student

What was the biggest hurdle, and how do you get over it? Perseverance. Everyone struggles from day to day. When I hit a plateau, I let my body rest. When it's time to get back to it, I do it. There is no time to overanalyze and beat my goals to death. My workout is the time to stop thinking.

How do you find the energy and time to work out with your busy schedule? I make sure to get at least 7 hours of sleep per night, even if that means sacrificing socializing from time to time. After I jot down my hectic schedule, I find a block of time where I can squeeze in my runs. I manage to get a good run in at 5 a.m. with over an hour to get ready for the day. Fit in your workout in the morning so you can get it out of the way. Plus, you'll most likely feel energized and you won't put it off by the time you get home.

What kinds of changes did you make to your diet? My biggest struggle is bingeing. I'm not eating unhealthy foods, I just eat a lot. The way I manage this is by staying busy. Oh, there are some homemade cookies on the counter? I'll walk the dog instead. Cravings go away in about 20 minutes, so if you can stay busy for 20 minutes, you won't think about food for long.

How did you manage your exercise and eating issues? Food has been my enemy since I was over 180 pounds in high school. I was always the "chunky girl" when I was younger. To this day, I struggle with eating. When I got into running, I did not feel the need to binge myself to death. The adrenaline from a good run helps put my cravings to rest. Instead of eating out of emotional deprivation, I eat to sustain my energy and fuel my body for runs. Mornings are when I binge. So when I run in the morning, I manage to eat much more balanced throughout the day.

What has been the biggest reward of your running life? Running was about taking control of my life during a time where I felt completely helpless. I cannot control what happens at work or school, but I can control how I take care of myself. Running makes me feel good overall. As a result, I feel more confident at school, work, and among my friends and family. I am rather shy, and I try to avoid conflict. But since I started running, I have felt more outgoing and tackle issues head-on. I'm not saying running is completely responsible for this, but it definitely contributes to my overall sense of self.

What advice would you give to a beginner? Start slow. Do not expect too much of yourself all at once.

Favorite motivational quotes: "If you're going through hell, keep going." —Winston Churchill

Bart Says . . .

 A lot of people see elite athletes or see models in magazines like *Runner's World* and say, "I'm not a runner." But a runner is someone who heads out the door and runs. A golfer is someone who golfs. It doesn't matter how fast you're going. The beauty of this sport is how accepting it is of people of all abilities. And it doesn't matter whether you're running, jogging, doing a run/walk, or sauntering.

even thinking most of the time," he says. "It's just another part of the day, like taking a shower. The fact that it's a habit keeps the desire going when times are tough. It becomes hard not to do it."

Here are some of Duhigg's best tips on how to make running a habit and how to make it stick.

Make a plan. According to Duhigg, every habit is made up of a group of cues (e.g., time, place, mood, music, certain other people), a reward (chocolate, massage, hot shower, smoothie), and a routine (the running). So pick some cues (e.g., the most convenient time to run or the best route to take) and rewards that will incentivize you to run. Then write out a plan with the cues and rewards and post it where you can see it. Let's say the best time to run is morning; you've got an energizing music mix on your iPod, and your reward is a

relaxing long, hot shower. Your plan would be: "If it's morning and I hear this music, I will run, because then I'll get a long, hot shower." Post the plan where you can see it. Try it for a week. If it doesn't work, try changing the cues or the rewards.

Keep it regular. Create a prerun routine to cue your body and mind that it's time to run, and repeat it every time you go. Always go at the same time of day. Place your workout clothes next to your bed. Play the same workout music before you go out. "In order to make something like running into a habit, you have to have cues to trigger you, and they have to be consistent," says Duhigg. "You're creating neural pathways that make the activity into a habit," he adds.

Reward yourself immediately. Right after your run, treat yourself to something you genuinely enjoy—a hot shower, a smoothie, even a small piece of dark chocolate—so your brain associates exercise with an immediate reward. "You have to get the reward right away for something to become automatic," says Duhigg. "You can't intellectualize your way to a reward. You have to teach the brain about reward through experience."

Build your own support system. Equip your running routine with the activities that will make you feel good about it and get you revved up to get up and go each day, says Duhigg. Meet up with friends so that the run doubles as socializing time; track your miles so that you can see the progress you're making and the fitness improvements.

Make Your Workout Happen Any Time of Day

What's the best time of day to work out? It's whatever time of day you're most likely to consistently get it done!

Whether you're a morning person, a night owl, or someone who looks forward to a midday break to split up the workday, what matters most is clearing whatever road-blocks get between you and your workout.

MORNING: Many people find that the morning is the easiest time to consistently work out. That's the only time when other family and work activities aren't likely to get in the way. But there are challenges. In the a.m., your body temperature and heart rate are at their lowest levels. If you skipped dinner the night before or ate fast-digesting carbs like rice, bread, or sugary desserts, your fuel stores will be depleted, which will make it hard to find the energy to get up. And if you skimped on sleep—8 hours is ideal—you're going to be more likely to hit the snooze button than to hit the road.

How to: Prep for an early-morning walk or run the night before. Eat slow-digesting carbs like broccoli, beans, and lentils. Set your automatic coffeemaker to brew before you wake. Turn off the computer and TV at least 30 minutes before you hit the sack and get blackout shades for your windows—the absence of light boosts production of melatonin, a hormone that makes you feel sleepy. Move your alarm clock across the room, so you'll have to get out of bed to turn it off. And once you're up, put on your exercise clothes in a brightly lit room: When light hits your eyes, it signals your pineal gland to stop producing melatonin, helping you wake up.

MIDDAY: Your body's level of melatonin, the sleepiness hormone, is at its lowest around noon, so physiologically that's when you're most alert. While it may be tempting to keep plugging away at work, it's time for a break. And if you haven't eaten, you may be more tempted to grab lunch rather than a workout.

How to: Schedule your walk or run like you would any other meeting; put it on your to-do list and cross it off for the confidence boost that comes from mission accomplished. Split your lunch in two: Eat half of it an hour before you go out, then have the remaining food afterward. Don't stress about missing work—exercise has been proven to increase work productivity.

LATER IN THE DAY: Many people save their workouts until the end of the day and rely on it to burn off stress. And for many people, that's the only opportunity to run. The good news is that research shows that your body is primed to perform its best late in the afternoon and early evening because that's when your core body temperature peaks. But if you've tried it, you know;

willpower can wane as the day goes on. Levels of the hormone cortisol, which helps your body get energy from the foods you eat, drop throughout the day. So while your muscles might be running-ready, your brain might talk you into bagging your workout.

Refuel. Low blood sugar levels can leave you feeling unfocused and in no mood for a workout. If you're a midday or evening runner, and the last meal you had was several hours ago, you may need to refuel your energy stores. Eat a high-carb snack (banana, pretzels) of 150 to 200 calories about an hour before you lace up.

Perk up. Caffeine releases dopamine and norepinephrine—two energizing neurotransmitters—into the brain, which boost alertness and motivation, says William R. Lovallo, PhD, professor of psychiatry at the University of Oklahoma Health Sciences Center. Caffeine also triggers the release of glucose into the bloodstream for extra energy. Studies show that 80 milligrams (a small cup of coffee) consumed 15 to 60 minutes before exercise can boost performance. But guzzle with caution. Caffeine stays in the system an average of 4.5 hours—in some people, it can have a half-life of up to 9 hours. So limit your consumption—or skip it entirely—if you run really late in the day so it doesn't interfere with your sleep.

Get inspired. Surround yourself with inspiration. Watch an energizing running video. Decorate your office with motivating running pictures, quotes, or bib numbers to create a similar effect, encouraging you to replicate the actions.

Stay accountable. Set a reminder on your smartphone to keep your afternoon run date. And using a mileage-tracking app that shares your progress with your friends can make you less likely to bail on a run.

Get into the habit. Create a routine that you can repeat before every run. An hour or so before you're supposed to head out, do the same exact sequence of events: Fill your water bottle, eat a banana, listen to a song that pumps you up, or watch an inspiring video. Going through the identical paces will help you condition yourself to crave your run.[37]

Get Over Mental Roadblocks on the Run

Regular exercise is supposed to relieve stress. So why can it sometimes feel so stressful? No matter how fit or fast we get, we're all vulnerable to fear, doubt, and insecurity when we venture out in our running gear.

As you become a runner, it's important to learn how to talk back to the negative voices that inevitably crop up when your body and brain tire out on the road.

Here's how to be your own cheering section.

PROBLEM: You feel overwhelmed by the distance you still have to do.

Solution: Break it down.

Studies have shown that about two-thirds of the way through any race, whatever the distance, runners tend to hit the wall. At that point, the excitement of the start has worn off, and the finish still feels like it's very far away. Anticipate that you're going to hit this tough stretch and prepare for it. Try doing a body scan. Are you in physical pain? Are you on the edge of your injury? Are you capable of taking just one more step? If so, keep going. Break the distance down into segments. Just focus on running to the next block or lamppost. Once you get there, pick another target just ahead.

PROBLEM: You get tired.

Solution: Slow down.

Ease back to a pace where you can maintain a conversation; you should feel relaxed, like you could run at that pace for an entire day if you had to. If you're huffing and puffing, you're going too fast. And do a body scan. Are you feeling acute pain? Is anything broken? Are you tensing nonrunning muscles? This is common when you're struggling, but it zaps the strength your legs and lungs need. Relax your brow and cheeks, unclench your jaw, move your shoulders away from your ears, and keep your hands loose and palms to the sky. Breathe.

PROBLEM: You feel discouraged.

Solution: Replay the "highlights reel" of the greatest moments of your life.

In a training log, keep a running tally of the number of miles and time that you've spent working out so you always know how much you've accomplished. It will make whatever distance you still have to cover seem much more manageable. Remember, all you can do is your best, and commit to be proud of whatever that amounts to.

PROBLEM: You feel demoralized because someone passed you.

Solution: Draw strength from others.

That runner who just whizzed by? He's showing you what's possible and how fast you can run. And remember that just by being out there, you're inspiring others who are still on the couch, and everyone who is driving by, and showing *them* what's possible. Keep moving.

Try to avoid comparing yourself to others. Remember: You're becoming a runner in order to be a better version of yourself— and to fulfill your own unique potential. George Sheehan, the author and longtime *Runner's World* columnist, once said, "The whole idea is not to beat other runners. Eventually, you learn that the competition is against the little voice inside you that wants to quit."

How to Break Out of a Rut

No matter how much you love to run, there are bound to be days when you're burned out, bored, frustrated, and want to throw your running shoes out the window. Sure, routine can help keep you consistent, but mixing things up every once in a while can help prevent you from falling—feet first—into a fitness rut. Here are six easy ways to revive your running desire.

1 Get a change of scenery. Find a new route. If you have a GPS, set out to run only on streets and routes that you haven't explored before. (Check out *Runner's World*'s route finder at runnersworld.com/routefinder.) If you're a roadie, hit the trails. The softer surface will give your bones and joints a break from the impact on the concrete. In the woods, the trees will provide the shade and breeze that you can't get in the city. Plus, focusing on navigating technical terrain (i.e., not falling face first over rocks and roots) will take your mind off the mileage. (For more, see "Your First Trail Run" on page 11.) Already run trails? Hit the road or the treadmill. (Find "Treadmill Training" on page 16.) Freed from worrying about your footing, you'll be able to get some quick work in.

2 Get some company. If you're committed to going solo, try hooking up with a buddy or joining a group. Choose your partners carefully; picking the perfect training partner can be tougher than dating.

Having company can make the miles roll by faster; you can explore new routes and run at times of day and in places that you might not feel safe covering alone. And knowing that you have to meet someone at 5 a.m. may be just the commitment you need to keep your training on track when it's so tempting to sleep in. Ask about group runs at a local running store or club (find clubs near you at runningintheusa.com/club). Friendly, informal runs are usually offered weekly and are open to runners of all abilities. Before joining a group for the first time, find out about the typical pace, route, and crowd. Are you likely to be the only newbie? Is it a bunch of grizzled veterans? (For more tips, see "Group Dynamics" on page 38.)

3 Reset your goals. Make some goals that have nothing to do with pace or the outcome of a race or any given run. You might start a workout streak, challenging yourself to do some sort of exercise every day. Or make a goal to run someplace new every day. Set some smaller short-term process goals that ultimately help you get fitter and faster. Do you always run out of energy? Aim to improve your pacing strategy, starting more slowly and finishing feeling strong. If you typically walk up hills, try running up them or maintaining the same pace as you do on even ground. (For more tips, see "Hills" on page 35.)

4 **Go race.** Even if you're a diehard long-distance runner, jumping into a 5-K is a great way to get a break from the monotony of training solo and rev up your competitive juices. There are usually 5-Ks in most areas on most weekends, so it should be easy to find one anytime near you. Find an event near you at runnersworld.com/race-finder. Learn more about racing in "Reasons to Race" on page 75.)

5 **Plug in . . .** Sometimes it's hard to gauge your effort level on your own, and the wind, fatigue, hills, and burnout can make your daily workout feel like a slogfest. If you usually run without technology, strap on a heart rate monitor and/or a GPS to determine exactly how far and how fast you're going. (Read more at "How to Gauge Your Fitness" on page 24.) On easy days, these devices can help ensure that you're going slow enough to give your muscles a genuine chance to recover, so you have more energy for quality workouts like speed sessions, tempo work, and long runs. During quality workouts, these devices can ensure that you're working hard enough to get the most benefit out of your workout so you can reach your race day goals. And you don't have to take technology so seriously: Strap on the GPS to run your errands, to find out how much distance you usually cover in the car. Run to a destination you typically drive to and have a friend pick you up. Even just hooking up some tunes can do you good.

Bart Says . . .

If you're lacing up the shoes and heading out the door, you're a mentor to others. You may not even notice it, but you are. Maybe a neighbor sees you running and thinks, for the first time, "Hey, maybe I can do this, too."

Studies have shown that listening to upbeat music will make the effort seem easier. (On the roads, keep the volume low enough to hear an oncoming vehicle, and wear only one earbud.) *Runner's World* has playlists at runnersworld.com/running-playlists.

6 **. . . or tune out.** If you tend to be a slave to the numbers, on one day each week take a tech timeout and run by feel. Sometimes, trying to boost the pace your training watch is displaying can spur you to override important signals your body is sending about how hard you're working. By leaving the devices at home, you can continuously scan your body to evaluate factors like how labored your breathing is. When you're running without a watch, it will be easier to bring yourself to adjust your effort if it's hot or if there's a headwind. Most important, freed from the stress of constant feedback on how fast or slow you're going, you may be able to enjoy your run more.

The Other Runner

By Ted Spiker, author of the *Runner's World* Big Guy Blog

The most challenging part about getting started running? Not the first steps, not the leg or lung pain, not the wall, not even learning the hard way that you may need lube or Band-Aids to prevent chafing in sensitive spots. It's a creature that can ease your mind, or mess with it. It's a creature that can drive you to the finish line, or drive you crazy. It's a creature that would rarely do anything to harm you intentionally, but may do so accidentally.

The Other Runner.

The Other Runner comes in all shapes, sizes, paces, and personalities (you're wearing neon for your shirt *and* your top *and* your compression socks *and* your shoes?). The Other Runner passes by us on our neighborhood runs. The Other Runner surrounds us in races by the hundreds, by the thousands. The Other Runner chimes in on message boards and in running clubs and may be your Uncle Josh, who has logged 37 marathons and does everything the way it's supposed to be done. The Other Runner has raced a lot, knows a lot, and—from your perspective—appears to zip through routes without an ounce of effort. The Other Runner has legs the size of my arms. The Other Runner can run 5, 6, 7, 8, whatever-many miles in the time I can do 4. For these reasons, the Other Runner can piss me off.

But the Other Runner can also help you—with advice, with encouragement, with a "we can do it" in the last two-tenths of a mile of the longest race you've ever run. The Other Runner has been through your struggles and many more, and the Other Runner—almost always—means well and wants you to succeed because, after all, the two of you aren't racing head-to-head. Unless you *are* in the last two-tenths of a mile and you haven't spoken a word up until this very moment, where you both want to see who has the most left in the tank.

As a bigger guy who has run a long time (and takes a long time to run), I think one of the hardest parts about running is getting out of your own mind. You see so much speed, you see so much grit, you see people who persevere, you see gazelles who log more miles on their feet than you could on your bike. And you get inspired. But you also get frustrated by bonking, by injuries, by size, by stride, by slower-than-you-want paces. Because it's hard *not* to compare yourself to others.

People will tell you that you need to stay in your own bubble. You run your race and compete only against yourself. Forget the rest. The minute you judge yourself based on the actions of others is the minute that you suffer from a sprained mojo—and go on the psychological DL. But how do you block it all out? How do you take the good stuff that the Other Runner can offer while not getting caught up in the things that can deflate you? Though I've far from figured it out, I try to plod forward, using my Other Runner Mantra, which goes something like this:

Other Runners have excellent advice and suggestions. They do not have The Only Answer. It's my job to ask questions, to listen, to experiment, and to thank them for their help.

Other Runners will be (a lot) faster than I will be. I have to stop thinking that has anything whatsoever to do with me.

Other Runners are always cool cats, who care about the well-being of their fellow runners, unless they don't look before they blow snot rockets.

Other Runners, in a race, can upset you because you can't keep up, but they can also get you going, if you can set your eyes on one or two of them running a few feet ahead of you and make it your mission to pick them off by the end.

Other Runners, ultimately, want you to feel the same joy that they do when they run. They want you to feel the force field that comes from being in the presence of Other Runners. They know that running is such a beautiful sport because while the final result is all about yourself, the sense of community and energy and passion is out of this world when you do it with others.

PART 2

NUTRITION AND WEIGHT LOSS

Two of the most important factors in determining your running success have to do with what's on your mind and what's in your stomach. In the previous chapter, we addressed how to manage your mind-set to become a runner. In the next section, we'll address how to eat like a runner.

If you don't have the proper amount and kind of fuel in your stomach, you'll feel sluggish when you exercise, or you might end up sidelined with GI distress and forced to make some unwanted pit stops during your workout.

But as we all know, exercise and eating are much more intimately related than that.

Some lucky people start working out and find that their sustainable eating habits naturally evolve to complement their new exercise routines. They find that the more they move, the less they crave junk foods and the less prone they are to overeating. But for many others, it's more complicated and more challenging to strike the right balance. In some cases, it's necessary for a person to change eating habits and shed pounds before even starting to exercise. Others struggle to balance cutting calories while increasing the amount that they move.

No matter where you are, it's critical to develop eating habits that support your running. That may require some hard work. And you might find that the work you do at the table is more mentally and emotionally taxing than anything you do on the road. Exercise happens in a separate dimension and setting, often removed from your everyday life. But eating is something that's tightly woven into every day, often in situations that may have led to unhealthy habits in the past.

In the next section, you'll find all the tools you need to lose weight and learn to eat like a runner. You'll learn what and how much to eat; how to navigate the grocery store; and how to shed unwanted pounds, avoid diet disasters, and get back on the wagon if you get derailed—something that happens to everyone. Plus, you'll find out everything you need to stay energized on the run without ending up with an upset stomach.

CHAPTER 4

EAT LIKE A RUNNER

Some of the best advice we ever got was from Budd Coates, a coach and exercise physiologist who coaches many of the staffers at *Runner's World*. "Act like a runner even when you're not exercising." Nowhere is that more important than when you're sitting down to eat.

I n an ideal world, the more you move, the more you'll crave healthy foods and the less you'll want junk or treats that do nothing for your running life. But it does take a little effort to tweak your eating habits so that they support your running—otherwise when you sit down with a fork and knife, you can undo all the hard work you do on the road.

When you start exercising regularly, you might have to revamp some of your everyday eating habits to feel your best while you're working out and to avoid unwanted bathroom stops. Here are some tips to keep in mind.

Go on empty (sometimes). What you eat before you hit the road or the gym depends on when you're exercising and what kind of workout you're planning. Many people don't have the time—or the stomach—to eat and digest food before a workout, especially if that workout is in the early morning. For an easy workout of 1 hour or less, going without food or drink probably won't do you any harm. (Just make sure you're staying hydrated.) But for any event that's longer or more intense, pre-workout fuel is critical. Go out on empty and you'll fatigue sooner, plus you'll have a much tougher time meeting your goals.

Keep it simple. So what's the perfect preworkout meal? Familiar foods that are easy on your system, low in fat and fiber, and high in carbs will boost your energy without upsetting your stomach. See our list of pre-run meals and snacks on pages 128–131.

Time it right. When it comes to fueling your workout, timing is everything. Before your workout, you'll want to have something that will give you a boost of energy without wreaking havoc on your gut. So focus on wholesome carbs and foods that are low in fiber and low in fat. In general, the bigger the meal the more time you'll need to digest. Each person is different, but most people need to eat at least 30 minutes before heading out to avoid GI distress on the road. Within 30 to 60 minutes of finishing your workout, have a protein-rich snack to repair muscle tissue, along with some carbohydrates to restock your spent energy stores. This will kickstart the recovery process so that you can bounce back quickly for your next workout. Learn more about postrun fueling on page 131.

Drink up. Hydration is important, and not just when you're exercising. Fluids regulate body temperature, remove waste from your body, ensure that your joints are adequately lubricated, and help flush out the damaged cells that can lead to inflammation. And proper hydration can help control cravings, which is important because it's often easy to mistake thirst for hunger. While there's no set recommendation for daily fluid intake, a good rule of thumb is to aim to drink about half of your body weight in ounces each day. (So if you weigh 150 pounds, drink 75 ounces of water.) And you don't have to just guzzle water. Fruits and vegetables can also help you stay hydrated. Plus, they're packed

MAKE YOUR GRAINS WHOLE

Whole grain foods include the bran, germ, and endosperm—the parts of the grain that contain nutrients such as B vitamins, iron, magnesium, and fiber. When whole grains are refined into foods like white bread, many nutrients are lost. So is the fiber. A diet rich in fiber helps lower cholesterol, reduce blood pressure, and decrease the risk of diabetes and heart disease. Fiber also helps your digestive system function well, slows the absorption of sugar, and keeps you feeling fuller for longer. And remember, just because a bread is brown doesn't mean it's whole grain. When you're searching for whole grains, look for the word "whole" in the ingredient panel as well as any (or all!) of the following ingredients:

- **BARLEY**
- **BROWN RICE**
- **BUCKWHEAT**
- **BULGUR**
- **CORNMEAL**

- **OATMEAL**
- **POPCORN**
- **QUINOA**
- **STONEGROUND WHOLE OATS**

- **WHOLE GRAIN**
- **WHOLE GRAIN PASTA**
- **WHOLE OATS**
- **WHOLE WHEAT**
- **WILD RICE**

with antioxidants, which boost muscle recovery and immunity.

Take out the trash. If you have a family to feed, it may feel like you're constantly surrounded by foods that threaten to derail your healthy eating aspirations. Your kids and partner may not be trying to get in shape, but eating more fruits and vegetables, and less junk, is good for them, too. So next time you're at the store, shop with a "clean kitchen" in mind. Limit the high-sugar, high-fat, highly processed foods you toss in your cart; if they're not in the house, you won't be tempted to eat them. Stock your fridge with fruits, veggies, and whole grains, so they'll be there when mealtime rolls around. Those foods will keep you feeling good when you're working out, plus they'll keep your heart healthy, your cholesterol low, and your blood sugar stable.

Get the balance right. Even if you're not exercising with a goal of losing weight, you still need the right mix of foods and nutrients to feel energized on your runs and to stay injury free. About 55 percent of your daily calories should come from carbohydrates, 25 percent should come from protein, and another 15 to 20 percent should come from unsaturated fats. But there's no need to start carrying around a calculator. Don't obsess. At each meal, simply devote half of your plate to carbs, one-quarter of your plate to protein, and another quarter to healthy fats. Here's what you need to know about each nutrient group.

Carbs

There are lots of low-carb diets out there. Diets like Atkins and South Beach urge you to curb carbs to help control spikes in blood sugar and insulin surges. But carbs are the main source of glucose, which is your muscles' main source of fuel. If you slash your carbs too much, you'll find yourself out of energy on your runs. Keep carbs in your diet and you'll be able to go faster and longer. But don't belly up to the bakery just yet. The key is to get the right types of carbs at the right time.

Some carbs are fast. That means that your body can digest them quickly and use them for energy right away. Foods like candy, plain bagels, and white bread will give you an energy boost right before a workout. And after a tough run, they can help restock your energy stores fast.

But beyond that, fast carbs don't offer you much benefit, and they often have calories and additives that you don't need. Plenty of folks start pounding the breads and baked goods as soon as they start working out—all in the good name of "carb-loading"—but the only times you need those fast carbs are right before and during your workouts.

Most carbs in your diet should be slow. These are high in fiber. They're digested slowly, so they help you maintain a steady level of energy throughout a run. Fruits, whole grains, vegetables, oatmeal, and beans are all good examples of slow carbs that provide vitamins, minerals, and antioxidants to help you stay healthy and recover quickly.

And remember, carbs don't come from grains alone. Fresh produce can also provide the carbs you need to run strong. In addition, they offer lots of vitamins, minerals, and antioxidants to keep your body in peak condition. To get the widest variety of nutrients, eat as many different kinds of vegetables as possible: carrots, tomatoes, leafy greens, and more. Among fruits, choose berries, melons, grapes, apples, and oranges. Eat the skin when possible;

it provides more fiber and nutrients. For ideas on the best carbs for you, see the guide below.

Protein

Runners need protein to aid recovery. Protein helps repair muscles and strengthen immunity. And because protein takes longer to digest, it helps keep you fuller for longer, which can help if you're looking to quiet

THE BEST CARBS FOR RUNNERS

FOOD	PORTION SIZE	CARBS (G)	EXTRA BENEFITS FOR RUNNERS
Bananas	1 medium	27	These contain potassium, which helps with muscle contraction.
Raisins	2 Tbsp	30	These are high in potassium and iron, which helps carry oxygen throughout the body.
Kamut, black rice, amaranth, and quinoa	$\frac{1}{4}$ cup raw	29	These ancient grains or grainlike products provide fiber along with protein, vitamins, and minerals.
Sweet potato	1 small, about $3\frac{1}{2}$ oz	28	This is a good source of vitamin A, vitamin C, potassium, iron, and manganese, which helps optimize muscle function.
Steel-cut oats	$\frac{1}{2}$ cup	27	With more fiber than other types of oatmeal, these help you stay fuller longer. They also contain beta-glucan, which can help improve cholesterol levels, along with protein, iron, fiber, calcium, folate, and vitamin A.
Berries	1 cup	20	Blueberries, blackberries, and raspberries all have antioxidants, which help ward off disease and muscle soreness.
Apples	1	19	The peel contains quercetin, a flavonoid that may reduce risk of coughs and colds, as well as fiber.
Whole grain pasta	$\frac{1}{2}$ cup cooked	20	It contains more fiber, vitamins, minerals, and protein than white pasta. Those nutrients help with muscle repair and heart health.
Whole grain bread	1 slice	15–20	This contains fiber plus essential B vitamins.
Orange	1 small	15	This provides 100 percent of the daily recommended intake of vitamin C, which helps lower cholesterol and prevent muscle soreness.
Tomatoes	$\frac{1}{2}$ cup canned	8	These are rich in vitamin C and lycopene, a phytonutrient that protects against some kinds of cancer.

THE BEST PROTEINS FOR RUNNERS

FOOD	PORTION SIZE	PROTEIN (G)	EXTRA BENEFITS FOR RUNNERS
Chicken	4 oz skinless, white meat	28	Chicken contains selenium, which helps protect muscles from free-radical damage that can occur during running, and niacin, which helps regulate how much fat is burned during the run.
Lean beef	3½ oz; look for cuts with loin or round or labeled 90% lean	26	Beef is rich in iron and zinc to keep your immune system healthy.
Pork	3 oz	22	Pork has iron levels similar to beef's, but with one-third less fat. It contains thiamin, riboflavin, and B vitamins that help you metabolize (use) the energy from your food.
Salmon	3 oz	22	In addition to being rich in inflammation-fighting omega-3s, salmon contains vitamin B_{12}. Choose canned salmon for additional calcium.
Tofu	4 oz, firm	20	Made from soy, it can be a great source of calcium and can help lower cholesterol and risk of heart disease.
Egg	1 whole	6	Eggs are rich in choline—a nutrient that boosts brain and memory power. Choose omega-3–enhanced eggs to increase healthy fats.
Lentils	1 cup, canned	18	These are also high in iron, which helps transport oxygen to legs and lungs.
Black beans	1 cup, canned	15	These provide fiber and folate, a B vitamin that boosts heart health and circulation.
Greek yogurt	6 oz	10–15	This packs more protein, calcium, and vitamin D than traditional yogurt. Aim for low-fat or fat-free varieties.
Low-fat yogurt, plain	8 oz	12	This provides calcium and vitamin D. Yogurts containing "live active cultures" or "probiotics" can help your digestive system work optimally and give your immune system a boost.
Kidney beans	1 cup, canned	13	Besides being rich in iron, kidney beans are rich in fiber, providing 11 g per serving.
Chickpeas	1 cup, canned	12–15	Chickpeas provide manganese, which helps build healthy bones and also helps regulate blood sugar, absorption of calcium, and metabolism.
Peanut butter	2 Tbsp	8	Peanuts provide more protein per ounce than other nuts, saving you calories while helping you rebuild muscles.
Quinoa	1 cup, cooked	9	Quinoa contains fiber, complex carbs, and amino acids, the building blocks to make more proteins and build muscles.
Almonds	¼ cup	8	These provide vitamin E, which helps build a strong circulatory system and acts as an antioxidant, which helps prevent cell damage. Almonds also have heart-healthy monounsaturated fats and help lower cholesterol.

your appetite and shed pounds. Choose products that are lower in saturated fat, such as skinless chicken, pork, and lean cuts of beef; fish (such as salmon and tuna); soy; low-fat dairy (like yogurt and cottage cheese); and beans and lentils.

A note on supplements: A ton of protein supplements, bars, shakes, and drinks are on the market, many of them containing protein from egg, soy, hemp, or whey. Do you need them? Probably not. Chances are, you're getting plenty of protein from your everyday diet. It's best to get protein from whole foods, which are naturally rich in nutrients like fiber and iron that these engineeered foods may lack. But if you can't tolerate solids after a hard workout or if you're not getting enough protein, they can be good alternatives. See the chart on page 105 for lean protein options.

Fats

Fats have gotten a bad rap in recent years. But fat is an essential nutrient and plays a key role in keeping you healthy. Polyunsaturated fats (PUFAs) have anti-inflammatory properties, so they may help repair the microscopic muscle tears and bone breakdown that happen after a hard workout. Dietary fat also helps the body absorb fat-soluble nutrients, including vitamins D and K, both of which are vital for bone health, and vitamin E, which acts as an antioxidant and helps keep the body from breaking down. Omega-3 fatty acids—the kind found in salmon, wal-

nuts, and ground flaxseed—help fight inflammation and soothe aches and pains. And because fats promote the feeling of fullness, they're good for runners who want to shed pounds. They also help prevent blood sugar spikes and crashes, as well as the cycle of craving and overeating that can trip up your training. But the key is to eat moderate amounts of the right kinds of fats at the right time. Focus on healthy unsaturated fats from avocados, nuts, seeds, and olive oil; these fats lower bad cholesterol and help reduce your risk of heart disease. Stay away from saturated and trans fats, because they raise your levels of bad cholesterol (LDL). Trans fats also lower good cholesterol levels (HDL) and increase your risk of heart disease. See the chart at right for a guide.

Monounsaturated Fat (MUFA)

WHAT IT DOES: Lowers total cholesterol and LDL (bad) cholesterol

WHERE IT COMES FROM: Vegetable and nut oils including almond, avocado, canola, olive, peanut, pecan, and pistachio

Polyunsaturated Fat (PUFA)

WHAT IT DOES: PUFAs such as omega-3, omega-6, and the essential fatty acids ALA, EPA, and DHA, have been found to lower

Fats and Protein

Protein is essential for building and repairing muscle and helping you develop strength. Healthy fats—also known as unsaturated fats—help keep your heart healthy, your cholesterol low, and your appetite in check. About 15 to 20 percent of your daily calories should come from healthy fats, and another 25 percent should come from lean protein. Here are the best sources of foods touting both protein and fat.

EGGS: Packed with protein, lutein (for eye health), and a handful of vitamins and minerals, eggs are an inexpensive option and are easy and quick to prepare. Need to limit your cholesterol? Just use the whites, or use an egg substitute.

GREEK YOGURT: This will help you pack in protein and calcium in your next meal or snack. Greek yogurt is thicker, creamier, and richer in protein than traditional yogurts. Try to select a brand with as few ingredients as possible and choose one that is low in fat or fat free.

NUTS: Many nuts—like peanuts, almonds, and pistachios—come equipped with antioxidants, phytosterols, and heart-healthy unsaturated fats. Be sure to watch portion size, as a few nuts can add up in calories fairly quickly. Looking for the most nuts with the fewest calories? Try shelled pistachios. One ounce (49 kernels) provides 160 calories, 3 grams of fiber, and 6 grams of protein and is cholesterol free. The most nutritious options are dry roasted and unsalted. Prolong their freshness by storing them in the freezer.

SKINLESS CHICKEN AND TURKEY BREAST: Lean poultry such as chicken and turkey breast is an excellent option if you want to boost protein—without packing on the calories. Skinless poultry is low in fat, high in protein (4 ounces contain more than 60 grams of protein), and full of essential nutrients like B vitamins and phosphorus, which are essential for healthy bones and teeth. You can buy it fresh, frozen, or canned. Skip the frozen, prepared, and breaded options, as they can be packed with salt, empty calories, and preservatives.

FISH AND SEAFOOD: Seafood is an excellent source of hard-to-come-by omega-3 fatty acids, which have been found to promote heart health and fight inflammation. Fish and seafood are also excellent sources of protein and many vitamins and minerals but are not overloaded with calories. For best health, try to consume fish or seafood at least once a week. If you're worried about mercury content, avoid larger fish like marlin, swordfish, and shark and instead choose fish such as anchovies, flounder, salmon, and sole. Shrimp, scallops, clams, and oysters are also good choices. If you're concerned about sustainability, check out the Seafood Watch resource offered by the Monterey Bay Aquarium.

Fruits and Vegetables

Fresh produce has a bounty of benefits: It provides a wide variety of vitamins and

THE BEST FATS FOR RUNNERS

FOOD	PORTION SIZE	FATS (G)	EXTRA BENEFITS FOR RUNNERS
Dry-roasted nuts	1 oz	12–15	These are rich in magnesium, which helps nerve and mu function. They also contain protein.
Olive oil	1 Tbsp	14	This is rich in monounsaturated fat, which can lower you risk of heart disease. Choose extra-virgin or virgin olive oil which are the least processed and contain the highest level of polyphenols, which promote heart health.
Canola and vegetable oils	1 Tbsp	14	These contain 62% MUFAs and 13% PUFAs, leaving little room for artery-clogging saturated fat.
Avocado	½ cup or ⅓ medium	11	Avocado is rich in vitamin B_6, which boosts immunity. It also contains lutein, which helps with eye health, and vitamin E, which protects cells from damage.
Salmon	3 oz, cooked	4–7	Any variety is rich in omega-3 fatty acids, which fight inflammation, boost heart health, reduce high blood pressure, and help control blood sugar.

total cholesterol including LDL (bad) cholesterol.

WHERE IT COMES FROM: Vegetable and nut oils including almond, avocado, canola, olive, peanut, pecan, and pistachio

Saturated Fat

WHAT IT DOES: Can lead to high cholesterol.

WHERE IT COMES FROM: Animal-based fats including full-fat dairy, butter, lard, and marbled meats (like bacon), and tropical oils such as coconut and palm

Trans Fat

WHAT IT DOES: Raises total cholesterol and risk for heart disease; also raises LDL (bad)

cholesterol while decreasing HDL (good) cholesterol levels

WHERE IT COMES FROM: Fried and baked foods, stick margarines, and foods that contain partially hydrogenated oils

How to Stock Your Kitchen

It's important to eat in a way that supports the exercise routine that you've worked so hard to develop. Keep your kitchen stocked with these bare essentials at all times so you stay energized for your workouts and healthy for the long run. Be sure to check out our recipe finder at recipes.runnersworld.com for ideas on quick, healthy dishes to whip up with these ingredients.

minerals to keep you healthy, and it's low calorie and high in fiber, so you can eat large quantities without packing on the pounds. About half of your daily calories should come from carbs, mainly from fruits and vegetables, along with whole grains. Here are some fruits and veggies that have extra benefits for anyone who regularly exercises.

BEETS: Beets are naturally high in nitrates, which some athletes consume to improve performance. Studies have shown that people who consumed baked beets before a tough workout ran faster with less effort. You can get beets raw or canned; you can even juice them to get the benefits. To glean the health and performance benefits that beets may provide, try juicing them or consuming them immediately after cooking.

CRANBERRIES: Cranberries contain powerful nutrients called proanthocyanidins that play a role in helping to maintain the health of the urinary tract, bones, teeth, and immune system. Whether you eat them fresh, canned, dried, or in juice, they protect against certain harmful bacteria that cause urinary tract infections.

CRUCIFEROUS VEGETABLES: Working out is taxing on the body, and cruciferous vegetables—such as cabbage, kale, broccoli, cauliflower, Brussels sprouts, and bok choy—can help boost the immune system and fight chronic disease. Cruciferous vegetables, whether you eat them fresh, cooked, frozen, or canned, have phytonutrients plus vita-

mins A and C, folic acid, and more. To retain the nutrients, avoid overcooking them.

SPINACH: Whether you use it as a topping for sandwiches, as an ingredient in dips, or as a foundation for a big salad, spinach is a classic example of a vegetable that delivers tons of nutrients you need with few calories. With less than 10 calories per cup, spinach is packed with iron, potassium, and antioxidant vitamins like A, C, and K. Spinach is also an excellent source of lutein, which protects the eyes from the sun's harmful rays and even diseases like macular degeneration. Keep spinach on hand fresh, frozen, or in a can.

POTATOES: The complex carbs in potatoes are easy to digest, making them a great preworkout source of energy. These inexpensive starchy vegetables are easy to prepare—simply microwave, boil, or bake—and provide nutrients like potassium and fiber. Sweet potatoes offer big doses of vitamin A and beta-carotene, which are excellent for the eyes.

Grains

If you're cutting calories or carbs, you may be tempted to eliminate whole grains from your diet. But these are important sources of the energizing vitamins and minerals you need for your workouts. About half of your daily calories should come from carbs that include vegetables, fruits, and whole grains.

WHOLE GRAINS: No athlete's pantry is complete without whole grain breads, pastas, and cereals. The term "whole grain" means that the food includes the bran, germ, and endosperm—the parts of the grain that contain the nutritious B vitamins, iron, magnesium, and fiber your body needs. When whole grains are refined into foods like white bread, the nutrients are lost, and so is the fiber. A diet rich in fiber helps lower cholesterol, reduce blood pressure, and decrease the risk of diabetes and heart disease. Fiber also helps keep the digestive system functioning well and keeps you feeling fuller for longer. Good sources of whole grains include bulgur, whole oats, cornmeal, popcorn, brown rice, barley, wild rice, quinoa, whole grain pasta, and buckwheat. Remember: Just because a bread is brown doesn't necessarily mean that it's whole grain. Look for labels that say 100 percent whole grain, or look for these terms on the list of ingredients: whole grain, whole wheat, stone-ground whole oats, and oatmeal. If you see terms like enriched flour, bran, or wheat germ, chances are the bread isn't whole grain.

Foods to Avoid

What you don't eat is just as important—if not more—as what you do eat. By leaving sodium, fat, and sugar-filled junk on store shelves and bringing home fruits, vegetables, and foods that are full of fiber, you won't have to go through the painful process of trying to resist temptation at home, and it will be easier to make a healthy choice when your stomach is growling.

So what, exactly, should be left at the grocery and stay out of the pantry? Follow this guide.

WHITE AND BROWN BREADS: Enriched white breads are highly refined and lack the nutrients of whole grain breads. The bran and germ have been removed from white bread for longer shelf life, and with that, also gone are the fiber, iron, and B vitamins you need. And just because bread is brown or is labeled "wheat" doesn't make it a whole grain choice. Be sure to check the list of ingredients to make sure that the bread does indeed include whole grain, meaning that the entire seed—which is what creates all the fiber and the vitamins—has been used. The first ingredient(s) in your loaf should include the word "whole," which means that the grain proven to reduce the risk of cancer, heart disease, type 2 diabetes, and obesity is still there.

CRACKERS, COOKIES, AND CAKES: These are filled with calories and added sugar and fat that will pack on the pounds. Plus, they don't have the nutrients, vitamins, and minerals your body needs to stay healthy. If you must have a snack, choose versions that are labeled low fat, whole grain, or reduced sodium. (See "Learning How to Read a Food Label" on page 154 for guidance on what these terms actually mean.)

JUICE Even if it's labeled 100 percent juice, it's best to avoid it altogether. Sure, there are vitamins and minerals, but juice is full of calories and sugar and devoid of fiber that will fill you up and keep you satisfied. It's harder for the body to register "I'm full" when you drink your calories. Instead, choose milk, water, or some other calorie-free beverages.

SOFT DRINKS: The regular versions are packed with sugar and a meal's worth of calories. And while the diet versions are free of calories, ingredients like caramel color and phosphoric acid aren't doing anything to help your weight-loss and healthy-eating goals.

OILS AND BUTTER: Avoid saturated-fat-laden butter and lard and any margarines that contain trans fats. They've all been linked to increased risk of obesity and heart disease. Instead, choose oils like canola, olive, and grapeseed. What to spread on your toast? Choose a vegetable-oil-based spread like Promise, which contains significantly less saturated fat and is almost always cholesterol free.

FULL-FAT DAIRY: Whole milk, cheese, and yogurt are packed with sugar and fat that you don't need. When looking for milk, choose fat-free or 1 percent versions or try other nondairy milks like almond and soy milk. Try low-fat cheeses and sour cream. With yogurt, choose brands with less than 5 grams of sugar per serving. Or better yet, buy plain Greek yogurt and sweeten it by adding your own fresh fruit.

CREAM-BASED SOUPS: Soups will fill you up and warm you up on a cold day. But the wrong bowl can pack on the pounds. Avoid cream of anything soup, like cream of broccoli or New England clam chowder. Instead, look for broth-based soups with less than 150 calories, less than 3 grams of fat, and less than 149 milligrams of sodium per serving.

FROZEN MEALS: Sure, they're convenient and the portions are measured out for you, but they can be filled with calories, fat, and sodium. Avoid any product with more than 500 calories, 10 grams of fat, or 500 milligrams of sodium per serving. And be sure to check the serving size before you dig in. Lots of meals that look like they're a single serving are actually two.

ALCOHOL: Avoid fruity mixed drinks. They're full of sugar and calories and will wreak havoc on your waistline (and your head if you enjoy too many). Choose beer, wine, or spirits instead. Studies have shown that one to two drinks per day may actually reduce risk of chronic diseases like cardiovascular disease and type 2 diabetes. Red wine has antioxidants that have been linked to heart health; beer offers protein, B vitamins, and a bit of soluble fiber.

NUTS: Nuts come packed with fiber, protein, vitamins, minerals, and antioxidants and have been linked to lower risk of heart disease. Avoid nuts that are roasted or coated in oil and that have empty calories coming from sugars or other ingredients. Avoid highly processed nut butters that contain a laundry list of preservatives and fillers like sugar, soy lecithin, and hydrogenated vegetable oils. Your best bet is to look for raw, ground, or dry-roasted nuts that are free of fillers and preservatives. Because nuts are calorie-dense, be sure to watch your portion size.

How Running Changed My Life

Running helped Ken Thomas quit smoking and begin a new life in retirement

As Ken Thomas was considering retiring from his 29-year career as a facilities manager, he was scared. He'd smoked for 45 years—two and a half packs a day. He couldn't walk up a flight of stairs without stopping to catch his breath.

"I'd seen so many people who had worked all their lives and now they couldn't enjoy what was left of it because they hadn't taken care of themselves," he says. "I wanted to be able to live a little bit. And I wanted to stop smoking."

He decided that every time he wanted a cigarette, he'd put on his running shoes and try to run to the mailbox—which was 25 yards away.

The first time, he huffed and puffed and felt like throwing up. But the next time he wanted to smoke, he put on his running shoes. And he did it again, and again, and again until he started making progress. He'd pick a lamppost to run to, then walk to the next one, and repeat that cycle. Eventually, he worked his way up to running around the block. Then a nearby trail.

"Running gave me something else to focus on," he says. "When you put your shoes on and take off running, and find that you can't run because you can't breathe, you

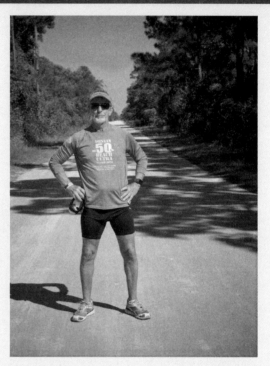

don't want to sit down and light another cigarette."

Thomas has run two ultramarathons and a slew of shorter races. He's dropped 30 pounds and now, in retirement, is at the same weight he was in junior high school. But the best part is how he's changed on the inside.

"I used to be a lot more reserved; now I'm more confident," he says. "I am more outgoing now because of running. Once you've run for so many hours straight, you realize it's possible to do anything you're determined to do."

AGE: 58

HOMETOWN: Mableton, Georgia

OCCUPATION: Retired senior facilities manager at Georgia Institute of Technology

What's your regular workout routine? Every day I get up at 5:30 a.m. and head out and run until I get tired. I log 70 to 90 miles a week.

What was the biggest hurdle, and how did you get over it? My biggest hurdle was gaining confidence in my ability to maintain a pace for a chosen distance without giving up. The entire time I am out there, I constantly recall where I started, and it gives me even more incentive to strive for improvement.

What kinds of changes did you make to your diet? My diet changes were drastic. The most important thing was to massively change my entire lifestyle, because that was actually what I was trying to do—go from a sedentary smoker to a runner. I stopped eating red meat and consuming sodas and artificial sugars, and I avoided processed foods. I started eating raw veggies and salads and drinking lots and lots of water.

What is the biggest reward of your running life? I can't begin to explain how good it is not to gasp for breath. I remember vividly lying in bed and taking very long, deep breaths at night for the first time, which is something I'd not been able to do in years. It was amazing to just lie there and breathe.

What advice would you give to a beginner? It's fun. It's not about speed; it's about just being out there. Slow as I go, I'm faster than my sofa. Too much focus on producing results will lead to too little focus on enjoying the experience!

Favorite motivational quote: "Run whenever you can, walk if you must, crawl if you have to—but never give up!" When I run and think about stopping short, I keep this going in my mind. Never, ever give up. You've come too far to give up.

YOUR ULTIMATE GROCERY SHOPPING GUIDE

Every time you walk into a grocery store, you face a daunting task: picking the healthiest, most nutrient-packed foods from thousands of choices. Supermarkets today carry an average of 38,718 items, according to the Food Marketing Institute. Colorful packaging, deceptive claims, and hidden ingredients confuse even the savviest shopper. Who wants to waste precious time dithering over yogurt?

This aisle-by-aisle guide, compiled by Matthew G. Kadey, MSc, RD, tells you exactly which nutritious (and delicious!) foods you should toss into your cart and which health food impostors you should run away from.[1] These expert tips will help you shop smarter, so you can get in, get out, and get back to your life—fast. Be sure to check out our quick guide on page 235, which you can cut out and take with you next time you make a grocery run.

STOP ONE
THE PRODUCE SECTION

"Fruits and vegetables are loaded with vitamins, minerals, and antioxidants runners need to support training," says Tara Gidus, MS, RD, an Orlando-based sports dietitian and marathoner. "In general, the more color in your shopping cart, the more antioxidants and nutrients you're going to get."

RED

BEETS: Natural vegetable-sourced nitrates found in beets can make your muscles work more efficiently during exercise by reducing the amount of oxygen they need.

RASPBERRIES: Eight grams of fiber in a single cup. "Higher fiber foods help runners maintain a healthy body weight and digestive system," says Gidus.

WHEN TO GO ORGANIC

If you're peeling or removing the rind (avocado, bananas, or onions), conventionally grown produce is fine. If you're going to eat the exterior (apples, peaches, bell peppers), buying organic will limit your pesticide exposure.

GREEN

KALE: Jam-packed with vitamin C, vitamin K, and vision-protecting beta-carotene. Add it to soups, sauté it for a side, or add it to salads and sandwiches.

AVOCADO: Nearly 70 percent of its fat is monounsaturated, "the same kind that makes olive oil heart-healthy," Gidus says. Half an avocado also delivers 7 grams of fiber.

YELLOW AND ORANGE

SWEET POTATO: One potato provides more than three times your daily need for immune-boosting vitamin A. "It's full of complex carbohydrates," Gidus says, "which helps keep your energy stores topped up."

MANGO: High vitamin C intake may reduce upper respiratory tract infections, as well as help lower your heart rate during exercise. One cup of mango delivers 75 percent of your daily need for C.

WHITE

BANANA: It brims with potassium and quick-digesting carbs. "Potassium plays a key role in muscle contraction, with low levels linked to muscle cramping," Gidus says.

TOFU: Usually located in the produce department, tofu is an inexpensive and low-fat protein source. Add it to stir-fries, chili, or even pasta sauce.

BLUE AND PURPLE

EGGPLANT: Eggplant, which has just 20 calories per cup, contains antioxidants with heart-protective qualities.

PLUMS: Studies show that plums contain as much antioxidant power as blueberries. "Consuming plenty of antioxidants," says Gidus, "may reduce postworkout muscle tissue damage, speed recovery, and boost immune function."

HEALTH FOOD IMPOSTORS

- **PRESLICED PACKAGED FRUIT:** Slicing ahead of time exposes more surface area, raising the risk of nutrient loss from oxygen exposure. And the packages are more expensive than whole fruit.

- **ICEBERG LETTUCE:** One of the most popular vegetables is also one of the least nutrient dense. In general, the darker the leafy green, the bigger the nutritional bang.

- **BOTTLED SMOOTHIES:** Many are sweetened with sugar or nutritionally poor juices like apple or pear. Plus, they almost always cost much more than making your own.

THE MEAT, FISH, AND DELI COUNTERS

FINS, SCALES, AND SHELLS

GOOD: Eat these two or three times a month.

TILAPIA: Protein rich and inexpensive, US-farmed tilapia is virtually free of saturated fat and is farmed in an environmentally sound way, but it's relatively high in omega-6 fats, which promote inflammation in the body.

SEA SCALLOPS: Populations are abundant and contamination risk is low, but harvesting methods can be harmful to the ocean. Farmed bay scallops are a more eco-wise option.

BETTER: Eat these two or three times a week.

RAINBOW TROUT: Less expensive than wild salmon, trout is rich in omega-3 fatty acids, which may help lower your risk for diabetes and heart disease and relieve achy joints. Almost all US rainbow trout available in supermarkets is grown at inland farms that follow environmentally responsible production methods.

WILD SMOKED SALMON: More sustainable than farmed varieties, wild smoked salmon is an easy way to add brain-boosting vitamin B_{12} and inflammation-reducing omega-3s to your meals.

MUSSELS: Inexpensive mussels are full of iron, vitamin B_{12}, and selenium—an antioxidant that may ease postexercise oxidative stress. They're farmed using eco-sound methods with little toxin risk.

WORST: Eat rarely or never.

IMPORTED SHRIMP: Overseas shrimp farms have destroyed coastal forests and often rely heavily on antibiotic use. Try US farmed or wild shrimp.

FARMED ATLANTIC SALMON: Ocean pens can pollute surrounding waterways, and contamination from PCBs may be a concern. Splurge on wild.

BLUEFIN TUNA: This pricey tuna is overfished and high in mercury. Domestic, line-caught skipjack or yellowfin tuna have lower contaminants.

Shop Smart!

Phone users can download apps to help them choose sustainable seafood with low contaminant levels. FishPhone, an iPhone app from Blue Ocean Institute, ranks fish choices, as does the Seafood Watch app from the Monterey Bay Aquarium, which also provides regional recommendations.

SLICED AND CURED

TURKEY BREAST: It's virtually fat free and a good source of protein. Fresh roasted tastes better and usually contains less sodium.

ROAST BEEF: A 2-ounce serving contains just 3 grams of fat, 110 calories, and 19 grams of protein.

CANADIAN BACON: One ounce of this lean cut contains about a third of the calories of regular bacon and 11 less grams of fat.

FROM THE FARMYARD
GOOD FOR YOU: HAPPY MEAT

Organic meat costs more but limits your exposure to the antibiotics and growth hormones used in conventionally raised livestock. "Free range" means only that animals have access to outdoor spaces. Grass-fed beef is a smart choice: A 2010 California State University study found that, compared to conventionally raised cattle, it's lower in saturated fat and richer in heart-healthy omega-3s and vitamin E.[2]

	BEST BUY	WHY?	AVOID	WHY?
Beef	Eye, top, and bottom round; sirloin; flank steak; 90 or 95% lean ground beef	Contains about 18 g protein per 3-oz serving and no more than 6 g fat	Rib-eye, porterhouse, and T-bone steaks; 80% lean ground beef	These cuts have the highest fat-to-protein ratio. Three ounces pack 12 g protein for every 18 g fat.
Poultry	Skinless chicken thighs; turkey legs	A 3-oz thigh contains 18 g protein and 3 g fat—just 1 more gram than breast meat. Remove the skin, and turkey legs have the same protein-to-fat ratio as chicken thighs.	Ground turkey; enhanced chicken breast	If it includes skin, ground poultry can have as much fat as ground beef. Enhanced chicken is injected with saltwater to keep it moist; 3 oz can pack more than 300 mg sodium.
Pork	Pork tenderloin; boneless pork loin chops	Contain 3 g fat and 18 g protein per 3 oz, making them nearly as lean as chicken breast	Premarinated cuts; pork blade chops	High sodium; pork blade packs about 21 g fat per 3 oz.

STOP THREE
THE PANTRY AISLES

THE PERFECT PASTA

WHOLE GRAINS: Whole wheat, brown rice, buckwheat, spelt, or other types of whole grains should appear first in the ingredient list.

5 GRAMS OF FIBER: Look for at least this much fiber per 2-ounce serving. "Choose a 100 percent whole grain product and it won't be hard to reach this mark," says Janis Jibrin, RD, author of *The Supermarket Diet*.

6 GRAMS OF PROTEIN: Look for this much per 2-ounce serving. Whole grains naturally contain some protein, which helps keep blood sugar levels steady.

THE PERFECT SAUCE

400 MILLIGRAMS OF SODIUM: No more than this per ½-cup serving. "Some brands can pack more than 600 milligrams," Jibrin says.

4 GRAMS OF SUGAR OR LESS: Look for this per ½-cup serving. "Ideally, there should be no added sugar in the ingredient list," says Jibrin. "The only sugar should come from the tomatoes themselves."

2 GRAMS OF FAT OR LESS: Look for this per ½-cup serving. Skip the creamy white sauces, like Alfredo, which pack the most saturated fat, says Jibrin.

Shop Smart!

"Grocery shopping when hungry can set the stage for unhealthy impulse buys," says Bonnie Taub-Dix, MA, RD, author of *Read It Before You Eat It*. With its high-fat doughnuts and pastries, the bread aisle can be particularly dangerous. Fortify your healthy resolve by eating before you leave home.

GOOD AND BAKED

TOSS OUT: Multigrain bread
TOSS IN: 100% whole grain

Multigrain bread is often made of enriched flour or wheat flour—which lacks the fiber and vitamins of 100% whole grain flour. "The first item should be a whole grain," says Bonnie Taub-Dix, MA, RD, author of *Read It Before You Eat It*. Look for 3 grams of fiber and no more than 200 milligrams of sodium per slice.

TOSS OUT: Spinach wraps
TOSS IN: Corn tortillas

Made mostly of refined white flour, many spinach wraps contain a scant amount of the actual leafy vegetable. Six-inch corn tortillas made with whole corn flour are higher in fiber and lower in calories.

TOSS OUT: Bagels
TOSS IN: Whole wheat English muffins

One hundred percent whole wheat English muffins contain less than half the calories of and more fiber than most bagels.

OILS AND VINEGARS

BEST FOR SALADS	WHY?	BEST FOR COOKING	WHY?
Extra-virgin olive oil	It contains an antioxidant called oleo-canthal, a natural anti-inflammatory that helps soothe sore muscles. Dark bottles preserve flavor.	**Canola oil**	This inexpensive oil has a high smoke point, making it ideal for stir-fries, and provides healthy amounts of omega-3 fats.
Hemp oil	Pressed from hemp seeds, this nutty-tasting oil adds artery-friendly omega-3 fats to your diet. Try it in tomato sauce and pesto.	**Avocado oil**	Buttery tasting, it provides an abundance of "good" monounsaturated fat. Use it to sauté vegetables. It's also delicious drizzled over pasta.
Balsamic vinegar	With just 14 calories per tablespoon, it adds a rich, intense, and slightly sweet flavor.	**Rice vinegar**	It's a low-calorie way to punch up the flavor of stir-fries, marinades, and vegetables.

MUSTARDS AND MORE

DIJON MUSTARD: Mustard seeds are a source of omega-3s and the antioxidant selenium. For few calories, Dijon adds tons of flavor to sandwiches, salad dressings, even mashed potatoes.

Keep it healthy: Look for brands without sugar and no more than 120 milligrams of sodium per teaspoon.

KETCHUP: Rich in lycopene, an antioxidant that helps protect skin from sun damage.

Keep it healthy: Splurge on organic, which has up to 60 percent more lycopene than conventional. Keep it under 5 grams of sugar and 180 milligrams of sodium per tablespoon.

HORSERADISH: This spicy root contains glucosinolates, compounds that can detoxify carcinogens. Use it to add kick to dips, sauces, and fish.

Keep it healthy: Brands with the word "sauce" in the name often contain sugar and low-quality oils. An ideal ingredient list includes only grated horseradish, vinegar, and salt.

SRIRACHA: The chile sauce adds low-calorie punch to scrambled eggs, soups, and pasta sauce. It gets its spice from capsaicin, a compound in chile peppers that may boost metabolism and curb appetite.

Keep it healthy: Avoid versions with more than 100 milligrams of sodium per teaspoon or with food coloring in the ingredient list.

MANGO CHUTNEY: Use it on fish, chicken, or cooked rice. Mangoes provide a kick of vitamin C and vitamin A.

Keep it healthy: Choose brands that list mango before sugar in the ingredient list.

SEEDS, NUTS, AND STAPLES

QUINOA: A fast-cooking whole grain loaded with fiber, B vitamins, and magnesium, a mineral that may improve muscle strength.

PUMPKIN SEEDS: Just ¼ cup of pumpkin seeds provides 30 percent of your daily need for iron.

PRUNES: Research from Oklahoma State University shows that dried plums contain polyphenol antioxidants that may fight bone loss.

IN-SHELL PISTACHIOS: These are high in protein, fiber, and vitamin B_6. A 2011 study in the journal *Appetite* shows you eat fewer if you shell them.[3]

BROWN RICE: Harvard scientists found that adults who eat two or more servings of brown rice a week reduce their risk of developing type 2 diabetes by about 10 percent.

WALNUTS: contain more inflammation-fighting omega-3s than other nuts.

HEALTH FOOD IMPOSTORS

- **YOGURT-COVERED NUTS AND PRETZELS:** This fake yogurt covering is made with added sugars and unhealthy fats.
- **SALTED NUTS AND SEEDS:** Eating too many will put you into calorie and sodium overload.
- **SWEETENED DRIED FRUITS:** Some dried fruits (e.g., cranberries) are bathed in extra sugars. Scoop unsweetened.
- **FAT-FREE DRESSINGS:** "Fat is often replaced with sugars or other fillers," says Bonnie Taub-Dix, MA, RD, author of *Read It Before You Eat It*, "so these dressings may contain nearly as many calories as regular versions." Plus, you need some fat—it helps your body absorb vitamins and antioxidants.

DRINKS

FLAVORED SPARKLING WATER provides bubbles without the sugar-packed calories.

HEMP MILK: This dairy alternative contains more heart-friendly omega-3s than soy and almond milk.

COCONUT WATER: Tangy coconut water contains natural sugars and electrolytes like potassium, making it ideal to drink before or after a run.

GREEN TEA is a rich source of catechins, antioxidants that can help lower cholesterol and protect against exercise-induced muscle damage.

TART CHERRY JUICE: The antioxidant-packed juice can reduce muscle damage.

SPREADS AND SWEETENERS

Nut Butters

GOOD

Natural-style peanut butter: Made with just peanuts, it contains heart-healthy fats and vitamin E without added sugar or hydrogenated oils.

BETTER

Almond butter: More expensive than PB, the almond version is a richer source of bone-building magnesium and calcium, as well as cholesterol-lowering monounsaturated fat.

WORST

Reduced-fat peanut butter: Most brands swap out unsaturated fats for extra sugar, which means they often have nearly the same calorie cost as and more sugar than the full-fat version.

Sweeteners

GOOD

Honey: The easily digestible carbs contain antioxidants and antibacterial properties. Stash a honey packet in your running shorts for midrun fueling.

BETTER

Maple syrup: It has about 20 percent less calories than honey, plus a wider array of antioxidants that may help muscle recovery. Use it to lightly sweeten plain yogurt and oatmeal.

WORST

Imitation maple syrup: Made of dyed and refined corn syrup, it contains empty calories with no redeeming health qualities.

Fruit Spreads

GOOD

Marmalade: It's made with whole fruit, including the orange rind. Stick with fruit-juice-sweetened varieties.

BETTER

Apple butter: Cooking down apples creates a spread with a buttery mouthfeel but no fat. Buy brands made without added sugars.

WORST

Sugar-packed jams: Avoid jams, jellies, and preserves that contain more added sugar than fruit. How do you know? Sugar is on the ingredient list before fruit.

CEREALS
Hot

OLD-FASHIONED ROLLED OATS: They cook up quickly without the sugar overload found in flavored instant brands. "Whole grain oats are a good source of soluble fiber, which is shown to reduce cholesterol," says Taub-Dix.

HOT MULTIGRAIN CEREAL: The healthiest choices contain fiber-rich whole grains, such as oats, barley, rye, and whole wheat, and no added sugars.

BROWN RICE FARINA: Made of finely ground whole grain brown rice, it's fast cooking and easy to digest, making it an ideal prerun choice.

INSTANT STEEL-CUT OATMEAL: These packets are just as convenient as regular instant oatmeal but provide more fiber, no added sugar, and that chewy texture you get only from steel-cut oats.

Cold

- **SERVING SIZE:** A hungry runner can easily eat more than the 1-cup serving commonly listed (some list a smaller serving). "Be realistic about how much you'll eat, and adjust accordingly," says Taub-Dix.

- **CALORIES:** Cap it at 200 per cup. Despite their health halo, granolas can pack twice that and lead to weight gain if eaten too liberally.

- **FIBER:** "It keeps you full and helps steady blood sugar levels," Taub-Dix says. Go with brands that pack 5 grams of fiber or more per cup.

- **SUGAR:** The Environmental Working Group found that 66 percent of cereals it tested were more than 25 percent sugar by weight. Choose one with less than 10 grams per cup, more if it contains fruit.

- **SODIUM:** Stick with those with 200 milligrams or less in 1 cup.

- **INGREDIENT LIST:** The first ingredient should be a whole grain. If sugar by any name (cane juice, dextrose, rice syrup) is near the top or if it lists hydrogenated oils (which contain harmful trans fat), skip it.

BAKERS' FRIENDS

PURE VANILLA EXTRACT is a nearly calorie-free way to boost the flavor of yogurt.

WHOLE WHEAT PASTRY FLOUR is milled from a softer variety of whole wheat. Use it as a 1-to-1 replacement for refined white flour.

NONFAT DRY MILK adds bone-building calcium to smoothies and hot cereal.

FLAXSEEDS: These tiny seeds brim with omega fats and fiber and can help lower cholesterol.

CINNAMON: Studies show regular consumption can help reduce type 2 diabetes risk.

CANNED FOODS

Sardines: This sustainable catch is loaded with omega-3s, vitamin B$_{12}$, and vitamin D, which may help fend off viruses. Sauté with onions and toss with pasta, parsley, and bread crumbs.

Salsa verde: Tangy tomatillos make a vitamin C–packed green salsa. Use it to brighten up fish tacos or baked chicken breasts.

Roasted red peppers: They're a rich source of beta-carotene. Add them to frozen pizza for a low-calorie flavor and nutrient boost.

Chicken: Quick and convenient, lean canned chicken gives fresh salads a hit of muscle-building protein.

Black beans: One cup provides 15 grams of fiber and a high dose of antioxidants. Use as a sandwich spread.

Applesauce: Eat it as a prerun snack or use it in place of some fat in baked goods. Unsweetened varieties have about half the sugar calories.

Butternut squash: A $\frac{1}{2}$-cup serving provides nearly half your daily need for immune-boosting vitamin A. Blend with broth and spices for an instant soup.

Salmon: It contains more heart-friendly omega-3 fatty acids and far less mercury than most brands of canned tuna.

Fire-roasted tomatoes lend a smoky flavor (plus potassium) to vegetarian chili or tomato sauce.

Pineapple chunks: Add them to yogurt or cottage cheese for blood pressure–lowering vitamin C. Choose only fruits packed in juices.

SNACK TIME

Popcorn: Crunchy and salty, whole grain popcorn packs antioxidants and fiber.

Hummus: Chickpeas, the main ingredient in hummus, brim with fiber, protein, and brain-boosting vitamin B$_6$.

Beef jerky: The high-protein snack keeps you feeling full between meals.

Dark chocolate: A 2011 British study found that people who regularly eat antioxidant-packed dark chocolate reduce their heart disease risk by a third. It's also a source of iron.[4]

Trail mix supplies antioxidants from dried fruit and healthy fats from nuts.

STOP FOUR
THE REFRIGERATOR AISLES
YOUR DAILY DAIRY

A Canadian study found that people who exercised daily and ate a high-dairy, calorie-controlled diet for 4 months lost fat and gained muscle. Researchers think that dairy products may regulate appetite and promote muscle growth.[5]

LOW-FAT KEFIR: "With protein and carbs, kefir is a good option when you need something easy to digest," says Marni Sumbal, owner of Trimarni Coaching and Nutrition in Jacksonville, Florida.

LOW-FAT PLAIN GREEK YOGURT: Thick and creamy Greek yogurt has about twice as much hunger-satisfying protein as traditional yogurt.

CHOCOLATE MILK: The perfect postrun snack. "The combination of protein and quick-digesting carbs helps repair exercise-induced muscle damage and refuel tired muscles," says Sumbal. But it's high in calories, so "choose low-fat varieties."

EGGS: Antioxidant-rich eggs are an inexpensive, nutritious, and quick-cooking alternative to meat for dinner. One large egg provides 6 grams of protein and 23 percent of your daily need for selenium.

LOW-FAT COTTAGE CHEESE: A 2012 study published in *Medicine & Science in Sports & Exercise* found that eating protein prior to sleep significantly improves recovery from exercise.[6]

THE CHEESE BAR

Thumbs-Up

PARMESAN: "A little freshly grated Parmesan packs potent flavor," says sports dietian Tara Gidus. Buy blocks or wedges of fresh Parmesan cheese. They provide better flavor than pre-shredded and won't contain any stabilizers or other additives.

FRESH MOZZARELLA: Thanks to its high water content, it's one of the lowest-calorie cheeses on the market.

SOFT GOAT: Studies suggest that goat milk is richer in omega-3 fats and bone-building calcium than cow's milk.

LIGHT RICOTTA: Reduced-fat ricotta cheese is still rich tasting and delivers good amounts of whey protein.

Thumbs-Down

CHEDDAR CHEESE: "This is an oilier cheese, so it will be higher in fat than many others," says Gidus.

BLENDED CHEESE MIXES: Bags of shredded cheese mixes often include higher-fat options like Cheddar.

AMERICAN CHEESE: Heavily processed American cheese is among the saltiest and fattiest options in the cheese department.

Hydration

How well you're hydrated can have a huge impact on how you feel during your workout, says Douglas Casa, PhD, who heads the University of Connecticut's Korey Stringer Institute, which studies heatstroke and other causes of sudden death in sports. When you're working out, your heart needs fluid to pump blood, your muscles need fluids to contract, and your skin needs fluids to sweat in order to cool you down. "If you're dehydrated, there's going to be a lot less fluid stores in the body," he says. "So your muscles aren't going to get as much bloodflow as they normally would, and your workout is going to feel harder. If you're well hydrated, your muscles will be happier and you'll perform better."

Each individual has different needs based on weight, sweat rate, and how hard you're working. Here is what you need to know to stay hydrated.

Stick to water. Simple water is the best way to go. "If you're working out for 30 to 60 minutes, you don't need a sports drink," says Casa. That said, if you prefer something with flavor, try one of the many flavored, low-calorie sports drinks or waters on the market. Be sure to read the nutrition label and avoid extra calories and sugar. If you want a natural option that's a little tastier, try adding a slice of orange, lemon, lime, grapefruit, a few mint leaves, or even cucumber to your water.

Develop a daily drinking habit. This is the best way to avoid a last-minute push to pound fluids before a workout, a sloshy or nauseous feeling while you're on the road, and unwanted pit stops on your run. So sip small amounts of water or calorie-free beverages with and between meals. "Get in the habit of trying to drink water throughout the day," says Casa. He recommends carrying a water bottle with you so you can drink between meals (keep one at your work station) and ensure that you're hydrated before your workout begins.

Do the bathroom check. When you're adequately hydrated, your urine will be the color of pale lemonade or straw. If it's clear, you're drinking too much. If it's the color of apple juice, drink more. "It's the easiest and cheapest way to assess your hydration status," says Casa. "It really does work."

Drink when you're thirsty. That's the advice from the International Marathon Medical Directors Association and Tim Noakes, MD, author of *Waterlogged: The Serious Problem of Overhydration in Endurance Sports*. The body's thirst mechanism is exquisitely tuned to tell you when you need to hydrate.

Drink more when it's hot and humid. Hydration becomes most important during intense exercise in the heat. When it's hot and you're sweating, it's easier to get dehydrated. Even slight dehydration can make the effort feel tougher. So drink extra water and electrolytes when it's hot and humid outside. The best bet for rehydration is to consume a low-cal beverage that contains electrolytes such as sodium and potassium. Good choices include low-calorie sports drinks, coconut water, or water with a slice of fruit. The refreshing hint of flavor may drive you to drink more. How much is enough? Try to drink to match your thirst. If you want to be technical about it, you can do the sweat test (see next column). You'll know you've consumed enough when your urine runs light yellow in color.

Know when it's time for a sports drink. In general, says Casa, there are three circumstances that would reap the benefits of a sports drink to replace the electrolytes you lose through sweat: if you're working out longer than 60 minutes, working out hard, or exercising in the heat.

Check the label before you sip. Many sports drinks look appealing, but they are also laden with calories and sugar, which makes it easy to consume all the calories that you worked so hard to burn. Avoid specialty coffee drinks, high-octane sports drinks, and even fruit juice, all of which can be high in calories. Unless your workout lasted more than an hour or caused you to sweat profusely, stick to something as simple as water with a slice of lime. If you're looking to replace electrolytes, choose a calorie-free sports drink

or even coconut water. Remember, if your goal is to stay hydrated while also shedding unwanted weight, choose a drink with less than 50 calories for every 16-ounce serving.

Get a jolt prerun. It's okay to drink coffee or caffeinated tea before a workout. In fact, studies have shown that caffeine boosts energy and alertness. Just be sure to leave enough time between your java and your run to hit the bathroom. The heat of the liquid gets the bowels moving, and you don't want to have to make an unwanted stop on the run.

Do the sweat test. If you want to know *exactly* how much fluid you lose during a workout, do the sweat test. Here's how: Weigh yourself naked before a workout, then again after you're done. If you lost 1 pound during the workout, you sweated 16 ounces (1 pound). Next time, when you're working out in similar conditions, aim for 16 ounces of fluids during the workout to replace what you lost through sweating.

Rehydrate postworkout. Do you have white streaks on your skin or clothes after your workout? It means you're a salty sweater. You've lost a lot of sodium. Have a sports drink or water with an electrolyte tablet. There are many types of sugar-free, low-calorie electrolyte tablets, which dissolve quickly in water and help replenish electrolytes. You might also try low-calorie vegetable juice, which is a good source of sodium.

Stay off the hard stuff. The night before a hard workout, it's probably a good idea to lay off the alcohol, says Casa. A little bit isn't harmful, but it can act as a diuretic, and it's not going to help your hydration or mental status. And it could interfere with your ability to adequately prepare for the workout. Also, stay off the carbonated drinks like soda, he suggests. The carbonation affects the comfort of your stomach, and that's going to have an impact on how much water you choose to drink. If you're drinking so much soda that you feel full and gassy, it's less likely that you're going to drink the water you need to stay adequately hydrated for your workout.

THE LOW DOWN ON SOFT DRINKS

For many people, the daily soft drink—or five—is a habit that feels as addictive as that to any food or drug. We hear lots of reports from people who call soft drinks their "drug of choice," and report feeling addicted to their daily swig.

So how bad is it for you if you're trying to lose weight? And how can you kick the habit?

If you drink a lot of regular (non-diet) soda, you're consuming hundreds of calories that are devoid of nutrients. Research has shown that your body doesn't recognize the energy you drink in soda the same way it registers calories that come from solid foods. That means you may finish your drink and still feel hungry, even though you just consumed a meal's worth of calories. So if you find a way to break free of the habit, chances are, you'll start shedding pounds.

If you're a die-hard diet soda fan, you don't have to worry about the calories. And most research shows that it won't affect metabolism or appetite. But many people report that they lose when the stop drinking diet soda as well.

So how to kick the habit? Try abstaining from soda for a day, and see how you feel. On that day, try some of the options listed below. After your soda-free day, try extending that to an entire week. Chances are you'll feel better, the cravings will subside, and you'll be free of your soda addiction for the long run.

Want to drop pop? Try some of the options below to satisfy your thirst and your craving for flavor.

- Water-flavored with slices of lemon, lime, cucumber, mint, or watermelon.
- Tea: herbal, black, or green tea are great options. Add a hint of honey if needed.
- Low-fat milk
- Coffee; regular or decaf with a splash of low-fat milk
- Water with a hint of fruit juice.

What to Eat Before You Run

Your body needs high-octane fuel to run its best. Here are some high-carb, low-fat, low-fiber meals and snacks that can provide the energy you need to run your best, for a variety of different workouts. These meals and snacks are packed with nutrients to keep you healthy.

Use the following two tables as a guide, but listen to your body. Each individual is unique in terms of digestion time, so you may need to eat closer to your workout or a few hours earlier than what's prescribed here.

Refueling While on the Road

Walk into any sports store or go to any race, and you'll see a buffet of energy gels, chews, bars, drinks, and other engineered sports foods that promise to make you run faster and go longer. But are they for you? When and why do you need them?

If you're working out for an hour or less, you won't need to consume any food while you're on the road. But anytime you're working out for 75 minutes or longer, you'll need to refuel while running. In general, runners need to add in 30 to 60 grams of carbohy-

FUELING UP FOR WORKOUTS OF 60 MINUTES OR LESS

If you're exercising for up to an hour at an easy effort, it's okay to run on empty. But having a small snack or meal ahead of time may help you feel energized and strong throughout the workout. These snacks are also ideal before shorter quality workouts, like speed sessions and hillwork.

FOOD	CALORIES	IDEAL TO EAT . . .	EXTRA NUTRIENTS FOR RUNNERS
1 cup low-fiber cereal with ½ cup fat-free milk	195	30 minutes before workout	The milk provides protein; both the cereal and the milk have carbs to keep you energized.
3 fig cookies	150	30 minutes to 1 hour before workout	Easy to digest, these are packed with high-energy carbs, vitamins, and minerals.
1 cup berries with ½ cup low-fat cottage cheese	160	60 to 90 minutes before workout	The berries offer carbs for energy, while the cottage cheese provides calcium, potassium, and vitamin D—all of which come in handy when training.
3 graham cracker squares with 1 tsp honey	98	15 to 30 minutes before a workout or a shorter speed session	Packed with carbs, this will keep you energized for your workout.
6 oz low-fat fruited yogurt 1 medium peach	275	1 hour before workout	This snack has calcium, vitamin D, and potassium to support bone and muscle health, plus antioxidants to boost immune function.

FUELING UP FOR 60- TO 90-MINUTE WORKOUTS

Going longer? You'll need more fuel so you finish the workout strong and don't tire out before you're done.

FOOD	CALORIES	IDEAL TO EAT . . .	EXTRA NUTRIENTS FOR RUNNERS
1 medium banana and 1 Tbsp nut butter	200	1 hour before workout	The potassium and fluid in the fruit help you stay hydrated; the nut butter offers heart-healthy fat plus carbs.
1 bagel with 1 Tbsp nut butter and 1 Tbsp jam or honey	390	1 hour before workout	The bagel and toppings offer long-lasting energy so you can stay strong.
½ cup steel-cut oats with fat-free milk, topped with 1 cup sliced strawberries	260	1 hour before workout	Packed with carbs and B vitamins, this is an excellent choice for pre- or postrun recovery.
2 oz pretzels 2 Tbsp hummus	265	1 hour before workout	The pretzels provide easy-to-digest carbs for fast energy plus sodium to keep you hydrated; the hummus offers iron for strength, plus protein.
2 whole grain waffles (frozen) 2 Tbsp maple syrup	270	1 hour before workout	The syrup and waffles both offer fast-digesting carbs to provide an energy boost; the syrup also offers B vitamins to boost energy and bolster recovery.
PB & B sandwich: 1 medium banana 2 slices whole grain bread 1 Tbsp peanut butter	360	60 to 90 minutes before workout	All the ingredients provide carbs for energy; the peanut butter offers extra protein to fend off hunger; the banana provides potassium to help stave off muscle cramps.
2 oz honey whole wheat pretzels dipped in 1 Tbsp natural peanut butter	230	1 hour before workout	The pretzels provide carbs for energy and sodium to help keep you hydrated; the peanut butter offers protein to help muscles recover.
16-oz sports drink	125	15 to 30 minutes before (or during) workout	This provides fluids and electrolytes to help keep you hydrated.
15 animal crackers dipped in 2 Tbsp peanut butter	390	30 to 60 minutes before workout	The animal crackers are easy to digest and provide carbs for long-lasting energy. Peanut butter has vitamins and minerals like potassium and has been linked to lower risk of coronary heart disease.
1 cup apple-cinnamon O's cereal with 1 cup fat-free milk and 1 medium banana	255	45 to 60 minutes before workout	The cereal and milk provide carbs for an energy boost; the banana provides potassium to support your muscles; the milk offers an extra boost of calcium for bone health.
3 oz deli turkey wrapped in a flour tortilla with 1 cup shredded veggies	275	90 minutes before workout	This offers long-lasting energy with extra protein to aid in muscle recovery.

drates each hour that they are running beyond 75 minutes. Here's what you need to know about how to get the nutrients you need so you can get a boost without upsetting your stomach.

Refuel early and often. Don't wait until you're hungry and tired to refuel. By that time, your tank will be empty, and it will be tough to recover. At first, try taking in a bit of fuel within 15 to 30 minutes of hitting the pavement. Take more fuel 15 to 30 minutes later—even if you don't feel hungry or tired. The idea is to keep your energy

level steady and stop fatigue and hunger before it stops you. By the time you feel like you need the fuel, it may be too late.

Start small. Some runners find that when they add in too much fuel—like an entire gel at one time—their digestive system is upset, and their energy levels shoot up and then plummet. Try half a gel or a few blocks or a few beans every 15 minutes until you determine how much your gut can take.

Just add water. Be sure to wash down those carbs with a sip of water. Do not chase an energy gel, chew, or any carb-heavy fuel

AVOIDING MIDRUN PIT STOPS

During your workouts, your body continually shunts blood away from your GI tract and into your legs and lungs so you can run. That reduces the bloodflow to your digestive tract, so it's harder to handle fluids or food.

There's no sure-fire way to prevent this. But you can take some steps that can help. Be sure to water down any fuel you take on the run. If there's a high concentration of sugars in your stomach—say from energy gels or sports drink—the body can't digest it and essentially dumps out the calories. The fuel goes right through you!

Make sure that your prerun meal is low in fiber and fat, both of which can contribute to GI distress.

If you have any food allergies, closely examine the labels to make sure that there are no allergens in the products. Many foods can have hidden allergens (for instance, whey

protein can cause problems for people with dairy allergies).

Also, take a look at your everyday diet. Is there a certain ingredient or food that is widespread in your diet or you're consuming a lot of close to your runs? If so, you might benefit from eliminating that ingredient from your diet, and seeing if that doesn't eliminate those runs to the bathroom.

Finally, you might try adding in a fish oil supplement. It may help with the inflammation your gut is experiencing. It certainly won't hurt. Aim for 1,000 to 3,000 milligrams per day and make sure the fish oil contains both EPA and DHA.

with sports drinks, which have carbs, too. Doing so dumps too many carbs into your gut at once and is likely to send you dashing for the nearest toilet.

Take good notes. As you try out fuel during your training runs, keep track of what you took and how you felt afterward. Did you get a burst of energy? Or did you feel sluggish? Were you able to keep your pace constant but then hit the wall toward the end of the workout? Did the fuel tie your stomach in knots? Or did it sit well?

Try everything. A variety of sports drinks and energy gels and chews are on the market. Figure out what you like and what you can stomach. Energy chews are bite-size products with about 5 grams of carbs per chew. Energy gels usually have 22 to 30 grams of carbs per packet, while energy bars typically have about 22 to 50 grams of carbs, plus some protein. Most all of these products offer a boost of electrolytes, too. Some people can't stomach anything solid and choose to rely on sports drinks, which can have 15 to 30 grams of carbs per 16 ounces. Each product has its own unique blend of sugar and other ingredients, so try as many different flavors and brands as you can to determine which product gives you a boost without upsetting your stomach. If you're training for a race, try the brand that will be offered at aid stations at the race to determine if that works for you.

Go natural if you need to. While a ton of engineered sports foods are on the market, there's a chance you may not be able to tolerate any of them. Luckily, a lot of more traditional foods can offer the same boost—without the unwanted side effects.

Eating After Your Workout

Come in from a tough workout and it's tempting to just hit the showers, collapse, or reach for some sort of edible treat to reward yourself for getting out the door. But the steps you take after you finish your run—especially a tough one—will have a big impact on how you feel for the rest of the day, on your next workout, and on your ability to steer clear of injuries.

The 30 to 60 minutes after your workout are peak time for recovery. That's when your body is superprimed to restock glycogen stores and start repairing muscle tissue so you can bounce back for your next workout.

After exercising, and particularly after a hard workout, bloodflow to your muscles increases. At that time, your body is more sensitive to insulin, which shuttles glucose into your muscles, where it's converted into glycogen and stored until your body needs it for fuel. Along with glucose, insulin also cues your muscles to pick up protein to jump-start muscle repair. Wait any longer, and your body won't absorb glucose and other nutrients as well, and you'll end up feeling more tired. You might not feel it right away, but the cumulative effect of weeks and months of working hard—without proper refueling—will wear you down.

Refueling is most important if you're out for an intense effort that taxes your muscles and drains your muscle glycogen stores. For a shorter, easy workouts of 30 minutes or less, refueling isn't going to be as critical. Even so, it's still a good idea to eat right away to get into the habit of tying your meals to your workouts. Scientists have nailed down an optimum formula for refueling.

Divide your weight in half and eat that many grams of carbs. (A 160-pound runner would aim for 80 grams.)

Aim to get a carbs-to-protein ratio of 2:1. (So that same 160-pound runner would aim for 40 grams of protein.)

Don't stress about hitting the exact ratio; just make sure you're getting both carbs and protein. If you aren't getting that many carbs, be certain to take in 20 to 25 grams of protein just to ensure you're getting enough to repair your muscles. And try to eat that same 2:1 balance of carbs and protein 2 hours later. For postrun meal ideas, check out the table on page 133.

How much should you drink? That will vary widely depending on your fitness level, the weather, and how much you sweat. When you're rehydrated, your urine will be the color of lemonade. If it's darker—say, the color of apple juice—or

you haven't gone for a few hours, drink more.

Rehydrating is probably the most critical step of the recovery process. Even if you don't feel thirsty, it's important to drink. Water supports so many of your body's critical functions, including bringing nutrients and oxygen to your cells via your blood and flushing waste products out of your muscles. If you're dehydrated, the body has to work harder to perform all those functions, and you're going to feel more tired.

These meals are packed with protein and carbs to help you bounce back strong. Most of them have the carbs-to-protein ratio that scientists have found is ideal to facilitate muscle recovery. Plus, they're packed with vitamins and minerals to keep you healthy in your everyday life.

If you're watching your daily calorie intake, be sure to time your workout so that your recovery meal replaces your usual breakfast, lunch, or dinner. If you just finished a hard workout but it's hours until your next meal, choose a recovery snack that contains less than 300 calories but at least 20 to 25 grams of protein.

How to Pick the Best Sports Foods

Energy bars are everywhere for good reason. They're tasty, convenient, and relatively healthy. But with hundreds of brands and flavors to choose from, which is best? That

WHAT TO EAT AFTER YOUR WORKOUT

MEAL	NUTRITION	HEALTH BENEFITS
8 oz low-fat chocolate milk + 1 serving fresh fruit	225 calories* 40 g carbs 9 g protein	Fresh fruit and milk help you rehydrate while providing calcium, vitamin D, and other vitamins and minerals.
1 oz pretzels dipped in 6 oz low-carb (protein-rich) yogurt	275 calories 59 g carbs 12 g protein	Pretzels offer carbs, plus sodium to help replenish electrolytes. Yogurt adds calcium and vitamin D.
Turkey sandwich that includes 2 slices whole grain bread, 4 thin slices of deli turkey, and veggies	310 calories 55 g carbs 17 g protein	The turkey provides protein, while the bread provides nutrients and minerals that support heart health.
1 medium banana with 2 Tbsp peanut butter + 8 oz recovery shake	380 calories 55 g carbs 12 g protein	The sports drink replenishes electrolytes and fluids. The banana provides potassium to help with muscle contraction. The peanut butter adds healthy fats, plus niacin, which helps recovery.
1 whole egg (cooked in a nonstick skillet) on a toasted whole wheat English muffin + 1 cup fresh blueberries 6 oz Greek yogurt	290 calories 37 g carbs 21 g protein	Blueberries contain antioxidants that help ease muscle soreness. The yogurt provides calcium and vitamin D to support bone health. The egg provides protein, B vitamins, and choline, which boost immunity.
Smoothie that includes 8 oz fat-free milk, 1 Tbsp peanut butter, 1 medium banana, 1 Tbsp fat-free chocolate syrup	340 calories 55 g carbs 14 g protein	This is easy on the stomach if you can't tolerate real food after a run. Milk provides calcium and protein. The peanut butter offers healthy fats and niacin. The chocolate syrup adds carb and a sweet treat.
3 cups air-popped popcorn + 8 oz low-fat chocolate milk	280 calories 46 g carbs 11 g protein	Popcorn provides carbs, fiber, and iron. Milk provides calcium and carbs. Together they can satisfy your sweet and salty craving.

Calories and nutrient counts are estimates based on USDA nutrition database; specific brands may offer nutrient counts that vary slightly from the values listed in the table above.

depends. "You need to consider when you plan to eat the bar," says sports dietitian Tara Gidus. Before a run, for example, you want the right amount and type of carbs for an energy boost—without a trip to a porta potty. Afterward, you need more protein. In general, if you're watching your weight, you may want to think twice before adding a couple hundred extra calories to your diet.

But regardless of your weight goals, there really is a best bar for every running situation. But be sure to check the nutrition label carefully: Many so-called "sports foods" have ingredients—not to mention calorie, fat, and sugar counts—that rival candy bars. Follow these tips, adapted from a guide put together by *Runner's World* contributor Kelly Bastone.[7]

A Prerun Boost

You're dashing out the door for a run when you realize you haven't eaten in hours, or you're in the middle of a workout and need a quick energy boost. Grab a bar with malto-dextrin. This lab-formulated carbohydrate is more quickly absorbed than other carbohy-drates, so it delivers a fast hit of fuel. "When you need a rapid rise in blood sugar, malto-dextrin is a good choice," says Gidus. It's also easier on the stomach than the concentrated glucose found in some sports drinks. Because maltodextrin is relatively tasteless, it's a use-ful choice when you want to avoid overly sweet gels and chews, which can leave an unpleasant aftertaste during your run.

Be sure to think twice if you only think you're hungry and are unwrapping a bar. Most runners find that if they skip the urge to snack before a shorter workout and sim-ply start running, their appetite subsides and they get through the workout without hitting any "wall."

Midrun Energy

During medium to longer workouts lasting 60 to 90 minutes or longer, you need easily digestible energy that won't send your blood sugar levels on a roller-coaster ride. Pick a honey-based bar. Honey contains carbohy-drates (glucose and fructose) that deliver fast and long-lasting fuel. "Fructose is absorbed relatively slowly," says Gidus, "so its energy is released over time, while glucose is fast act-ing." Plus, studies show that consuming those two types of carbs at once increases the amount of energy your muscles can use and improves performance, says Gidus. Unlike table sugar, honey contains trace amounts of B vitamins, calcium, and iron. Be sure to avoid bars that are high in protein or packed with

WHAT'S THAT STUFF?

Some mysterious ingredients are good—and some aren't.

GOOD	WHY	BAD	WHY
Protein isolates	Whey and soy proteins are first extracted from a food and then added to bars to boost protein content. Hydrolyzed proteins undergo further processing that may remove vitamins but makes the protein more digestible.	**Sugar alcohols, such as sorbitol, xylitol, and malitol**	When consumed in excess quantities, these low-calorie sweeteners can cause diarrhea.
Glucose syrup	It's another term for corn syrup. It's used because it bonds easily with dry or solid ingredients. Its short, simple sugar chains are rapidly absorbed, so it offers instant fuel that's ideal for pre-run energy.	**Brown rice syrup**	This sweetener is a bit higher in nutri-ents and slower burning than corn syrup. But organic versions can contain traces of naturally occurring arsenic. Its health threats haven't been confirmed, but some companies may stop using it.

fiber. Your body doesn't use much protein for fuel during the run, and both of these nutrients take longer to digest. For obvious reasons, eating a lot of fiber right before or during a run is probably not the smartest choice.

Lunch Replacement

If back-to-back meetings mean you'll have to skip a sit-down meal, grab a high-calorie bar complete with extra fiber and protein. It should contain 250 to 400 calories, 9 grams of protein or more, and high-fiber carbohydrates, such as seeds, whole oats, and dried fruit. You also want some healthy fat (from nuts, for example), which, says Christine Gerbstadt, MD, RD, a spokesperson for the Academy of Nutrition and Dietetics, "helps you absorb vitamins more effectively and keeps you feeling satisfied."

Postrun Immunity Boost

After a long hard workout, you need foods that are packed with antioxidants, which will help you bounce back strong. "There's good research suggesting that selenium, vitamin E, and other antioxidants help protect the immune system," says Gidus. Nuts and dried fruits are rich in these antioxidants; cherries and berries in particular contain phytochemicals, which help protect against cancer and heart disease and help reduce inflammation.

Postworkout Recovery

When you want a nutrient-rich recovery snack but don't have time to seek out the perfect whole food, eat a carb-rich bar with moderate doses of protein and fiber (10 to 15 grams of protein, 2 to 5 grams of fiber for a bar with about 200 calories). "Postrun, these nutrients can help improve recovery and curb hunger," says Gidus. For the greatest recovery benefit, eat a bar within 30 minutes of your workout. If your workout was particularly hard or long, follow that with a light meal of protein and whole grain carbs 1 to 2 hours later.

CHAPTER 5

LOSING WEIGHT AND KEEPING IT OFF

Lots of people start working out to lose weight. And for some people, once they start exercising, especially if they're doing it for the first time, the pounds just melt off.

But if you're like most folks, it will take as much diligence at the dinner table as you practice when you're on the road. And studies have shown that it takes both exercise and healthy eating to shed pounds and make that weight loss last.[8] Here's how to lose weight and keep it off when you start to work out.

1 **Do some detective work.** Take some time to identify the most likely culprits for the unwanted weight. Are fried or sugary foods too tough to resist? Is it hard to avoid noshing whenever free food is within arm's reach? Are you too tired and busy to shop and cook healthy meals? Or do emotions—like boredom, anxiety, nervousness, depression, and joy—send you straight to the fridge? For most people, a wide variety of factors lead to unwanted pounds. The answers can lead you to your best first steps. If intense emotions are driving you to eat, identify alternate routes that will offer relief without derailing your weight-loss goals. You might reach out to a friend, get more sleep, or sink into the distraction of a good book or movie.

2 **Get moving.** It's difficult to lose weight by just cutting calories. Reducing calorie intake through diet *and* exercise is the most effective way to shed unwanted pounds and keep them off. It's ideal to develop a regular exercise routine of three to four times a week. But also try to incorporate more activity whenever you can. Take the long way to the restroom, take the stairs rather than the elevator, park your car as far as you can from the front door. Set a timer to chime every hour so that you get up from your seat.

3 Plan ahead. Everyone has their weak moments—situations where they find it tough to make healthy choices. Make a list of those occasions and settings where your diet tends to take a detour. No healthy lunch options at work? Pack your own. Devour everything in the fridge in the 10 anxious minutes after you walk in from work? Have a snack on the way home and precook a dinner you can reheat right when you get there. If you go off the rails late at night, once the kids are in bed and you finally have a chance to decompress, think of another activity far from the kitchen that helps you relax. Try a book, a shower, a call to a friend, a hot bath, a fun movie. Hate to cook or don't have time for it? Plan ahead and order premade foods or convenient healthy foods.

4 Fill up on fruits and veggies. Compared with other foods, produce is low in calories and high in nutrients, fiber, and water, all of which will help you lose weight without being hungry. Fill half your plate at every meal with fruits and vegetables. Divide the other half between whole grains, heart-healthy fats, and lean protein—lean cuts of meat, beans, tofu, or low-fat dairy—to keep you feeling fuller for longer.

5 Don't drink your calories. Stick to calorie-free beverages like water or hot tea. A 20-ounce soda can pack 240 calories and 65 grams of sugar. Even a 16-ounce hot chocolate with fat-free milk can have up to 360 calories. Add whipped cream, and you have an entire meal's worth of calories before you've taken your first bite. If you love specialty drinks, choose a smaller size with fat-free or low-fat milk and skip the whipped cream and syrups.

6 Don't do anything drastic. It's hard to feel bad about your body or have a burning desire to be leaner. Everyone wants to get thin now. But crash diets that promise to help you do that—by limiting you to a small group of foods, drastically reducing your calorie intake, or requiring you to buy certain engineered foods—won't work. Even if you lose weight fast, you'll likely regain the weight and then some. If you want the weight loss to last for life, you need to make changes that you can sustain for life.

7 Set smart calorie targets. Eating three meals each day keeps your metabolism revved, keeps you burning calories, and prevents you from getting so ravenously hungry that you eventually eat everything that's not tied down. If you restrict your meals to fewer than three per day, you'll be more likely to go overboard as soon as anything edible is within arm's reach.

- **WOMEN:** Aim for 300 to 500 calories a meal.

- **MEN:** Aim for 400 to 600 calories a meal.

- **WOMEN AND MEN:** Aim for 100- to 200-calorie snack(s).

8 **Keep track.** Studies show that people who track the calories they consume lose weight and keep it off more than those who don't. And there's good reason. When you have to track your calories, you see the sources of empty calories that are low on nutrients. To accurately track calories, you have to measure out portions—another practice that's proven to aid weight loss.

9 **Do not make weight the only measure of success.** Even as you get fitter, you may not see results on the scale. Keep in mind: Muscle weighs more than fat, and hydration, hormones, time of day, and other factors can all have an impact on the numbers on the scale. Don't measure success with the scale alone. Are your pants getting looser? Are you getting more compliments? Do you have more energy? What about your blood pressure, cholesterol, and other markers of chronic disease: Which way are they moving?

10 **Just practice; don't try to be perfect.** Realize that it's okay to indulge on occasion; one extra treat will not doom

your dieting efforts. Everyone goes overboard from time to time. When you do, try not to wallow in guilt or anxiety about it. You can't control the past; all you can control is the choice you can make right now. Work in enough foods that feel like rewards so that you don't feel deprived and primed to binge on a regular basis. Remember, it takes time, effort, and practice to form new, healthy eating habits.

Which Diet Is Right for New Runners?

Google "diet" or "quick weight loss" and you'll get hundreds of options, from supplements to books to detoxes, diets, and magic plans that make bold promises for instant, permanent results, with little work required by you.

You won't be hungry! Eat whatever you want! Indulge! Lose 25 pounds by the end of the week!

While deep down we all know that to lose weight you must eat less and move more, it's hard to resist the lure of these diets. So what place does each of them have in your new, active running life?

The truth is that diets are a lot like training plans. There's no ONE diet that's best for everyone. Only one healthy eating strategy is best for a particular person at a particular time. Each diet has its benefits and drawbacks for new runners. The most important factor in any diet is how well it helps you meet your goals and fits your needs, and how well you can maintain the healthy eating habits for life. Here is a comparison of some of the more popular diets on the market now, and their benefits and potential drawbacks for new runners.

Low-Carb Diets

A number of popular diets fall under the umbrella of carbohydrate-restricted diets. The Zone Diet, Carbohydrate Addict's Diet, the South Beach Diet, and probably the most famous, the Atkins Diet, advocate low-carb eating with generous portions of protein and fat.

Any low-carbohydrate diet—technically—is defined as an eating plan consisting of less than 20 percent of a day's calories from carbohydrate, or approximately 20 to 60 grams per day. Each has a slightly different twist. Atkins calls for perhaps the most drastic reduction—less than 40 grams of carbs per day at first—reasoning that this forces the body to burn stored body fat and release an energy source known as ketones. Another popular plan, The Zone Diet, restricts carbs to 40 percent of daily calories and calls for the balance to be split equally between protein and fat.

PROS: Proponents claim that weight loss will naturally follow elimination or restriction of sugars and carbohydrates. And

indeed, you'll see fast results. Carbs cause your body to retain water. So when you slash carbs, you retain less water, and the water in your system is flushed out. (Plan for lots of extra pit stops.) And you'll see numbers you like on the bathroom scale. Also, because many of these diets allow you unlimited fats and protein, you can indulge in carb-free, animal-based foods you might have previously written off as off-limits, such as eggs and bacon. And because fat and protein are digested more slowly in the body, you'll feel fuller for longer and avoid feelings of deprivation that can lead to a binge down the road.

CONS: Short-term, these diets appear to be safe, but there are lingering concerns about long-term safety, and research has yet to determine the impact of such diets on the development of chronic diseases like type 2 diabetes, osteoporosis, cardiovascular disease, and kidney disease, not to mention nutrient deficiencies. Because you eliminate many food groups when you go low carb, you can develop deficiencies of vitamins A, B_6, C, and E, as well as thiamin, folate, calcium, magnesium, iron, potassium, and fiber. In addition, you might find yourself suffering from headaches and constipation, which are common complaints among people following low-carb diets. And you might be wondering what happens when you start adding carbs back into the diet. Alas, some of the weight you lost is sure to return, and you're bound to experience the frustration of "yo-yo dieting."

Are they safe and healthy for runners? Carbs are your body's preferred source of fuel. That is, it's the nutrient that your body can most efficiently convert into the energy you need to run strong, without leaving you with any GI distress. (It's generally recommended that runners get 50 to 70 percent of their daily calories from carbs.) The body digests fats and protein more slowly. So you won't feel as energized on the run, and to avoid GI distress, you may have to be more careful about what you eat prerun.

High-Protein Diets

In recent years, high-protein diets that fall under the "paleo" umbrella have become more popular. Many of them focus on replacing carbohydrates with protein, reasoning that the body digests it more slowly—so you feel fuller for longer—and that it helps build and repair your working muscles.

These diets, which generally stress foods that can be hunted, gathered, or fished, is based on the theory that our bodies are designed to eat like our caveman ancestors; they're not designed to digest the processed foods that are the basis of the standard American diet. Advocates say that the packaged processed foods lead to inflammation and chronic diseases, from

heart disease to diabetes and joint pain. They generally advocate sticking with various grass-fed meats, wild fish, poultry, eggs, nuts, fruit, and vegetables—which are generally high in protein and fiber and low in carbohydrates—and avoiding grains and starchy vegetables. Healthy fats (olive oil, fish oil, avocado, herbs, and spices) are also recommended. Generally off-limits are dairy, grains, legumes, starches, alcohol, processed foods, sugars, and sugar substitutes.

PROS: You may feel better overall and lose some inches around the waist as you cut out empty calories and trans fats—all of which are from the processed foods. You won't go hungry. Studies have shown that people who eat more protein—about 30 percent of total calories—are less hungry and take in less calories. Not to mention, your body has to spend more energy—burn more calories—to digest protein than it does for carbs and fat—which is another way it promotes weight loss. And studies have shown that those who upped their protein intake were 50 percent less likely to regain the weight they'd lost. They also lowered their percentage of body fat.[9]

CONS: Because these diets are so high in fiber, your digestive health may improve, but it may be tough to get through a long run without a few pit stops, or hitting the wall. Though lots of protein can be taxing on the kidneys, many health experts consider a higher protein diet safe. It's common for those following high-protein diets to report feeling deprived at first, when they start slashing carbs (and junk foods) from their diet. But over time, many report becoming accustomed to eating cleaner.

Are they safe and healthy for runners? Because these diets are very low in carbs and higher in fat, they are not the best choices for runners. The body runs most efficiently when it's using carbs for fuel; the body has a harder time converting fat to fuel. So you may feel sluggish while you're adjusting to this new diet. And if you're running longer distances—say up to a half-marathon or a 10-K—it may be challenging to find any sports energy gels or chews that meet the parameters of the diet.

Detox Diets

The concept of cleansing the body of a buildup of toxins is not new. Indeed, detoxification and cleansing practices have been around for centuries, and they become popular again every now and again. Historically, detoxification-type diets were based in religion or self-purification and commonly involved fasting. Ancient Ayurvedic medicine, dating back prior to 400 BC, frequently recommended diets that cleansed the body of impurities by eliminating various food groups and instead focusing on eating plants.

Today a diet is commonly classified as "detox" if it involves a change of eating patterns with the goal of ridding the body of toxin buildup. These types of diets vary from those that involve a 2-day fast to others that call for a 21-day detox, during which time dieters must eliminate certain food groups or even drink "cleansing" beverages on a daily basis. Generally, these diets promise quick weight loss, healing, and cleansing and a renewed sense of better health. The idea is that by eliminating certain food groups, some of the toxins linked with those foods—like caffeine or alcohol—are eliminated, and the detox purportedly gives the body a break from foods that are considered hard to digest and absorb, like meat, cheese, and processed foods. In theory, as a result of avoiding these food items, the body uses less energy to digest food and fight off toxins and frees up energy to heal. While not all detox diets are solely focused on weight loss, the eating is so restrictive that weight loss often follows.

PROS: Quick results; because you're consuming so little, the weight immediately drops off.

CONS: Generally speaking, it's best to avoid these kinds of diets. While you may lose weight in the short term, they don't nurture the kind of lifestyle change and nutrition improvement that are essential to losing weight and keeping it off in the long term. Plus, you won't have the energy you need to exercise, which is critical to sustainable weight loss. Probably the most frustrating part of these diets is that once you finish the detox and return to your old eating habits, the weight you worked so hard to lose is certain to return.

Are they safe and healthy for runners? Some serious, negative, long-term consequences can come from detox diets. Short term, you might suffer from negative drug–nutrient interactions or you may even find some potentially toxic components in so-called "cleansing" products. And if you are suffering from a chronic disease like type 2 diabetes, these diets could put you at risk for other complications. As a runner, detox diets are likely to derail your training. You're likely to feel fatigued due to too few nutrients, and you may spend extra time darting for a porta potty thanks to the "cleansing products." Bottom line, think twice before jumping into a detox diet with both feet.

Commercial Diets

Many people turn to commercial programs like Weight Watchers, Medifast, or Jenny Craig for weight loss.

PROS: Some commercial weight-loss programs can be very effective in not only helping with weight loss but also helping to encourage general lifestyle changes. For instance, in Weight Watchers, foods and drinks are assigned point values according to the nutrients they provide and overall calorie contribution. This encourages people to learn how nutritious certain foods are. They also require members to weigh their foods—which teaches portion control, another important tenet of long-term weight loss. Some programs also include weekly meetings led by trained instructors and require weekly weigh-ins and accountability. This type of program also encourages exercise, as working out can "earn" you more points. All of this includes the social support and counseling that research has proven can be so helpful to weight loss. A recent study published in the *British Medical Journal*,[10] which compared six different weight-loss programs, found that people who use these programs are just as successful at weight loss—and sometimes more so—than if they'd simply joined a health club or sought one-on-one counseling. In the studies, people kept the weight off for a year. Many of the programs provide online support in addition to in-person meetings, so people can take advantage of that even if they don't live near a regular meeting place.

CONS: Some commercial diets—namely those where you have to buy that diet brand's food either in the grocery store or through the mail—can be difficult to sustain. Once you stop buying the food (which has controlled portions) and return to eating regular food that you prepare, the weight is sure to creep back. The foods on the system don't come cheap either, so you

(continued on page 146)

How Running Changed My Life

Andy Aubin started running, lost 133 pounds, and gained confidence

Andy Aubin had come to accept his size—and his extra weight—as a fact of life.

But once his daughter Tessa was born, "It just wasn't acceptable to be that overweight anymore," he says.

Aubin had tried lots of diets—from Weight Watchers to a chicken soup diet—and the diet would always work for a little bit, then fizzle out. "I'd lose interest and end up back where I started," he says. The same went for exercise. "I tried to start a Couch to 5-K plan a half-dozen times, but I was in such poor physical condition that I could never keep up with the first workout of the first week. I would repeat it over and over and just get frustrated and quit."

Then one day, he got winded going up a flight of stairs.

"That was the tipping point," he says.

He started with a training plan to build up to running 1 mile. That got him accustomed to exercise and gave him the confidence that he could do it. He progressed and

now runs 3 miles three times a week, cross-trains, and strength trains.

He went from 328.8 pounds to 195. He's now 20 pounds lighter than what he weighed in high school. But even more important is the confidence he gained along the way.

AGE: 36
HOMETOWN: Hatboro, Pennsylvania
OCCUPATION: Insurance broker

How did you get started? I couldn't focus on just the eating or just the working out. I needed to focus on the food and exercise at the same time. I knew I needed something different, even more introductory than Couch to 5-K. I found a plan that let me build up to 1 mile in 4 weeks with workouts three times per week. It eased me into running a mile, got me used to being active, and showed me that I can do it. I finally experienced some success, which gave me the confidence to try the Couch to 5-K workout.

What was the biggest hurdle, and how did you get over it? Lack of information. I was so far out of shape that I just didn't know where to start. It was really overwhelming.

What is the biggest reward of your running life? I'm doing things that I used to think were impossible. I finished the 10-mile Broad Street Run and two half-marathons. It's empowering to be able to do something you never thought was possible. Now I don't view anything as undoable. Nothing is off the table. That doesn't make it free or easy. But now I have the confidence to know if I'm willing to put in the work, there's nothing that can't be done. It carries over into work and relationships and everything else in real life. Running really showed me that.

What was your weight-loss goal? I started at 328.8, and my target was 225, which was what I weighed in high school. I hit my goal weight within 6 months, then I lost another 20 pounds. I am holding stable at 195.

What is the secret to your weight-loss success? Getting active and cutting calories at the same time. I wanted multiple ways to measure and motivate myself so that if I had a crappy week on the scale, I still could draw confidence from some great runs. I started counting calories using the MyFitnessPal app. That helped me determine how many calories I should be eating without slapping me in the face with it. It doesn't say, "You have to have broccoli," but when you eat two slices of pizza and see that an entire bag of broccoli has less calories than a half slice of pizza, you learn. I adjusted what I ate so I could stretch the calories and feel full all day, rather than being so ravenous by mealtime that it was a feeding frenzy. I started eating tons of fruits and vegetables, air-popped popcorn, lean meats, and turkey.

What advice would you give to a beginner? It's easy to get overwhelmed. It's going to take some time and break it down to manageable pieces. Don't focus on 3.1 miles; it feels impossible. Just focus on running for 60 seconds. But trust the plan and trust yourself. And it will really surprise you what you can do.

(continued from page 143)
may see your grocery bill swell. And one other drawback: Mail-order diets are not designed family style. So you can expect to receive your food in the mail and still need to prepare a meal for the rest of the family. Finally, if the diet cuts calories too rapidly, you may not have the energy you need to work out. And that can make the weight loss more difficult.

Why Some Calories Matter More Than Others

If you've been trying to lose weight, you've probably heard this rule: It's just a matter of calories in, calories out. That is, simply burn more calories than you consume, and the pounds will melt off. Right?

Unfortunately, it's not that simple—or that easy. Some calories actually do count more than others. Sure, there are 100 calories in 2 tablespoons of chocolate chips, and the very same 100 calories in 2 cups of baby carrots. But there's a huge difference in the way that those two different foods affect your appetite, your energy level, and your long-term health. Here's what you need to know.

Look for colors. About half of each meal should be fruits and vegetables. Not only are they low in calories, high in fiber, and filling, but a wide variety of produce will provide nutrients and minerals that help stave off diseases like cancer and keep your bones, muscles, metabolism, heart, and lungs in top form. Dark green veggies like kale and spinach will give you iron to maintain the health of red blood cells, which deliver oxygen-rich blood to the body; oranges and strawberries provide vitamin C to help the body absorb the iron. Red tomatoes and peppers have vitamin C, lycopene, lutein, potassium, beta-carotene, and vitamin B_6. Blueberries, blackberries, beets, and eggplants are sources of potassium—which helps the muscles contract properly—and anthocyanins, which help prevent cancer. Orange and yellow fruits and vegetables like corn, butternut squash, pineapple, yellow peppers, mangoes, carrots, pumpkins, sweet potatoes, and apricots are rich in beta-carotene, lutein, potassium, manganese, copper, folate, and vitamins C, A, and B_6.

Find the fiber. Found in fruits, vegetables, beans, and whole grains, fiber fills you up fast with less calories, and because it takes longer to eat and digest, it keeps you feeling satisfied longer. Aim for 25 to 35 grams of fiber each day. Spread your fiber intake throughout the day and try to consume at least 5 grams of fiber per meal. Water-soluble fiber, found mostly in fruits, vegetables, and beans, helps lower cholesterol and blood sugar levels. Insoluble fiber, found mostly in whole grains, keeps the colon clean, which may help prevent cancer and digestive disorders. To avoid an upset stomach, be sure to get the timing right. It takes about 2 hours for fiber to leave the stomach and get to the intestine. So save high-fiber foods for after your workouts, or consume them at least 2 hours beforehand.

Don't fear fat. In recent years, low-fat and fat-free products have flooded the market. But we now know that unsaturated fats like the ones you can get from olive oil, avocados, canola oil, nuts, seeds, and almonds actually help boost your heart health. They also leave you feeling fuller for longer and even lower risk of injuries like stress fractures. Stay away from saturated fat and trans fat; they raise your "bad" cholesterol levels and decrease your "good" cholesterol levels, and that can raise your risk for heart disease. You still want to keep fats in moderation. Learn more about the difference between good and bad fats on page 106.

Watch the sugar. Sure, a few tiny hard candy treats seem harmless enough—after all, one bag has only 250 calories and 2.5 grams of fat. But the 47 grams of sugar per serving has a cascade of negative side effects: You'll get a sugar high and crash that will send your energy levels on a roller-coaster ride and set the stage for more cravings down the line. Indulging those cravings can lead to weight gain and health problems like type 2 diabetes and high blood pressure. Look for products with the fewest grams of sugar and aim for less than 2.5 grams of sugar per 100 calories. The World Health Organization recommends keeping sugar intake to no more than 10 percent of daily calories. For many folks that's a limit of 50 grams of sugar per day. Aim much lower if you're trying to shed pounds. Your best option for a sweet treat is fresh fruit, which provides vitamins and minerals along with fiber. If you must indulge in candy, enjoy it right after a tough workout. In the 20 to 30 minutes immediately following a run that's longer or faster than you usually go, your body is especially efficient at metabolizing sugar. In fact, pairing these carbs with protein will help your muscles recover.

Measuring Weight-Loss Success

With all the choices out there, it's hard to figure out which measure of weight-loss success matters most. The scale isn't always the best one. After all, on any given day, factors like how much water and salty foods you consumed, the timing of your last meal, and hormone fluctuations can have a big impact on what the scale says. And yet these factors have nothing to do with how your healthy eating habits are going. Here's everything you need to know about how to measure weight-loss success, from M. Nicole Nazzaro, *Runner's World* contributor.[11]

The Bathroom Scale

What it measures: How much you weigh.

PROS: By watching this number from week to week, you can see trends and determine if your exercise habits and diet are leading you down the right path. Also, by carefully watching the trends (from week to week—there's no need to step on the scale more than a few times a week), you can put a quick stop to "falling off the weight-loss wagon" rather than realizing a month later that those late-night ice cream cones totally derailed your efforts. It's okay if your scale doesn't cost hundreds of dollars and isn't precisely calibrated; the important thing is to watch the trends (is it going up, down, or holding steady?), not the actual number.

CONS: Not every scale is calibrated, so if you jump from scale to scale, you might see numbers that are higher or lower than reality. It's best to use the same scale and watch the trends. The numbers can fluctuate from hour to hour (depending on what you ate or drank). Weigh yourself just after a heavy lunch, and that may be enough to ruin your day. If it plummets, you may feel free to go back for seconds (and essentially undo all of your hard work!). Finally, optimal health isn't all about the number on the scale. A scale can't tell you other important health factors such as cholesterol and blood pressure measurements. Some can tell you your percentage of body fat, but unless you laid down quite a bit of money for the scale, don't bet your life on the accuracy those metal pads report.

Body Mass Index (BMI)

What it measures: This is a measure of how much you weigh in relation to your height. A BMI of 25 or higher means you're at high risk for weight-related chronic diseases. The most healthy levels are between 18.5 and 24.9. Research suggests that BMI is most closely related to percentage of body fat.

PROS: It is a good tool to use to monitor whether or not your weight may be increasing your risk for future diseases.

CONS: You can have a very low percentage of body fat, a high percentage of muscle mass, be completely healthy, and still have a BMI that registers in the overweight or obese range. In addition, if you're under 5 feet tall, you might have a high BMI that doesn't accurately depict overweight or fatness. Adult BMI values should not be applied to children or adolescents or pregnant or lactating women (they have unique BMI standards), frail elderly, or even highly muscular individuals.

Body Fat Percentage

What it measures: Also known as "body composition," body fat percentage can range from 2 to 70 percent of body weight. For men, the ideal body fat is 8 to 24 percent of body weight; for women, the ideal is 21 to 35 percent. Some athletes have even lower levels of body fat. (It is not recommended that men dip below 5 percent; women below 12 percent.) Reducing your body fat percentage can help you run faster, as extra body fat can slow you down and put additional stress on your joints. That said, insufficient body fat can lead to injury and other health complications. The most accurate ways to assess body fat, unfortunately, can be expensive. A DEXA scan (which stands for dual-energy x-ray absorptiometry) is available at some hospitals, doctors' offices, research centers, and universities. Another method, The Bod Pod (which is air displacement plethysmography), is available at some universities, community colleges, and gyms. Other methods are less expensive and more accessible but not as accurate. The scales (or handheld devices) often used at gyms use bioelectrical impedance analysis (or BIA) to assess body composition. Essentially, the tool is based on the conductive properties of different tissues in the body. It sends a painless, low-energy electrical current to and from the body, and, theoretically, fat tissue resists the flow of this current whereas muscle tissue (which has a higher water and electrolyte content) does not offer much resistance. The machine converts this resistance into an approximation of total body fat as long as hydration is normal. So if you take the tests while dehydrated or waterlogged, the results will be off. At a gym, a personal trainer can use calipers to measure skinfold thickness to measure your body composition. This is based on the theory that subcutaneous fat represents a certain proportion of total body fat and you can measure it by checking a few select sites on the body (including the chest, abdomen, triceps, and midthigh). This fairly inexpensive test can be somewhat accurate if the technician who is using the calipers has experience, uses high-quality calipers, and uses the right equation to translate all of those measurements into a total body fat percentage.

PROS: Body composition can be used to monitor your health and to track changes over time. If you hit a weight plateau, while the number on the scale may not be moving, you can still see success as your percentage of body fat decreases while your percentage of lean body mass increases.

CONS: Many methods are used to measure body fat percentage, but not all of them are accurate. Even under the best conditions, most methods still have a margin of error of 3 to 4 percent, which means you might get a value that either inflates your ego or offers you false reassurance. Remember, every person has his or her own optimal level of percentage body fat and weight for top performance, so no all-encompassing number should be applied to everyone.

The Dream Jeans Test

What it measures: How many inches you've lost and how well you're toning up based on the ability to fit into your favorite pair of skinny jeans, or any other coveted, make-you-feel-great piece of clothing.

PROS: There's no pressure to hit a certain number on the scale, and there's no temptation to check back again and again to see if your body fat percentage has changed overnight. This test also requires very little equipment to run.

CONS: Just like the number on the scale, the fit of your clothes throughout the day can vary based on simple factors like your beverage intake. Additionally, this method is not as easy to monitor and track for progress's sake. Finally, the way your clothes fit doesn't necessarily tell you how healthy you might be. Plenty of people with

high cholesterol and blood sugar levels fit nicely into a size 2.

Running and Diabetes

Ask any runner, and they'll tell you that if you want to get going, you will likely have to make quite a few major changes. That includes adjustments to schedule (those early morning runs require a predawn wake-up call), diet (more nutrients, less junk food), and overall attitude toward eating and exercise. But for the runner with diabetes, even more adjustments need to be made in planning and timing meals, medication, and exercise to maintain stable blood sugar levels before, during, and after the activity—and to stay safe and healthy.

There are many types of diabetes. Two of the forms of the disease are type 1 (also known as insulin-dependent diabetes mellitus or juvenile-onset diabetes) and type 2 (also known as non-insulin-dependent diabetes mellitus or adult-onset diabetes).

Type 2 is the most common type of the disease; it accounts for 90 to 95 percent of diagnoses according to the American Diabetes Assocation. While athletes with type 2 often make their own insulin and rely on changes to the diet and exercise (and in some cases oral medications) to manage the disease, those with type 1 have absolute insulin deficiency, so they are treated with diet, exercise, and insulin injections.

If you're overweight or obese and at risk of developing type 2 diabetes (or already suffer from the disease), one of the best things you can do for your health is to stay active and lose weight. (Exercise also benefits those with type 1 diabetes, even if weight loss isn't necessary.) A regular exercise routine can reduce cardiovascular risk factors, improve body composition, improve insulin sensitivity, and even improve blood glucose control.

If you're a runner with type 1 or type 2 diabetes, keep the following tips in mind to exercise safely and improve your overall health.

Talk to your doctor. This should be your first stop before starting any exercise program. You're likely to get a pat on the back for your hard work, and get some guidance on how to tweak your medication schedule as you become more active or adjust your fueling to prevent extreme blood sugar highs or lows. A certified diabetes educator (CDE) or a registered dietitian (RD) can offer helpful advice as well.

Watch the sports foods. You may want to think twice before reaching for sports nutrition bars, drinks, and supplements that promise to make you faster or recover better. While the readily available carbs in these products can help to treat hypoglycemia, experts say that for athletes with type 2 diabetes, frequent consumption of extra calories while working out may cancel out the calorie burning effects of the exercise.

Plan ahead. If you have type 1 diabetes, it's critical that you plan ahead and take precautions when working out long or hard to prevent extreme blood sugar fluctuations. This means that you may have to adjust your basal insulin or daily injections, or your pattern of eating. So talk to your doctor about your training regimen, goals, and blood glucose levels to see if your insulin regimen should be modified as you start working out. And be sure to regularly monitor blood glucose levels so you understand your body's response to exercise.

Preempt low blood sugar. If you have type 2 diabetes and control it with diet and exercise, you're not at increased risk of hypoglycemia when running. Participating in exercise while taking certain oral diabetes medications can lower your blood sugar, but that's unlikely to cause hypoglycemia. However, some meds can lead to hypoglycemia, so check with your doctor to find out how exercise might impact your dosage. But if you have type 1 diabetes, you are at risk of hypoglycemia—especially when you have an unexpected opportunity to squeeze a workout in and your last meal was a while ago, or you covered your meal with insulin and now you want to exercise. Carbohydrate

(continued on page 154)

How Running Changed My Life

Aurea Nicolet-Dones became a runner, lost 40 pounds, and managed type 2 diabetes

Aurea Nicolet-Dones's running life began in the emergency room. Coworkers had noticed that she was slurring her words; the typing on her screen was nonsensical. A colleague advised her to check her blood sugar, and it was three times higher than normal levels.

Nicolet-Dones had been diagnosed with type 2 diabetes years earlier. She had gone to the doctor with blurry vision, expecting to leave with a prescription for eyeglasses. Instead, she left with a diagnosis. She was put on oral medication and a low-carb diet and told to check her blood sugar four times a day.

But by the time she ended up in the ER, she had become less vigilant in managing the disease. In the midst of working, getting a cold, and taking care of her 5-month-old daughter, she stopped taking her medicine and checking her blood sugar. Her family and friends had been concerned that she wasn't taking diabetes seriously.

At the ER, a doctor explained that high blood sugar could lead to coma or even death and put her on insulin. That, she says, was eye-opening. She started walking regularly, then running on a treadmill, then entering some local 5-Ks.

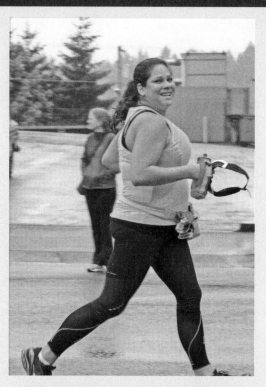

"I decided I was not going to let this disease beat me," she says. "I was not going to spend the rest of my life taking insulin."

Now Nicolet-Dones weighs 179 pounds. She has gone from a size 22 to a size 10. She has finished a few half-marathons and is training for a marathon. She is now off insulin, oral medications, and the daily blood sugar checks and able to manage the diabetes with diet and exercise.

"But knowing that my children will watch me be a healthy and physically fit adult is the greatest reward," she says.

AGE: 29

HOMETOWN: Puyallup, Washington

OCCUPATION: Program manager for state government

What's your regular workout routine? I work out 6 days a week. I do 1 hour of personal training twice a week (weight training, TRX training, high-intensity interval training, and/or Zumba), run three weekdays, and then do my long runs on the weekends. My endurance has increased; the same activities don't require as much of a recovery period.

What was the biggest hurdle, and how did you get over it? Finding time to work out is always a struggle for a full-time-employed, nursing mother with an infant and a toddler. During the week, I'll run during my lunch hour, while my husband is cooking dinner, or after the kids are in bed. For my long runs, I run when my husband can watch the kids. If there isn't time, he'll take the kids out in a bike trailer while I run so that we can all get out. When we need to go somewhere (like the store or a family member's house), my husband gets the kids ready, and I'll run to wherever we're going and meet them there.

What's the secret to your weight-loss success? I donate the clothes that have gotten too big for me and then I refuse to buy those sizes again. This forces me to maintain or lose weight in order to continue fitting into my new, smaller-size clothes.

What kinds of changes did you make to your diet? I went from eating fast food every day to eating healthier foods in smaller portions more often. The rule I follow is: If you can't tell what plant or animal it came from, don't eat it.

What is the biggest reward of your running life? I was able to able to get my [type 2] diabetes under control—free of constantly worrying about my blood sugars! As I started to lose weight, I was able to reduce and then eliminate the need for insulin. As the weight loss continued, my doctor allowed me to reduce and eliminate all oral medications. I currently manage my diabetes with only diet and exercise, with my doctor's monitoring.

Are there any special precautions you have to take to manage the type 2 diabetes? I still need to be cautious of letting my sugars get too low during a long run or intense workout. I do keep a blood glucose meter with me and check my blood when I am not feeling well. I only have to follow up with my doctor every 6 months to ensure that my diabetes is still under control.

What advice would you give to a beginner? Find what motivates you. Make small goals and when you reach them, reward yourself, and then make a new small goal. For example, each time I met a small weight-loss goal, I would get a relaxing massage.

supplements can be useful in this type of situation and also when heading out the door for longer workouts. Added bonus? If you're out on the road for much longer than 60 minutes, this extra carbohydrate can help maintain blood glucose levels, delay fatigue, and help you meet your pace and distance goals. How much fuel do you need during your workout? Experts generally recommend starting with 15 to 30 grams of carbohydrate every 30 to 60 minutes. Anytime you work out, be sure to take a sports drink, honey packet, or another fast-acting fuel in case you start to feel like your blood sugar is getting low.

Be prepared for an emergency. Anytime you go out on a run, be sure to wear identification that provides your name, your address, emergency contacts, and diabetes information.

Talk to your doctor about your medications. Individuals treated with insulin injections are more likely to see blood sugar fluctuations and hypoglycemia and therefore need to adjust meals, insulin, and exercise timing accordingly. These adjustments are highly personal, so be sure to work closely with your doctor, CDE, or RD to make the right adjustments.

Get the timing right. The beneficial effects of exercise on insulin sensitivity last for 24 to 72 hours (depending on intensity and duration of the workout). If you exercise relatively soon after a meal, the meal may not cause blood sugar to rise as much as it would have had you not worked out. So if you're accustomed to a blood sugar spike in the hour or two following dinner, an evening run might be the way to keep blood sugar from spiking and—as an added benefit—you're less likely to experience exercise-related low blood sugar. Again, talk with your doctor.

Learning How to Read Food Labels

The old saying goes, Don't judge a book by its cover, and when it comes to buying food, you really do have to look beyond the labels. It seems that most packaged foods claim to be "healthy" or "natural" or good for you in some way. But you really do have to drill down into the nutrition facts and lists of ingredients to find out if the product has the nutrients that you need, without the extra calories and junk that you don't. Studies have shown that those who read food labels are more likely to lose weight than those who don't. But labels can be confusing. Use the chart on the next page to figure out how healthy an item is.[12]

SERVING SIZE: Read this first. Some foods that look like they contain a single serving are actually two.

FATS: Total fat should be no more than 30 percent of total calories.

SODIUM: Aim for less than 200 milligrams per serving.

FIBER: Aim for approximately 25 to 35 grams of fiber daily.

SATURATED FAT: Less than 10 percent of calories should come from saturated fat.

TRANS FATS: Avoid them completely. If you must consume them, keep it to less than 2 grams per day.

INGREDIENTS: These are listed in descending order by weight. If an ingredient is near the beginning of the list, the product contains a large amount of it compared to the others. If the ingredient is toward the end of the list, the product contains only a small amount. A product with sugar near the end of an ingredient list is usually a healthier choice than a product with sugar as one of the first three ingredients.

DECODING FOOD LABELS

WHAT IT SAYS	WHAT IT MEANS
All natural	The food is minimally processed and contains no artificial colors or ingredients. May still be high in sodium, fat, and salt.
Reduced fat	Contains at least 25 percent less fat per serving than the original version. Watch for added sugar.
Low saturated fat	Contains 1 g or less of saturated fat per serving
Low cholesterol	Contains 20 mg of cholesterol or less per serving. Contains 2 g or less of saturated fat.
Low fat	Contains 3 g of fat or less per serving
Light	No standard definition. Sometimes means lower in fat and calories than similar products.
Cholesterol free	Contains less than 2 mg of cholesterol per serving. But unless it contains eggs or milk, it didn't have any to begin with.
Low calorie	Contains 40 calories or less per serving
Reduced sodium	Contains at least 25 percent less sodium than the original version
Low sodium	Contains 140 mg of sodium or less per serving
Very low sodium	Contains 35 mg of sodium or less per serving
Reduced sugar	Contains at least 25 percent less sugar than the original version
Low sugar	No standard definition
No sugar added	Contains no table sugar, but there may be other added sugars or sweeteners like corn syrup, dextrose, fructose, glucose, maltose, or sucrose
Sugar free	Contains less than 0.5 g of sugar per serving
Fortified	Nutrients have been added that weren't in the original ingredients.

Kicking the Sugar Habit

No matter how health conscious you are, you're bound to crave sweet things from time to time. But overloading on sugar can lead to lots of unwanted pounds and a wide range of health problems, including heart disease, diabetes, and high blood pressure.

In addition to sending your energy levels soaring. then crashing, overdosing on sugar sends your hunger hormones into overdrive. The satiety hormones that tell your brain "I'm full!" aren't properly triggered, which means you end up eating more than you need to. Not only that, but sugar triggers a rush of endorphins, the feel-good hormone. Nice as that instant gratification might be in the short term, if you overdo the sugar too often, you're likely to develop a craving for that sugar rush, which will lead to more extra calories and more excess weight gain.

So it's no wonder that experts recommend limiting sugar intake. If you're a woman, limit your intake of added sugars to 25 grams per day. (That's about 100 calories, or 6 teaspoons.) Most men should limit added sugars to 38 grams per day, which is about 150 calories per day, or about 9 teaspoons.

Here's how you can shake the sugar habit.

Know where to find it. You can find sugar by checking the ingredient list printed below the Nutrition Facts panel on most packaged foods. Added sugar goes by many names and often ends in "ose," such as lactose or maltose or sucrose. Other names for sugar include:

- **BROWN SUGAR**
- **CANE SUGAR**
- **CORN SYRUP**
- **CORN SUGAR**
- **DEXTROSE**
- **FRUIT JUICE CONCENTRATE**
- **HIGH FRUCTOSE CORN SYRUP**
- **HONEY**
- **MALTODEXTRIN**
- **MOLASSES**
- **SUCROSE**
- **RAW SUGAR**
- **TURBINADO SUGAR**

Scan the ingredients. If sugar (or a sugar from the list above) is one of the first three ingredients, think twice before choosing this food. Ingredients are listed by weight, so the ingredients that are listed first make up a greater percentage of the product.

Add it up. To determine if a food has added sugars (and how much), you have to do a little math. First, look at the Nutrition Facts panel and the line for total sugars.

There are 4 calories in each gram of sugar, so if a product has 20 grams of sugar per serving, that's 80 calories just from the sugar alone. How do you know if any of that is "added sugar"? Look at the ingredient list and see whether it contains any added sugars (like those from the list on the left). If it does not, the food doesn't contain any added sugars. The sugars that come from a natural sugar like lactose (milk sugar) or fructose (fruit sugar) are often considered "healthier" simply because they come from a food that offers other nutritional benefits like calcium and vitamin D (in milk) or fiber and vitamin C (in fresh fruit). But if you see an added sugar among the first three ingredients, the product contains significant "added sugars," and it's best to avoid it.

Aim low. Choose products with the least amount of added sugar. On any product, aim for no more than 2.5 grams of added sugar per 100 calories.

Go natural. Choose fresh fruit to satisfy a sweet craving; it provides vitamins, minerals, and fiber in addition to some hydration, so it will keep you feeling fuller longer.

Time it right. If you absolutely need a sweet, have it in the 20 to 30 minutes after a hard workout. During that time, your body is hyperefficient at digesting the sugar. Pair the sweet with protein, and this will kick-start muscle repair.

Choose an alternative. If you're looking to add flavor to your food, reach for herbs and spices instead of sugar. Cinnamon and cloves add flavor to oatmeal, while oregano and rosemary add flavor to marinara sauce.

Know where it's hidden. Foods like salad dressings and yogurt may not taste sweet, but sugar is often added to low-fat versions of products to make them tastier. Even foods like multigrain bread contain about 2 grams of added sugar per slice. Look for brands that have the label "no added sugar."

Watch the substitutes. With all these dire warnings about sugar, it's tempting to reach for calorie-free artificial sweeteners. Low-calorie sweeteners have led to the creation of a wide range of low-calorie products, which offer a healthier alternative for anyone watching their weight and those with diabetes, who must carefully monitor their carbohydrate and sugar intakes. Low-calorie sweeteners have been the subject of extensive scientific research and are generally recognized as safe by the FDA. While the research suggests that artificial sweeteners won't make you eat more, many people report sugar cravings and a need for more food after consuming "diet" foods sweetened with sugar substitutes. In addition, many report that once they cut back on the artificial sweeteners, their cravings ebbed, and it was easier to resist sweet temptations and lose weight.

How to Make Your Favorite Meals Healthier

There are many ways to change your favorite recipes to make them lower in cholesterol, fat, sugar, and calories. For instance, you can save nearly 200 calories per serving by baking or grilling meat rather than frying it. You can save nearly 300 calories simply by replacing 1 cup of sour cream in a recipe with 1 cup of plain, low-fat yogurt.

The following tips will allow you to cut calories and fat while still enjoying your favorite recipes. In fact, you probably won't notice a difference with many of these simple substitutions.

Avoid the Deep-Fry

Here are some healthier alternatives.

BAKE IT

GOOD FOR: Meat

WHY: Requires no oil, butter, or added fat

HOW TO: Use a covered container in the oven. If the cut of meat that you're using is very lean, try adding a fat-free liquid, such as vegetable or chicken broth, to help keep it moist.

POACH IT

GOOD FOR: Fish, chicken, and eggs

WHY: No frying or high-calorie cooking additives required

HOW TO: Cook the food in a small amount of simmering water or broth. Be careful not to leave foods in simmering liquids too long. Overcooking will dry them out.

STEAM IT

GOOD FOR: Vegetables and fish

WHY: Helps maintain their vitamins and minerals

HOW TO: Arrange foods in a steamer. Add a small amount of water. You can also steam foods in the microwave in a covered dish.

SAUTÉ OR STIR-FRY

GOOD FOR: Meats and vegetables

WHY: Cuts or eliminates the amount of oil and butter used

HOW TO: Avoid butter, shortening, or grease. Depending on the amount of meat and vegetables, add 1 to 2 tablespoons of oil to lightly coat the pan and add more if the food begins to stick. Or use a nonstick skillet and eliminate the need for a lot of fat. Cook for a short time at high heat.

GRILL IT OR BROIL IT

GOOD FOR: Meats, poultry, fish, and vegetables

WHY: Reduces or eliminates the need for butter and oil

HOW TO: Coat the broiler or grill with vegetable oil (use tongs and a paper towel) to prevent sticking. You can keep the skin on the meat while cooking to keep the item moist, but your best bet is to remove the fat before serving.

ROAST IT

GOOD FOR: Meats and vegetables

WHY: Reduces need for butter and oil

HOW TO: Preheat the oven to 350° to 400°F. Keep the meat moist by occasionally basting with wine, fruit juice, stock, or fat-free chicken or beef broth.

Stealth Swaps

Skim your soup. After cooking soups, stews, sauces, and broths, chill and spoon off hardened fat. This can save 100 calories per tablespoon of fat removed.

Go lean. Trim fat from meat before cooking. Remove the skin from poultry before eating it. Substitute lean ground turkey or ground round for regular ground meats such as hamburger.

Switch your dressings. Substitute low-calorie versions of your favorite sauces and dressings. Use vinegar, mustard, tomato juice, or fat-free bouillon instead of creams, fats, oil, and mayonnaise.

Avoiding Weight Gain When You Start Working Out

Being active every day and piling up the miles and minutes on the road burns a serious number of calories. But many folks step on the scale after they start an exercise routine only to discover that instead of dropping pounds, they've actually added some—a reality that seems both unfair and wrong. In some cases, it's because the amount of food consumed has gone up along with—or even beyond—the mileage. In other cases, it has to do with factors beyond a person's control, like hormonal fluctuations. Here's why the numbers can go up and how to avoid weight gain when you're on the run.

Think Harder about Hunger

If you have been sedentary in the past and are just starting to exercise on a regular basis, it makes sense that your appetite has climbed, too. "Your body is trying to help fuel your increased activity," says Jenna Bell, PhD, RD, a nutrition consultant and fitness expert in New York City. "One of the ways it does this is by making you hungry." It's worse for women—researchers from the University of Massachusetts discovered that this heightened sense of hunger is stronger in women than men because exercise accelerates the production of appetite-regulating

SMART SUBSTITUTES

Make these smart swaps to reduce calories and fat from your favorite foods.

REPLACE THIS	WITH THIS
1 whole egg	• ¼ cup egg substitute • 1 egg white plus 2 tsp oil • 2 egg whites
1 oz cheese	• 1 oz low-calorie or part-skim cheese, such as farmer's, mozzarella, reduced-calorie cheeses, or any cheese with less than 5 g fat per oz • 2 Tbsp Parmesan or Romano cheese
Whole milk ricotta cheese (1 cup)	• 1 cup low-fat cottage cheese • 1 cup low-fat ricotta cheese (low fat is less than 2% milk fat)
Meat	• Tofu cubes • Cooked dried beans • Cooked grains and starches
• Sausage • Bacon • Deli meats • Ground hamburger, ground chuck, or ground round • Spare ribs	• Ground sirloin • Lean pork • Ground chuck • Deli turkey • Chicken breast • Tenderloin
Whole milk yogurt, plain (1 cup)	• 1 cup low-fat or fat-free yogurt
Whole milk (1 cup)	• 1 cup fat-free milk

hormones, which prompts them to eat more. Men are not as vulnerable to hormonal fluctuations, making them less likely to put on extra pounds.[13]

So what should you do? If you have just finished a hard workout, by all means, have a recovery meal with a healthy mix of carbs and protein, or even a recovery smoothie made with fresh fruit and protein powder. Your muscles need fuel to restock your energy stores and speed recovery. But if

you're still looking for food beyond that, then it's time to ask some hard questions, says Leah Sabato, MPH, RD, a nutrition expert specializing in obesity treatment and prevention. Are you truly hungry? Or are you actually thirsty, tired, or feeling some emotion that is prompting you to reach for food for distraction or comfort? "When your body truly needs food," says Sabato, "you'll experience fatigue, a rumbling stomach, or hunger pangs that accu-

REPLACE THIS	WITH THIS
Sour cream (1 cup)	• 1 cup blenderized low-fat cottage cheese with 1 Tbsp lemon juice • 1 cup low-fat or fat-free yogurt • 1 cup low-fat sour cream
Shortening (1 cup)	• 1 cup margarine • 1 cup light or low-calorie margarine • $^3/_4$ cup vegetable oil
Butter (1 cup)	• $^7/_8$ cup vegetable oil • 1 cup tub margarine, reduced calorie • 2 sticks margarine, reduced calorie • Use butter-flavored powders to flavor foods instead of butter or margarine.
Light cream (1 cup)	• 3 Tbsp vegetable oil plus fat-free milk to equal 1 cup
Buttermilk (1 cup)	• 1 cup fat-free milk and 1 Tbsp vinegar or lemon juice. Beat briskly and let stand 5 minutes. • 1 cup low-fat buttermilk
Cream cheese (1 cup)	• $^1/_4$ cup margarine blended with 1 cup dry, low-fat cottage cheese. Add small amount of fat-free milk to blend. Salt to taste. • 1 cup low-fat cream cheese
Heavy cream (1 cup)	• $^2/_3$ cup fat-free milk and $^1/_3$ cup vegetable oil • 1 cup evaporated fat-free milk

mulate over time." If you have a craving for a specific food or feel the desire to eat come on suddenly or after an upsetting thought, chances are you're not actually hungry, says Sabato.

To keep cravings at bay, remove temptations from your sight—if nacho cheese Doritos aren't on the counter, chances are they won't call your name. You can also try a diversion, like taking a walk. In fact, a walk may be just what you need if weight maintenance or loss is your goal. If you can't fathom adding more activity in a day, trying using your stopwatch. Rather than engaging in a mental wrestling match between your urge to eat and your desire to "be good" and deny it, just wait for 20 minutes. Rather than the firm battle between "yes" and "no," you just have to tell yourself "not yet." Usually after 20 minutes have lapsed, the craving will likely not be as strong. It may even disappear.

Avoid Entitlement Eating

You go for a hard workout, come home starving, and reward yourself with a stack of whole grain pancakes, scrambled eggs, a smoothie, and a side of bacon and toast. Before you know it you've consumed nearly 900 calories—quite a few hundred more than what you burned on the run.

To limit the effects of overcompensation—that is, eating above and beyond what is needed for recovery and eating back all the calories you just burned during the workout—it's important to make smarter food choices throughout the day. Stick to whole, minimally processed foods that are rich in fiber and protein, which take longer to digest, keeping hunger at bay. Try to avoid falling into the "I deserve it" mind-set. Sadly, going for a run does not give you license to eat an entire batch of cookies.

The timing of the meals you eat can also help you avoid falling into the overcompensation trap. Schedule your meals so that you provide your body with enough energy to fuel workouts and your recovery, without overdoing it. If you eat a meal 2 to 3 hours before a workout, your body will be properly fueled for your run and you won't feel hungry on the road. After a run, skip the recovery snack and instead sit down to a full meal within 30 minutes.

Think Beyond the Bathroom Scale

When you start exercising, you gain muscle and lose body fat. Muscle does weigh more than fat (which explains why the scale may have crept up a few pounds).

But there's another common reason for weight gain in your workout life—you're retaining fluid. Not only do runners typically drink more fluids in the days when they're exercising more, but they also tend to eat more carbohydrates. And carbohydrate attracts water. This extra fluid ensures that you're hydrated and well fueled. Fluid gains often disappear when you're no longer loading up on carbs or hydrating quite as diligently.

Avoiding Weight Gain When You *Can't* Work Out

If it's easy to fall into weight-loss traps when you're working out, then you know it's *really* easy to gain weight when you're sidelined. It can be hard to stay motivated to eat healthy when you can't work out because you're injured, busy, or just can't get on the road. But it's not impossible. Here's what you can do to prevent the weight gain—and the emotional toll—during your time off.

Hide the scale. When you're regularly working out, it's a good idea to check in with the scale once a week, to see progress or to stop a landslide before it starts. But during your time off, try to stay off the scale every day, since your weight can fluctuate wildly throughout the day, depending on how much you drank, the amount of sodium you've consumed, and how much fat, protein, or carbs you've had. If the number on the scale consistently upsets you, be kind and hide the darn thing. Remember, progress also comes in the form of looser-fitting jeans and healthier cholesterol levels.

Treat yourself with a nonfood reward. Rather than rewarding yourself with food—even if it's sugar free, fat free, or calorie free—pat yourself on the back with something lasting and nonedible. Get a pedicure, buy a new outfit, meet up with friends, get a new book or some new tunes.

Don't stop moving! Light activity will help alleviate stiffness and soreness. If you are able, consider cross-training activities that don't stress your aching joints but still help you maintain the fitness you worked

so hard to develop. Even walking around the block will help burn more calories than sitting on the couch. Also, take advantage of opportunities to be active throughout the day: Take the stairs instead of the elevator. Park in the farthest spot in the lot. Walk your errands in your neighborhood instead of driving them. Have a stress fracture? Get in the pool. The nonimpact activity will burn calories and build strength.

Cut back on calories. If you're not working out like you usually do, you're burning less calories. That means you need to cut back on how many calories you take in. So think twice before going in for seconds. Before you have yet another snack, ask yourself, "Am I really hungry?"

TIPS TO AVOID WEIGHT-LOSS TRAPS

FUEL UP . . . WITHIN REASON. You need to eat before a workout, but you probably have enough stored energy to fuel you for a 3-miler, so skip the snack. Plus, it's okay to be mildly hungry before a short workout. Research shows that exercise suppresses the appetite (so your stomach will stop growling once you start running).[14]

DRINK FLUIDS. Staying hydrated can help you feel better on the run and keep you from feeling hungry. Remember to hydrate before and after a workout and sip on (calorie-free) fluids throughout the day. For more on hydration, see page 125.

FILL UP ON FIBER. High-fiber foods (fruits, vegetables, and whole grains) are low in calories but filling, which makes them great for weight control. But they also keep your diges-

tive system moving, so avoid eating a high-fiber meal right before you run.

MAKE YOUR CARBS COUNT. Don't fill up on junk carbs like those from simple sugars, sweets, and processed grains. Instead, carb-load with whole grains like brown rice, quinoa, whole wheat bread, and vegetables, which are more filling and full of the nutrients you need for long-term good health.

Don't eat your emotions. So often, we're eating not to soothe a growling stomach but to relieve boredom, anxiety, stress, sadness, or some other uncomfortable emotion. So find a solution that eases your discomfort without leaving you with extra pounds (and the regret that goes along with it). Go outside, knit, weed the garden, write a letter, call a friend, listen to some beautiful music, or just leave the kitchen so food will be out of sight and out of mind. On the fridge or the pantry, keep a list of safe alternatives to eating that you can refer to whenever a snack attack takes hold. (For more on this, see "How to Manage Emotional Eating" on the next page.)

Downsize portions and slow down. There are ways to eat less without feeling deprived. Use smaller plates, for instance. If you always serve dinner on a dinner plate, you're bound to fill it up and even ask for seconds. Choose a smaller plate and you won't be able to pile on quite as many calories. And slow down! Research has found that when people eat slowly, they actually take in less calories. Try chewing each mouthful at least 10 times. By the time your mouth is finished chewing, your stomach will have registered a full feeling and your brain will have gotten the hint that it's time to stop chowing down.

Set a calorie goal and stick to it! Lots of resources are available to help you determine how many calories you need each day. You can guesstimate your calorie needs by searching on the Internet (which is not always accurate),

logging in to an app (which is better but not always accurate), or calculating your needs based on your resting metabolic rate. Once you know your calorie "budget," start keeping a journal and write down everything that passes your lips. Next to each food item, record the calories. Toward the end of the day, add up your calories to see how close you are to your limit. If you're over, consider taking a walk to burn off some energy, and when dessert comes around, politely pass. If you finish the day with a calorie deficit, congratulations! You're one step closer to losing weight. If you have lots of calories left over each and every evening, then it might be time to add a fruit or veggie (or some other healthy snack). You don't want to be missing so many calories you miss out on vital nutrients, too.

Tracking Your Food Intake

Ruffin Rhodes reached his get-up-or-give-up moment at the age of 49. He was carrying 250 pounds around on his 5'6" frame; he was taking blood pressure medication and feared a diagnosis of type 2 diabetes was around the corner.

Some of the changes were easy to make immediately: He eliminated fast-food stops and lunch meetings.

But about 1 year into the effort, he hit a plateau. So he started using a calorie calculator and bought a digital food scale. And he was in for a surprise.

"I realized that my guesses on portion

size were about 20 percent off the mark," he says. "Measuring and tracking my food intake helped me to break that first weight-loss plateau."

He has a scale at work and at home and tries to avoid eating out as much as possible. When he does, he looks up the caloric information online before he goes to decide what he's going to eat. At business and social functions, he tries to stick to basic, nonprocessed foods. But the best part is, now that he's used the scale for so long, he can more accurately estimate portion sizes when he doesn't have the scale.

"I do get tired of the weighing sometimes and fall off the wagon every now and then," he says. "But when I'm not tracking my portion sizes or weighing my foods, I do see a weight gain."

Indeed, what Rhodes found confirms what scientists have said: One of the most powerful things you can do to shed pounds will happen when you're not on the road or at the dinner table: That's keep a food log.

One study published in the *American Journal of Preventive Medicine* found that among 1,700 overweight individuals, those who kept a food diary more than 5 days a week lost almost twice as much weight as those who didn't, and they kept the weight off.[15] There are plenty of apps on the market. Here is some of the information that you should include.

- **FOOD**
- **CALORIES**
- **FAT**
- **CARBS**
- **PROTEIN**
- **FIBER**
- **SODIUM**
- **ACTIVITY**

How to Manage Emotional Eating

To be sure, losing weight and keeping it off requires you to spend a lot of mental and emotional energy on food. Thinking about portion sizes, counting calories, adding up miles, and tracking calorie burn all consume a lot of thought.

But sometimes it's hard to know: What's the fine line between being conscientious and becoming obsessed? Here are some frequently asked questions and answers to help you find the mental and emotional balance involved with weight loss.

Now that I've got my weight under control, how do I keep it from returning to where it once was? Remember where you once were and how you got to where you are now, and keep your eye on where you want to go. Remember all of the hard work, sweat, and determination you've invested to get to where you are now. In the past, you might have lost control around certain foods or spent lots of time being sedentary, which might have led to the weight gain. But if you're currently at a weight where you feel great, ask yourself, "How did I get here?" Chances are you arrived by saying no to indulgences, by making healthy choices more often than not, and by getting moving on a regular basis. Keep in mind that you didn't reach your goal by making perfect choices about food and exercise all the time—just most of the time. None of us can avoid every single trigger food or resist every single offer of dessert or a second helping. Aim for balance, not perfection.

I'm in a terrible cycle. I am good about healthy eating for a while, then after a while, I inevitably end up feeling entitled to reward myself with the treats that I've been depriving myself of. Then I overindulge and end up destroying the progress I've made. What do I do? Think it through. If you just worked out for an hour and at the end of the workout, someone offered you a supersize serving of french fries, would you have it? Probably not. That's because you'd be very aware that you'd be undoing all the progress you just sweated so hard to make. At the end of the day, we all have to learn how to strike the balance between knowing when to indulge and when to restrain ourselves. If you've been busting your butt because you didn't like how you looked, how you felt, or how hard it was to do any physical activity, don't undo all of your hours of sweat and sacrifice. Certainly, there is always room for indulging on occasion, but there's a huge difference between that and completely falling off the wagon.

We do need to celebrate our efforts—and our successes—in order to keep up the good work. Otherwise, it's too easy to dwell on the negative. But there are many other ways to "treat" yourself for all your diligence and hard work. Incentivize yourself with a new pair of jeans that fit your new figure, since your others are too big. Get some new running shoes, because you put too many miles on your last pair. Get a new haircut to match your new figure. Treat yourself to a massage to ease your sore muscles, or a manicure and pedicure. Whatever reward you choose, make sure that it nourishes and encourages your healthy habits—and weight—in the future rather than reversing all the hard work you did.

How often is it okay to indulge? Every day? Every week? Special occasions like birthdays, etc.? I am restricting my food but I am constantly feeling deprived. Then I end up ultimately justifying treats and losing control because I feel like I deserve it after so much deprivation. What do I do? It's only natural to feel deprived when you are constantly saying no to your favorite foods. While some people may find that they do best on an "all-or-nothing" kick and simply must eliminate their trigger foods altogether, the majority finds that to reach their long-term weight-loss goals, they have to allow for a few treats now and then. This is fine to do. But set for yourself; a certain number of calories, or a certain number of days per week, or only on holidays. Pick a limit that you can stick with and feel good about. If you notice that over time you've allowed yourself more calories and more and more occasions for treats, then it might be time to try a no-treats detox for a few days, simply to get back on track.

What happens when I do fall off the wagon? I get frustrated and tempted to give up altogether, because it all feels too difficult and too overwhelming. What do I do? If you do get off track, acknowledge it and get back on as soon as possible. Ask yourself: Am I going to keep overdoing it? And ultimately regain the weight? Or am I going to get back on track and try again? Give yourself a deadline to restart your healthy-eating effort. When that time arrives, press the reset button and start again. You can't rewrite the past, but you can control the future by taking the reins over what you do in this moment. And it is never too late to start again and make a healthy choice that will improve your physical health and self-image.

I often overeat—or eat unhealthy things—because I feel emotional. Sometimes it's when I'm sad, angry, bored, depressed, lonely, or tired, or even when I feel excited and happy. Sometimes it happens so quickly I feel helpless to stop it. How do I avoid it? One way to avoid letting strong emotions prompt eating decisions that you regret is to avoid situations where you're going to be likely to act out in this way. Leave the room, step outside, or do anything you can think of to break the momentum between the strong emotion and your reach for the refrigerator door. Write down 10 things you can do when you are feeling very emotional and have been prone to overeat in

the past. This list needs to include simple tasks that would genuinely offer you relief, distract you, be easy to do on the spot, and break the momentum, but that don't leave you with the hangover of regret (and unwelcome news on the scale). For instance, you might clean the bathroom, make some scrapbook pages, take the dog for a walk, vacuum, step outside and look at the sky, count to 10, call or write a letter to a friend, pick up a favorite book, etc. Avoid making any of these tasks too big or so overwhelming that they're too daunting to try.

How often should I get on the scale? I don't want to let it ruin my day, and yet I don't want to fall off the wagon completely. It's a good idea to get on the scale once a week and at the same time of the day each time. Hop on the scale in the early morning, after you've used the restroom. The readout will be the most accurate, because during the day your weight will fluctuate depending on what you ate (salty foods?) and what you drank (too much water?). It's best not to get on the scale multiple times a day; the wide fluctuations are not only false, they're not good for your ego either.

The idea of eating healthy and exercising and losing all the weight I need to lose is just so daunting. I don't know where to begin, and it's easier to just say "I don't care." I've been eating this way for so long, and I fear and doubt I'll be able to do it. How do I start? Take it in baby steps. Set a small goal for yourself. Research shows that even minimal weight loss—such as 5 to 10 percent of your body weight—can improve your health and reduce your risk of chronic diseases such as type 2 diabetes. This means that if you weigh 200 pounds, you might think that you need to lose 50 pounds to be at your goal weight, but you need lose only 10 pounds to be closer to better health. This is much more doable. So set yourself some goals and make them reasonable. If they are too grandiose, you're likely to fail and give up. But when the goal is achievable—say 1 pound a week or maybe ½ pound a week, you'll be able to get a confidence boost as you meet the goal (and maybe even surpass it). And keep in mind that sometimes our markers of success don't need to be the number on the scale. Maybe you need to improve your cholesterol by eating less saturated fat. Or maybe you need to reduce your blood pressure and so start eating more foods with potassium and less salt. Start with one meal, one day at a time.

You might try a clean-eating day in which you avoid—for just 24 hours—the food items and lifestyle choices that are derailing your fitness and performance goals. Maybe your trigger is alcohol, maybe it's ice cream, maybe it's huge bowls of pasta. Whatever it is (and it could be multiple items), set aside a time frame (say, 24 hours) to completely avoid this trigger. If you feel better after this time, then expand this clean-eating day to include not only your trigger foods but

any food that's not whole, not pure, and essentially not good for you. What should you avoid? Any processed foods, convenience items, or foods with a laundry list of ingredients. For just one day, maybe more, promise yourself that you will eat clean and focus on quality calories that do something for your body, your health, and your confidence. A clean-eating day is sometimes just the jumpstart you need to get back on track when your dieting efforts go away.

Soft Drinks

When you do stop downing the sodas, you'll likely feel better and you might be surprised cravings for it will subside. You might also experience another positive side effect—weight loss. When you regularly drink regular (nondiet) soda, you're drinking hundreds of calories that are devoid of nutrients. Research has shown that your body doesn't recognize the energy you drink in soda. That means after you drink it, you're not full and you're still hungry, even though you just consumed a meal's worth of calories!

Sure, diet soda saves you the calories. And the majority of research suggests it doesn't affect metabolism or appetite, but many people find that they lose weight when they drop diet soda.

But that doesn't make it any easier to kick the habit. If you're trying to stop drinking so many soft drinks, it's important to have a plan in place for how you're going to satisfy your thirst and your craving for flavor. Here are a few options to consider.

- Water flavored with slices of any of the following: lemon, lime, cucumber, mint, watermelon (consider keeping this mix in your fridge)

- Herbal/black/green tea. Add a hint of honey if needed.

- Low-fat milk

- Coffee—regular or decaf with a splash of low-fat milk (optional)

- Water with a hint of fruit juice

Promise yourself that you will not drink soda for a short period of time, like a day or a week and see how it goes. In that time, try out some of the beverages listed here. Chances are you'll feel better, the cravings will subside.

SHOULD I TAKE VITAMINS?

Most nutrients should come from real food. Why? Real food offers a host of nutrients—and health benefits—that you won't find in any pill. That said, in some cases there is a real need for vitamin supplementation. Research shows that certain populations—including pregnant and nursing women, women of childbearing age, endurance athletes, and vegans—have a greater need for nutrients and are at risk for certain vitamin and nutrient deficiencies.

And research shows that most people don't get enough vitamin D (which boosts bone health because it helps the body absorb calcium) or omega-3 fatty acids (important for heart health). People who run a lot tend to be deficient in calcium, zinc, iron, and other nutrients.

But there's no need to rush out and stock up on supplements just yet—unless your doctor has specifically recommended it. Popping individual vitamin pills may lead to overdosing on certain nutrients, which can have harmful side effects.

That said, almost all people can benefit from a basic daily multivitamin. These pills are like an insurance policy. They ensure that you get the nutrients your food isn't providing, and any nutrients you don't need will be flushed out of your body when you go to the bathroom.

You may not need a multivitamin if you consume a lot of meal replacements—like energy bars or shakes. Those items are fortified with all sorts of vitamins and minerals.

So which brand is best? Look for a product that is manufactured by a reputable company and has been lab tested for purity. Many of these pills carry the seal of the USP (US Pharmacopia), but not all do. Choose a vitamin that meets close to 100 percent of your daily needs (100 percent of Daily Value) in one dose or two. Don't buy into a supplement that says it will help you lose weight. Those types of products may have harmful stimulants and side effects.

ESSAY
SOBRIETY TEST

By Caleb Daniloff, *Runner's World* contributing editor

On most days from the ages of 15 to 29, I was either drunk or hungover, usually both. Drunkenness was my calling, and I worked hard at it—at bars, on the streets, behind the wheel. Needless to say, the only part of me that ran back then was my mouth, whether I was begging for a drink, fighting with a girlfriend, or trying to cajole a store clerk who had caught me stuffing a bottle of wine down my pants.

It's been 9 years since I last wiped Budweiser foam from my lips. I don't wake up hungover anymore, but I do wake up haunted—by who I used to be, by the people I've done wrong. On the days I don't run, it's worse.

Down by the river, the rain was coming down in sheets. The dirt paths were filled with long puddles. My gloves and socks were soaked, and without my glasses, the horizon was a blur. I just had to keep moving, one sloshing step at a time.

During my drinking career, I had been court-ordered to AA meetings, drug counselors, and group therapy, and I'd developed an aversion to these settings. So when I finally quit the bottle, I chose to go it alone, and at first, muscling through seemed to work. But as each sober year passed, the details of my offenses were dissolving, while my guilt calcified. The past had become a hard lump in my throat.

When I took up running, I discovered a powerful healing agent—a therapist's couch, confessional, and pharmacy counter rolled into one. The head space that opened up during my predawn runs allowed me to embrace all the people I used to be, even the ugly ones, replacing callousness and narcissism with humility and clarity. I found not only a new central rhythm to my life, but a forum in which to confront myself.

Was it cowardly to write apology letters rather than look people in the eye? Have I avoided AA all these years because I'm afraid to say "I'm an alcoholic" in a roomful of people? The concrete sidewalk represented the hard facts I had to accept—that I'd cheated on girlfriends and abandoned friends. The bottle-strewn homeless camps I saw were cautionary tales.

Every lung-squeezing hill reminded me of the pain that precedes reward. One foot in front of the other, one run at a time. My apologies to those I'd harmed were all drafted at 6 miles per hour.

Some might suggest I've simply swapped one addiction for another. Yes, there is the swoon of endorphins, but what I'm hooked on is forward motion and progress, on overcoming and becoming. With its demand on the body and mind, there's no room for false thoughts. I sweat out my anxieties and insecurities and parse through job and family challenges instead of drowning them in booze. Grinding out miles has never turned me into a monster, never once filled me with shame or regret.

I don't know whether I'll ever fully calm the waters of my past, but the steady drumbeat of my feet on the ground and my arms sawing through the rain help. For an hour at a time, I arrive at a place where I can throw my arm around that shy, insecure 15-year-old boy, where I can sit down that cocky 22-year-old, and where I can try to forgive the 38-year-old with sore ankles and sweat stinging his eyes.

No longer am I running from my demons. We pace each other, the past and me. And some days, I go faster.[16]

PART 3

STAYING HEALTHY AND MANAGING INJURIES

If you've already started running, family and friends have probably warned you: Running is bad for your knees. Though studies have proven that this is a myth, it's easy to see why so many people believe it's true. *So many* people get hurt when they first start running—and not just in their knees. Common complaints include sore feet, blisters, chafing, side stitches, stiffness, muscle soreness, shin splints, and niggling pains that seem to defy description.

And that's to say nothing of the countless *Oof!*s *Ah!*s *D'oh!*s and other calamities that go along with braving the elements—traffic, humidity that makes you feel like you're standing inside a hair dryer, or those treadmills at the gym that force you to face the embarrassing prospect of running in front of other people.

But we've got good news.

Many of these injuries and calamities are as easy to prevent and avoid as they are to succumb to. Regardless of your age, weight, level of fitness, and innate athletic predisposition—or lack there of—many of these issues can be sidestepped with a change of shoes and a healthy dose of patience.

"When you're just starting out, the toughest thing to do is to take a step back," says physical therapist and elite marathoner Clint Verran, "But just start over and don't give up."

In this section, you'll find all the tools you need to stay safe, healthy, and injury free. And you'll find the insights you need to figure out what to do when you do get hurt and how to come back feeling strong.

CHAPTER 6

RUN SAFE AND INJURY FREE

When Melissa Althen was pushing her youngest son in a stroller around the neighborhood, she was amazed by what she noticed.

Many drivers would not stop for us at parking lot entrances," says Althen, a mother of four from Bedford, Texas. So when she started running, "I assumed that no one saw us."

Now she takes precautions. She sticks to neighborhood roads instead of busy streets; she plans her runs for times when traffic is light, like dawn; she always runs against the flow of traffic; and she looks in all directions several times when crossing the street or a parking lot entrance.

Althen isn't alone. In a poll on the Web site runnersworld.com, 50 percent of people said that they'd had close encounters with cars. Here are a few rules you can follow to stay safe on the roads.

Leave word. Tell somebody or leave a note at home saying where you plan to go and how long you plan to be out. That way, your loved ones will know to come look for you if they need to.

Identify yourself. Run with proper ID and carry a cell phone with emergency contacts taped to its back.

Pretend you're invisible. Don't assume a driver sees you. In fact, imagine that a driver can't see you, and behave accordingly.

Face traffic. It's easier to see, and react to, oncoming cars and other vehicles. And motorists will see you more clearly, too.

Make room. If traffic gets heavy or the road narrows, be prepared to move onto the sidewalk or shoulder of the road.

Be seen. Wear high-visibility, brightly colored clothing. When out near or after sunset, reflective materials are a must. (If you don't own reflective clothing, a lightweight reflective vest is a great option.) Use a headlamp or handheld light so you can see where you're going and drivers can see you. The light should have a bright LED (drivers see blinking red as a hazard).

Make sure you can hear. The safest option is to avoid wearing headphones so you can hear approaching vehicles. But if you do use headphones, run with the volume low and just one earbud in.

Understand the conditions. Factors like sun glare can interfere with drivers' ability to see you.

Beware of trouble spots. Steer clear of potential problem areas like entrances to parking lots, bars, and restaurants, where there may be heavy traffic.

Watch for early birds and night owls. At odd hours, be extra careful. Early in the morning and very late at night, people may be overtired and not as alert and as careful to avoid people who are on foot.

Mind your manners. At a stop sign or light, wait for the driver to wave you through—then acknowledge with your own polite wave. That polite exchange will make the driver feel more inclined to do it again for the next walker or runner. Use hand signals (as you would on a bicycle) to show which way you plan to turn.

Working Out in the Heat

A lot of people decide to start working out once the weather warms up. And it's easy to understand why. More daylight before and after work means more time to get outside. What's more, with vacations, it's easier to be more active in the summer. That said, there are plenty of obstacles to running in warm-weather months. Heat can make the same distance and pace feel harder than they do in cooler conditions. And a variety of heat ailments, from sunburn and chafing to heat stroke, can make for some serious discomfort. Here's everything you need to know to stay safe, healthy, and happy when you're working out in the heat.

Get fit first. Make sure that you've been exercising regularly for 4 to 6 weeks *before* you start doing any workouts in the heat, says Douglas Casa, PhD, who heads the Korey Stringer Institute at the University of Connecticut, which studies heatstroke and other causes of sudden death in sports. "The most important thing is to get fit first," says Casa. "The heat is basically another stress, just like the exercise. So if you're unfit and you start exercising in the heat, it's like throwing two swords at you at the same time." When you get fit, he explains, you're increasing blood volume, sweating more (so you're able to more efficiently cool off your body), and developing a higher stroke volume (which means that each heartbeat is pumping more blood out to the body), so your heart rate doesn't have to go as high during your workout. "All of these ways that you get in shape are going to be vital when you start working out in the heat," he says. "When you're introducing the unique stress of exercise, adding the extra stress of heat is a lot to handle."

Listen to your body and back off! If you don't feel well—whether you have a headache, feel nauseous, or the workout just feels harder than usual—always back off. If you're running hard, go easy. If you're running easy, walk. If you're walking, then stop and get in the shade. "Listen to your body, lower your intensity, and have fluids available when you need to hydrate," says Casa.

Stay hydrated. Dehydration can make you more prone to heat illnesses, so it's important to keep your thirst quenched. When you don't drink enough, "your blood volume drops, so your heart has to work harder to power your muscles and keep you cool," says Casa. As a result, the workout is going to feel tougher and likely be slower. Stay hydrated throughout the day and drink low-calorie sports drink when it's hot outside. If your urine is pale yellow, then you're well hydrated. If it's darker—say the color of apple juice—drink more. If it's clear, back off. Use thirst as your guide; experts have established that thirst will guide you to drink when you need to. "If you stay hydrated, that's going to keep your body temperature lower in the heat," says Casa. "You're going to be safer and feel better." During intense exercise in the heat, your body temperature rises about half a degree Fahrenheit for every 1 percent of body mass you lose through sweat. So if you're 4 percent dehydrated, your core temperature is going to be about

2 degrees higher. "When you are well hydrated, you'll recover better from exercising, and you won't have to worry about rehydrating as much at the end of the workout." (For more, see "Hydration" on page 125.)

Give yourself time to adjust to the heat. Don't do long or higher-intensity workouts during the heat of the day. If you must do a high-intensity run at midday, pick routes with shade or do them indoors.

Start outside workouts in cooler conditions in the winter, fall, or spring; in shady areas; at the coolest time of day; or at a gym, says Casa. Once you've done that, you'll be ready to start exercising in the heat. It can take 7 to 10 exercise sessions over the course of a couple weeks to adjust to the heat. But even then, "don't do the hardest workout in the hottest time of day," says Casa. "Keep it easy when it's hot; go hard during cooler parts of day."

Dress for the occasion. Wear apparel that's light in color and lightweight with vents or mesh. Microfiber polyesters and cotton blends are good fabric choices. Also be sure to wear a hat, sunglasses, and sunscreen with an SPF of 30 or higher.

Watch your alcohol and meds. Alcohol, antihistamines, and other medications can have a dehydrating effect. Using them just before a run can make you have to pee, compounding your risk of dehydration. Talk with your doctor about how these medications may impact your running.

Be patient. Give yourself 8 to 14 days to acclimatize to hot weather, gradually increasing the length and intensity of your training. In that time, your body will learn to decrease your heart rate, decrease your core body temperature, and increase your sweat rate.

Seek grass and shade. It's always hotter in cities than in surrounding areas because asphalt and concrete retain heat. If you must run in an urban or even a suburban area, look for shade—any park will do—and try to go in the early morning or late evening.

Check the breeze. If possible, start your run going with the wind and then run back with a headwind. Running into the wind has a cooling effect, and you'll need that in the second half of a run.

CLOSE ENCOUNTERS WITH MEAN DOGS

When Mandy Hubbard started running, she had an awesome paved loop she loved to do. Then one day, she looked up and found a huge English mastiff barking at her. She swung wide to give him his space, but he bolted toward her from the open gate to his driveway.

"I skidded to a stop, slowly backed up, but the dog continued toward me, barking," she says.

She stared toward the ground and kept backing up, but the dog kept coming and brought along his buddy. "I thought, 'I am so screwed.'" The dog finally stopped, and she kept backing away until she was far enough away that she could turn and run. She hasn't run that route.

Maybe it's happened to you, or perhaps it's just your greatest fear: A barking dog comes racing at you unleashed. "Typically, a dog who is aggressive is doing it more out of fear than anything else," says Maui-based dog trainer and runner Jt Clough. "When you just tell it what to do, it will back down." Follow these tips from Clough on handling an encounter with a dog when you're on the run.

KEEP YOUR DISTANCE. On many occasions, the dog is not going to attack you—it's just guarding its property, says Clough. Chances are, as long as you don't approach, the dog will stop barking and go back home.

CROSS THE STREET. If you hear a dog barking up ahead, cross the street. Most dogs won't cross the street to chase you, because they know the danger of getting hit by a car.

TELL THE DOG, "SIT!" Even the most untrained dog typically understands this simple command. "Typically, that's the one thing they've been taught," says Clough.

KNOW THE TERRITORY. Scout out any new routes for loose dogs before you head out on it alone. The "surprise factor" is a big part of what can make these encounters so frightening, says Clough.

DON'T RUN EMPTY-HANDED. Take a water bottle to spray a dog with water if necessary, says Clough. You can throw a water bottle in the dog's direction—just to distract it

Head out early or late. Even in the worst heat wave, it cools off significantly by dawn. Get your run done then and you'll feel good about it all day. Can't fit it in? Wait until evening, when the sun's rays aren't as strong—just don't do it so late that it keeps you from getting to sleep.

Run in water. Substitute one weekly outdoor walk or run with a pool-running session of the same duration. If you're new to pool running, use a flotation device and simply move your legs as if you were running on land, with a slightly exaggerated forward lean and vigorous arm pump. (For pool-running workouts, see page 14.)

and diffuse its aggression, not to hit it, she says. "Try to entice the dog to go after something other than you," says Clough, "while using a low, authoritative voice to command them away by saying something like 'Go get it!'"

DON'T GET EMOTIONAL. If you cower or jump when you see the dog and your voice gets screechy, the dog will go into attack mode, Clough says. "Dogs pick up on emotion before anything else." Get authoritative, drop your voice, and say 'Go get on home' like you mean it," she suggests. "If you get hysterical, they're going to come after you," she says.

KNOW THE SIGNS. When you're startled by the loud bark of a dog, it can be hard to tell if it's just saying a rather loud "hello" or if it's ready to attack. Signs that the dog is about to charge include:

- A stiff, pointed tail
- Raised hair, particularly behind the shoulders and neck
- Snarling
- Baring teeth, with lip raised on both sides

DON'T RUN AWAY. "If you think you're going to outrun the dog, that's a mistake," says Clough. "They will catch you."

DON'T STARE. Keep the dog in the corner of your eye, be aware of what it's doing, and back away from it. If you turn your back and take off, it's highly likely the dog will run after you.

PUT OUT YOUR HANDS AND FEET. If you come across a really unruly dog or you're seriously worried about an attack, put your hand or foot out in front of you, just as you would to protect yourself if a person lunged at you. Drop your voice and be authoritative.

HOW HEAT CAN HURT

Take steps to prevent the following hot-weather illnesses.

HEAT CRAMPS

- **Cause:** Dehydration leads to an electrolyte imbalance.
- **Symptoms:** Severe abdominal or large-muscle cramps
- **Treatment:** Restore salt balance with foods or drinks that contain sodium.
- **Prevention:** Don't run hard in the heat till acclimatized and stay well hydrated with sports drink.

HEAT FAINTING

- **Cause:** Often brought on by a sudden stop that interrupts bloodflow from the legs to the brain.
- **Symptoms:** Fainting
- **Treatment:** After the fall, elevate legs and pelvis to help restore bloodflow to the brain.
- **Prevention:** Cool down gradually after a workout with at least 5 minutes of easy jogging and walking.

HEAT EXHAUSTION

- **Cause:** Dehydration leads to an electrolyte imbalance.
- **Symptoms:** Core body temperature of 102° to 104°F, headache, fatigue, profuse sweating, nausea, clammy skin
- **Treatment:** Rest and apply a cold pack on head/neck; also restore salt balance with foods and drinks with sodium.

- **Prevention:** Don't run hard in the heat till acclimatized and stay well hydrated with sports drink.

HYPONATREMIA

- **Cause:** Excessive water intake dilutes blood-sodium levels; usually occurs after running for 4 or more hours.
- **Symptoms:** Headache, disorientation, muscle twitching
- **Treatment:** Emergency medical treatment is necessary; hydration in any form can be fatal.
- **Prevention:** When running, don't drink more than about 32 ounces per hour; choose sports drink over water.

HEATSTROKE

- **Cause:** Extreme exertion and dehydration impair your body's ability to maintain an optimal temperature.
- **Symptoms:** Core body temperature of 104°F or more, headache, nausea, vomiting, rapid pulse, disorientation
- **Treatment:** Emergency medical treatment is necessary for immediate ice-water immersion and IV fluids.
- **Prevention:** Don't run hard in the heat until acclimatized and stay well hydrated with sports drink.

Sun Safety

When you're exercising outside in the summer, some of the biggest discomforts you may encounter may have nothing to do with how hard your muscles were working but instead how much you've exposed your skin to the sun's searing rays. "You run to be healthy, but all that outdoor time is not so great for your skin," says Brooke Jackson, a Chicago-based dermatologist and runner. "You need to do what you can every time you run to protect yourself. A little bit each time will benefit you in the long run!" Here are Jackson's tips on how to stay safe in the sun.

Preventing Sunburn

- Avoid running between 10 a.m. and 4 p.m., when the most potent ultraviolet rays shine.

- Wear a hat and sunglasses to protect your face and eyes.

- Avoid running shirtless; your clothes offer protection from the sun.

- Look for running shirts and shorts that offer UV protection or wear darker colors, which block more UV rays than light colors do.

- Use a sunscreen with an SPF of 30 or greater. It should be labeled "broad spectrum," which means it will protect you from both UVA and UVB rays.

YOUR SKIN CARE KIT

When you're going out for a warm-weather workout, stash these supplies in your gym bag or car.

- **BODYGLIDE OR VASELINE:** Prevents chafing and blisters

- **ANTIBIOTIC OINTMENT:** Keeps chafing wounds and popped blisters from getting infected

- **SUNSCREEN:** Prevents sunburn. Apply sweat-proof formulas with a broad spectrum SPF of at least 30. Reapply each hour that you're outside.

- **MOLESKIN:** Covers hot spots to prevent blisters from developing

- **ANTIFUNGAL POWDER OR SPRAY:** Helps prevent athlete's foot

- **ALOE VERA:** Soothes sunburn

- Apply enough sunscreen to fill up a shot glass to cover your entire body before you go outside.

- Apply sunscreen at least 20 minutes before you go out so it has time to absorb into your skin. Reapply once each hour that you're outside.

CHAFING

Skin-to-skin and skin-to-clothing rubbing can cause a red, raw rash that can bleed, sting, and make you yelp during your postrun shower. Moisture and salt on the body make it worse. Underarms, inner thighs, the bra line (women), and nipples (men) are vulnerable spots. To help prevent it, wear moisture-wicking, seamless, tagless gear. Fit is important—a baggy shirt has excess material that can cause irritation; a too-snug sports bra can dig into skin. Apply Vaseline, sports lube, Band-Aids, or NipGuards before you run. To treat chafing, wash the area with soap and water, apply an antibacterial ointment, and cover with a bandage.

- If running with others, offer to spray one another's backs. This area often gets missed because it's difficult to reach and apply sunscreen to your own back.

- Use a lip balm with SPF; men in particular have a higher risk of sunburn on the lips than women do.

Treating Sunburn

- Get inside to cool off.

- Apply a cold compress or some refrigerated aloe.

- Take a cool shower or soak in an oatmeal bath.

- Take an over-the-counter pain reliever like Tylenol to relieve discomfort.

- If the burn is severe enough to develop blisters, you might be susceptible to infection, so it's best to see a dermatologist.

- Stay away from gels, which are alcohol based and can further dry out the skin. Moisturizer works just as well.

- If you develop blisters covering a good portion of your body or face, or start to get chills, go to the emergency room for treatment.

You should also keep an eye out for skin cancer. Studies have shown that marathoners and outdoor athletes have a higher risk for all skin cancers.[1]

- Know what your moles look like.

- Look for any changes in size or color.

- A pimple, scratch, or bug bite should heal within a week. If it's not healing, or it's bleeding or growing, see a dermatologist.

- Get an annual skin cancer screening by a dermatologist who can examine the nuances and pick up early warning signs.

- If you have a history of skin cancer, get checked every 6 months.

Working Out in the Cold and Snow

Winter can be a challenging time to stick to an exercise routine, and not just because of the weather. Aside from the ice, slush, snow, and far fewer hours of daylight to get those workouts in, you have to juggle it with holiday and family commitments.

So it can be easy to let things slide. Below you'll find all the strategies you need to stay fit until spring, when daylight hours and temperatures are more agreeable.

Warm up inside. Before you head out the door, move around indoors enough to get the blood flowing and gradually raise the heart rate, without breaking a sweat. This will help your workout feel easier sooner. Run in place, walk up and down your stairs, do some jumping jacks, use a jump rope . . . whatever it takes to get warmed up.

Head into the wind. If you can, start your walk or run facing the wind and finish with it at your back. Otherwise, you'll work up a sweat and then turn directly into a cold blast. Not fun! To avoid a long, biting slog, you can break this into segments, walking or running into the wind for 10 minutes, turning around to walk or run with the wind at your back for 5 minutes, then repeat.

Run with others. Exercising with a friend even once a week can help you get out the door, as it's harder to blow off a workout if you know that someone is waiting for you. And you don't necessarily have to run or walk. Making dates to lift weights at the gym or take a yoga or Pilates class can help you stay on track with these activities.

Stay visible. When the days are short, you're more likely to be walking or running in the dark. Wear reflective, fluorescent gear and use a headlamp or carry a flashlight so you can see where you're going. (As always, remember to walk or run against the flow of traffic.)

Forget about pace. Snow and ice-covered roads can be tricky. When you do run or walk, don't worry about how fast or slow you're going. Just focus on getting in time on your feet, enjoying some fresh air, and getting home safe. Get into a rhythm that feels easy and comfortable.

Find stable footing. Look for snow that's been packed down—it will provide better traction. Fresh powder can cover up ice patches. Run on the street if it's been plowed, provided that it's safe from traffic, and watch out for areas that could have black ice. Use the sidewalk if it's clear of ice and slippery snow. Find a well-lit route, slow down, and make sure you're familiar with areas of broken concrete. Use products like Yaktrax to reduce your risk of falling.

Take short steps. When you're running on ice or snow, shorten your stride to help prevent slipping and falling.

Be flexible. Winter is not the time to be rigid about when, where, and how far you go. If you're a morning exerciser, you may need to switch to lunchtime workouts, when the air is warmest and the sun is out; if you usually hit the trails, you may need to stick to well-lit roads or even the treadmill.

Run indoors. If the roads are covered with ice, it's better to exercise inside than risk hurting yourself. (See page 16 for tips on working out on the treadmill.) The treadmill doesn't have to feel like torture. Play around with the speed and incline to fend off boredom. Most treadmills come with preprogrammed workouts that do the changing for you, so try those, too. If you can't bear the treadmill, use the elliptical trainer or stair machine or "run" in deep water for the same amount of time that you'd spend running.

Get dry and warm postrun Damp clothing increases heat loss. Immediately after your workout, remove your sweaty clothes and get into a hot shower—or, if you aren't ready for a shower, slip into something dry and warm.

Don't forget to drink. Even when it's cold, you lose water through sweating. So it's important to stay hydrated throughout the winter. Drink half your weight in ounces throughout the day (e.g., if you weigh 150 pounds, aim for 75 ounces of fluids per day).

Dressing for Cold-Weather Workouts

Cover your extremities. Your nose, fingers, and ears are the first to freeze, so be sure to keep them well protected from wind, wet, and freezing temperatures. Balaclavas—knit masks that cover the whole head, with holes for nose and eyes—are the way to go. Or try a heavy synthetic knit cap pulled down low, with a scarf or neck muffler pulled up high.

Wear wool. Wool retains much of its insulating properties even when it's wet, thanks to air pockets in the fiber that trap warm air. Socks made from merino wool won't make your feet feel itchy.

Protect your private parts . . . Wind robs your body of heat. That's why briefs or boxers with a nylon wind barrier are so important for guys on cold days. The nylon panel on the front keeps the wind out.

. . . and your hands. Mittens keep your hands warmer than gloves by creating a big, warm air pocket around your entire hand. Pick a pair with a nylon shell or wear glove liners underneath. If your hands start to feel numb and look pale, warm them as soon as possible, as these are early signs of frostbite.

Wear a shell. On wet days, look for a shell that will not only keep you dry and protected from the snow or sleet but will also vent the moisture you create as you sweat. Many jackets are made from waterproof, breathable fabrics and have large midback and underarm vents.

When Winter Weather Becomes Dangerous

As long as you're dressed for the conditions and continuing to move (at least 60 percent of maximum heart rate, or roughly equivalent to your easy level of effort), you can produce enough body heat to offset the cold. Still, when it is severely cold, be sure to watch out for these two dangerous conditions, hypothermia and frostbite

- **HYPOTHERMIA:** Hypothermia strikes when your body loses more heat than it can produce and your core temperature falls below 95°F (35°C). Symptoms can vary widely but typically start with shivering and numbness and progress to confusion and lack of coordination. You're most at risk when it's rainy or snowy and your skin is damp. That's because water transfers heat away from your body much more quickly than air.

- **FROSTBITE:** Frostbite happens when the skin temperature falls below 32°F (0°C) and most commonly strikes the nose, ears, cheeks, fingers, and toes. It can start with tingling, burning, aching,

and redness, then progress to numbness. Windy and wet days are the riskiest times for frostbite. When the wind chill falls below −18°F (−27°C), you can develop frostbite on exposed skin in 30 minutes or less.

Side Stitches

Many runners find that the big problem when they start running has nothing to do with their legs—it's their lungs: They can't catch their breath, or they get side stitches.

If you are having problems breathing, consult with your doctor first to rule out any medical issues. Asthma or exercise-induced asthma and allergies are very common; wheezing and feeling like you can't catch your breath can be common symptoms of those conditions.

Side stitches—a sharp pain in the right side, immediately below the ribs—are considered a muscle spasm of the ligaments that support the diaphragm, a muscle associated with breathing, says Susan Paul, an exercise physiologist and *Runner's World*'s "For Beginners Only" columnist.

Like other muscle cramps or spasms, diaphragm spasms or side stitches are thought to occur from the strain and fatigue associated with working and breathing harder. As your overall conditioning improves, muscles tend to get less tired, and side stitches tend to go away, too.

CATCHING YOUR BREATH

Going about your everyday life, you don't think much about breathing. It happens automatically, so unless something interferes with your inhale and exhale, you don't have to. But many people find that when they start working out, they get out of breath quickly.

Budd Coates, coach, exercise physiologist, and senior director of employee fitness and health at Rodale, developed a system of controlling your breathing—and preventing injury—called rhythmic breathing. He has used this program to help scores of runners—many of them beginners—breathe easier and stay injury free. You can read more about rhythmic breathing in his book, *Running on Air*.

The more air you inhale, the more oxygen is available to be transferred through your circulatory system to your working muscles. Many people breathe from their chest and take in less oxygen. The chest muscles (the intercostals) fatigue sooner than the diaphragm. That's why it's a good idea to learn how to breathe from the belly. Here's how.

- Lie down on your back.
- Keep your upper chest and shoulders still.
- Focus on raising your belly as you inhale.
- Lower your belly as you exhale.
- Inhale and exhale through both your nose and your mouth.

You can also practice this sitting, standing, and during the activities of your everyday life.

Some research indicates that side stitches may also be related to running posture. In a 2010 study published in the *Journal of Science and Medicine in Sport*,[2] side stitches were more common in runners who slouch over or hunch their backs. So improving your posture by strengthening your core may help the side stitches go away.

Asthma

When B.J. Keeton started working out, the soreness in his legs was expected. After all, he weighed 310 pounds and had been sedentary all his life. But what he didn't expect was the metallic taste in his mouth, and the breaths that would feel cold in his chest. "I felt like a weight was sitting on my chest as I ran," he says. "I would start to cough and wheeze, and there'd be a lot of excess mucus I'd be coughing up for hours afterward, and a metallic taste I couldn't get rid of.

"It wasn't uncommon for me to be out of breath walking from my car to my office," he says. "If I did anything to get my heart rate up, I'd be worthless for the rest of the day."

His doctor diagnosed him with exercise-induced asthma.

Though his doctor didn't limit his activities at all—just advised him to take along his Albuterol inhaler—he was hesitant to keep working out at first.

"Mainly, I was scared I would collapse with no one around and suffocate," he says. And the lingering effects—having a hard time breathing after exercising—"made me feel like being active wasn't worth suffering through the side effects."

It can take a while before breathing on the run feels like second nature. Many people go out so hard that they huff, puff, and end up with a side stitch a few minutes into the run. It can take time to get into a rhythm that feels natural and comfortable enough to hold a conversation.

But if you keep working out and find that you consistently wheeze, cough, feel a tightness in your chest, or just can't catch your breath when you run, you might have asthma, a condition where the tubes that bring air in and out of your lungs tighten, says Dr. Stanley Fineman, founder of the Atlanta Asthma and Allergy Clinic. Asthma can be triggered by allergies, infections, and other substances like mold, pollen, and pet dander. And some people have exercise-induced asthma (EIA), in which the symptoms are triggered by, well, exercise. With EIA, you may start to wheeze, cough, and have difficulty breathing about 8 to 10 minutes into a workout, says Fineman.

Typically, air will be warmed and moistened when it's inhaled through the nose. But when you're running, or exerting yourself through any exercise, you tend to breathe more rapidly and breathe through your mouth, says Clifford Bassett, a New York University–affiliated allergist who is the medical director of New York Asthma and Allergy Care of New York. When this happens, cold, dry air gets to the airways and lungs, and this can trigger asthma symptoms. Many people with asthma tend to be particularly sensitive to substances like seasonal pollens and indoor allergens (like cat dander and dust), grass, and air pollutants (like ozone and smoke). So running outside, exposed to those substances for a long period of time, may create a greater risk of an asthma attack, particularly in a more sensitive individual.

But that doesn't make it a good excuse to hang up your running shoes. Fineman says he encourages those with asthma to exercise.

"It builds lung capacity and improves overall quality of life," he says. "I see asthmatics who are competitive runners all the time and manage their symptoms. I think the main thing is to make sure you have a good diagnosis, check your lung function, find out what the triggers are, and make sure you have an asthma management plan once you start an exercise program."

Indeed, that's what Keeton found. He started walking, then running, and shed 145 pounds from his 310-pound frame. His

(continued on page 190)

How Running Changed My Life

Running helped Chris Keating manage his epilepsy and regain his independence

Chris Keating had a charmed childhood. He played three varsity sports, made straight A's, and held down a part-time job. But when he was 15, that all changed. In a wrestling tournament, he hit his head and had his first seizure.

He started having up to six seizures a week. Each one would last from 5 to 25 minutes. "My self-esteem quickly diminished," he says. "I could barely even tell if I had any left."

He lived at home throughout college, so his parents could drop him off and pick him up.

Through it all, the seizures drained him, and so did the medications he took to manage them. To get his driver's license, he had to go 6 months without a seizure. He was 20 before that happened. But shortly after he got the license, he had another seizure and had to wait another 6 months to drive again.

"Learning to cope with not being able to participate in the social norms has been a huge obstacle," he says.

After losing his license for the third time, Keating vowed to find some independence. Doctors had suggested that exercise could reduce seizures.

He started cycling everywhere he wanted to go, to class or to the grocery store. He started running 13.1 miles to class each day.

A month after he started, Keating finished his first sprint triathlon, then a half-marathon. Now he has completed two half-marathons and a marathon. He's had fewer seizures and struggles less with the side effects of medications. "My energy levels are higher and I have fewer mood swings that are not as drastic."

What's more, running "has given me an escape and a way to find myself," he says. "There is no one to tell me I can't. And nothing can stop me."

AGE: 23
HOMETOWN: Dawsonville, Georgia
OCCUPATION: Full-time Nike+ Athlete at Nike Factory Store

What was the biggest hurdle, and how did you get over it? The hardest thing for me to get over was the side effects of the medications I am taking. With every medicine change, I would have to start over. After I took my medicine, I would become extremely tired and almost pass out; it took everything I had to get out the door and start running or biking. I viewed this as a mental block, not a physical hurdle, so I used this as a time to work on my discipline. I began to structure my daily schedule around my workouts and would wake up at 5:30 every morning to start my day. This helped me learn how to persevere, and how to make a schedule and stick to it, no matter what.

What precautions do you have to take while running to manage your epilepsy? The main precautions have to do with my diet and my sleep. I make sure I get at least 8 hours of sleep a day. If I don't, I take a nap to make up for it. I also don't run on days that I feel sluggish in any way. If I feel anything out of the ordinary, like tingling fingers, migraines, or any possible preseizure signs, I rest. On those days, if I do run, I'll just run a very short distance on a track or a nearby 1-mile loop, and I will have my mom or dad watch me for a little while. Also, I always wear my RoadID, which states that I am epileptic, and I carry my medicine and cell phone with me with directions on how to administer it. I try to remain as hydrated as possible so that I don't self-induce a seizure. I always carry water and Gatorade chews when I run.

What advice would you give to a beginner? Don't stop, whatever you do. Don't get discouraged, because results don't happen overnight; it takes time, motivation, determination, and inspiration to keep going.

What advice would you give others who have epilepsy and would like to start running? Consult your doctor first. Honestly, epilepsy can hold you back in a lot of ways. It can wear out you and your family members or close friends. But it can only wear you down if you let it. When you're running, everyone is equal. It doesn't matter how fast you are or how far you run. It just matters that you put on your shoes and walk out your front door. Running instills confidence, and it provides a way to cope with life's struggles.

Favorite motivational quote: "Do a little more each day than you think you possibly can."—Lowell Thomas

(continued from page 187)

doctor prescribed an Albuterol inhaler, from which he takes two puffs 15 to 20 minutes before he runs. Since he's been doing that, he hasn't had a single attack. When running in moderate weather, he doesn't even use the inhaler. But in extreme heat, cold, or humidity, he keeps it handy or takes a few puffs before he heads out.

"Exercise has completely changed my exercise-induced asthma," says Keeton, an English professor and author from Lawrenceburg, Tennessee. "Before starting to run, I had very little endurance because of my diminished lung capacity. But now, as long as I'm staying active, I don't have any problems." And now he is training for a half-marathon. "I've started telling people that you can't beat having EIA, but you sure can outrun it."

Here are some tips for managing asthma symptoms with your running life. For more information, please contact the American College of Allergy, Asthma and Immunology (acaai.org).

Get tested. Asthma and allergies can develop at any age. But cases often go undiagnosed because some of the symptoms— like coughing during exercise in the case of allergies or shortness of breath in the case of asthma—are so common to so many other ailments. "If you're having shortness of breath, it's important to get an accurate diagnosis," says Fineman. Be sure to note how often and in what settings you have the symptoms and how severe they are. When

you get tested, you will be given a variety of lung function tests including spirometry, which assesses how much air you can exhale after a deep breath and how fast you can breathe out, and a peak flow test, which measures how hard you can breathe out. For allergies, you will likely get a variety of blood or skin tests, where a small amount of an allergen (like mold or grass) is placed on or below the skin to test for a reaction.

Warm up and cool down. This has been known to reduce symptoms. It helps the body more efficiently deliver oxygen to the working muscles.

Have a plan. If you do have asthma, create an asthma management plan with your doctor. Some people need to take maintenance medications a few times a day, bring rescue inhalers with them on runs, or both, says Fineman. Others are prescribed fast-acting medicines like an Albuterol inhaler, which relaxes the muscles around the airways.

Know your prime times. Avoid running outside when pollen and mold counts are at their highest. You can get daily alerts about local pollen and mold levels from the American Academy of Allergy, Asthma, and Immunology (aaaai.org). If you can't avoid your triggers, or if the air is particularly cold and dry, hit the treadmill. Avoid workouts when you have a viral infection, temperatures are low, or pollen and air pollution levels are high. Warm and somewhat humid air is generally more tolerated than cool, dry air.

Cross-train. Swimming, walking, cycling, and hiking are good cross-training activities for those with asthma. Swimming helps strengthen the upper body, and swimmers are exposed to warm, moist air during the workout. Swimming also helps strengthen upper-body muscles.

Breathe through your nose. Breathing in and out of your nose—rather than your mouth—allows air to be warmed and humidified before it reaches your airways, which can prevent an attack. Wearing a face mask or balaclava in cold conditions also warms the air you inhale.

Keep it steady. Sudden bursts of activity are more likely to provoke asthma attacks than continuous efforts. So maintaining a steady pace could help you avoid an attack.

Stay hydrated. Start by getting hydrated with H_2O and low-calorie sports electrolyte drinks before, during, and after a workout, says Bassett. This is particularly important when it's hot outside. Good hydration may help prevent the airways from getting too dry and shutting down, causing an asthma attack. For more information, you can visit allergyandasthmarelief.org.

Stretching

You've seen the iconic image of a runner bent over and touching his toes. You've probably seen plenty of runners doing this. So it may surprise you to hear that this so-called static stretching—attempting to lengthen muscles and tendons to increase flexibility—is generally not recommended before a run.

Stretching has been hotly debated in recent years. There is no evidence that static stretching prevents injury or improves performance, experts now say. In fact, there's some evidence that it can hurt. When it comes to staying injury free, functional range of motion is more important than flexibility.

"If you can run comfortably, and without injury, there is no need to stretch," says William O. Roberts, professor in the department of family medicine and community health at the University of Minnesota Medical School. He's also runnersworld.com's "Ask the Sports Doc" columnist.

Before your workout, your time is better spent warming up with dynamic stretching. (See page 21 on warming up.)

These moves, which include butt kicks and walking with high knees, improve range of motion and loosen up muscles that you're going to use on the road. They also increase heart rate, body temperature, and bloodflow so you feel warmed up sooner and run more efficiently.

After your run, if you have an area that still feels tight—the calves, hamstrings, IT bands, and quads tend to be tight after running—you may want to try the static stretches featured on pages 194 to 195. But it is not necessary. Each stretch should give you the feeling of slight discomfort in the muscle. But do not stretch to the point that you feel a sensation that is sharp or intense. If you do, back off.

(continued on page 194)

ESSAY

RUNNING WITH ASTHMA

By Caitlin Giddings, *Runner's World* web producer

Exercise-induced asthma: It sounds like something a nerdy kid like me might dream up to get out of gym class, but it's a real condition and the scourge of my running life.

When I set out too fast—or the day is hot and sticky, or there's a chill in the air, or something (anything!) triggers my delicate race day emotions—the wheezing starts, panic sets in, and I immediately begin the process of having an asthma attack.

It happens almost without notice. One minute, I'm darting toward a finish line, high on endorphins, life, and triumph of the human spirit. Then some small, imperceptible shift takes place in my lungs, and I'm hit by a wave of powerlessness and panic, like a fish out of water, or a hamster in a shoebox without airholes.

It took me decades to break through that panic and become a runner, particularly because my asthma wasn't diagnosed until I was in my late teens. All I knew back then was no matter how hard I tried, running felt flat-out impossible. My mom—a fitness-obsessed marathoner—didn't know what to do with her nonathletic, comic-book-obsessed kid and used to torture me with organized family "fun runs" and laps around the block in exchange for Nintendo time. But it wasn't that I was trying to disappoint her or reject her active lifestyle. I just

wanted jogging a single mile to feel more like the first level of a video game and less like being sucked out of a space station's airlock.

I just wanted to take deep breaths and fly.

So how did I end up carrying the family running baton? My transformation from teenage sloth to running addict wasn't easy, and like everything else about me, it wasn't fast.

It started with my exercise-induced asthma diagnosis and an Albuterol inhaler, which enabled me to work up to 2 miles. Just knowing I had help in my pocket made it possible to slowly and steadily increase mileage without the snowballing panic I get when my ability to take in oxygen decides to take a nap. It was scary, but I persisted, imagining each short, little run to be a snapshot in my superhero-training montage. Then after more than a year of side stitches and struggle, one day running 6 miles felt as comfortable and effortless as doing a Monday *New York Times* crossword puzzle.

There was no conscious thought. My limbs just locked onto the same radio frequency and started 10-4'ing back and forth like they had their own CB channel. It felt better than anything has a right to. My first runner's high—I almost couldn't believe it was actually good for me.

Today—eight marathons later—I carefully manage my asthma with an inhaler, a long warmup before working up to full speed (particularly in the winter), and a lot of patience with my strengths and weaknesses as a runner. I've learned to always carry a phone and inhaler when I'm going out on a long run. I've learned to run at inhumanely early hours and hydrate like water is going out of style when the weather is hot and humid, and not beat myself up if I have to take a walking break. And I've also learned to accept that my mile pace won't deviate too far from my 5-K pace, which won't be too far off my half-marathon pace. Like an old computer, it takes me a while to whir into action.

But it's taken me so long to get here that there's no way I'm stopping now.

If anything, my asthma only makes me more determined to keep running so I don't have to start all over again from scratch, coaching my breathing into taking on more

and more. And anytime I feel sorry for myself after a bad race, I try to remember that everyone on the course has his or her own hurdles to overcome.

So if you have exercise-induced asthma, don't write yourself out. It might take you a bit longer to reach the point where running feels safe and comfortable, but once you build up endurance, your breathing anxiety will begin to fade, along with the snowballing panic that can trigger the worst of your symptoms. At least that's been my experience—as I've grown more and more confident of my ability to prevent a midrun attack, I've faced those attacks less and less frequently. Racing with asthma can be scary, but it reminds me of a great quote by Ronald Rook: "I do not run to add days to my life, I run to add life to my days."

So take a deep breath and a risk, build strong lungs, and try not to compare yourself to runners who might not be facing the same breathing challenges you're facing.

For a few minutes, just see if you can fly.

Five Key Postrun Stretches

Try this five-stretch routine after your workout to reduce stiffness. Hold each stretch for 2 seconds.[3]

QUAD STRETCH

While standing on one leg, bring your opposite heel back toward the rear of the body and grab your ankle or foot. Keep your knees aligned and your back straight. You should feel this stretch down the front of your thigh. Repeat on the opposite leg. If necessary, hold on to a stable object for balance.

HAMSTRING STRETCH

Place your leg straight out in front of you. Bend your knee and slowly extend and lower your hips back as if you're sitting in an imaginary chair. Make sure you keep your grounded foot parallel to your outstretched leg. Repeat on the other side.

GLUTE STRETCH

Cross your ankle just above your knee and lower down into a squatting position. If comfortable, gently push down on the knee. Repeat on the opposite side. If necessary, hold on to a stable object for balance.

CALF STRETCH

Stand with both feet on a curb or step. Lower your heel down so you can feel a stretch in your calf. Keep both knees bent so you can deepen the stretch. Repeat with the other leg.

CHEST STRETCH

Stand with your feet shoulder-width apart. Lace your fingers together behind your head above your neck. Squeeze your shoulder blades together while trying to bring your elbows out to the sides behind you.

How Running Changed My Life

Running helped Tara Cuslidge-Staiano change her entire identity

Tara Cuslidge-Staiano reached her get-up-or-give-up moment the day after Christmas in 2009. She was getting ready for dinner, and no clothes fit.

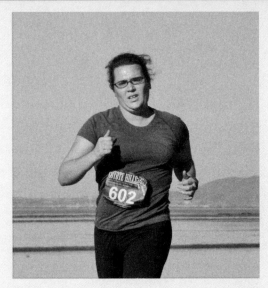

Her weight had ballooned to 200 pounds. She was tired all the time, the doctors had said she was prediabetic, and she was taking medications to control her cholesterol and blood sugar.

"I just decided enough is enough," she says.

The next day, she got on the treadmill and set it for 15 minutes per mile. Afterward, she told her husband, "I'm never going to do that again."

But the next day, she did do it again. She ran 1.1 miles. And the next day, she did it again. She kept coming back. The day she set her sights on covering the 5-K distance on the treadmill—and succeeded—was the turning point when she fell in love with running.

"Wow," she remembers thinking. "I just ran my first 5-K, and it wasn't as bad as I thought it would be."

From then on, running morphed to something that felt like pleasure, not pun-ishment. She started running on days when she hadn't planned to, and set her sights on long distances.

Four years later, Cuslidge-Staiano has finished 14 half-marathons and two mara-thons. She's lost 35 pounds and is com-pletely off medications to control her blood sugar, cholesterol, and diabetes. But the best part is the transformation in how she feels and how she sees herself.

"I have more energy. I want to do more," she says. "And I just became somebody else—someone who wants to be out there and active, not someone who wants to be on the couch eating bonbons."

AGE: 28

HOMETOWN: Stockton, California

OCCUPATION: Journalist, community college instructor

What's your regular workout routine? On Sundays I do a long run of a minimum of 10 miles. I'll do a tempo run on Monday; on Tuesday run 6 miles with a friend; cross-train and do core work on Wednesday; run 6 to 8 miles on Thursday with a friend; rest on Friday; and on Saturday, cross-train or rest, depending on what else I've done that week.

What is your weight-loss goal? I was at 200. My lowest was 150. When I started training for a half-marathon, I packed back on some weight. I've been able to maintain [at 165 pounds] for more than a year. That said, my husband and I are also hoping to have kids, so I'm trying to lose some weight to avoid diabetes rearing its ugly head again when and if I get pregnant.

What kinds of changes have you made to your diet? I let myself splurge from time to time. At the beginning, I made the mistake of limiting everything. When I'd see a cupcake, which is my biggest weakness, I would feel as if I couldn't eat it because that one cupcake would bring back all the weight. Now I indulge in the cupcake but know I can't do it every single day. I actually splurge on cupcakes now during race weekends, because I know I'll be burning off those calories (and more). My biggest issue is overeating. It's something that doesn't go away; I just get better at controlling it. I watch my portion sizes now. If I go out to dinner, I look at the low-calorie options as well. I never realized how little food I needed to actually feel "full" until I started eating less. Now I stock up on 100-calorie snacks or fruit as go-tos for when I start to feel hungry.

What advice would you give to a beginner? The first mile is always the hardest. And that's true if it's your first run, or if you're out on a 10-mile run. Just get past that point. It always feels better after the first mile. It's not going to get easier, but every day you get stronger and better.

Favorite motivational quote: "You must do the thing you think you cannot do."—Eleanor Roosevelt. I actually have "you must do the thing" engraved on my RoadID I wear when I run. I bought it before my first half-marathon, and it's kind of inspired every step of my journey.

Is Yoga for You?

The health benefits of yoga have been well established: Studies have shown that yoga reduces stress, aids weight loss, helps you manage pain, and can help you stick to an exercise routine. A July 2005 study in the *British Journal of Sports Medicine* even showed that yoga helped runners get faster.[4] But the impact of yoga on running performance has not been widely studied. That said, coaches and experts say that the strength and flexibility you develop on the mat—namely in the core, quads, and hip flexors—can help you run more efficiently and stay injury free.

"When you're on the mat, engaging the transverse abs helps stabilize the core and lower back and translates well to running," says Adam St. Pierre, a coach, biomechanist, and exercise physiologist for the Boulder Center for Sports Medicine. "If you have a strong and stable core, you won't get a lot of excessive rotation in the pelvis, so you'll be more efficient."

Runners tend to be tight in the hip flexors, which can lead to weakness in the calves and hamstrings and excessive pronation, says St. Pierre. "That can set off a cascade of other issues, like lower-back injuries, IT band syndrome, plantar fasciitis, Achilles problems, and shin splints."

Additionally, tightening the mind-body connection, as you do in yoga, helps you tune in to how hard you're working so that you can better manage your efforts when you're running, says yoga instructor Sage Rountree, an RRCA-certified coach and author of *The Runner's Guide to Yoga*. Yoga helps you tune in to areas where you're needlessly tensing up, so you can relax them and free up strength that your legs and lungs need. "It lets you notice where you're wasting energy, so you can run more efficiently, and that's the key to endurance," says Rountree.

That said, many people insist that they're too tightly wound—in body or mind—to practice. And if you're not careful, you can end up hurt, frustrated, and even more stressed out than you were before. Here's a guide that will help you find the right place for yoga in your running life.

Shop around. From yin yoga to vinyasa, and from gyms to spalike studios, there are a dizzying array of yoga styles and settings to choose from. And different teachers can have a radically different effect on your experience. No single style of yoga is the best for everyone. As with a good training plan, different styles can be the best fit for different runners at different times. So if on your first try you're turned off by the teacher, the vibe, or the poses, keep searching until you find the right fit for you, says Johnny Gillespie, owner of

Empowered Yoga, a Wilmington, Delaware–based studio with four locations. "It's not the type of yoga you practice, as much as the consistency of practice, that counts," he says. "The most important thing is finding a place where you feel comfortable, where you're connecting with your teacher—like you would with a coach—and where that teacher is helping you to pay attention to yourself." Rountree recommends starting at a dedicated yoga studio rather than a gym. Many studios have classes that are geared specifically to runners, focusing on areas where runners tend to be weak and tight, like the core, glutes, quads, and hip flexors.

Time it right. Practice the most-intense yoga during the least-intense periods of running. As you ramp up your mileage, run faster, and get closer to race day, you should practice yoga less frequently and with less intensity, says Rountree. If you pile on an intensive daily practice on top of your toughest running weeks, "you're undermining yourself," she says. "You're interfering with the ability of the body to recover, and you run the risk of hurting yourself." By the same token, don't

YOGA ETIQUETTE

Dos and don'ts for your first time at the yoga studio, from *Runner's Guide to Yoga* author Sage Rountree:

GET THERE EARLY so you can tell the teachers you're a runner, areas of tightness and injury, and whether you want them to help you adjust or get into postures.

DITCH YOUR DEVICES. Don't take cell phones or iPads into the room to watch while you practice.

PASS THE SNIFF TEST. You'll be taking deep breaths close to others, so go easy on the cologne and perfume.

OFF WITH YOUR SHOES. Since all yoga is practiced in bare feet, you don't want to track in dirt and debris from the outside. Most studios will designate places near the door for leaving your shoes.

DON'T TALK during class unless the teacher allows it.

DON'T GET UP. Resist the urge to leave during Savasana, the final resting pose. No matter how busy you are, it's distracting to others who are trying to relax and meditate.

FIND THE TIME. No time to get to a yoga class? It doesn't have to be an all-or-nothing proposition. There are online yoga classes that you can download or do anytime, try ours at **runnersworld.com/yogaseries**.

do an intense yoga practice on the same day as a hard workout.

Take it easy. Rountree suggests that runners practice restorative yoga, postures that are held for several minutes at a time, with the support of blankets, blocks, and other props. This can be a tough sell to many people who equate intensity with progress.

Don't get hurt. The last thing you want is to inflict an injury on yourself in the process of trying to prevent one. Runners' high pain thresholds, paired with competitive natures, may make them more prone to injury, warns St. Pierre. "You've got to come to terms with the fact that you might not be able to do this pose right away," he says. Indeed, many runners, eager to loosen up tight hamstrings, end up overextending or tearing the tendons just beneath the sitting bone, says Rountree. Another reason to steer clear of the hamstrings: And it's not just the hamstrings you have to be wary of. St. Pierre got too aggressive in Pigeon pose, trying to stretch out his glutes and piriformis, and ended up not being able to run for 3 weeks.

Be humble. Just as it takes years to master running, it can take years to master yoga postures. So don't go into your first class—or your first 20 classes—expecting to achieve an Olympic A standard in yoga. It may be daunting; you might be self-conscious and worry about what everyone else is thinking.

"You're not going to go in there knowing everything," says Rountree. But remember that everyone is focused on themselves, not you. And rest assured that with enough practice, you'll be okay with less-than-perfect performance.

Strength Training for New Runners

Strength training can help you run more efficiently and stay injury free. Research "points clearly in the direction of weakness of the hip stabilizing muscles and the inability to properly control lower-extremity joint motion," says Reed Ferber, associate professor at the University of Calgary and the director of the Running Injury Clinic. To avoid getting hurt, says Ferber, is to follow a training plan to avoid doing too much too soon, and to strengthen the muscles that stabilize your hips—like the gluteus medius and the hip abductors.

Heather K. Vincent, PhD, director of the Human Performance Laboratory and Sports Performance Center at the University of Florida, says that those who want to begin running may benefit from starting a strengthening-routine program before they even hit the road. Increasing the strength and control of the smaller muscles in the feet and larger muscles in the lower limbs helps control movement at the pelvis, hips, and knees so you can maintain proper running form and stay injury free. "Strengthening the muscles can help runners land with more control and less risk of injury," Vincent says. Start by doing the following routine, designed by Vincent, four times per week. After you've been at it for about 2 months, you can ratchet it back to three times per week.

Unless otherwise noted, for each of the following exercises, start by doing as many repetitions as you can on each side while maintaining proper form. You might start with one set of 20 reps and build up to three sets of 20 reps, resting for 45 to 90 seconds in between sets. Then increase the resistance so the effort feels harder and you can get keep getting stronger. Maintaining proper form is the most important thing. When your form starts to fall apart, that's a sign that you're tiring and have done your final rep. "Doing improper form puts you at risk of injury," says Vincent. Not to mention it's a waste of time!

Foot and Leg Strength

These exercises will help build strength in your hips, legs, and feet so you can maintain good running form and avoid common overuse injuries like runner's knee, IT band syndrome, and foot pain. To perform many of these, you'll need a rubber resistance band. These can be found in most sporting goods stores or online. Rubber strip bands are the least expensive, and they can be cut to different sizes. Tube bands come with handles and can be held during exercise. Bands typically come in varying levels of resistance: light (which provide 3 to 5 pounds of resistance), medium (which provide 8 pounds of resistance), and heavy and extra-heavy bands (which provide 12 to 20 pounds of resistance). Heavy and extra-heavy bands are designed for people who are already trained. To feel whether the band is right for you, test it out in the store. Look for extra features that matter to you, like clips, handles, cuffs, or rings. Consider buying two different resistance levels for different exercises.

SEATED HIP EXTERNAL ROTATOR

- Attach a resistance band to the left end of a bench or a stable object and loop the other end around your right foot.
- While sitting on the exercise bench, keep your knees together, lift your right leg out to a count of two, then release it back down to a count of two. Repeat on the other leg.

STANDING HIP FLEXOR

- Tie a resistance band to a stable object.

- Put your right foot in the resistance band and turn so you are facing away from the band's anchor.

- Keeping your right leg straight, lift it forward to a count of two, then release it back down to a count of two. Repeat on the other leg.

STANDING HIP ABDUCTOR

- Tie a resistance band to a stable object.

- Loop the other end around your right foot so the band crosses in front of you.

- Standing with your left leg slightly behind you, keep your right leg straight and lift it out to the other side. Lift it to a count of two, then release it back down to a count of two. Repeat on the other leg.

SIDE-LYING LEG RAISE

- While lying on your side on the floor, raise one leg straight up and lower it back down.
- Do not let your leg cross your midline (move in front of your body or go behind your back).
- Raise the leg 15 times. Repeat on the other leg.

PELVIC DROP EXERCISE

- Use a stair or a step from a step exercise class.

- Stand on the step on one leg. This is your support leg. Keep that leg straight and keep your abdominals engaged.

- Allow your other leg to hang off the edge of the step. Let that leg slowly lower toward the ground by allowing your pelvis to slowly drop down. Do not let that foot touch the ground. Just control the movement with a slow, steady drop. When you've gone as low as you can without touching the ground, hold this position for two counts, keeping your abs tight.

- Keep your support leg as straight as possible as you lower the other leg. Don't let it bend.

- Raise your pelvis up to raise the foot up. When the pelvis is level and your hips are even, that's one rep.

- Do 10 to 15 reps on each side. When it becomes easy, build up to two or three sets of the exercise or hold a lightweight dumbbell in your hand to increase the resistance.

Foot Strength

Anytime you're sitting down, you can work on strengthening your feet. You can do these exercises while you're watching television, sitting at your desk, or taking a break. Perform 15 reps of each exercise. Do each of these exercises three to four times per week. Choose four from the group and rotate different exercises each day.

HEEL RAISE

- With your feet on the floor lift your heels up while keeping the balls of your feet on the ground.
- Lower your heels.
- Repeat.

TOE GRIP

- With your feet flat on the floor, act as if you were raking your toes backward and curling up the arches of your feet.
- Flatten your foot again.
- Repeat.

DORSIFLEXION AND PLANTARFLEXION

- With your legs stretched straight out in front of you, push down your toes like you are pointing them (plantarflexion).
- Then bring your toes back (dorsiflexion).
- Repeat.

TOE SPREAD

- With your feet flat on the floor, envision spreading your toes like you would spread the fingers of your hand.
- Relax your toes.
- Repeat. This is tricky and takes some practice.

TOE TAP

- With your feet flat on the floor, tap each of your toes up and down on the ground in sequence like you would tap your fingers on a table.
- Repeat.

EXAGGERATED INVERSION AND EVERSION

- Starting with your feet flat on the floor, drop your arches in and lift the sides of your feet outward.
- Hold for 2 seconds, then lift your arches while you push the outsides of your feet firmly down on the ground.
- Hold for two counts. Repeat.

GRABBING AND PASSING A TOWEL

- Place a small hand towel on the floor.
- Alternate which foot will pick up the towel using the toes.
- Pass the towel from the toe grip of one foot to the other foot and hold in place for two counts to strengthen the grip.

CHAPTER 7

PREVENTING AND COPING WITH INJURIES

A few years ago, *Runner's World* set out to answer some of the most pressing questions on every runner's mind: How can you get fit without getting hurt?

Our author Amby Burfoot did an exhaustive examination of hundreds of studies. But he came up with more questions than answers. "I learned," he wrote, in the March 2010 issue of *Runner's World*,[5] "that injuries can be caused by being female, being male, being old, being young, pronating too much, pronating too little, training too much, and training too little. And to get rid of blisters, you should drink less and smoke more."

He's joking, of course, but the point is that science doesn't have any firm answers that apply to all people. He interviewed the world's top injury experts—in biomechanics, sports podiatry, and physical

therapy. Like the studies, they didn't always agree. But the more he talked with them, the more he was able to identify certain universals.

From these, he developed some golden rules of injury prevention that seem to work for most people most of the time. There's no guarantee they'll prevent you from ever getting hurt. But if you incorporate these guiding principles into your exercise routine, you'll be more likely to enjoy a long and healthy running life.

Avoid the terrible toos. Doing too much too soon and too fast is the number-one cause of running injuries. The body needs time to adapt to increases in mileage or speed. Muscles and joints need recovery time so they can handle more demands. If you rush that process, you could break down rather than build up. So be the tortoise, not the hare. Increase your weekly and monthly running totals gradually.

Use the 10 percent rule as a guide. Build your weekly mileage by no more than 10 percent per week. So if you run 5 miles the first week, run 5.5 miles the second week, about 6 miles the third week, and so on. There may be times when even a 10 percent increase proves too much. Use the 10 percent rule as a guideline, but realize that it might be too aggressive for you.

Let the body be the boss. Most running injuries don't just come out of nowhere and blindside you. Usually, there are warning signs—aches, soreness, and persistent pain. It's up to you to heed those signs. If you don't, you could hurt something else as you try to change your gait to compensate for the pain.

Get good shoes. Running shoes have changed a lot over the years, and there's a dizzying variety of models, brands, and types to choose from. There are even minimalist shoes designed to mimic barefoot running (although there's no scientific evidence that forgoing shoes decreases injury risk).

There's no single best shoe for every runner—your goal is to find the one that offers the best support and fit for your unique anat-

omy and biomechanics. Don't buy a shoe just because it's the cheapest, because it "looks fast," or because it matches your favorite workout gear.

You should replace your shoes every 300 to 500 miles. Note the date that you bought your shoes in your training log so that later you'll know when it's time for a change. And when it's time to buy, visit a specialty running store—the staff there will ask you lots of questions, watch you walk or run, and take other steps to help you find the right shoe. (For more on buying shoes, see "Get Good Running Shoes" on page 9.)

Take good notes. A detailed workout log can help keep you motivated and injury free. Take some time after each workout to jot down notes about what you did and how you felt. Look for patterns. For instance, you may notice that your knees ache when you run on consecutive days, but you feel great when you rest in between running days. This will help you determine the best routine for you. Plus, it will help get you out the door when the going gets tough. You can draw confidence from seeing all the miles pile up. And the next workout doesn't seem as daunting when you see how much you've already accomplished. There are lots of online training logs available, but a notebook and a pencil work just as well. Here are some data that you should consider including in your training diary.

1. Daily or weekly goal

2. Mode of exercise (run, elliptical, swim, bike, etc.)

3. Distance (in miles or kilometers)

4. Workout time in minutes

5. Weather conditions

6. Time of workout (this can influence how you feel)

7. Route and terrain (hills, treadmill, track, trail)

8. How you feel before, during, and after the run

9. Shoes and gear used

10. Music

11. Interesting things you saw along the way

12. Notes about the people you worked out with

Cross-train. Running is hard on your body, there's no doubt about it. So experts agree that most runners can benefit from cross-training activities to help improve muscle balance and stay injury free. Swimming, cycling, elliptical training, and rowing will burn a lot of calories and boost your aerobic fitness. (For more, see "Cross-Training" on page 29.)

Respect your limits. Each person has his or her own unique "orthopedic threshold"—that is, how far and fast you can go before you get hurt. This threshold is as one of a kind as an individual's fingerprint. It's determined by genetics, anatomy, biomechanics, age, level of fitness, history of injury, gender, lifestyle, time in your schedule to work out, and a whole host of other factors, many of which you can't control. And unfortunately, there's only one way to find it. By crossing that threshold, i.e., getting hurt. Some people find that they break down if they take one step beyond 25 miles a week. Others can run at an easy pace forever but are left aching for days after speedwork. Figure out where your threshold is and respect it. If you can only run 4 days per week before you get injured, but want to exercise more, cross-train with activities like cycling or working out on the elliptical machine.

Increase your stride rate. Increasing your stride rate has been linked to a lower rate of injuries. Ideally you'll have 170 to 180 steps per minute. But a shorter stride should produce lower forces with each footfall. Overstriding is a common mistake that can lead to decreased efficiency and increased injury risk. See "How to Increase Your Stride Rate" on the next page.

HOW TO INCREASE YOUR STRIDE RATE

Increasing your stride rate has been linked to a lower rate of injuries. Ideally, you'll have 170 to 180 steps per minute. But the best way to increase yours is to find your current stride rate (by counting your steps) and aim to boost it by 5 percent at a time, says running coach Jeff Gaudette, founder of RunnersConnect, a Boston-based online training service. Once that new stride feels natural, try boosting it by another 5 percent. "It's going to feel uncomfortable at first," he says. Count your steps on two or three runs a week. Then focusing on using it on every other run. If you count steps during a speed session (see page 68 on why you should run faster and page 69 for speed workouts), it has the added benefit of distraction, Gaudette says. "Because you're counting, it takes your mind off the fact that it's hard."

Below are Gaudette's tips on how to count your stride rate and improve it.

1 Warm up with 10 minutes of easy running.

2 Count how many steps one foot takes for 30 seconds.

3 Double this number. That's how many steps that foot takes in 1 minute.

4 Double that number. That's how many steps both feet take in 1 minute. That's your stride rate.

5 Repeat this every 10 minutes of the run.

The Most Common Running Injuries

Working out can be uncomfortable (especially when you're just getting started), but it should never hurt. Aches and pains in the feet, ankles, and shins are common among new runners, says Clint Verran, an elite marathoner and physical therapist in Lake Orion, Michigan.

"Most people don't realize how easy it is to overstep their training," he says. To be sure, it takes times for the musculoskeletal system to adapt to the impact of running and walking.

"The bones, muscles, and connective tissues are not used to hitting the ground. They're not hardened to the stress of training," he says. "There's an adaptation process. And the only way to overcome it is to start slow, with short workouts, and gradually progress."

Indeed, the best way to avoid injury is to gradually increase your time spent running, run on soft surfaces as much as possible, and make sure you've got shoes that offer the fit and support your feet need, and orthotics if you need extra support. Go to a specialty running store where you can get guidance in finding the pair that works best for you.

Below are some of the most common injuries for new runners. If you do feel any of these aches and pains, Verran recommends taking 2 days off, icing for 15 to 20 minutes a day twice a day, starting back again, and building up slowly. "When you have pain, you just have to dial something back—distance, intensity, or both," he says.

You may be able to cross-train to keep up your fitness while you give your running injuries time to heal. (To find out which forms of cross-training are safe for which injuries, see "Cross-Training," page 29.)

And when in doubt, rest and have your pain checked out. It's better to spend a little time and money seeing the doctor than to be sidelined for months by an injury that you could have prevented or minimized. (For a more detailed guide on which pains to run through and which pains require medical attention, see "Should I Run or See the Doctor?" on page 215.)

Shin Splints (Medial Tibial Stress Syndrome)

Shin splints happen when there are small tears in the muscles around your shinbones. You might feel a tight, aching pain when you first start running or just after you're done. Shin splints are common among new runners, those returning after an extended layoff, and those who have built up mileage too quickly. Overpronation, running on cambered roads, and wearing worn-out running shoes can also lead to shin splints. "About 90 percent of the time, it goes away with some rest," says Verran. "It's just a matter of backing off, starting slowly, and letting the body adapt to hitting the ground."

HAMSTRINGS HURT?

Achiness and tightness in the back of the thighs isn't a common injury for new runners, but it can crop up. At first, it might force you to slow down and shorten your stride. As it gets worse, the pain can become sharp. Overstriding, overextending your legs while trying to speed up, or bending forward from the waist too much to increase your forward lean can all contribute to hamstring strains. Going too far or too fast too soon or doing too many hills can also strain the hamstrings. Sticking with easy runs and shortening your stride can help alleviate the strain. Avoid stretching your hamstring when it's sore, which can worsen the strain. To avoid overstriding, see "How to Increase Your Stride Rate" on the opposite page.

Foot Pain (Metatarsalgia)

If you suddenly start running a lot, you can develop pain and achiness in the forefoot that's due to inflammation around the metatarsals, the small bones in the front of the foot that run from the arch to the toe joints. That's the area that absorbs the force when you run. Carrying around extra weight can also contribute to the condition, because the extra pounds put added pressure on the metatarsals. Shoes that have a toe box that's too narrow or that don't offer proper support can also make your feet hurt. "New runners' feet are just not used to getting pounded against the concrete," says Verran. "There's an adaptation process, and [you need time to] build up your tolerance for hitting the ground."

Plantar Fasciitis (PF)

PF is an inflammation of the plantar fasciae, tendons on the bottom of the foot, from the heel to the toes. It feels like a dull ache or bruise along the arch or on the bottom of the heel, and it can be most painful first thing in the morning and at the beginning of a workout. Overpronation and wearing worn-out shoes are the most common causes of PF. A sudden mileage increase in hill running can also set it off, as can long periods of standing. Those with high arches are more at risk of PF, and often it's made worse if you wear shoes with no arch support or often walk around barefoot. PF can get worse and more difficult to treat if you let it linger. To prevent it, stick to soft surfaces, rest and reduce your mileage, and go to a specialty running store to make sure you have the shoes that offer your feet the support and fit they need.

Iliotibial (IT) Band Syndrome

This is a strain within the IT band, the connective tissue that runs along the outside of your thigh, from your hip to your shin. When your knee flexes and extends during running, the IT band can rub against the bone, causing irritation. It can feel like a dull pain on the outside of your knee. As it gets worse, it can radiate up and down your leg, even while you're walking downstairs or down a hill. Piling on too many miles too quickly can irritate the IT band, as can running on cambered roads. Your best bet is to rest, decrease your mileage, and replace worn-out shoes.

Achilles Tendinitis

This condition is the tightening and irritation of the Achilles tendon, which connects the two calf muscles to the back of the heel. It may start as a dull ache. As it progresses, you may develop severe pain and swelling—even when you're not running. It's caused by doing too much too soon, doing too many hills, or wearing the wrong shoes. It's important not to try to run through this; doing so can make it last for months. Avoid aggressive stretching and wearing high heels and flip-flops, both of which can irritate the Achilles. Resting and icing can help alleviate symptoms.

Runner's Knee (Patellofemoral Pain Syndrome)

This is a soreness or pain around the front and inside of the kneecap that can get worse during a workout or while going down hills and stairs. It's often caused by inflammation in the tendons around the knees or in cartilage under the kneecap. It's often linked to running in worn-out shoes, inadequate footwear, or overpronation (excessive inward foot rolling). It is also linked to weakness in the quads or the glutes, which can lead to poor tracking of the knee. You may feel twinges early in the workout that go away only to reappear later. As it worsens, the pain may be on the inside or outside of the knee (toward your other knee or toward the outside of your leg) and may persist even after you're done with your workout. Take 2 or 3 days off. Avoid downhills and leaning too far forward during your workouts, which can add stress to the knees. And strengthen your quads and glutes, which control the tracking of your knees. When you start running, you're introducing "a new force, and the body just isn't used to it," says Verran. "It's just like going into the gym and doing a whole bunch of bench presses when you'd never done it before."

Should I Run or See the Doctor?

It can be tough to determine which pains to run through and which pains demand surrender. Bruce Wilk, a physical therapist, coach, and owner of The Runner's High specialty shop in Miami, has developed a five-point checklist that you can use to determine whether you should run, walk, rest, or rush to a doctor.

Stages one to three encompass the normal discomforts that go along with pushing your body farther and faster than it's gone before. Take 2 or 3 days off from working out, ice five times a day, and use compression and elevation.

But if you see a red flag, or you reach stage four or five, stop working out and seek professional help ASAP. See a sports medicine specialist or orthopedist, preferably someone who has experience working with runners. A local running club or store may be able to recommend someone.

STAGE ONE: An unfamiliar and disconcerting pain while running—*It hurts when I run; it stops hurting when I'm done.*

    Red flag: It forces you to alter your stride.

STAGE TWO: An unfamiliar or disconcerting pain at rest—*It may hurt when I run, and it definitely aches when I'm done.*

    Red flag: The pain interferes with your rest.

STAGE THREE: Pain during normal daily activities—*It hurts when I walk or climb the stairs, or when I'm sitting at my desk after I run.*

    Red flag: The pain forces you to avoid the stairs, walk barefoot, or alter any other normal daily activities.

STAGE FOUR/RED FLAG: Pain that makes you take medication, including shots or prescription or over-the-counter meds—*It hurt, but once I took the ibuprofen (or got a cortisone shot), it went away.*

STAGE FIVE/RED FLAG: Pain that stops you from running or even walking without pain

Blisters

Annoying and painful, blisters are caused by friction, usually your shoes or socks

MAKING A COMEBACK

So you get hurt and take time off. You're pain free and ready to start back. What do you do? "Do not start again where you left off," says Reed Ferber, associate professor at the University of Calgary and director of the Running Injury Clinic. "Start at a point that allows you to complete the run injury free." Use the checklist on page 215 ("Should I Run or See the Doctor?") to determine the length of your run. This may mean that you start a few weeks behind the rest of the group, but you can adjust the schedule, and with the help of a coach, "catch up" in a reasonable amount of time. The other important thing is to strengthen the muscles in the site that are injured. For instance, if your Achilles is hurt, with the guidance of a physical therapist or athletic trainer, do heel raises and strengthen the hip-stabilizing muscles. Use "active rest," that is, no running but improving muscle strength to get back on the wagon and prevent the injury from reoccurring.

rubbing against your skin. Anything that intensifies rubbing can start a blister, including a faster pace, poor-fitting shoes, and abnormalities such as bunions, heel spurs, and hammertoes. Heat and moisture intensify friction by making your feet swell.

AMBY'S ADVICE

Runners aren't defined by how much they run; they're defined by their attitude about exercise. Even when injured and unable to run as much as they would like, runners find alternative ways to stay fit or even build fitness. When your legs hurt so much that you can't run, you can still train your upper body in the gym. And you might be able to exercise your legs on a bike, rowing machine, elliptical trainer, or in the pool. All these alternatives are good examples of "cross-training," but you don't even have to think of it as training. Just think of it as "moving," and be sure to get in an hour or so a day. The easiest way to do this: Turn off the TV and head outside.

wet. Both methods form a protective shield between your skin and sock.

- **Double up.** Wear two pairs of socks so the friction occurs between the two socks, rather than between the sock and skin. If your shoe now feels too tight, go up a half size as long as your foot doesn't slide around, making blisters a possibility.

- **Wear shoes and socks that fit.** Shoes that are too small will cause blisters

under the toes and on the ends of the toenails. There should be a thumb's width of space between the toes and end of the toe box. Your socks should fit smoothly, with no extra fabric at the toes or heels.

How to Treat Blisters

If you have a large blister, drain it. If you don't drain it, your blister will hurt, and it could puncture on its own.

To drain the blister, wash your hands, then wipe a needle with alcohol to sterilize it. Don't skip this step; serious infections can result when one uses a dirty needle to pop a blister.

Once you've punctured the blister, carefully drain the liquid by pushing gently with your fingers near the hole. Keep the skin or the roof of the blister on to help prevent infection. Then cover the blister with a tight bandage to keep bacteria from getting in.

You can take the bandage off periodically and soak your foot in Epsom salts (follow package directions) to draw out the fluid. After soaking, put on a fresh bandage. It's a good idea to keep a bandage on until the skin closes up again.

If you've got a small blister—say smaller than the size of a pencil eraser—leave it intact. The skin acts as a protective covering. Leave small blood blisters intact

HOW TO STAY ACTIVE WHEN YOU CAN'T RUN

Cross-training can help you stay fit when you can't run, but choose wisely, says runner and sports podiatrist Stephen Pribut, DPM, of Washington, DC. Some activities may worsen an injury. Below is a table of common running injuries and what cross-training activity is safe to do with the injury's symptoms.

INJURY	SWIMMING	STATIONARY BIKE	ELLIPTICAL	ROWING MACHINE
Runner's knee	Usually	Sometimes	Sometimes	No
IT band syndrome	Usually	Sometimes	Sometimes	Sometimes
Calf pain, Achilles strain	Usually	Usually	Usually	Usually
Plantar fasciitis	Usually	Usually	Usually	Usually
Shin splints	Usually	Sometimes	No	No
Stress fractures	Usually	Sometimes	No	No

That explains why many runners only suffer blisters during races or in the summer.

The body responds to the friction by producing fluid, which builds up beneath the part of the skin being rubbed, causing pressure and pain. A blood blister occurs when the friction ruptures tiny blood vessels.

While most blisters don't pose a serious health risk, they should be treated with respect. A painful blister can cause you to change your gait—so you avoid aggravating it—and that can lead to injury. The biggest risk is that the blister gets infected, which can lead to a need to see a doctor.

How to Prevent Blisters

- **Moisten your feet.** Just like sweaty skin, dry skin is also more prone to friction. Use skin creams and lotions liberally on a daily basis to maintain proper moisture.

- **Choose blister-free socks.** Synthetic socks wick moisture away from the skin. Cotton may be lighter, but it retains fluid. Socks with reinforced heels and toes also help reduce friction.

- **Run with slick skin.** Coat your feet with Vaseline or another lubricant before you run. Or use Second Skin, a padded tape that stays on even when also. Otherwise you risk getting bacteria into your bloodstream. Cut a hole the size of the blister in the middle of a piece of moleskin, then place it over the blister and cover it with gauze. The blister will dry out and heal on its own.

If you develop a blister under the nail bed, it's best to see a doctor to get it treated. You never want to deliberately remove the toenail. That could lead to a serious infection.

How Running Changed My Life

Running helped Jodi Edwards gain control over MS and lose weight

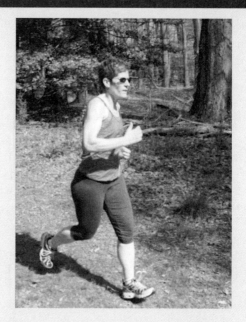

Jodi Edwards had lost about 80 pounds and had another 30 pounds to lose when she was diagnosed with multiple sclerosis, a chronic, often disabling disease that attacks the brain, spinal cord, and optic nerves and can lead to numbness and paralysis.

She kept working out even after the diagnosis, but because she struggled with balance, she had been sticking with spinning classes and the elliptical machine. When a personal trainer suggested she try the treadmill, she was terrified. The first few sessions, she set the treadmill at 4 miles per hour and held on to the handrails.

"Even at that pace, I was getting so tired and winded," she says. She fell off the treadmill once and landed on her face. Her legs would cramp up.

"It took me a long time to realize that the runner's high wasn't total crap," she says.

Still, something kept bringing her back. "Every day, I was able to go out a little bit longer or feel a little bit better afterward. So I'd go in the next day, talk myself down from the fear again. And there was a sense of freedom, even when it was hard, because I could make my legs work like that. I was so thrilled that I was able to do it. Not only was I not walking with a cane, I was running."

Eventually, she was able to finish a half-marathon and then full marathons.

"Running was a way of thumbing my nose at MS," she says. "I figured if I could do this, nothing could stop me."

AGE: 43

HOMETOWN: Lexington Park, Maryland

OCCUPATION: Veterinarian

What was the biggest hurdle, and how do you get over it? Sometimes I don't want to get dressed and go, but I make myself do it anyway. A short run is always better than no run. There is sometimes a time issue. I work 10-hour days and work evenings. Sometimes it is hard to keep myself on a regular schedule so I can get the runs in and do the things I need and want to do around the house and have some time with my wife. (She is not a runner; she cycles.)

Did you have a weight-loss goal? My goal was to be healthier. Before I was diagnosed with MS, I was at 240 pounds. Now I am 134. It is a whole lot easier to push the chair when you weigh less. My family has a genetic predisposition to high cholesterol. Even now, mine runs toward the high end of normal. I ultimately wanted to be feel better. Looking back, I realize I didn't really feel good.

What kinds of changes did you make to your diet? We have limited the times we eat out. We go out once, sometimes twice on the weekend, and usually it's for a good reason. We eliminated high fructose corn syrup, which makes you hungrier after you are finished than when you started. We eat chicken or fish and avoid red meat. Everyone's MS is different, but a steak will cause muscle spasms in my legs that make me unable to walk. I stick to a low-fat, higher-protein diet. I feel better on a higher-protein diet than the typical runner diet that is a little higher in carbs. I eat a lot of veggies, and we stay away from prepackaged and convenience foods. One of my personal mantras is "Self-discipline is remembering what you really want." It is hard when someone brings cake to work, and the next day there is ice cream. I am a big-time sweets junkie. One of the biggest things I do is I don't keep this stuff in the house. If I want it bad enough, I have to get up and go get it. That means there have been a few 9 p.m. ice cream runs, but more often, I skipped it.

What advice would you give to a beginner? Invest in good shoes and socks. Don't just pick out a pair that looks good. Take the time and spend the money to go to a running store. The first time I went into the store I was embarrassed. But the new shoes made a huge difference. You may have sticker shock at a pair of $15 socks. But when your feet are dry in the summer or warm in the winter, you'll be glad you did.

Favorite motivational quotes: One is my own, an answer to someone who asked me once why I ran a marathon—"I run because I can."

PART 4

APPENDIX

THE STARTING LINE

STEP ONE:
START WALKING PLAN

The *Runner's World* Start Walking plan will help you get in the habit of exercising regularly and stick with it.

With this 7-week plan, you can build up to and beyond 150 minutes of exercise per week—the amount of exercise that the American College of Sports Medicine (ACSM) says will stave off diabetes, heart disease, and stroke; lower blood pressure and cholesterol; increase energy; and improve depression and anxiety. By the end of the plan, you'll be able to complete a 60-minute walk.

- These walks should be brisk—not a race walk, but not a window-shopping walk either.

- You can substitute time on a stationary bike or an elliptical trainer, but walking is the best foundation for running.

- If you don't have time for the longest workout of each week, it's okay to split it in half. You'll get the same health benefits.

- If you have a BMI of more than 25, are 60 years or older, or if you'd like to take a more gradual approach, you can repeat any week, or every week, and stretch this out to an 8-, 10-, or 12-week plan.

- If you're 40 or older, or have a family history of heart disease, diabetes, or other chronic illnesses, see a doctor before starting any exercise routine.

START WALKING PLAN

WEEK	MON	TUES	WED	THURS	FRI	SAT	SUN	TOTAL MINUTES (ESTIMATED MILEAGE)
1	15 min	25 min	Rest or optional 15 min walk	25 min	Rest	35 min	Rest	100–115 min (5–7.7 miles)
2	15 min	28 min	Rest or optional 15 min walk	28 min	Rest	38 min	Rest	109–124 min (5.4–8.3 miles)
3	20 min	30 min	Rest or optional 15 min walk	30 min	Rest	40 min	Rest	120–135 min (6–9 miles)
4	20 min	35 min	Rest or optional 15 min walk	35 min	Rest	45 min	Rest	135–150 min (6.7–10 miles)
5	20 min	40 min	Rest or optional 20 min walk	40 min	Rest	50 min	Rest	150–170 min (7.5–11.4 miles)
6	20 min	40 min	Rest or optional 20 min walk	40 min	Rest	55 min	Rest	155–175 min (7.8–11.7 miles)
7	20 min	45 min	Rest or optional 20 min walk	40 min	Rest	60 min	Rest	165–1815 min (8.25–12.3 miles)

KEY

- On Monday of the first week, 15 minutes (min) means that the total workout time is 15 minutes.
- The distance for each day is an approximation based on a 10- to 20-minute-per-mile walking pace.

THE ▶ STARTING LINE

STEP TWO:
START RUNNING PLAN

The *Runner's World* Start Running plan will help you start adding short bouts of running to your regular walks. At the end of this plan, you'll be able to complete 175 minutes of exercise per week, running for about twice the amount of time that you spend walking.

This plan begins with a 20-minute walk and builds up gradually, so that in 7 weeks you'll be able to comfortably complete a 55-minute workout that combines running and walking.

- These walks should be brisk—not a race walk, but not a window-shopping walk either.

- If you don't have time for the longest workout of each week, it's okay to split it in half. You'll get the same health benefits.

- If you have a BMI of more than 25, are 60 years or older, or if you'd like to take a more gradual approach, you can repeat any week, or every week, and stretch this out to an 8-, 10-, or 12-week plan.

START RUNNING PLAN

WEEK	MON	TUES	WED	THURS	FRI	SAT	SUN	TOTAL MINUTES (ESTIMATED MILEAGE)
1 Walk only	20 min	40 min	Rest or optional 20 min walk (no running segments)	40 min	Rest	55 min	Rest	155–175 min (7.8–11.7 miles)
2 Walk only	20 min	40 min	Rest or optional 20 min walk (no running segments)	40 min	Rest	60 min	Rest	165–185 min (8.25–12.3 miles)
3 1:4 Run/ Walk	**20 min—**Walk 5 min; run 1 min then walk 4 min for 15 min	**35 min—**Walk 5 min; run 1 min then walk 4 min for 25 min; walk 5 min	Rest or optional 20 min walk (no run-ningseg-ments)	**35 min—**Walk 5 min; run 1 min then walk 4 min for 25 min; walk 5 min	Rest	**50 min—**Walk 5 min; run 1 min then walk 4 min for 40 min; walk 5 min	Rest	140–160 min (8.5–10 miles)
4 1:3 Run/ Walk	**20 min—**Walk 3 min; run 1 min then walk 3 min for 15 min; walk 2 min	**40 min—**Walk 5 min; then run 1 min then walk 3 min for 30 min; walk 5 min	Rest or optional 20 min walk (no running segments)	**40 min—**Walk 5 min; run 1 min then walk 3 min for 30 min; walk 5 min	Rest	**55 min—**Walk 5 min; run 1 min then walk 3 min for 45 min; walk 5 min	Rest	155–175 min (10–11.25 miles)
5 2:3 Run/ Walk	**20 min—**Walk 3 min; run 2 min then walk 3 min for 15 min; walk 2 min	**40 min—**Walk 5 min; run 2 min then walk 3 min for 30 min; walk 5 min	Rest or optional 20 min walk (no running segments)	**40 min—**Walk 5 min; run 2 min then walk 3 min for 30 min; walk 5 min	Rest	**55 min—**Walk 5 min; run 2 min then walk 3 min for 45 min; walk 5 min	Rest	155–175 min (10.5–11.75 miles)
6 2:2 Run/ Walk	**20 min—**Walk 3 min; run 2 min then walk 2 min for 15 min; walk 2 min	**40 min—**Walk 5 min; run 2 min then walk 2 min for 30 min; walk 5 min	Rest or optional 20 min walk (no running segments)	**40 min—**Walk 5 min; run 2 min then walk 2 min for 30 min; walk 5 min	Rest	**55 min—**Walk 5 min; run 2 min then walk 2 min for 45 min; walk 5 min	Rest	155–175 min (10.9–12.1 miles)
7 2:1 Run/ Walk	**20 min—**Walk 3 min; run 2 min then walk 1 min for 15 min; walk 2 min	**40 min—**Walk 5 min; run 2 min then walk 1 min for 30 min; walk 5 min	Rest or optional 20 min walk (no running segments)	**40 min—**Walk 5 min; run 2 min then walk 1 min for 30 min; walk 5 min	Rest	**55 min—**Walk 5 min; run 2 min then walk 1 min for 45 min; walk 5 min	Rest	155–175 min (11.3–12.6 miles)

KEY

- On Monday of the first week, 20 minutes (min) means that the total workout time is 20 minutes. Starting week 3, the total time of the workout is listed at the top of each workout in **bold**.
- The workout pattern for each week is listed in the WEEK column. So in week 3, "1:4 Run/Walk" means that each of the workouts includes alternating between running for 1 minute and walking for 4 minutes.
- The distance for each day is an approximation based on a 10- to 20-minute-per-mile walking pace and an 11.4-minute-per-mile running pace.

THE > STARTING LINE

STEP THREE:
RUN NONSTOP PLAN

The *Runner's World* Run Nonstop plan will help you to transition from run/walk workouts to running without walk breaks. You'll gradually build up from a 3:2 run/walk ratio up to a 30-minute run without walk breaks. Each run should be done at a comfortable, conversational pace. If you're huffing and puffing, you're going too fast.

    This plan begins with a 25-minute run/walk and builds up gradually over 7 weeks, so that by the end you'll be able to run for 30 minutes—without stopping!

- The walking portion of your workouts should be brisk—not a race walk, but not a window-shopping walk either.

- Before you start each workout, and after you finish, walk for 3 to 5 minutes to warmup and cooldown.

- If you don't have time for the longest workout of each week, it's okay to split it in half. You'll get the same health benefits.

- If you have a BMI of more than 25, are 60 years or older, or if you'd like to take a more gradual approach, you can repeat any week, or every week, and stretch this out to an 8-, 10-, or 12-week plan.

- If you're 40 or older, or have a family history of heart disease, diabetes, or other chronic illnesses, see a doctor before starting any exercise routine.

RUN NONSTOP PLAN

WEEK	MON	TUES	WED	THURS	FRI	SAT	SUN	TOTAL MINUTES (ESTIMATED MILEAGE)
1 3:2 Run/Walk	25 min— Walk 3 min; run 3 min then walk 2 min for 20 min; walk 2 min	40 min— Walk 5 min; run 3 min then walk 2 min for 30 min; walk 5 min	Rest or optional 20 min walk (no running segments)	40 min— Walk 5 min; run 3 min then walk 2 min for 30 min; walk 5 min	Rest	55 min— Walk 5 min; run 3 min then walk 2 min for 45 min; walk 5 min	Rest	160–180 min (11.6–12.9 miles)
2 4:1 Run/Walk	25 min— Walk 3 min; run 4 min then walk 1 min for 20 min; walk 2 min	40 min— Walk 5 min; run 4 min then walk 1 min for 30 min; walk 5 min	Rest or optional 20 min walk (no running segments)	40 min— Walk 5 min; run 4 min then walk 1 min for 30 min; walk 5 min	Rest	55 min— Walk 5 min; run 4 min then walk 1 min for 45 min; walk 5 min	Rest	160–180 min (12.2–13.4 miles)
3 5:1 Run/Walk	25 min— Walk 3 min; run 5 min then walk 1 min for 20 min; walk 2 min	40 min— Walk 5 min; run 5 min then walk 1 min for 30 min; walk 5 min	Rest or optional 20 min walk (no running segments)	40 min— Walk 5 min; run 5 min then walk 1 min for 30 min; walk 5 min	Rest	55 min— Walk 5 min; run 5 min then walk 1 min for 45 min; walk 5 min	Rest	160–180 min (12.2–13.4 miles)
4 6:1 Run/Walk	25 min— Walk 3 min; run 5 min then walk 1 min for 20 min; walk 2 min	40 min— Walk 5 min; run 6 min then walk 1 min for 30 min; walk 5 min	Rest or optional 20 min walk (no running segments)	40 min— Walk 5 min; run 6 min then walk 1 min for 30 min; walk 5 min	Rest	55 min— Walk 5 min; run 6 min then walk 1 min for 45 min; walk 5 min	Rest	160–180 min (12.4–13.6 miles)
5 8:1 Run/Walk	25 min— Walk 3 min; run 5 min then walk 1 min for 20 min; walk 2 min	40 min— Walk 5 min; run 8 min then walk 1 min for 30 min; walk 5 min	Rest or optional 20 min walk (no running segments)	40 min— Walk 5 min; run 8 min then walk 1 min for 30 min; walk 5 min	Rest	55 min— Walk 5 min; run 8 min then walk 1 min for 45 min; walk 5 min	Rest	160–180 min (12.5–13.7 miles)
6 10 min: 30 sec Run/Walk	25 min— Walk 3 min; run 20 min with 30 sec walk at halfway; walk 2 min	40 min— Walk 5 min; run 30 min with 30 sec walk every 10 min; walk 5 min	Rest or optional 20 min walk (no running segments)	40 min— Walk 5 min; run 30 min with 30 sec walk every 10 min; walk 5 min	Rest	50 min— Walk 5 min; run 10 min then walk 1 min for 40 min; walk 5 min	Rest	155–175 min (12.4–13.6miles)
7 Run a 5-K! (or 30 minutes without stopping)	20 min— Walk 3 min; run 15 min with short walk breaks as needed; walk 2 min	30 min— Walk 5 min; run 20 min with short walk breaks as needed; walk 5 min	Rest	20 min— Walk 3 min; run 15 min with short walk breaks as needed; walk 2 min	Rest	5-K Fun Run– Get there early enough to warm up with some walking. Or run 30 min without walk breaks.	Rest or optional 20 min walk (no running segments)	100–120 min (8–10 miles)

KEY

- The workout pattern for each week is listed in the WEEK column. So in week 1, "3:2 Run/Walk" means that each of the workouts includes alternating between running for 3 minutes and walking for 2 minutes.

- The distance for each day is an approximation based on a 10- to 20-minute-per-mile walking pace and an 11.4-minute-per-mile running pace.

THE ▶ STARTING LINE

STEP FOUR: RUN LONGER PLAN

The *Runner's World* Run Longer plan will help you build up the endurance to run 6 miles without walk breaks, and the strength to race a 5-K (3.1 miles) or finish a 10-K (6.2 miles). The first workout is a 1-mile run, and by the end of the 7-week program, you'll be able to race a 5-K or comfortably finish a 10-K race.

- Before you start each workout, and after you finish, add a 3- to 5-minute warmup and cooldown.

- If you have a BMI of more than 25, are 60 years or older, or if you'd like to take a more gradual approach, you can repeat any week, or every week, and stretch this out to an 8-, 10-, or 12-week plan.

- If you're 40 or older, or have a family history of heart disease, diabetes, or other chronic illnesses, see a doctor before starting any exercise routine.

RUN LONGER PLAN

WEEK	MON	TUES	WED	THURS	FRI	SAT	SUN	TOTAL MINUTES
1	1 mile	2 miles	Rest or optional 1 mile	2 miles	Rest	3 miles	Rest	8–9 miles
2	1 mile	2 miles (hills)	Rest or optional 1 mile	2.5 miles	Rest	3.5 miles	Rest	9–10 miles
3	1 mile	2.5 miles (hills)	Rest or optional 1 mile	2.5 miles	Rest	4 miles	Rest	10–11 miles
4	1 mile	3 miles (hills)	Rest or optional 1 mile	3 miles	Rest	5 miles	Rest	12–13 miles
5	2 miles	3.5 miles (hills)	Rest or optional 1 mile	3.5 miles (fartlek)	Rest	5 miles	Rest	14–15 miles
6	2 miles	4 miles (hills)	Rest or optional 2 miles	4 miles (fartlek)	Rest	6 miles	Rest	16–18 miles
7	2 miles	4 miles (no hills)	Rest	2 miles	Rest	Race a 5-K or run 10-K to finish	Rest	11.1–14.2 miles

KEY

- Each run should be done at a comfortable, conversational effort. Don't worry about your pace, just focus on covering the distance. Start slow with the goal of finishing your workout feeling strong.
- **HILLS** Simply run the mileage for the day on a course that features hills with a variety of inclines and descents. After a warmup, run on the hills, maintain an easy effort on the climbs and the descents. Don't charge the hill; you don't want to be spent by the time you get to the top. On the descent, try to keep your toes under your nose. As you build fitness, progress to steeper and longer hills. Then work toward maintaining an even pace on the inclines and descents.
  - ▶ If you don't have easy access to hills, you can do this workout on a treadmill, varying the incline.
- **FARTLEK** Fartlek is Swedish for "speed play." It is an unstructured speed workout that alternates hard efforts with easy recovery efforts.
  - ▶ You can do this workout on a track, treadmill, or any traffic-free stretch of road.
  - ▶ After a 3- to 5- minute walk or jog to warmup, ease into your easy-run pace. Then alternate between running at a faster pace for 1 minute and running easy for 3 minutes. Repeat that three more times. Then walk or jog for 3 to 5 minutes to cooldown.
  - ▶ How fast should your fast bouts of running be? Don't worry too much about specific paces. Gradually accelerate to 80 to 90 percent of your effort. After your 1 minute of fast work, smoothly decelerate into an easy jog to recover. Cooldown with 3 to 5 minutes of walking.

THE > **STARTING LINE**

STEP FIVE:
RUN FASTER PLAN

The *Runner's World* Run Faster plan will help you boost your speed and fitness and will introduce you to track workouts.

The plan begins with a 2-mile run and builds gradually, so that by the end of the 8-week program you'll be able to comfortably complete a 9-mile run and do speed sessions at the track.

RUN FASTER PLAN

WEEK	MON	TUES	WED	THURS	FRI	SAT	SUN	TOTAL MINUTES
1	2 miles	4 miles	2 miles	4 miles	Rest	6 miles	Rest	18 miles
2	2 miles	4 miles (hills)	2 miles	**4.25 miles TRACK—** 1 mile easy warmup 4x100m @ 10-K w/ 100 jog recovery 4x200m @ 10-K w/ 200 jog recovery 2x400m @ 10-K w/ 400 jog recovery 1 mile cooldown	Rest	7 miles	Rest	19.25 miles
3	2 miles	4 miles (hills)	2 miles	**5.25 miles TRACK—** 1 mile easy warmup 4x100m @ 10-K w/ 100 jog recovery 4x200m @ 10-K w/ 200 jog recovery 1x400m @ 10-K w/ 400 jog recovery 3x400m @ 5-K w/ 400 jog recovery 1 mile cooldown	Rest	7.5 miles	Rest	20.75 miles
4	2 miles	5 miles (hills)	2 miles	**5.75 miles TRACK—** 1 mile easy warmup 4x100m @ 10-K w/ 100 jog recovery 4x200m @ 10-K w/ 200 jog recovery 1x800m @ 10-K w/ 400 jog recovery 4x400m @ 5-K w/ 200 jog recovery 1 mile cooldown	Rest	8 miles	Rest	22.75 miles

- Before you start each workout, and after you finish, add a 3- to 5-minute warmup and cooldown.

- If you have a BMI of more than 25, are 60 years or older, or if you'd like to take a more gradual approach, you can repeat any week, or every week, and stretch this out to an 8-, 10-, or 12-week plan.

- If you're 40 or older, or have a family history of heart disease, diabetes, or other chronic illnesses, see a doctor before starting any exercise routine.

WEEK	MON	TUES	WED	THURS	FRI	SAT	SUN	TOTAL MINUTES
5	3 miles	5 miles (hills)	3 miles	**6.2 miles TRACK—** 1 mile easy warmup 4x100m @ 10-K w/ 100 jog recovery 4x200m @ 10-K w/ 200 jog recovery 2x800m @ 10-K w/ 400 jog recovery 2x800m @ 5-K w/ 400 jog recovery 1 mile cooldown	Rest	8 miles	Rest	25.2 miles
6	3 miles	5 miles (hills)	3 miles	**6.2 miles TRACK—** 1 mile easy warmup 4x100m @ 10-K w/ 100 jog recovery 4x200m @ 10-K w/ 200 jog recovery 2x800m @ 10-K w/ 400 jog recovery 2x800m @ 5-K w/ 400 jog recovery 1 mile cooldown	Rest	9 miles	Rest	26.2 miles
7	3 miles	6 miles (hills)	3 miles	**6 miles TRACK—** 1 mile easy warmup 4x100m @ 10-K w/ 100 jog recovery 4x200m @ 10-K w/ 200 jog recovery 2x800m @ 10-K w/ 400 jog recovery 2x800m @ 5-K w/ 400 jog recovery 1 mile cooldown	Rest	8 miles	Rest	26 miles
8	3 miles	**5 miles TRACK—** 1 mile easy warmup 4x100m @ 10-K w/ 100 jog recovery 4x200m @ 10-K w/ 200 jog recovery 1 mile cooldown	2 miles	4 miles easy	Rest	Race 5-K or 10-K	Rest	17.1–20.1 miles

KEY

- Unless otherwise noted, each workout should be done at a level of effort that feels comfortable and conversational. Don't worry about your pace, just focus on covering the distance for the day. Start slow with the goal of finishing your workout feeling strong.

- **HILLS** Hills build leg and lung power and give you the foundation you need to get faster. For these workouts, simply run the mileage for the day on a course that features hills with a variety of inclines and descents. Find hills that take 30 to 60 seconds to climb at an easy effort. After a warmup, run on the hills, focusing on maintaining an easy level of effort on the climbs and the descents. Don't try to charge the hill; you don't want to spend all your energy by the time you get to the top. On the descent, try to keep your toes under your nose. Don't let your feet slap the pavement or try to brake with your quads; doing so could lead to injury. As you build your fitness, progress to steeper and longer hills. Then work toward maintaining a more even pace on the inclines and descents.

  ▸ If you don't have easy access to hills, you can do this workout on a treadmill, varying the elevation with the incline.

- **TRACK** On Thursdays, the total distance you'll cover for the day is listed at the top of the workout in **bold**. So in week 2 on Thursday, the total mileage for the day is 4.25 miles.

  ▸ For each track workout, you'll do bouts of fast running at your 5-K and 10-K pace. To find your 5-K and 10-K pace, go to our training calculator at runnersworld.com/tools.

  ▸ After each bout of fast running, you'll recover by jogging at an easy pace for the same distance that you ran fast. So for "4 x 100m @ 10-K with 100 jog recovery," you would run at your 10-K pace for 100 meters, then recover with 100 meters of easy jogging. Then you'll repeat that cycle three more times. Run easy to cooldown.

  ▸ You can do the workout on a treadmill or a flat stretch of road, but a track is the ideal site for speedwork because it's flat, traffic-free, and the distance is measured.

  ▸ Many schools open their tracks to the public during times when school isn't in session.

  ▸ Plan your workout around open hours.

  ▸ Most runners take a track counterclockwise. To avoid collisions, you should, too.

  ▸ Leave the headphones at home so you can tune in to what's going on around you.

  ▸ The innermost lane of the track (lane 1) is typically the place for the fastest runners. If you're warming up, cooling down, or running slower, move to an outside or middle lane.

  ▸ Most tracks are 400 meters around; that's about equivalent to one-quarter of a mile. Four laps around the track is roughly equivalent to 1 mile.

A GUIDE TO COMMON RUNNING TERMS

A

Achilles tendon: The tendon along the back of your foot that attaches your calf muscles to your heel bone. Achilles tendinitis can occur in new runners who increase their distance and/or intensity too quickly. This is especially true of new runners who have been inactive in recent years and who often wear heeled shoes (which can make the Achilles tendon shorter and tighter). Good flexibility in your calves and ankles can help to take some of the load off the Achilles tendon.

aid station: Also called a water stop. Any point along the course that offers water and sports drinks, handed out by volunteers. Often at longer races like marathons and half-marathons, people also hand out energy gels and other items.

altitude training: Elite runners train at altitude to increase their number of red blood cells, improving oxygen delivery to their muscles. At altitude, the amount of oxygen in the blood is reduced because there's less oxygen in the air. The kidneys then secrete more of a hormone called erythropoietin (EPO), which causes the body to create more red blood cells. Runners find they can train harder and perform better for several weeks after they return from an extended stay at altitude. If you're heading to an area at a higher altitude than what you're accustomed to, start your run slower and build intensity gradually. Expect to be slower. Dehydration can occur at altitude because the air is thinner and drier, so drink plenty of fluids. Get plenty of rest.

aqua jogging: Running against the water's resistance in the deep end of the pool, where you can't touch the bottom, provides many of the benefits of running on land. A flotation belt will help keep you upright and give you stability.

Athena: Races will often have divisions designated as "Athena" or "filly" for female runners who are over a certain weight. The minimum weight to qualify for that division varies from race to race.

B

bandit: Someone who is participating in the race unofficially, without having registered or paid for an entry.

bib: The sheets printed with numbers (called "bib numbers") used to identify each runner in a race.

black toenails: Lots of downhill running and too-small shoes can cause these, because both situations cause your toes to slam into the front of your shoe. They typically heal on their own within a few months and do not require medical attention.

bloody nipples: These are often caused by chafing, friction caused by the rubbing of the nipples against the shirt while running. They're more common in men and during cold weather, and they can be remedied by covering the nipples with adhesive bandages or nipple guards, which are sold in many specialty running stores.

body mass index (BMI): An estimation of body fat that can be used to determine whether or not your weight is healthy. BMI is derived by comparing your height to your weight. It can be used by men and women of all ages. Use *Runner's World* BMI calculator at runnersworld.com/bmi to determine your body mass index.

BQ: Shorthand for Boston Qualifying time. Often used to describe a marathon or half-marathon finish time that qualifies a person for entry into the Boston Marathon.

brick workout: A workout that includes consecutive biking and running. Often used by triathletes and duathletes to prepare for their goal events.

C

carb-loading: The practice of increasing the percentage of carbs in your diet during the days leading up to an endurance event that lasts 90 minutes or longer, such as a marathon or half-marathon. Carb-loading stores glycogen in the muscles and liver so that it can be used during the race; it is most effective when done along with a taper. It has been shown to improve runners' performance and help prevent them from running out of energy during the race.

certified course: Most marathons and half-marathons, and many 5-Ks and 10-Ks, are certified by USA Track & Field, which ensures that the distance of the race is accurately measured. For any running performance to be accepted as a record or for national ranking, it has to be run on a USATF-certified course.

chafing: Bloodied, blistered, irritated skin caused by friction that happens after clothing-on-skin or skin-on-skin rubbing.

chip: A small plastic piece attached to a runner's shoelace that's used to track a runner's progress and record times during a race. Timing chips are activated once you step over the electronic mat at the start and finish of a race, and at various points in between. At most races, if you forget your timing chip, your race time will not be officially recorded.

Clydesdale: Races often have divisions designated as "Clydesdale" for male runners who are over a certain weight. The minimum weight to qualify for that division varies from race to race.

cooldown: A period of light physical activity, like walking, after a longer or harder run. Done to help bring the heart rate down gradually and prevent the blood from pooling in the legs.

corral: A sectioned area at the lineup of a race that helps separate athletes into different pace groups. The faster an individual is, the more likely he or she will end up in one of the first few corrals. These corrals are especially important at large races, such as marathons, where elite athletes are running.

E

endorphins: Brain chemicals long credited with producing a "runner's high," the sense of elation that runners report experiencing during exercise. More recent research attributes this to endocannabinoids, molecules created by the body that are said to reduce pain and anxiety and promote well-being.

F

fartlek: A Swedish term meaning "speed play." Fartlek is a speedwork format in which you run faster for however long (or short) you want.

5-K: A race that's 3.1 miles long. It's the most popular race distance in the United States, and a good distance for your first race.

G

glycogen: The form of carbohydrates that is stored in your muscles and liver and is converted to glucose for energy during exercise. The amount of stored glycogen depends on your level of training and the amount of carbohydrates in your diet. The glycogen that is stored (so it can be made available for use during a race) if you have to carbo-load.

GPS: Many running watches now have a GPS function that tracks your distance with a fairly high degree of accuracy. This can be helpful when you're running new routes.

H

half-marathon: A race that's 13.1 miles long. The half-marathon has been the fastest-growing race distance in the United States in recent years.

Many runners like the challenge of extending their endurance without having to do the training necessary to finish a marathon.

hamstrings: The long muscles along the back of your legs. Strong, supple hamstrings are crucial for running your best, because they help to flex your knees and extend your hips. Weak or tight hamstrings shift some of the work of running to other body parts that aren't as well equipped for the job. New runners whose daily lives involve a lot of sitting should include hamstring-strengthening and flexibility exercises in their routine from the start.

heart rate: The number of times your heart beats in a minute. Training by heart rate accounts for many variables that affect how you feel from day to day. This makes it a better way to monitor how hard you're working than an arbitrary measure such as your pace. The key is to know what your maximum heart rate is; once you know that, you can figure out the range of heart rates that correspond to the effort level you want for a given run.

heat index: A combined measurement of temperature and humidity that shows how hot it feels outside. When humidity is high, it interferes with the body's ability to sweat—the body's self-cooling mechanism—so the body retains more heat and it's riskier to be outside. High humidity also increases the risk for conditions like heat cramps, heat exhaustion, and heatstroke. The National Weather Service issues an alert when the heat index is expected to exceed 105° to 110°F for at least 2 consecutive days.

hill repeats: A workout that includes sprinting uphill fast, jogging downhill at an easy pace to recover, and then repeating the sequence. It's thought to be an efficient way to build leg strength, speed, and aerobic capacity. Hill repeats may reduce your injury risk because they limit fast-running time and because the incline of a hill shortens the distance your feet have to fall, reducing the impact of each step.

I

ice bath: Typically taken after long runs, races, and hard workouts, ice baths involve immersing your legs in ice water for 15 to 20 minutes. The ice constricts blood vessels and decreases metabolic activity, which reduces swelling and tissue breakdown. Once you get out of the cold water, the underlying tissues warm up, causing a return of faster bloodflow, which helps flush waste products out of the cells.

iliotibial band: A thick, fibrous band that connects your hips and knees. It helps to flex and rotate your hips and stabilize and extend your knees. It can easily become strained, leading to iliotibial (IT) band syndrome, if you increase your mileage too quickly. The IT band is also often irritated if you regularly run on canted roads.

interval training: Technically, this refers to the time you spend recovering between speed segments. But the term is commonly used to refer to track workouts in general or fast bouts of running.

L

long slow distance (LSD) runs: Any run that's longer than a weekly run, which is the foundation of marathon and half-marathon training. These workouts help build endurance and psychological toughness that can help you get through race day.

M

marathon: A race that's 26.2 miles long. Most experts agree that you should have a year of regular running under your belt before you start training for your first marathon.

minimalism: A recent movement in running shoes away from the highly cushioned, thickly heeled models that have become the norm over recent decades. Proponents of minimalism say that lower, lighter models allow you to run with better, more natural form once you've adjusted to them. Many experienced runners find that running in a variety of shoes, including some minimalist models, is better than doing all of their running in the same shoes.

N

negative splits: Running the second half of a race faster than the first half.

O

orthotics: Devices worn inside running shoes to help treat or prevent injuries. Orthotics can be hard or soft and of varying length, depending on what injury they're trying to address. You should wear orthotics only if advised to by a sports medicine professional who says you need one to address a specific underlying imbalance or weakness.

out-and-back: A course that entails running out to a turnaround spot, then running back to the starting point. Out-and-backs are a convenient way to get in runs in unfamiliar locales. They're also a good option when you're trying to run a little farther than you have before, because you don't have the option of cutting the run short.

overpronation: Excessive inward roll of the foot, which can cause pain in the foot, shin, and knee.

overtraining: A collapse in performance that occurs when the body gets pushed beyond its capacity to recover. It can lead to fatigue, stale training, poor race performance, irritability, and loss of enthusiasm for running. Serious overtraining can cause sleep disturbances, hampered immune function, poor appetite, and the cessation of menstrual periods in women.

overuse injury: Any injury incurred from doing too much mileage or too much intensity before the body is ready. Examples of common overuse injuries among runners include runner's knee, iliotibial (IT) band syndrome, and plantar fasciitis.

P

pace: How fast you're running, usually expressed in terms of minutes per mile. Your running pace at a given effort level will vary greatly from day to day, depending on the weather, your fatigue level, and numerous other factors. While it's good to have a general idea of how fast you're running, it's best not to assess your fitness based on hitting certain paces all the time. Doing so usually leads to working too hard and can drain much of the enjoyment from your running life. When you're first starting to work out, it's better to base your workouts on duration, or the time you spend exercising. As you gain fitness, you'll naturally speed up.

personal record (PR): Term used to describe a runner's farthest or fastest time in a race. Also called a personal best (PB).

plantar fascia: Thick connective tissue that runs along the bottom of your foot from the heel bone to the base of your toe bones. It can easily be inflamed by many of the same things that irritate the Achilles tendon, including too-rapid increases in distance and/or intensity and poor flexibility of the calf muscles.

Q

quads/quadriceps: The four main muscles in the front of your legs. They help to stabilize your knees after your foot hits the ground when you're running. New runners whose lives involve a lot of sitting often have tighter and shorter quad muscles than are ideal for running. Good quad strength and flexibility helps to relieve strain on your knees.

quality workouts: Any workouts that are faster or longer than daily runs. Within the context of marathon and half-marathon training, the term usually refers to workouts such as long runs, speed sessions, and tempo runs, which all require a day or two of recovery.

R

recovery: When talking about a specific workout, recovery refers to walking or easy jogging between faster-paced segments. Recovery lets your heart rate return to the point where you're ready to run fast again, and it helps you regain the energy you'll need for the next burst of speed. In the context of a general running routine, the term recovery is used to refer to a day of rest or easy running taken to give the body a chance to adapt to the stresses of training and get stronger.

repeats: The fast segments of running that are repeated during a workout, with recovery in between. If you're training for a marathon, you might run 1000-meter repeats six times. For shorter races, like 5-Ks, you might do shorter repeats of 400 meters or so at your goal race pace.

RICE: Refers to Rest, Ice, Compression, and Elevation. These measures can relieve pain, reduce swelling, and protect damaged tissues, all of which speed healing. They're most effective when done immediately following an injury. RICE is the standard prescription for many aches and pains, such as strained hamstrings and twisted ankles.

runner's knee: A common running injury marked by inflammation of the underside of the kneecap. The technical term for this is chondromalacia. A common cause in new runners is building up mileage too quickly. Being at a healthy weight and having strong, flexible quad and hip muscles help to lessen your risk for developing runner's knee.

run/walk: Method popularized by Olympian Jeff Galloway, columnist and author of *Runner's World*'s monthly "Starting Line" column. Walk breaks allow a runner to feel strong to the end and recover fast, while providing the same stamina and conditioning as a continuous run. By shifting back and forth between walking and running, you work a variety of different muscle groups, which helps fend off fatigue. To receive the maximum benefit, you must start the walk breaks before you feel any fatigue, during the first mile. If you wait until you feel the need for a walk break, then you've already let yourself get fatigued and defeated the purpose of the walk break.

S

side stitch: Also called a "side sticker," this is a sharp pain usually felt just below the rib cage (though sometimes farther up the torso). It's thought to be caused by a cramp in the diaphragm, gas in the intestines, poor posture, or food in the stomach. Stitches normally come on during hard workouts or races. To get rid of a side stitch, notice which foot is striking the ground when you inhale and exhale, then switch the pattern. So if you were leading with your right foot, inhale when your left foot steps. If that doesn't help, stop running and reach both arms above your head. Bend at your waist, leaning to the side opposite the stitch until the pain subsides.

specificity: Training should be relevant and appropriate to the sport for which you're training in order to maximize performance. Long runs, for instance, as opposed to cycling, are specific training for marathons and half-marathons because they prepare your muscles for the specific activity that you'll be doing during the race: covering a long distance for hours at a time.

speedwork: Also called intervals or repeats, speedwork refers to any workout run at a faster-than-normal pace. Speedwork is often done at a track but can be done on a treadmill or a flat stretch of road. It's performed to increase cardiovascular fitness.

splits: The time it takes to complete any defined distance. If you're running 800 meters, or two laps, you might check your split after the first lap to shoot for an even pace.

streaker: Typically refers to someone who has completed a race multiple years in a row. Also used to refer to someone who has run a certain number of days.

stride rate: The number of times your feet hit the ground during a minute of running. This measurement is often used to assess running efficiency. Having a high stride rate—say 170 steps per minute or more—can reduce injuries and help you run faster. Typically, the number used refers to the total number of times either foot hits the ground. So for a person with a stride rate of 170, the right foot and the left foot would each have hit the ground 85 times.

strides: Also called striders or "pickups," these are typically 80- to 100-meter surges that are incorporated into a warmup or a regular workout. Strides increase heart rate and leg turnover; they get your legs ready to run. Strides are run near 80 percent of maximum effort, with easy jogging in between.

supination: The insufficient inward roll of the foot after landing. This places extra stress on the foot and can result in iliotibial (IT) band syndrome, Achilles tendinitis, and plantar fasciitis. Runners with high arches and tight Achilles tendons tend to supinate.

T

talk test: A way to see if you're running at a comfortable effort level. During most of your runs, you should be able to carry on a conversation, which means you've passed the talk test. If you can't say more than a few words at a time, you're probably running too hard. Back off to where you can say a sentence at a time, and you'll be able to run longer and better advance your fitness.

technical clothing: This typically refers to clothing made of synthetic fibers that wick moisture away from the skin. These fibers do not absorb moisture like cotton does, and they help prevent uncomfortable chafing.

tempo: When runners talk about doing a "tempo run," they usually mean a sustained, faster-than-usual run of 3 to 6 miles at the pace they could sustain for an hour in a race. Tempo runs are said to feel "comfortably hard"—you have to concentrate to keep the effort going but aren't running with as much effort as a sprint or 5-K race. Tempo runs are a good way to boost your fitness without doing hard track workouts.

10-K: A race that's 6.2 miles long. Most runners cover the distance at least 15 seconds per mile slower than they do a 5-K.

10 percent rule: Don't increase mileage or intensity by more than 10 percent from one week to another. This is a classic injury-prevention rule meant to prevent a runner from doing too much too soon and getting injured. While this formula works well for many people, it is not universal. Some people find that they cannot increase mileage more than 5 percent week over week before getting injured.

track: Most tracks are 400 meters long. Four laps, or 1600 meters, is approximately equivalent to 1 mile. Many runners use the term "track" to refer to a speed session done on a track.

trail running: Doing some or all of a run off-road. Trail running has become increasingly popular in part because running in the woods or mountains is usually more appealing than sharing the road with distracted drivers. Trails' softer surfaces are also a nice change from asphalt. Expect to run slower than usual on trails. Focus on running at a comfortable level of effort, rather than pace.

U

ultra/ultramarathon: Any race that's longer than a marathon. The most popular ultra distances are 50-K (31 miles), 50 miles, and 100-K (62 miles). A lot of ultras are run on trails or in other natural settings, and almost all ultras have much smaller fields than the average half-marathon or marathon.

USATF: USA Track & Field (usatf.org), the governing body of track and field, long-distance run-

Loss and Lean Mass Gain in Overweight and Obese Premenopausal Women," *Journal of Nutrition* 141, no. 9 (September 2011): 1626–34 .

6   P. T. Res, B. Groen, B. Pennings, M. Beelen, G. A. Wallis, A. P. Gijsen, J. M. Senden, and L. J. Van Loon, "Protein Ingestion before Sleep Improves Postexercise Overnight Recovery," *Medicine & Science in Sports & Exercise* 44, no. 8 (August 2012): 1560–69.

7   Kelly Bastone, "How to Pick the Best Sports Foods," *Runner's World* (October 2012): 33.

8   Karen E. Foster-Schubert, Catherine M. Alfano, Catherine R. Duggan, Liren Xiao, Kristin L. Campbell, Angela Kong, Carolyn E. Bain, Ching-Yun Wang, George L. Blackburn, and Anne McTiernan, "Effect of Diet and Exercise, Alone or Combined, on Weight and Body Composition in Overweight-to-Obese Postmenopausal Women," *Obesity* 20, no. 8 (August 2012): 1628–38.

9   M. S. Westerterp-Plantenga, M. P. Lejeune, I. Nijs, M. van Ooijen, E. M. Kovacs, "High Protein Intake Sustains Weight Maintenance after Body Weight Loss in Humans," *International Journal of Obesity and Related Metabolic Disorders* 28, no. 1 (January 2004): 57–64.

10   K. Jolly et al. "Comparison of Range of Commercial or Primary Care Led Weight Reduction Programmes with Minimal Intervention Control for Weight Loss in Obesity: Lighten Up Randomized Controlled Trial," *British Medical Journal* (November 3, 2011); 343:d6500.

11   M. Nicole Nazzaro, "Weight Loss by the Numbers," *Runner's World* (November 2009): 54–58.

12   Food and Drug Administration, "Guidance for Industry: A Food Labeling Guide (9. Appendix A: Definitions of Nutrient Content Claims)," October 2009. http://www.fda.gov/Food/GuidanceRegulation /GuidanceDocumentsRegulatoryInformation /LabelingNutrition/ucm064911.htm

13   Hagobian, T. A., C. G. Sharoff, B. R. Stephens, G. N. Wade, J. E. Silva, S. R. Chipkin, B. Braun. Effects of

exercise on energy-regulating hormones and appetite in men and women. *Am J Physiol Regul Integr Comp Physiol.* 2009 Feb; 296 (2): R233–42.

14   David R. Broom, James A. King, David J. Stensel, and Rachel L. Batterham, "The Influence of Resistance and Aerobic Exercise on Hunger, Circulating Levels of Acylated Ghrelin and Peptide YY in Healthy Males," *American Journal of Physiology-Regulatory, Integrative and Comparative Physiology* 296, no. 1 (January 2009): R29–35.

15   Jack Hollis, Christina Gullion, Victor Stevens, Phillip J. Brantley, and Lawrence Appel et al., "Weight Loss during the Intensive Intervention Phase of the Weight-Loss Maintenance Trial," *American Journal of Preventive Medicine* 35, no. 2 (August 2008): 118–26.

16   Caleb Daniloff, "Sobriety Test," *Runner's World* (March 2009): 48.

Part 3

1   Christina Ambros-Rudolph, Rainer Hofmann-Wellenhof, Erka Richtig, Manuela Muller-Furstner, Peter Soyer, and Helmut Kerl, "Malignant Melanoma in Marathon Runners," *Archives of Dermatology* 142 (2006): 1471–74.

2   Darren P. Morton and Robin Callister, "Influence of Posture and Body Type on the Experience of Exercise-Related Transient Abdominal Pain," *Journal of Science and Medicine in Sport* 13 (September 2010): 485–88.

3   Nicole Falcone, "Happy Endings," *Runner's World* (June 2013): 54.

4   B. Donohue, A. Miller, M. Beisecker, D. Houser, R. Valdez, S. Tiller, and T. Taymar, "Effects of Brief Yoga Exercises and Motivational Preparatory Interventions in Distance Runners: Results of a Controlled Trial," *British Journal of Sports Medicine* 40 (2006): 60–63.

5   Amby Burfoot, "The 10 Laws of Injury Prevention," *Runner's World* (March 2010): 50–58.

INDEX

CABLE

Son of Cyclops, **Nathan Summers** was born with powerful telepathic and telekinetic powers. But he was sick with a rare virus that limited his abilities. To save his son, Cyclops sent him into the future, where they would have a cure for his illness. Grown up, Nathan returned to the present as Cable to protect a mutant named Hope.

To save him from the virus that threatened him, Cable had to be partially rebuilt with robotic parts. Now part man and part machine, Cable is strong in body and mind.

CANNONBALL

Can you imagine being trapped deep within the earth? That's what happened to Sam Guthrie when a coal mine collapsed with him inside. Trying to escape, Sam discovered the ability to fly at supersonic speeds while encased in an unbreakable force field. He used those powers to free himself and become the teen hero Cannonball.

Cannonball formed a close friendship with his fellow New Mutant Sunspot. While the two have very different personalities, they work together well!

CAPTAIN AMERICA

Q&A

with Captain America:

Q: Being frozen in ice for decades...it must have come as quite a shock waking up.

A: It was a surprise, but in many ways it was a blessing. How many people would want to see what the future is like? Well, for me...I'm living in it.

Q: It's been quite an adjustment, I'm sure.... Cell phones, the Internet, space exploration...

A: Many things are different, it's true. But there's so much that's the same, too.

Q: What do you mean?

A: Human beings still want the same things, to love one another and to be free. And there are still those that would take that freedom from us. We still have to fight for it.

Captain America's famous shield is built largely from the rare metal vibranium, which allows it to absorb any energy that hits it.

Captain America fighting Arnim Zola's army of soldiers.

The Avengers celebrate the holidays.

A young man during World War II, **Steve Rogers** wanted to join the army and fight for his country. Unfortunately, Steve was too small, and military doctors told him he'd never be allowed to become a soldier. However, a brilliant scientist named **Dr. Abraham Erskine** created a Super-Soldier Serum that granted Steve the strength, speed, agility, and power he needed to help the war effort!

During a World War II battle with the Red Skull, Captain America was launched on a rocket into the freezing waters of the Arctic. The world thought he died, but decades later, the Avengers found Captain America's body frozen in ice, and revived him. From that day forward, Captain America fought as a member of the AVENGERS!

Top 5 Cap Villains:
5) *Crossbones*
4) *Baron von Strucker*
3) *Arnim Zola*
2) *Baron Zemo*
1) *The Red Skull*

CAPTAIN AMERICA

The first Super-Soldier, Captain America fought for freedom and justice. Known as Cap by his fellow soldiers, he traveled the world fighting the evil organization known as Hydra and its leader, Red Skull. After being frozen in ice for decades, Cap was finally freed by the Mighty Avengers. He joined them in their conquest for peace on Earth and now fights alongside them as a fellow Avenger!

CAPTAIN MARVEL

Carol Danvers was an officer in the United States Air Force when she became involved in a struggle between two alien warriors. Caught by the blast of an exploding extraterrestrial machine, Carol survived what could have easily killed her, but instead gave her special abilities.

Captain Marvel once helped Star-Lord fight a Skrull on Knowhere.

The hero known as Ms. Marvel picked that name in honor of Carol Danvers.

The accident that gave rise to Captain Marvel's powers caused her human DNA to combine with alien DNA. Now part human and part alien, Captain Marvel has superhuman strength and speed, power blasts, and the ability to fly.

CLOAK

On the way to prom, high-school student **Ty Johnson** and his date, **Tandy Bowen**, were critically injured in a car accident. The evil corporation **Roxxon** used the opportunity to have the teens declared clinically dead so it could experiment on them using dark matter. The experiments gave Ty the ability to travel into the Darkforce Dimension and teleport anywhere on Earth he wants!

The darkness inside Cloak is like a hunger that needs to be filled. Whatever enters the cloak can stay there for all eternity.

*Together, Ty and Tandy fight crime as **Cloak and Dagger**!*

COLOSSUS

One of the strongest **X-MEN**, the metal-plated giant known as Colossus is a quiet and thoughtful person, but when it's time to fight bad guys he lets his actions speak for him. Born in Russia, **Piotr Rasputin** believes that mutants must work for the betterment of everyone on Earth.

Colossus can control his body's transformation from its normal state to its metal-covered state. However, he cannot encase only one part of his body in metal at a time—it's all or nothing!

Mutant family connection: Colossus's sister is a mutant named Magik.

COULSON
(AKA AGENT PHIL COULSON)

When S.H.I.E.L.D. Director Nick Fury needs something done right, he calls on his most effective agent—**Phil Coulson**. As the liaison between **S.H.I.E.L.D.** and the **AVENGERS**, Coulson has a lot of experience managing people with extraordinary abilities. A dedicated member of S.H.I.E.L.D., Coulson has led several teams of agents and occasionally finds himself in the midst of battle.

I heard the Hulk didn't want to cooperate with the mission.

I got it under control, sir.

How did you "control" the Hulk?

Let's just say we're going to need a new Helicarrier.

Send Stark the bill for that.

Agent Coulson has no super powers, but his combat training, his leadership skills, and his raw intelligence have combined to prove, time and time again, that he deserves to fight on the same field of battle as Iron Man, Captain America, Hulk, and Thor.

CRYSTAL

Have you ever felt alone, like you needed a friend? That's how Crystal, one of the mysterious race of beings called **INHUMANS**, felt when she was forced to leave her home and travel in the world of human beings. Just when Crystal most needed friendship, she found the **FANTASTIC FOUR** and was able to help them defeat criminals using her control over earth, wind, fire, and water.

Crystal's earth ability can make small earthquakes. Her wind ability can cause tornados to quickly form. Her fire ability allows her to instantly create flames. And her water ability can bring rain on a clear day.

Inhuman relations:

Crystal is the sister of Medusa, Queen of the Inhumans.

She is the distant cousin of Black Bolt, King of the Inhumans.

CYCLOPS

After running away from his orphanage, **Scott Summers** was found by Professor X, who was looking for mutant children to attend his school. The professor became like a father to Scott. The professor asked him to lead the **X-MEN**.

Cyclops can shoot energy beams from his eyes. Scott doesn't always have complete control of them; he can only stop them with ruby glasses.

"Even though some humans fear, or even hate, mutants, it's our job to show them that mutants can be heroes!"
—Cyclops

DAGGER

On the way to prom, **Tandy Bowen** and her date, **Ty Johnson**, were injured in a car accident. Declared dead, the teens were experimented on by scientists from the evil corporation Roxxon. These experiments gave Tandy the ability to create daggers out of pure light.

Working together, Tandy and Ty escaped from Roxxon. Known by the name Dagger, Tandy fights crime with Ty, now called Cloak, by her side.

DAREDEVIL

As a boy, **Matt Murdock** was just playing in his New York City neighborhood, **Hell's Kitchen**, when a passing vehicle splashed radioactive waste on him, leaving him blind. Without his eyesight, Matt soon realized all his other senses, especially hearing, had become heightened. He grew up to use these powerful senses as the hero Daredevil.

Did you know? Daredevil is a master of twelve forms of martial arts, including kung fu, ninjutsu, and aikido. He uses his specially designed billy clubs as his primary weapons.

Daredevil's hearing is so good he can listen to an individual person's heartbeat from a block away. His sense of touch is so sensitive he can read a normal-print book by feeling the ink on the page.

DAZZLER

Growing up, **Alison Blaire** always dreamed of being a famous singer. When she started performing music professionally, Alison took the stage name Dazzler. A mutant, she used her ability to manipulate light to help her stage shows really shine, but after witnessing a fight between the **X-MEN** and the **Hellfire Club**, Dazzler realized she couldn't just use her powers to become famous. . .she had to become a hero as well.

In combat, Dazzler can use her control of light to create intense flashes that blind her enemies, or create lasers that zap them. She can even create a pulsing light that can hypnotize some enemies, putting them completely in her control.

Best of Disco Dazzler

Dazzler's Top Hits of All Time:
3) *"From Madripoor with Love"*
2) *"I Light up Your Life"*
1) *"Let's Have a Blast"*

THE DEFENDERS

When the **Sorcerer Supreme**, **Dr. Strange**, needed help protecting the planet from an invasion of mystical beings called the **Undying Ones**, he turned to the **incredible Hulk** and **Namor**, the Sub-Mariner. The team-up worked so well that the three began working together regularly, and soon they were known by the team name the **Defenders**.

The original three defenders were soon joined by other heroes, like Valkyrie, the Silver Surfer, and Power Man. While teams like the Avengers and the X-Men almost always have a core list of members, the Defenders' membership is looser and more casual, allowing heroes to come and go as needs fluctuate.

DR. STRANGE

Q&A
with Dr. Strange:

Q: You use specific spells to fight your enemies, is that correct?

A: Yes, I pull my spells from *The Lesser Book of Vishanti* and other mystical texts.

Q: So what would you do if you were being attacked by, say, Ultron, for example?

A: I would cast a spell known as the Seven Suns of Cinnibus to conjure an energy blast of intense heat.

Q: And then?

A: Then I would cast the Crimson Bands of Cyttorak to bind him.

Dr. Stephen Strange was a brilliant brain surgeon, but when an accident damaged his hands, leaving him unable to perform surgeries, he turned from medical science to magic. Stephen trained to become a sorcerer with a powerful mystic, and his natural talent for magic soon became evident. Before long, Dr. Strange inherited the title of Sorcerer Supreme of Earth's Dimension, making him our planet's primary protector against any and all magical threats.

I summon you for an important meeting.

 Dr. Strange? You have a cell phone?

No, I do not.

 Then how are you texting me?

The mystical arts hold many powers.

 Do the mystical arts get free nights and weekends?

Dr. Strange has an incredible range of magical abilities at his command. He uses a cloak of levitation to give him the power of flight, and he can use various spells from ancient books to create powerful bolts of energy, mystical flames, and other kinds of attacks.

DRAX THE DESTROYER

Q&A
with Drax:

Q: What's it like being a member of the Guardians of the Galaxy?

A: It is good to have companionship in my quest for justice.

Q: Have you ever been a member of any other teams?

A: I also serve as a member of Infinity Watch, a team devoted to hiding the location of the Infinity Stones from Thanos.

Q: Where are the Infinity Stones now?

A: Why do you ask? Who sent you?! Was it THANOS?!

Rocket Raccoon thinks Drax can beat the Hulk in an arm wrestling match.

Drax's tattoos sometimes glow when he is angry.

His home...His family...Everything was taken away from Drax by the evil intergalactic villain known as **Thanos**. On that day, Drax swore an oath to destroy Thanos so that no other families would have to suffer the way Drax did. Drax joined a group of space heroes known as THE GUARDIANS OF THE GALAXY.

Finally we have a day off. What do you want to do today?

Seek and destroy Thanos.

Yeah, we're always on the lookout for that guy. But what should we do with our day off?

I already told you: seek and destroy Thanos.

Does this guy have a one-track mind or what?

Drax's powerful alien body has superhuman strength, speed, and stamina. Drax's body can even survive in the vacuum of space without a space suit. He can go long periods of time without food, water, or even air.

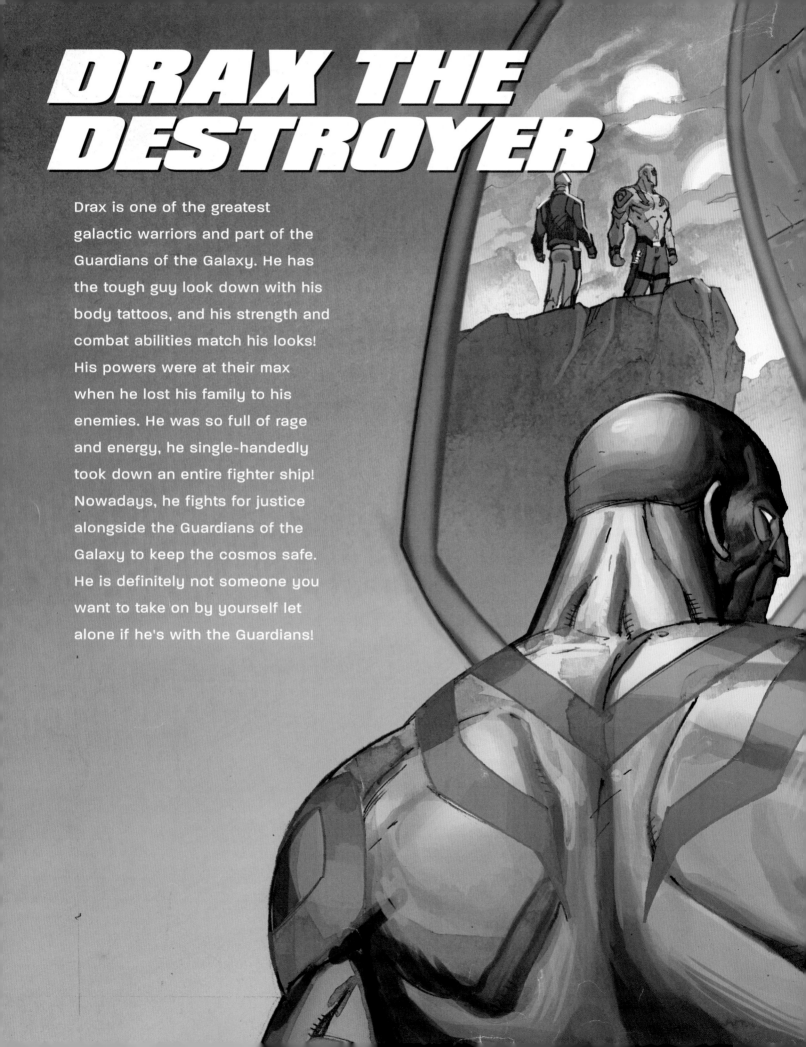

DRAX THE DESTROYER

Drax is one of the greatest galactic warriors and part of the Guardians of the Galaxy. He has the tough guy look down with his body tattoos, and his strength and combat abilities match his looks! His powers were at their max when he lost his family to his enemies. He was so full of rage and energy, he single-handedly took down an entire fighter ship! Nowadays, he fights for justice alongside the Guardians of the Galaxy to keep the cosmos safe. He is definitely not someone you want to take on by yourself let alone if he's with the Guardians!

ELEKTRA

In the jungles of China, a blind martial arts instructor named Stick trained a young woman, **Elektra Natchios**, to become a **kunoichi** female ninja master. Elektra sought to avenge the death of her father, **Hugo**, and was willing to fight crime with extreme violence until her friendship with Daredevil taught her the value of mercy.

Elektra has no real super powers, but she is the perfect weapon. She has above-normal strength and over the years she has mastered several martial arts. Her favorite is ninjutsu. Elektra's main weapon of choice is her trademark twin sais.

Elektra likes to work alone, but when she does team up, it's usually with Daredevil or Wolverine.

EMMA FROST

How can you trust a leader who used to be a villain? Emma Frost, a powerful mutant psychic, was known as the **White Queen** of the **Hellfire Club**, an organization of Super Villains. After seeing the results of the bad things the club was doing, Emma joined the fight for good, eventually becoming one of the leading members of the **X-MEN**.

Emma Frost can use her mental influence to give other mutants' powers a temporary boost.

Emma Frost is a powerful psychic who is able to read minds, put ideas in people's heads, and even make them freeze in place by seizing control of their brains. In addition, she can convert her body into a hardened diamond form, but when she does so, she loses her telepathic abilities.

FALCON

Q&A
with Falcon:

Q: What's it like being best friends with Captain America?

A: Steve's cool. People think he must be uptight or something. He's not.

Q: It was Cap who invited you to become an Avenger, is that right?

A: Yeah, I was very surprised when that happened, but now I'm glad it did.

Q: Some say that when Steve Rogers decides to step down from being Captain America, that he'll probably ask you to take his place.

A: Well, let's just hope he never steps down. . .for all our sakes.

Sam crashes into Black Widow while fighting the Skrulls.

Falcon has teamed with Cap and Black Widow numerous times.

When Captain America suggests you become a hero, you'd better become a hero. After a plane crash, **Sam Wilson** found himself trapped with Captain America on a tropical island run by the villainous **Red Skull**. After the two escaped, Cap was so impressed by Sam's skill that he suggested Sam train with him. Sam and Cap soon became best friends.

Sam uses a flight harness given to him by the Black Panther to take to the air as Falcon! In addition to his suit, Falcon has a telepathic connection with Redwing, a real falcon that Sam has trained to work with him.

Falcon can see everything that Redwing sees, making Redwing a living spy cam!

FANTASTIC FOUR

It was only supposed to be a short, simple mission to space. But when the brilliant scientist **Reed Richards**, his future wife, **Sue Storm**, her brother, **Johnny Storm**, and their best friend, **Ben Grimm**, were subjected to cosmic rays, they were changed forever. Reed, with the power to stretch his body, became known as **Mr. Fantastic**. Sue, with the powers to become invisible and project force fields, became known as the **Invisible Woman**. Johnny, with the power to turn into living flame, became known as the **Human Torch**. And Ben, whose body turned to hard rock, became known as **the Thing**!

As soon as Reed and his family gained their powers, they knew they needed to use them for good. They formed the Fantastic Four and began looking for ways to make the world a better place. The team based itself out of a Manhattan skyscraper called the Baxter Building.

The Fantastic Four's Top 5 Villains:
5) The Super-Skrull
4) *Mole Man*
3) *Annihilus*
2) *Galactus*
1) *Doctor Doom*

FANDRAL THE DASHING

Brave and adventurous, Fandral is a romantic at heart and is always willing to jump into a quest if it means there's excitement to be had. A skilled **swordsman** and experienced soldier, Fandral is one of the famous **WARRIORS THREE** of **Asgard**, who are loyal friends of Thor. There's usually a smile on his face, even in the direst situations, to the annoyance of his friend **Hogun the Grim**!

Some people believe that Fandral, who, like all Asgardians, has lived a very long life by human standards, might have been the inspiration for the legend of Robin Hood.

The Warriors Three first joined forces as students in the Asgardian Learning Hall, where they had to compete in three-person trials of bravery.

FIRESTAR

Angelica "Angel" Jones was always bullied in school by the other kids. As Angel grew, she discovered her mutant ability to create and control flames, and she had a chance to make those bullies pay for what they'd done to her. But instead, she turned away from revenge and became the hero known as Firestar.

At different times, Firestar has been a member of the X-MEN, the Avengers, and even the New Warriors. She is also an "amazing" friend of Spider-Man's, and the two have teamed up on many adventures.

GAMBIT

Remy LeBeau grew up on the streets, using his energy powers to steal. One day he found **Storm**, an **X-Man**, hurt. Instead of walking away, he helped save her life. Storm and the other **X-MEN** showed him that he didn't have to use his powers for crime; instead, he could become a hero!

Gambit's mutant ability allows him to charge small objects with energy, which he likes to throw at his enemies, creating explosions. His choice of weapon is playing cards. He always has a deck handy!

GAMORA

Q&A
with Gamora:

Q: Is it true that you're sisters with the alien Super Villain Nebula?

A: She was adopted by Thanos. I was adopted by Thanos. The similarities stop there.

Q: Okay. . . .Sounds like you two don't get along?

A: That's an understatement. Can we stop talking about her?

Q: What made you decide to join the Guardians of the Galaxy?

A: They may seem pretty strange, but they take care of one another. . . unlike certain adopted Super Villain sisters I could name.

Q: I thought you didn't want to talk about her.

A: I don't.

Gamora practices martial arts with Star-Lord.

Gamora is also known as the most dangerous woman in the galaxy.

From a very early age, Gamora was trained to do the will of the villain **Thanos**, but as she grew older, Gamora realized that she didn't want to hurt people—she wanted to help them. Enraging Thanos, she threw aside everything he had taught her to join **THE GUARDIANS OF THE GALAXY**, a team of space heroes!

To: Gamora@gotg.net
From: Cosmo@Knowhere.gal
Subject: Fear in the streets

Gamora,
As head of security for Knowhere, I need you to stop practicing with your sword in public. You're scaring people and driving business away from the shop Please practice on your ship, or on some deserted asteroid— anywhere really, just not here.

Thanks,
Cosmo

Gamora's alien species is known as the Zen-Whoberi. This species is naturally stronger and more powerful than human beings. In addition, Thanos trained her in many forms of fighting from various planets. Gamora also received alien medical treatments from Thanos to increase her speed and to enhance her healing factor.

GAMORA

She is one of the fiercest and most dangerous galactic warriors in the universe. She is also the last of her alien race. When she was only a girl, the Badoon plundered and destroyed her people. She managed to hide and survive, only to be found by Thanos, the most sinister of all villains. However, Thanos took Gamora as his daughter and trained her to be a deadly assassin. Learning about her adoptive father's evil ways and how he was even worse than the Badoon, Gamora turned her back on Thanos and joined the Guardians of the Galaxy to fight for good.

GROOT

Q&A
with Groot:

Q: Your name is Groot, correct?

A: I am Groot.

Q: Have you gone by any other name?

A: I am Groot.

Q: Can you say anything else?

A: I am Groot.

Q: I know. You said that already. I assume no, then?

A: I am Groot!!

The Guardians ready for battle.

I AM GROOT!

The Guardians are proud to have strong and loyal Groot by their side, even though most of them have trouble understanding him. All Groot ever says is "I am Groot." But those three words might mean something different every time.

Groot, a treelike alien, comes from a mysterious world known only as **Planet X**. Members of Groot's species are so rare that almost no one in the galaxy has ever seen one. In fact, some people don't believe Groot's race even exists, thinking it's just a legend. Groot enjoys traveling with his adopted family, **THE GUARDIANS OF THE GALAXY**. Groot can instantly grow to incredible sizes and shoot out sharp branches, which he uses in combat.

I am Groot!

 Sure, I'm up for anything. What are you thinking?

I am Groot!

 I know where it is. I'll meet you there.

I am Groot!

 Oh, yeah, I won't forget.

GROOT

Groot does not say anything more than "I am Groot." He's the perfect example of why not to judge anyone by their appearance. Don't take his limited vocabulary as a sign of his strength or intelligence. He can grow into a giant and even regrow from a single leaf. He is from Planet X, a world filled with sprawling forests and treelike beings. With a heart to match his size, he loves his family, the Guardians of the Galaxy.

GUARDIANS OF THE GALAXY

There are those who are born heroes. . .and there are those who have to stretch to become heroes. The members of the Guardians of the Galaxy are all **misfits** in one way or another— some of them are the last of their species, and some of them have made mistakes in their pasts. Together, the members of this unlikely family support one another as they travel the stars helping the helpless and protecting the innocent.

The members of the Guardians include: Star-Lord, from the planet Earth; Drax the Destroyer, a warrior bent on revenge; Gamora, an assassin trained for evil who decided to become a hero; Groot, a rare treelike alien; and Rocket Raccoon, an experimental life form with a bad attitude.

The Guardians' main base is on the space station Knowhere, which was once the living skull of a celestial being!

HAVOK

You think you have a weird family? Well, **Alex Summers** probably has you beat. One of his brothers is **Scott Summers**, the **X-MEN** leader also known as **Cyclops**. His other brother is **Gabe Summers**, also known as the evil space villain **Emperor Vulcan**. And their dad? He's **Christopher Summers**, a swashbuckling space hero.

At first, Havok could only use his power when he was in great danger. However, with the help of the X-Men, he soon learned how to better control it.

Alex was born with a mutant power that lets him absorb cosmic energy and release it as super-heated plasma. The plasma shoots out in very recognizable circular patterns. Alex's powers, when unleashed, have caused such chaos that he chose "Havok" as his Super Hero code name.

HAWKEYE

For many, the circus is fun to visit, but for **Clint Barton** it was home. Clint was raised in a traveling circus known as Carson's Carnival of Traveling Wonders and was taught from an early age to be a master archer. People came from all around to see the boy archer perform. Later, as an adult, Clint used his skills to become the costumed hero known as Hawkeye.

Hawkeye uses a variety of trick arrows, including:

- *Explosive arrows*
- *Net arrows*
- *Frost arrows*
- *Hook arrows*
- *Quick-hardening foam arrows*

Hawkeye joined S.H.I.E.L.D., where he was considered one of the most valuable agents Director Nick Fury had under his command. He later went on to become a central member of the AVENGERS.

HEIMDALL

Heimdall holds an important role in the realm of **Asgard**. As guardian of the **Rainbow Bridge**, Heimdall controls the ability of people to travel from Asgard to other realms by means of the Bifrost bridge. He also uses a special form of sight to see things happening throughout the universe. Without Heimdall, Asgard would be vulnerable to surprise attack from its enemies.

You can see everything in the universe, right?

Aye, I can.

Great! Can you help me find my keys? I lost them!

My legendary powers are not to be used for such things.

You're a real by-the-book kind of guy, huh?

Tell me about it.

Odin has entrusted Heimdall with a special sword so powerful it is rumored to contain the cosmic force of an entire universe! Heimdall's sword is made of uru, a mystical metal found only in Asgard. Thor's hammer is made of this same metal.

HERCULES

"Anything that Thor canst do—Hercules canst accomplish more mightily!"
—Hercules

Everybody's heard of the ancient hero Hercules, famous in **Greek mythology**. But did you know he also joined the **AVENGERS**? Once, an evil witch named **Enchantress** gained control of Hercules's mind, forcing him to leave **Mount Olympus** and fight the Avengers. But Hawkeye was able to free Hercules from the spell, and ever since, he's fought alongside the Avengers whenever they need him.

While Hercules's friend and sometimes rival Thor carries a battle hammer, Hercules carries a mace made of adamantine.

HOGUN THE GRIM

Hogun, a champion fighter from **Asgard**, is short-tempered, pessimistic, and downright gloomy. . . .But that doesn't mean he's not also a hero. One of Thor's closest friends from childhood, Hogun is willing to take on all odds in order to defend what's right. He's a member of the famous **WARRIORS THREE**.

Though he is not a trained healer, Hogun has some skill in battlefield first aid, and is always willing to help out people who are injured, even under dangerous circumstances.

As a student in the Asgardian Learning Hall, Hogun's talent for composing poetry and ballads was widely noted.

HOPE SUMMERS

Some humans fear and hate mutants because they are different, but a message from the future told the **X-MEN** that a girl would be born who was destined to join mutants and humankind in peace. Hope Summers is that girl. Imagine being just a **teenager**, but knowing everyone expects you to inspire world peace. Talk about pressure!

The hero known as Cable has taken a vow to protect Hope from those who do not want peace between mutants and humans. Hope looks to Cable as a father figure.

Hope's mutation is the ability to mimic the powers of those around her. If Hope is near a mutant who can shoot fire, she will also be able to shoot fire. If Hope is around a mutant who can make arctic blasts, Hope will also be able to make arctic blasts.

HULK

Q&A
with Hulk:

Q: So, um, should I call you Dr. Banner?

A: Hulk is not Banner. Hulk is Hulk.

Q: But, I mean, you are both the same person, right?

A: Puny Banner is not Hulk.

Q: But your other persona, Dr. Banner, is one of the smartest men on the planet. Are you proud of that side of yourself?

A: Banner smart, but Banner weak. Banner not an Avenger. Hulk, an Avenger.

HULK . . . SMASH!!!

Hulk loves the holidays!

How strong is the Hulk? As he would say: **"Hulk is the strongest there is."** But it's difficult to measure Hulk's strength exactly, because it changes. The angrier Hulk gets, the stronger he is!

Brilliant scientist **Dr. Bruce Banner** was testing an experimental gamma bomb when an innocent bystander wandered onto the testing range. Bruce was able to push the man to safety, but was caught in the blast himself. The gamma rays flooded Bruce's body, changing him into a massive creature known as the Hulk! When Bruce is calm, he's able to stay his normal self, but whenever he gets angry, he turns back into the Hulk!

Hey, Hulk, how are those anger management classes working out for you?

 AUGHHHHH!!!

I can see they're really doing the job.

 AUGHHHHH!!!

Kidding. . . .

71

HULK

When Dr. Bruce Banner was zapped by gamma radiation, he got the ability to turn into the incredible Hulk whenever he's mad! However, staying calm is not as easy as it seems when you're a misunderstood green giant. He protects the innocent, but because of his appearance, people usually think he's one of the bad guys. Despite saving many lives and being a hero, Hulk finds that people are still scared of him. As a result, Hulk usually kept to himself until he found his family with the Avengers. He's always ready to SMASH when the Avengers are called to assemble!

HUMAN TORCH

Long before he became a Super Hero, **Johnny Storm** lived a flashy life. He loved fast cars, and he never met a party he didn't like. Johnny was the kind of guy people called a real hot shot—and how right that nickname proved to be! After being exposed to cosmic rays while on a test space flight, Johnny found he was able to create a ball of flame around his body without harming himself. Johnny became known as the Human Torch.

The Human Torch can control the flame around his body, so he can make sure no one standing near him is hurt by the heat he generates. His flames also give him the power of flight.

Johnny is the younger brother of Sue Richards, the Invisible Woman. The two work together as members of the Fantastic Four.

ICEMAN

Bobby Drake proves that being an **X-MAN** can be a lot of fun! Even while fighting dangerous villains or facing possible destruction, Iceman manages to smile and joke. He uses his incredible power of spontaneous ice creation to send arctic blasts at his enemies. Bobby's motto: If it's worth doing, then it's worth having fun doing it!

Iceman can't fly like his friend the Human Torch, but he uses his ice powers to create a continuous line of ice slides in order to travel quickly.

@IcemanX: Today's bad guys? Kicked to the curb. Now? Time to par-tay! #XmansionRave #VillainsNotInvited

THE INHUMANS

Many millennia ago, visiting aliens experimented on a population of early humans. The experiments created a new race, called the Inhumans. Inhumans have been living on Earth, hiding away from humans, for countless ages. When a young Inhuman is old enough, he or she undergoes a process called **Terrigenesis**, which grants each Inhuman a unique power.

A small group of Inhuman leaders has occasionally come into the human world and fought the forces of evil. These Inhuman heroes include Black Bolt, Medusa, Triton, Lockjaw, and Crystal.

Most Inhumans live in a floating city, called **Attilan**, that sometimes flies among the clouds but is normally situated in one spot—like right above Central Park!

INVISIBLE WOMAN

When **Sue Storm**, her future husband, **Reed Richards**, her brother, **Johnny Storm**, and her friend **Ben Grimm** took an experimental space flight, they were accidentally exposed to cosmic rays that turned them into the **FANTASTIC FOUR!** Sue developed two powers: the ability to turn invisible, and the ability to create force fields with her mind. She uses those powers to protect the FF as they go on amazing adventures!

When Sue Storm and Reed Richards went on their experimental space flight, they were still just dating. Eventually, Sue and Reed married and started a family.

The Invisible Woman's force fields can either be launched like weapons or used for defense. When an attack is headed her way, she can create a force bubble around herself for protection on all sides.

IRON FIST

Danny Rand is the latest in a long line of martial artists to hold the title of the Iron Fist. Trained in the mystic city of **K'un-Lun**, where he gained his powers by fighting and defeating the dragon **Shou-Lao**, Danny now fights crime in **New York City** and sometimes teams up with his best friend, **Luke Cage**.

Iron Fist can summon his body's internal chi energy, focusing it into his fists. When he does this, his fists take on a supernatural glow and become as hard as metal.

*Iron Fist and Power Man formed a partnership called **Heroes for Hire**.*

IRON MAN

Q&A
with Iron Man:

Q: Many Super Heroes keep their identity secret. You, on the other hand, have publicly admitted to being Iron Man. Why?

A: If you were Iron Man, wouldn't you want to tell other people all about it?

Q: It's rumored that villains like Titanium Man, Shockwave, and the Crimson Dynamo are using suits based on Iron Man technology.

A: It's true that some villains have stolen my tech, but they should be warned. . .I will get it back.

Q: What's the best thing about being Iron Man?

A: The theme song.

Iron Man tries to pick up Thor's hammer, but only Thor can use Mjolnir.

Tony Stark working on adjustments to his armored suit.

An American billionaire weapons manufacturer, **Tony Stark** was traveling overseas when a group of armed international criminals kidnapped him, held him in a cave, and tried to force him to create a bomb for them. Tony tricked his captors, however, and instead invented a suit of armor capable of helping him escape. Once back home, Tony used his Iron Man suit to help him become a Super Hero!

Iron Man's armor can fly, fire repulsor blasts, and use additional weapons and hardware as Tony adds them. In fact, Tony has an entire hall filled with armor suits created to serve specific purposes.

Iron Man has many specialty armors including:

1) *Prototype armor*

2) *Underwater armor*

3) *Heavy combat armor*

4) *Space armor*

IRON MAN

Tony Stark is a billionaire genius inventor and the owner of Stark Industries, who enjoys the finer things in life. But when he injured his heart, he created an arc reactor to wear within his chest along with a suit of armor. He continues to work on and perfect his suit, and when he puts it on, he is invincible. And now he can add Avenger to his list of occupations.

IRON PATRIOT

What would it be like to be best friends with a Super Hero? **James "Rhodey" Rhodes** knows. He was best friends with **Tony Stark**, the invincible Iron Man. Then, once when Tony was in trouble, Rhodey put on the Iron Man armor and saved him! That's why Tony made Rhodey his own suit of armor. Now Rhodey fights crime as the Iron Patriot!

The Iron Patriot armor has all the capabilities of a normal Iron Man suit, but it also has the capability to interface with any U.S. satellite in orbit.

Hey—you never told me what this red button does.

Oh. . . .Don't touch that! Red = Self-destruct.

There's a self-destruct button and YOU NEVER TOLD ME?!

Of course not! Kidding! Kidding!

But seriously, don't press that button.

JUBILEE

As a little girl, **Jubilation Lee** was an impressive **gymnast** with a chance of competing in the Olympics, but her dreams were crushed when criminals murdered her parents. Jubilation became even more terrified when she found out she was a mutant with the ability to launch blasts, like fireworks.

One day Jubilation followed the X-Men back to their headquarters, surprised to find out how loving and supportive they could be. The X-MEN became Jubilee's new family.

 # KARMA

Life has always been hard for **Xi'an Coy Manh**, who, at an early age, lost both her parents and was forced to take care of her younger siblings on the mean streets of New York. Later, Xi'an discovered that she had a mutant power that allowed her to take over the minds and bodies of others.

Discovered by Professor X, Xi'an became Karma, one of the first members of the group of teenage mutant heroes known as the NEW MUTANTS.

KITTY PRYDE

Kitty Pryde was born with incredible mutant abilities, but perhaps her most important talent is being a good friend. Because Kitty was the youngest person to ever join the **X-MEN**, many of the other heroes began to think of her as a younger sister. Caring, kind, and a good listener, Kitty often helps other X-Men work through their personal problems. Kitty has a small pet dragon named **Lockheed**.

Kitty has the mutant ability to "phase," or travel, through solid objects. She can also bring other people through solid objects by touching them while she is phasing. Kitty can also destroy any electronic device by passing through it.

Kitty Pryde has used several Super Hero code names during her time in the X-Men, including Sprite, Ariel, and Shadowcat.

LADY SIF

Lady Sif is a warrior from the realm of **Asgard**. She is the sister of **Heimdall**, and grew up playing with **Thor**, his brother **Loki**, and Balder of the **WARRIORS THREE**. While Lady Sif still lives in Asgard, she has visited Earth many times in order to help Thor and other heroes defend the planet.

Lady Sif was born with golden-colored hair, but her childhood playmate Loki was jealous of it, and cut it all off while she was sleeping. Loki replaced Sif's hair with enchanted dwarf hair, which Lady Sif has had ever since.

Ever since she was very young, Lady Sif has shown amazing skill at fighting. While still a student, she excelled in swordplay, defeating many masters of the art. As she grew, all of Asgard acknowledged that she was one of the realm's most powerful warriors.

LOCKJAW

Lockjaw is a magical dog-like creature who serves the **INHUMANS**. Lockjaw can **teleport** himself—and any nearby living creatures—anywhere on Earth, in space, and even in other dimensions. He serves as the official provider of transportation for **Black Bolt**, king of the Inhumans, and other important members of the Inhuman race. Additionally, Lockjaw is a loyal protector, and would defend Black Bolt with his life.

Unknown to the other Inhumans, Lockjaw has, at times, teamed up with the pets of various heroes to form the Pet Avengers. Members of the Pet Avengers include Falcon's pet bird, Redwing; Kitty Pryde's pet dragon, Lockheed; and Firestar's pet cat, Ms. Lion.

Much like a hunting dog with a scent, Lockjaw can get a fix on the energy patterns of a missing person, and then track that person across space. Plus, Lockjaw's jaw muscles are powerful, so once he's got ahold of the person he's looking for, he never lets go.

MAGIK

Illyana Rasputin was kidnapped from her native Russia when she was still a little girl, but she was freed by **Professor X** and the **X-MEN**, who brought her to Xavier's School for Gifted Youngsters. Magik's mutation allows her to use magic spells and to teleport herself and others by passing through a gateway into a mystical dimension called **Limbo**.

Magik uses a weapon known as the soulsword, which she created from her own life energy. Whenever she uses the soulsword, Magik is instantly covered with a magical armor.

Magik is the younger sister of the mutant strongman Colossus. The two are very close. Colossus would give anything to keep his sister safe.

MAN-THING

Dr. Ted Sallis was desperately trying to recreate the Super-Soldier Serum that gave **Captain America** his powers when he was attacked by villains who wanted to steal his work. Ted injected himself with his last batch of experimental serum so that no one else could get it. But when his car crashed in the Everglades, the serum fused Ted's body with the swamp, turning him into a **swamp monster**!

Man-Thing is known to roam freely in the swampland of the Florida Everglades.

Man-Thing is sensitive to human emotions. When Man-Thing senses human fear, his body secretes a dangerous chemical. If Man-Thing touches someone who is afraid, that person will start to burn.

MARIA HILL

From childhood, Maria Hill's strongest desire was to serve in the military. As soon as she was old enough, she joined the **United States armed forces**. During a mission on the Asian island of **Madripoor**, a known haven for super-powered pirates, Hill was able to take down an entire terrorist organization almost single-handedly. It was not long after this that **S.H.I.E.L.D.** snapped her up and made her a lead agent.

When Nick Fury, director of S.H.I.E.L.D., needed to go into hiding, there was only one person he was willing to call on to take his place—Maria Hill. She has served as acting director and director multiple times.

Maria Hill has no super powers, but her forceful leadership and keen intellect command the respect of those around her.

MARVEL GIRL

One of the founding members of the **X-MEN**, **Jean Grey** is a mutant psychic so powerful that Professor X can't even measure the upper level of her powers. Jean can read, influence, and even control the minds of others. When her powers first appeared, Jean had trouble using them, but the more time she spends exercising them, the better she gets at it. Jean has also been a conduit for the **Phoenix**, a mighty cosmic force of life and death, and struggles to control its hold on her destiny.

X-Men love triangle: both Cyclops and Wolverine have been in love with Jean.

In addition to being telepathic, Jean is also telekinetic—meaning she can move objects, large and small, with her mind! By lifting herself with her mind, Jean can give herself a form of flight.

MISTER FANTASTIC

By the time **Reed Richards** was a teenager, it was obvious to everyone that he was a genius. Already a college student when most kids were still in junior high, Reed met **Ben Grimm**, who would become his lifelong friend. Ben was the pilot on the spaceship Reed designed when it was hit with cosmic rays. Reed, Ben, Reed's girlfriend, Sue, and Sue's brother, Johnny, all got super powers from their cosmic exposure.

The leader of the FANTASTIC FOUR, Mister Fantastic can stretch his body to amazing lengths, and even use it to contain explosions or stop bullets. But his more important power is something he's had since birth—his incredible intelligence.

Top 5 Super Hero Scientists:
5) *Bruce Banner*
4) *Beast*
3) *Ant-Man*
2) *Tony Stark*
1) *Mister Fantastic*

MEDUSA

Medusa is queen of the powerful beings known as **INHUMANS**. The key to Medusa's Inhuman ability is in her long red hair. Her hair is incredibly long, capable of lifting great weights, and can stretch to almost twice its normal length.

Medusa can control every strand of her hair as if each is a separate arm. Medusa relies heavily on her hair when in battle.

MOCKINGBIRD

An agent of **S.H.I.E.L.D.**, **Bobbi Morse** was assigned the secret task of uncovering double agents working for both S.H.I.E.L.D. and **Hydra**. Bobbi assumed the identity of Mockingbird. Though it took a lot of work, Bobbi discovered many corrupt agents!

Mockingbird has no super powers, but she is trained in hand-to-hand combat and often uses her signature weapon, a pair of batons that combine to make a single bowstave.

MOON KNIGHT

While traveling in **Egypt**, American **Marc Spector** got into a fight with a mercenary who left him for dead. Kind locals, upon discovering the gravely injured Spector, carried him to a temple of the **Egyptian moon god Khonshu**. When Spector's heart stopped, Khonshu offered him a second chance at life if he would agree to fight villains on Khonshu's behalf.

Khonshu granted him supernatural powers like super strength and reflexes. However, Moon Knight's powers are linked to the phases of the moon. The fuller the moon, the stronger Moon Knight is.

MOONSTAR

A Native American from the **Cheyenne Nation**, **Dani Moonstar** was alone when her parents suddenly disappeared. But **Professor X**, a good friend of Dani's father, took her in at his school. She joined the NEW MUTANTS, a team of teenage heroes.

Her mutant ability allows her to reach inside the brains of her enemies and then create hologram-like projections of their worst fears.

MS. MARVEL

Q&A
with Ms. Marvel:

Q: What's the hardest thing about being a new Super Hero?

A: Sneaking out to fight crime without my parents finding out.

Q: What?

A: Oh, nothing. I was just kidding. I totally have my own apartment in the city and everything.

Q: So, if you got your powers through Terrigen, does that mean you're an Inhuman?

A: Hmmm...I don't think so. I'm from Jersey City.

Q: Is it true that Captain Marvel is your inspiration?

A: Yeah, isn't she great? She's just so...Hold on, I need to take this....What, Mom? Yes, I'll take out the trash when I get home, OK?...Fine. I'm coming now.

Kamala Khan, the child of Pakistani immigrants to the United States, often felt like she didn't fit in. She always loved Super Heroes, because having special powers seemed like a form of freedom. Then one night, while walking home from a party, Kamala ran into a cloud of **Terrigen Mist** released by the **INHUMANS'** city of **Attilan**. The mists granted her special abilities.

Ms. Marvel is a shape-shifter—so she can grow, stretch, expand, twist, and compress her body any way she pleases. This means she can grow the size of her fists to deliver super-heavy punches. She also has an increased healing factor.

Kamala's favorite Super Hero was Carol Danvers, who used to be known as Ms. Marvel, but then changed her name to Captain Marvel. In order to honor her favorite hero, Kamala adopted Carol's old title.

NAMOR

Captain America wasn't the only superhuman to fight during **World War II**. In many important battles Cap fought alongside Namor, the prince of the under-water kingdom of **Atlantis**. While the people of Atlantis have no love for the surface world, they have a special grudge against **Hydra**, which experimented with under-water missiles by targeting Atlantean colonies. Because of this, Namor joined Cap on the American side of the conflict.

Although Namor is prince of Atlantis, he is only half Atlantean by birth. Namor's mother, a princess of Atlantis, fell in love with and married a human mutant sea captain.

NAMORITA

Biologically, Namorita is a distant cousin of **Namor, prince of Atlantis**. When Namorita became curious about the surface world, she traveled to New York, where she decided to attend a human college, primarily to learn what "surface dwellers" were really like. After meeting **Nova** and a few other human heroes, Namorita decided to join the **NEW WARRIORS**, a team of young heroes.

On land, Namorita is stronger and faster than most humans, but when in water, her abilities are even more enhanced. She can also produce a corrosive acid from her skin.

Namorita joined and eventually became the leader of the New Warriors. Nova and Firestar both served on the team.

NICK FURY

Q&A
with Nick Fury:

Q: As director of S.H.I.E.L.D. you've been criticized for using excessive force. Any comment?

A: The world is a dangerous place. Sometimes that means doing dangerous things.

Q: What is S.H.I.E.L.D.'s relationship with the Avengers?

A: We have a reciprocal relationship. They help us, we help them.

Q: There are rumors that sometimes S.H.I.E.L.D. and the Avengers don't see eye-to-eye.

A: When that happens, S.H.I.E.L.D. takes the steps needed to keep the peace... whether the Avengers like it or not.

Director Fury runs S.H.I.E.L.D. from his command center on board the floating fortress known as the Helicarrier.

Fury commands hundreds of S.H.I.E.L.D. agents at any given moment.

How did a man without any super powers rise to lead the most important security agency in the world? Sheer grit, determination, and force of will.

The Strategic Homeland Intervention, Enforcement, and Logistics Division (better known as **S.H.I.E.L.D.**) is an international organization devoted to discovering and containing threats to the planet and her people. S.H.I.E.L.D. is commanded by a single leader, Director Nick Fury. With a long history of military service, an incredible intellect, and a vision for world security, Fury is one of the most trusted commanders on the planet.

Top 5 S.H.I.E.L.D. Agents Commanded by Nick Fury:

5) *Mockingbird*

4) *Phil Coulson*

3) *Maria Hill*

2) *Hawkeye*

1) *Black Widow*

NIGHTCRAWLER

Born with abnormalities like blue skin and a tail, **Kurt Wagner** was abandoned by his parents, **Mystique** and the **demon Azazel**. He was raised in a circus. While he looked different his whole life, it wasn't until he was a teenager that he realized he could teleport. His teleportation became a real asset to the **X-MEN**.

Nightcrawler can teleport up to two miles at a time if he needs to; however, traveling such long distances can leave him worn out. He can teleport a passenger short distances if needed.

NIGHTHAWK

Looking for adventure, **Jack Norris** joined a team of criminals. But when they nearly defeated the **Hulk**, it was Jack who brought Hulk to safety. Because of his kindness, Jack was asked to join the **DEFENDERS**! Now he could have the adventure he was seeking while fighting for good!

Nighthawk's costume includes jet-powered wings, mini-laser cannons, and artificial claws.

NORTHSTAR

A native of **Montreal**, **Jean-Paul Beaubier** was tragically separated from his twin sister, **Jeanne-Marie**, when the two were still very young. Years later, Jean-Paul was surprised when his **mutant powers** began to appear. He considered using these powers for personal gain, but instead chose to join the Canadian Super Hero team called **ALPHA FLIGHT**. It was on the team that Jean-Paul was reunited with his sister, who now goes by the name **Aurora**.

Northstar's mutant body generates a form of atomic energy that he can use to fly so fast that he can almost reach the speed of light. This same energy also allows him to punch at incredible speeds and gives him increased reflexes.

Aurora can sense when her brother is in danger.

NOVA

Q&A
with Nova:

Q: Where do you get the name Nova?

A: There used to be all kinds of Novas from different planets. . . .But now I'm the last one, I think.

Q: What were the other Novas like?

A: The Nova Corps was like the police department of space, but with awesome powers.

Q: What happened to them all?

A: I'm not really sure. I think there was a huge space war.

Q: What made you want to be a Nova?

A: I didn't do it on purpose. My dad was one before me. . . .Maybe it's the family business.

Q: Where is your dad now?

A: Somewhere lost in space, I think. But don't worry, I'll find him.

Nova loves to play tag with Spider-Man.

Nova with Iron Man.

Sam Alexander grew up listening to his father's crazy stories about once having been a space-traveling hero named Nova, but Sam never believed him. However, when Sam's dad went missing, alien heroes named **Gamora** and **Rocket Raccoon** came looking for him. The aliens confirmed that all of Sam's dad's crazy stories were true. And when Sam tried on his dad's old space helmet, he, too, got Nova powers!

While wearing the Nova helmet, Sam Alexander can survive in space, fly faster than light, project energy beams, and translate any alien language. Through his helmet he gets access to the Nova database, one of the largest sources of information in the galaxy.

@NovaCorps1—I make this helmet look good! #AlienTechRules, #LastOfTheNovas

ODIN

Thor's father, Odin, is the **King of Asgard**, the **magical realm** where Thor was born. Knowing that his son Thor would one day take his place on the **throne of Asgard**, Odin grew concerned when Thor seemed to be selfish and prideful. For this reason, Odin cast Thor down to Earth, in hopes that time among the humans would teach him humility.

 toorooll attk onn svartlhhhem

I have no idea what you mean, Father.

 whe mmust tto arrrmsk

Father, if you are having trouble texting, just ask Heimdall to summon me.

Just as Thor has Mjolnir, a magical Asgardian battle hammer, his father, Odin, has Gungnir, a magical Asgardian battle spear. Gungnir channels the "Odin Force," a mystical source of energy that comes from the king himself.

PEPPER POTTS/ RESCUE

When **Tony Stark** needed to go off the grid for a while, he named Pepper Potts the new **CEO** of his company, **Stark Industries**.

Pepper's Rescue armor is similar to the Iron Man armor, except that it uses a special portable magnetic super-field generator to control metal. Rescue's magnetic powers are so strong that she can stop a falling jet from hitting the ground.

TODAY'S AGENDA FOR PEPPER POTTS:

6 a.m.—Combat training

8 a.m.—Meeting with the board of Stark Industries

10 a.m.—Rescue kidnapped politician

Noon—Remind Tony Stark about upcoming tax filing

3 p.m.—Attempt to locate the villain known as Titanium Man

5 p.m.—Tour Stark Industries factory in midtown

7 p.m.—Dinner reservations with Tony Stark

POWER MAN

Q&A

with
Power Man:

Q: So Iron Fist is your partner, correct?

A: Correct.

Q: And who is the leader of the duo?

A: Me, of course.

Q: And does he know that?

A: Of course he does, and if he doesn't, he knows now.

Q: I sense you're getting upset. Are you upset?

A: I sense you're getting under my skin. Are you getting under my skin?

Q: Uh, that is all for now. Thank you, Mr. Power Man.

When a villain attacked a crowd, **Victor Alvarez** discovered that he could draw chi from the people around him and become super strong! He took the name Power Man and started fighting crime with other heroes like **Luke Cage** and **Iron Fist**. Some day, he wants to start his own team of heroes!

Victor once absorbed chi from multiple sources simultaneously, briefly growing giant-sized with increased strength. He sometimes experiences memories of those whose chi he has absorbed.

J. Jonah Jameson, publisher of *The Daily Bugle, once hired Power Man to capture Spider-Man. Jameson told Luke Cage that Spidey was a "menace" and needed to be brought in. However, once Cage actually met Spider-Man, he realized he was a good person and refused to take him to Jameson. Instead, he just returned Jameson's money.*

PSYLOCKE

The ninja clan known as **the Hand** trains one assassin at a time in the fatal art of **ninjutsu**. The **X-MAN** known as Psylocke received this training, making her a deadly martial arts master even without her mutant powers of **telepathy**. Despite being trained as a remorseless killer for hire, Psylocke now will only fight to defend herself, or protect her friends.

Psylocke's telepathy allows her to read other people's minds, make them see visions, or even control them. When Psylocke uses her mutant power, a telltale butterfly-shaped energy pattern appears around her face.

Because their powers are similar, Psylocke and Jean Grey have shared a special bond.

QUASAR

Trained by **S.H.I.E.L.D.**, **Wendell Vaughn** was guarding Stark Industries the day scientists were testing newly discovered alien artifacts called **Quantum Bands**. When a band of super criminals broke into the building to steal the bands, Wendell had no choice but to put the bands on himself and fight the villains. Wendell quickly discovered that he was a natural at using the powers of the bands.

The Quantum Bands allow Quasar to pull an unlimited amount of energy from another dimension, called the Quantum Zone. Quasar can turn this energy into heat and force blasts!

The Quantum Bands were made by an alien species known as the Kree.

QUICKSILVER

Q&A
with
Quicksilver:

Q: Quicksilver, I'm told that you—

A: Can we hurry this up?

Q: Hurry? But we just started. I haven't asked my first question yet.

A: I know. That's the problem. Pick up the pace.

Q: Well, I was just going to ask— Hey, where did you go?

A: Sorry, I'm back. I just had to run to Canada for a moment.

Q: Canada? How did you—?

A: Oops, out of time. Gotta go!

Q: Where are y—

A: France. Just got back. Picked you up a crepe

Q: ??

Some say that Quicksilver and his sister, the **Scarlet Witch**, were born to be villains. But Quicksilver didn't like the feeling that he got when he saw innocent people being taken advantage of. Born with an incredible power, Quicksilver decided to fight for justice... something he'd do very effectively if he joined the **AVENGERS**!

Quicksilver is very quick indeed. His mutant ability allows him to run many times faster than the speed of sound. He can run so fast that he can run up buildings, run across water, and even whip up hurricane-force winds by running in circles.

Quicksilver is the twin brother of the Scarlet Witch, who also served with the Avengers.

RED HULK

Q&A
with Red Hulk:

Q: You are often seen carrying guns into combat.

A: Yes. What's so strange about that?

Q: Well, you're a Hulk. It wouldn't seem like you'd need weapons other than your fists.

A: I like weapons. You got a problem with weapons?

Q: Uh. . .No, I guess not.

A: Good, then I don't have a problem with you.

When it was first reported that there was a **red version** of the Hulk on the loose, hunting the normal Hulk's old enemies, not many people believed the story. But as the normal Hulk investigated further, he found that it was true. What was the mysterious identity of this new Red Hulk? None other than the normal Hulk's old enemy **General Thunderbolt Ross**, who had taken treatments to give him super powers and help him become the Red Hulk.

The Red Hulk has almost as much strength and crushing power as the original green Hulk, but in addition he has a cool head for battle strategy. Unlike the normal Hulk, Red Hulk often uses weapons, including **massive guns** and **rocket launchers**.

Okay. I've got a strategy. . . .

 Let's SMASH!

My plan is, you come around on the left flank, while—

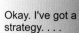 Less think, MORE SMASH!

Ugh. Okay, fine. SMASH!!!

ROCKET RACCOON

Q&A

with Rocket Raccoon:

Q: Where do you spend most of your time?

A: When we're not on a mission, the Guardians of the Galaxy and I usually hang out on a space station called Knowhere.

Q: "Knowhere"? That's an unusual name.

A: It's built inside the giant floating skull of a celestial being.

Q: What do you do there?

A: Depends. Go to the Orlani races sometimes. Or hang out with folks like Cosmo, the talking Russian space dog, or that guy Howard the Duck.

Q: So in your spare time you hang out inside a skull, talking to a dog and a duck?

A: You say that like it's weird.

Rocket in the shop working on his latest weaponry creation.

Rocket fires blasts using his own designed weaponry.

Rocket is a genius engineer and weapons designer. A pile of rusting spare parts might look like junk to everyone else, but give Rocket a few minutes, and he'll be able to use those parts to make a deadly blaster.

Rocket Raccoon has been known to say, **"Ain't no one like me, except me."** He is, in fact, one of a kind. Rocket was **genetically** and **cybernetically enhanced** to human-level intelligence by a mad scientist. Sassy and sarcastic, Rocket's aggressive personality fits in well with his teammates, **THE GUARDIANS OF THE GALAXY.**

GUIDE TO ROCKET-SPEAK
Rocket has his own slang, including:

Humie = Human being

Filthy humie = An unlikable human being

Toaster-heads = Robots

Chokey = Prison

Flark = Oh, no!

Don't call him "raccoon." While Rocket, an intelligent alien being, may look like an Earth raccoon, he doesn't appreciate the comparison. Any earthling who actually calls him that to his face better be ready to run from a blast of laser fire.

ROCKET RACCOON

Do not call him a raccoon! He is from the planet Halfworld, where he was created to become the snarky, highly intelligent inventor and skilled fighter he is today. He can create weapons out of just about anything! His talents make him an excellent fit for the Guardians of the Galaxy. One of his other skills is that he speaks Groot and is often the translator for his good friend.

ROGUE

Q&A
with Rogue:

Q: Because of your mutant ability to absorb the super power of others, you've tried out lots of different powers, right?

A: I guess so.

Q: What's your favorite super power to use?

A: "Favorite"? It's not like that. Sometimes I have to take other people's powers during battle, but I never like it.

Q: Why not?

A: Because it just feels too personal, like an invasion of privacy. I would rather not do that to someone else if I didn't have to.

The mutant known as Rogue hates her super power because it drives her away from other people. When Rogue's skin touches another person's, she uncontrollably absorbs the memories, physical strength, and super powers of that other person. Because of this, Rogue often wears gloves and other clothing that protects her from accidentally touching other people. As a member of the **X-MEN**, Rogue uses her abilities to fight evil mutants.

Rogue's heavy Southern accent indicates that she's from rural Mississippi. She calls herself a Southern belle.

In battle, it can be a helpful thing to take away your enemy's power and then use it against them.

Rogue has a crush on her fellow X-Men member Gambit, but the two can never touch, not even to hold hands.

SCARLET WITCH

Q&A
with
Scarlet Witch:

Q: You were once in the Brotherhood of Evil Mutants, but now you're an Avenger?

A: I'm so happy that Cap, Iron Man, and the others took me in and gave me a second chance.

Q: What's it like being on a Super Hero team with your own brother?

A: Sometimes he can be overprotective, but other times it's really good.

Q: How can it be good?

A: Just. . .there's always someone who knows me, who really knows me.

Do you believe in magic? **Wanda Maximoff** didn't. Wanda was born with a very logical mind, and she grew up thinking all magic was just made up of stage tricks. Then, as she grew older, her mutant abilities kicked in. Suddenly, she could control magic and **cast spells** and **hexes**. Like her brother, Quicksilver, Wanda joined the **AVENGERS** where she became known as the Scarlet Witch!

The Scarlet Witch has a mutant ability to control magical spells called hexes. These hexes include **hex-bolts** and **hex-spheres**, which can be hurled at enemies.

The Scarlet Witch is the twin sister of Quicksilver, who also served with the Avengers.

SHANG-CHI

There is one name that the finest fighters in history bow down before: Shang-Chi. Shang-Chi's training began as a young child. But when he learned he was being trained for a life of evil, he turned against all those who would corrupt others. Having gone up against Shang-Chi in the past, the likes of **Spider-Man** and **the Thing** are very, very happy to now have **the Master of Kung Fu** on their side.

Although he has no super powers, by the time he was an adult, Shang-Chi's martial arts skills were so well developed they were practically superhuman.

You want to head down to the Midtown Dojo and train?

They won't let me in there anymore.

Why not?

Last time I was there, I broke all their practice dummies.

Okay, let's go over to Power Man's place. He's invulnerable. He can be our practice dummy!

SHE-HULK

Jennifer Walters is **Bruce Banner's cousin**. She's also a brilliant lawyer devoted to putting criminals behind bars. One day Jen was attacked and injured by one of the crooks she was trying to convict. Jen needed an emergency blood transfusion, so Bruce donated some of his. Because they are family members and **share DNA**, Bruce's blood transferred powers that are similar to the Hulk's.

Unlike the Hulk, She-Hulk is able to keep her normal personality and intelligence when she is in a Hulked-out state. Jen continues to practice law.

Because of her She-Hulk powers, Jen cannot be harmed by gamma radiation.

SILVER SURFER

The brilliant alien scholar **Norrin Radd** was one of the most important thinkers on his planet, **Zenn-La**. One day the giant cosmic villain **Galactus** came to Zenn-La expecting to feed on its life energy, draining the planet and killing everyone on it. In order to save his world, Norrin sacrificed himself, promising to spend his life in the service of Galactus. Eventually, he escaped the grasp of Galactus and became a servant of good.

When Norrin became the herald (or servant) of Galactus, his body was covered in a silvery material to protect him when traveling in space. Additionally, he has the ability to blast cosmic energy. His surfboard-like space vehicle obeys his mental commands.

Silver Surfer has joined the **Fantastic Four** *in several key battles against Galactus.*

SMASHER

Izzy Dare is the granddaughter of British World War II hero Dan Dare. So it was only natural for Izzy to become a Super Hero when she discovered alien goggles that gave her powers. Dan was proud to see her follow in his footsteps. He introduced Izzy to his wartime friend, **Captain America**, who asked Izzy to join the **AVENGERS**.

Smasher's goggles give her the power to draw **cosmic energy** from the universe into herself and use it to achieve incredible feats of strength. She also uses alien antigravity patches to fly.

SPECTRUM

Monica Rambeau was a hard-as-nails cop in **New Orleans**. When she busted a criminal scientist experimenting with cosmic energy, Monica was exposed to the cosmic rays, which gave her powers. Though she was unsure how to use them, Monica knew she wanted to use them for good. She decided to join the **AVENGERS**.

Monica has the power to transform herself into any form of energy on the electromagnetic spectrum, which is how she gets her name: Spectrum. In her energy form, Spectrum can turn invisible.

SPIDER-MAN

"With great power comes great responsibility."
—Peter's Uncle Ben

Q&A

with Spider-Man:

Q: What's the best thing about being Spider-Man?

A: Helping people. That and the costume. It's a pretty great costume, right?

Q: What's the worst thing about being Spider-Man?

A: J. Jonah Jameson. He's the publisher of *The Daily Bugle* newspaper, and he's always calling me a "menace." If people read that enough, they'll believe it!

Q: Are you a menace?

A: Of course not! I'm just the friendly, neighborhood Spider-Man!

Spider-Man on the Roosevelt Island Tram, making his way to Manhattan.

Peter's former love interest, Gwen Stacy, studying for an exam.

Peter soon discovered that he had gained the proportionate strength and speed of a spider. He could stick to walls and easily climb buildings. Peter invented "web-shooters" to wear on his wrists. Spidey can shoot webs to capture bad guys and swing across the city.

The bullies at Midtown High called **Peter Parker** "Puny Parker" and made fun of him for being small, bad at sports, and really into science. Peter was able to put up with the bullying because he had a wonderful home life with his loving **Aunt May** and **Uncle Ben**. One day, while attending a science exhibition, Peter happened to be **bitten** by a **radioactive spider**. The spider bite gave Peter amazing powers!

Where are you, Peter? You were supposed to meet me and the gang ten minutes ago!

MJ. SORRY! The Goblin showed up.

Goblin? As in the Green Goblin?

Oh, uh, sorry. I meant, I'm GOBBLIN' up my food and will see you soon!

You're already eating? You're a bad friend!

129

SPIDER-MAN

Peter Parker was an ordinary teenager living with his Aunt May and Uncle Ben until he was bit by a radioactive spider! It gave him amazing strength and abilities. Initially, he used his powers for himself. One day, he witnessed a robbery but did nothing to stop it, despite his powers. The same robber he let go later killed his Uncle Ben in another crime. Since then, Peter has realized that with great power comes great responsibility and has become known as Spider-Man, leaving his ordinary teenage life behind.

SPIDER-WOMAN

While **Jessica Drew** was still in her scientist mother's womb, she was hit by a **wave of radiation** that was patterned after the DNA of several spiders. Jess was born with powers similar to those of **Spider-Man**. Once she was older, Jess was brainwashed by the evil organization known as **Hydra** and forced to go on missions for them, but thanks to **the Thing**, Jessica was able to break her mental programming and become a hero.

Like Spider-Man, Spider-Woman has the proportionate strength and speed of a spider, and can stick to surfaces. Unlike Spider-Man, Spider-Woman has heightened senses of hearing and smell, and can send jolts of electricity into people by touching them.

Hey—crazy story. This reporter asked me if we were dating.

Just because we have the same powers? LOL!

I KNOW.

I mean, can you imagine? Me. . .dating you? LOL! LOL!

Wait . . .why is that so funny?

SQUIRREL GIRL

Have you ever found that people weren't taking you seriously? Squirrel Girl had that same problem. Her mutant abilities made her look and act like she was **part rodent**, which seemed silly to other heroes. But when she was able to command a **small army of squirrels** to take down the evil **Doctor Doom**, people realized that she was a true hero.

Squirrel Girl is a mutant with enhanced abilities similar to those of a common squirrel. She has a long bushy tail that she can use to perform gymnastic moves, she has large buckteeth capable of chewing through almost anything, and she has the ability to communicate with squirrels.

Hey, girl, we should hang out.

 Uh, okay. . .What do you want to do?

I was thinking a forest hike!

 I'm more of a city person. Wanna grab coffee?

Okay, I guess. You think they'll have an acorn latte?

STAR-LORD

Q&A
with Star-Lord:

Q: What was it like to find out you were half alien?

A: Of course I was surprised at first. But once I thought about it, it made sense. I always felt like I was a little different from the people around me.

Q: People have said that the Guardians of the Galaxy is just a band of misfits.

A: Who said that? What are their names and addresses?

Q: But seriously, there doesn't seem to be much in common between the members of the Guardians. What makes you guys stay together?

A: Well, I guess it's true that we are all different from one another. But maybe different isn't always bad?

Q: Is it hard working on a team with a crazy space raccoon?

A: Don't let Rocket hear you call him a raccoon.

Captain Marvel, Star-Lord, Yon Rogg, and Cosmo on Knowhere.

Captain Marvel stops by to see Star-Lord about a dangerous mission.

Star-Lord uses a special weapon called an Element Gun. Based on the setting, Peter can project powerful blasts of earth, wind, fire, or water. Peter is half human, but he's also half Spartax.

Even when **Peter Quill** was a little boy on Earth, he always defended people in need. When he was a little older, Peter finally learned from his mother that his father was from another planet, called **Spartax**. Knowing that he had a father out in the stars drove Peter's life from that point on. He studied hard, designed his own spaceship, and eventually took off from Earth to explore space.

What have you done to my ship?

 Improved it!

You stripped it down to a pile of parts!

 Out of those parts I built, like, thirty different blasters.

I want my ship back!

 Settle down, humie. I'll give you one of the blasters.

STAR-LORD

Peter Quill always stood up against bullies no matter their size. And when he left Earth at a young age, he continued doing exactly that and defended the helpless throughout the galaxy. Soon, he became the leader of the team the Guardians of the Galaxy, which includes Rocket Raccoon, Groot, Drax, and Gamora.

STORM

Some of **Ororo Munroe's** ancestors, who were **Kenyan princesses**, had the ability to **control weather**. It was a power that was passed down to Ororo. Ororo always believed that her powers were born of magic, but when she met **Professor X**, he was able to explain that they were actually natural mutant abilities. Ororo joined the **X-MEN** in order to better train herself to control her powers. She quickly became one of the team's leaders.

Storm can **control all forms of weather**, creating rain, hail, lightning, thunder, wind, snow, heat, cold, and humidity at will. She can even make a sunny, clear day for picnics if she needs to.

I'll wager I can create more lightning than you.

I don't waste my powers on silly games.

Sounds like someone's afraid of losing a wager.

Taunting me won't trick me into doing what you want me to.

It always works on Hulk.

SUNSPOT

In his native country of Brazil, **Bobby da Costa** was a rising soccer star. One day when a close friend was attacked by a mob, Bobby jumped in to defend him. To Bobby's surprise, he became engulfed in black solar energy, which gave him incredible strength and speed. Bobby decided to skip out on his sports dreams and join the **NEW MUTANTS**.

When Bobby's body shifts into solar form, it takes on a solid black appearance that could be harmful to a normal human.

THE THING

Growing up in a tough New York City neighborhood, **Ben Grimm** developed a thick skin. But Ben's skin got even thicker when he was exposed to cosmic rays on an experimental space flight, which caused him to transform into a **rock monster**. Part of the **FANTASTIC FOUR**, Ben uses his rocky fists to land blows for justice!

Unlike the other members of the Fantastic Four, the Thing can't turn off his powers and look like a normal person.

THOR

Q&A
with Thor:

Q: Thor, you're a god from Asgard. What makes you stay on Earth?

A: I never meant to come to Earth, but once I did, I learned to love the people here.

Q: Will you ever return to Asgard to stay?

A: Aye, I am prince and will one day need to serve as king. But Odin is strong, and I do not expect to replace him for many centuries.

Q: Why join the Avengers?

A: The Avengers are valiant warriors. I am proud to call them comrades-in-arms!

Q: Who is stronger, you or your good friend Hulk?

A: Hulk is, of course. . . . HA! I jest! I am, clearly.

Thor in a battle fighting alongside the Avengers.

Thor and Wasp enjoying a holiday party with fellow Avengers.

Even for an Asgardian, Thor is incredibly strong. As the God of Thunder, Thor can use his battle hammer, called **Mjolnir**, to summon lightning blasts at will. Thor can also spin and hurl Mjolnir in a way that gives him the power of flight.

Thor, **the God of Thunder**, was born the son of **Odin**, the ruler of a magical realm called **Asgard**. As a prince, Thor knew that one day he would be **king**. Thor grew up to be a brave warrior, and he thought that his accomplishments on the battle-field meant that he would be a great king. But Odin saw that his son was prideful and self-ish. Odin exiled his son to Earth in hopes that living among humans would teach him the humility he badly needed.

Thor's greatest enemy is his own brother. Loki grew up in the shadow of Thor. Thor was so good at everything, and Loki always took second place. Loki even believed that their father, Odin, loved Thor more than he loved Loki.

THOR

Before he joined the Avengers, Thor was a mighty opponent and a haughty Asgardian prince not worthy of the throne. His father, Odin, banished him to Earth until he proved worthy. During his time on Earth, he went under the name of Donald Blake and learned to be humble. Once he proved himself, Thor returned to Asgard to the dismay of his brother, Loki. Sibling rivalry is a bit different when your younger brother decides he wants your throne for himself—and Earth, too! The thunder god has sworn to protect Earth, his new home, with his hammer, Mjolnir.

TRITON

Triton is one of the **INHUMANS**, a species of beings that shares ancestors with modern humans, but who are granted special powers by means of a substance called the **Terrigen Mists**. A skilled tracker both on land and in water, Triton is trusted by **King Black Bolt** to find any Inhumans who might go missing.

Exposure to the Terrigen Mists granted Triton an amphibian-type body, gills, and the ability to breathe underwater. However, now when traveling on land, Triton must wear a hydration suit in order to breathe.

Inhuman relations:
Triton is the brother of Karnak.
A cousin of Crystal.
A cousin of Black Bolt, king of the Inhumans.

VALKYRIE

The Valkyrior is a race of winged **Asgardian warriors**. Chief among them is a powerful soldier named **Brunnhilde**. Brunnhilde has the unique ability to become a spirit form and enter into the body of human hosts. Several human beings have served as manifestations of Brunnhilde through the years.

Valkyrie has a special sword named **Dragonfang**, which was carved from the tooth of an extra-dimensional dragon. The indestructible sword was given to Valkyrie by the sorcerer **Doctor Strange.**

Valkyrie has used her powers in order to support members of the Super Hero team known as the Invaders, including Captain America, Namor, and the Human Torch.

VISION

Q&A
with Vision:

Q: You're just an android, but you claim to be actually alive?

A: I don't have to make any claims, I just am.

Q: But how can you prove that you are a living being?

A: How can you prove that you are?

Q: I'm a human being. I think. I feel.

A: I do those things, too.

Q: You were created by Ultron. How can we know you can be trusted?

A: As a hero, I choose to let my actions speak for my character.

Ultron, a robot Super Villain, wanted to replace **"flawed humans"** with an android of his own creation, named Vision. Ultron saw Vision as an improved version of humanity, but Vision knew that destroying humankind was wrong. He joined the **AVENGERS** in order to defeat Ultron. Vision is such an advanced form of machine that he is the first true artificial life form with independent thoughts and feelings.

Vision can fly, pass through solid objects, become hard as a diamond, and use heat vision to melt through steel. He is a loyal and trusted member of the Avengers.

VOLSTAGG

Like the other members of the **WARRIORS THREE**, Volstagg loves travel, adventure, and valiant combat. But unlike the others, Volstagg also appreciates the finer things in life—**like a good meal**. Always ready for feasting and merriment, Volstagg has a boastful mouth that often gets him, and his companions, into trouble. Volstagg has accompanied **Thor** on many adventures.

Volstagg's Top 5 Favorite Meals:

5) Roasted mutton

4) Roasted goat

3) More roasted mutton

2) Roasted bilgesnipe

1) Roasted anything, anytime, anywhere

Like all Asgardians, Volstagg is stronger, tougher, and longer-lived than the average human. He was trained in the arts of war in the Asgardian Learning Hall.

WARLOCK

The mysterious cosmic entity known as Warlock is devoted to protecting the universe from those who wish to rule or destroy it. Warlock focuses on ensuring that the most powerful items in the universe, called the **Infinity Stones**, are never used for evil. This has brought him into direct conflict with **Thanos**, an **intergalactic warlord** who seeks the Stones.

When the intergalactic warlord Thanos tried to gather the most powerful items in the universe, the Infinity Stones, it was Adam Warlock who assembled the universe's most powerful beings in order to stop him.

Warlock uses **Quantum Magic** to manipulate energy, create force fields, teleport, produce wormholes, and travel faster than light. If badly injured, he can create a healing cocoon around himself.

WASP

Q&A
with Wasp:

Q: Wasp! Is it true that there was once a time when everyone thought you were dead?

A: Yeah, that was a crazy time.

Q: What happened?

A: A while back we were fighting an invasion of shape-shifting aliens called the Skrull and I got sucked through a portal, but to those watching it looked like I'd disintegrated.

Q: Where were you?

A: I shrank down to a size smaller than an atom and slipped into a dimension called the Microverse.

Q: Whoa, what's down there?

A: More bad guys, it turns out!

Q: There's never any rest for an Avenger, I guess.

A: Guess not.

Wasp celebrating with fellow Avengers at a holiday party.

Black Widow and Wasp exchanging gifts at Avengers mansion.

Thanks to Dr. Pym, Janet gained the ability to both shrink to **insect size** and to grow to **giant size**. She also grew wings, giving her the ability to fly, and started to shoot small blasts from her hands that acted like a bee stings.

Janet Van Dyne needed help solving the mysterious murder of her father, a famous scientist, so she went to **Dr. Hank Pym**. Pym, the original **Ant-Man**, was a fan of Janet's father's work and wanted to assist her. He gave her some of the same **Pym Particles** that he used to shrink to the size of an ant. Once she had shrunk down, Janet found evidence that the police had missed and brought her father's killer to justice.

*Like Ant-Man, Wasp joined the **Avengers**, proving that even the smallest among us can make a big difference in the world.*

WHITE TIGER

For generations, there has been a hero known as White Tiger, wielding tiger-like abilities in order to protect the world. The current White Tiger, teenager **Ava Ayala**, is the fifth person to assume the role. Her father, who was the third White Tiger, passed on to her the **mystical tiger amulet** that grants super powers after her brother, the fourth White Tiger, died in combat with the villain known as **Kraven the Hunter**.

White Tiger's mystical amulet grants her superhuman strength, speed, stamina, balance, endurance, and reflexes. White Tiger must hold on firmly to her amulet. If she ever loses it, her powers instantly disappear.

White Tiger is known to regularly team up with:

Spider-Man

Iron Fist

Power Man

Nova

WINTER SOLDIER

As a U.S. soldier in World War II, **James "Bucky" Barnes** fought side by side with his childhood friend, **Captain America**. During an important battle, Bucky gave his life to save Cap. . . .Or at least he thought he was giving his life. Instead, a mysterious villain retrieved Bucky, brought him back to life, and brainwashed him into becoming a deadly assassin known as the Winter Soldier.

To revive the Winter Soldier, doctors gave him the best simulation they could make of the **Super-Soldier Serum** that gave Cap his strength. The serum wasn't perfect, but it did enhance the Winter Soldier's natural abilities.

After several attempts, Captain America was finally able to break through the Winter Soldier's mental conditioning and remind him of the hero he really is.

WOLVERINE

"I'm the best at what I do, and what I do isn't very nice."

—Wolverine

Q&A
with Wolverine:

Q: I've been told that you're a real loner.

A: That's right, bub. I prefer to work alone.

Q: And yet, you're a member of the X-Men, a team?

A: Professor X asked me to join. I owe that man a lot, and I believe in loyalty. I'm not going to turn him down.

Q: So now that you have to work with a team, what do you think of it?

A: I think I work better alone.

James "Logan" Howlett
was born in Canada in 1882.
Because of his special mutant
healing factor, the hero that
came to be known as Wolverine
can survive otherwise fatal
injuries with ease. Evil men who
wished to use Wolverine as a
weapon kidnapped him and
erased his memory. They also
put him through an extremely
painful process in order to
bond the unbreakable metal
adamantium to his skeleton.
Adamantium now covers even
Wolverine's bone claws.

Because of his advanced healing capability,
Wolverine has lived an incredibly long life. Watching
all the people he's loved grow old and die made
him believe he would always be alone, but then
Professor X found him and asked him to join the
X-MEN. Professor X helped Logan get his memory
back and finally gave him a home.

Many members of the X-Men,
including their leader, Cyclops,
questioned Professor X's decision to ask Wolverine to join them.
But through his heroic actions,
Wolverine has proven many times
over that he is one of the greatest
X-Men of all.

155

WONDER MAN

A business rival of Tony Stark's, **Simon Williams** hated Iron Man so much that he agreed to undergo radiation treatments from the evil **Baron Zemo**. The treatments gave Simon super strength, speed, and the ability to fly. Wonder Man attacked the Avengers, but lost so badly that he wound up in a coma. When he woke, the Avengers actually helped him get better. Wonder Man was so grateful that he not only changed his ways, he actually became an **AVENGER!**

Super powers don't have to be used only for heroics. Simon, a handsome man, used his fame as a Super Hero to land leading roles in major **Hollywood** movies. Studios loved working with Wonder Man, because, since he used his own super powers, they didn't have to spend as much money on special effects.

Wonder Man's Top 5 Movie Roles:

5) *The Termanoid in* Robot Attack

4) *Sheik Painful in* The Fighting Sheik

3) *Robin Hood in* Robin Hood Meets the Mummy

2) *Himself in* Wonder Man: A True Story

1) *Himself in* Wonder Man 2

XAVIER
(AKA PROFESSOR X)

While he was still just a little boy, the powerful mutant telepath **Charles Xavier** learned that he could **read minds**. Concerned about the way humans and mutants were struggling to get along, Charles decided to devote his life to creating a peaceful mutant-human coexistence. He founded **the Xavier School for Gifted Young-sters** to train mutants in how to best use their powers. Professor X is an inspiration to mutants everywhere.

Professor X started both the ***X-Men*** *and the* ***New Mutants*** *because he believed that if humans could see mutants acting as heroes, they might become more accepting of his kind.*

With the help of a device called **Cerebro**, Professor X has used his mind to locate mutants across the globe in hopes of recruiting them for his school. He has tried to give young mutants a comfortable place to call home, so they can become the best people they can possibly be.

THE X-MEN

Because humans seemed readier than ever to hate and fear the X-Men, **Professor Charles Xavier** created a team to help train mutants in how to use their powers and to help prove to humans that they could be heroes. The X-Men quickly became the most influential team of **mutants**, serving as an inspiration to countless others just like them, and helping humans and mutants to better get along.

The founding members of the X-Men were **Cyclops**, the leader; **Marvel Girl**, the psychic; **Beast**, the monstrous scientist; **Angel**, the winged warrior; and **Iceman**, one cool dude.

Later additions to the team included:

1) *Wolverine*

2) *Nightcrawler*

3) *Psylocke*

4) *Storm*

5) *Gambit*

6) *Rogue*

7) *Banshee*

Among many others

INDEX

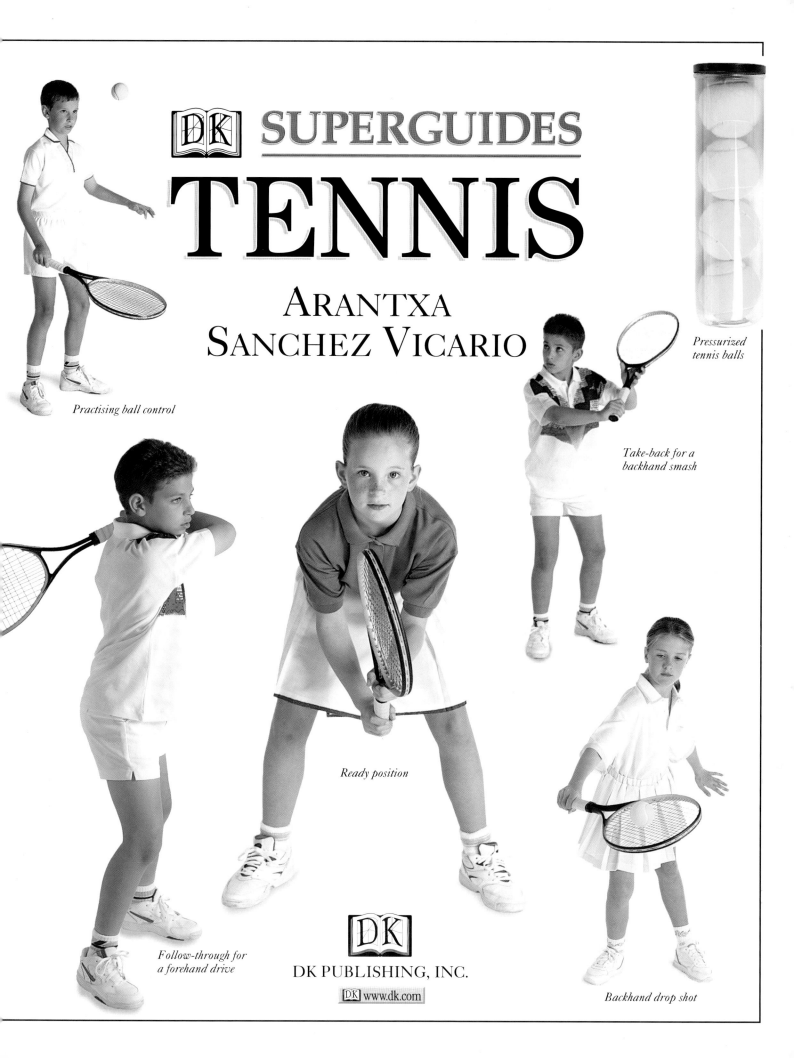

DK SUPERGUIDES
TENNIS

ARANTXA
SANCHEZ VICARIO

Practising ball control

Pressurized tennis balls

Take-back for a backhand smash

Ready position

Follow-through for a forehand drive

DK
DK PUBLISHING, INC.

DK www.dk.com

Backhand drop shot

A DORLING KINDERSLEY BOOK

DK www.dk.com

Editor Francesca Stich   **Art editor** Rebecca Johns
Project editor Fiona Robertson
Photography Matthew Ward
Picture research Sharon Southren
Production Charlotte Traill
Deputy editorial director Sophie Mitchell
Deputy art director Miranda Kennedy

The young tennis players
Nick Çava Day, Tom Cowley, Bea Guard, Nick Hamnabard, Jessica London,
Faye Mason, Vishal Nayyar, Namita Shah, and Steven Vance

First American Edition, 2000
2 4 6 8 10 9 7 5 3

Published in the United States by
Dorling Kindersley Publishing, Inc.
95 Madison Avenue
New York, NY 10016

ISBN: 0-7894-5434-3

Color reproduction by Colourscan, Singapore
Printed and bound in Italy by L.E.G.O.

Contents

To all young players

" TENNIS HAS ALWAYS BEEN part of my life. As the youngest in a family with four professional tennis players, I began to play tennis when I was four years old. I valued the time and advice that people gave me and began to spend every spare minute on a tennis court. I decided to make a career out of the game and turned professional ten years later, at the age of 14. When I was 17, I won my first Grand Slam title, the French Open. In 1994, I won the French Open again, as well as the US Open, and was ranked Number One in the world that year. If you are a tennis enthusiast, I know you'll enjoy reading this book. Tennis is a 'sport for all,' and whatever your ability, this book will improve your understanding and increase your enjoyment of the game. "

Arantxa Sánchez Vicario

Buzzing with confidence

Determination is one of the most important skills a professional tennis player must learn. My opponents nicknamed me "the Bumblebee" because of my determined spirit and the speed with which I move around the court.

This is a cross court shot with topspin.

This shows the flight of a short, angled shot.

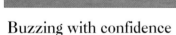

Talking tactics

In addition to the amazing step-by-step photography throughout this book, you will see these diagrams. I have tried to give you tactical advice on each of your shots. Remember, however, that as your game improves, you will learn your own strengths and weaknesses and develop your favorite shots.

Left-handed players

Whenever you see this sign, the pictures show a left-handed player.

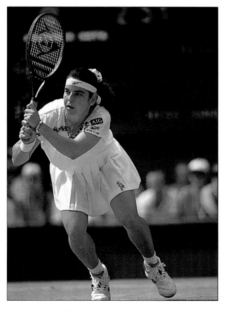

Olympic Games

When I was at the 1992 Olympic Games, Conchita Martinez and I won a silver medal in the doubles competition. I also earned a bronze medal in the women's singles. This was especially nice since the 1992 Olympics were held in my home country.

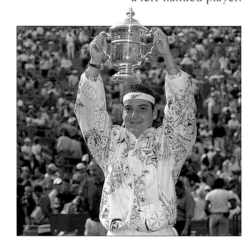

At the US Open

Here I am holding the trophy at the US Open. In 1994, I won both the singles and the doubles titles at the US Open. I am the first player to achieve both wins at once since Martina Navratilova in 1987.

History of tennis

FROM THE GREEK wall paintings of Themistocles we know that an ancient form of tennis was played as far back as 500 BC. During the 15th century Real, or Royal, tennis was developed in France from a game called *Jeu de Paume* (game of the palm). Real tennis was originally played in monastery cloisters and is still occasionally played by enthusiasts. Lawn tennis, or tennis as we know it today, became popular during Queen Victoria's reign, when it was played on the lawns of stately homes. It was not until the early 1870s that tennis was played as a serious sport. The first tennis championships were held at the All England Croquet and Lawn Tennis Club at Wimbledon, London, in July 1877. Some 200 spectators watched the first men's final. More than 15,000 fill the center court stands at Wimbledon now.

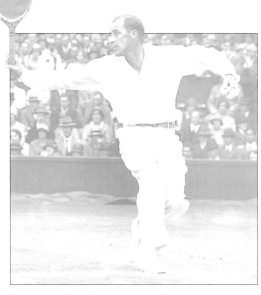

International team tennis
The first international team competition was the Davis Cup in 1900. During the 1920s, Bill Tilden of America never lost a singles match in the Davis Cup challenge rounds. For many years only Britain, France, Australia, and America took part. Today, more than 100 countries participate in the Davis Cup.

Young Americans
May Sutton of America was only 18 years old when she won her first Wimbledon title in 1905. Here, you can see just how much tennis equipment and clothing have changed over the last century.

Skirt sensation
In the 1920s, tennis became very popular. Suzanne Lenglen of France, seen here winning the women's singles at Wimbledon in 1922, was the first woman to wear a shorter dress and short sleeves. Lenglen was also one of the first players to turn professional.

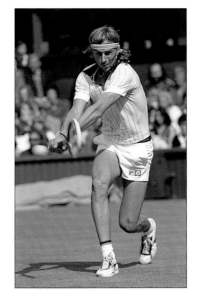

Sporting hero
Bjorn Borg of Sweden won the Wimbledon men's singles for five years running (from 1976 through 1980). Only two other men have achieved this.

19th century tennis set
Most early racket frames were made from one solid piece of ash wood like the one above. Today they are made from carbon graphite or fiberglass. Rackets can still be any weight or shape, but must measure less than 32 in (81.28 cm) long and 12.5 in (31.75 cm) across.

Tennis today
For professional players, tennis is a way of life. Some professionals will travel the world 20 times in their career. There are dozens of tournaments every year and I have even represented my country at the Olympics. I miss my home in Andorra, but playing tennis is very satisfying and the rewards compensate for the time I dedicate to the game.

Getting started

ANYONE CAN START to play tennis. All you need is a borrowed tennis racket, an old tennis ball, and a wall to hit against. If you enjoy this, then invite a friend to play on a court at your local playground or park. To become more experienced, you may want to join a tennis club that has a good junior coaching program. As you start to play more regularly, your game will improve. At this stage you might want to get your own equipment. The two most important items are your racket and suitable tennis shoes.

If you have long hair, keep it tied back away from your face.

Polo shirts are traditional and popular tennis wear.

Boys' clothes
Tennis clothes should be loose-fitting and made from natural, lightweight materials. In order to keep within the standard rules of most tennis clubs, you should wear mainly white shorts, socks, and a shirt. Sometimes you can wear patterned shirts or partially colored clothes. To begin with, your school sports gear will probably be fine.

Tennis shoes
Comfortable, well-made tennis shoes are extremely important. Cushioning in the sole will reduce the amount of vibration to your ankles and legs when you are running. The shoes should also support your insteps and the tendons at the backs of your heels. Buy shoes that are suitable for indoor and outdoor court surfaces.

Shorts should have pockets to keep a spare ball.

A leather upper will be more hard-wearing than canvas.

Reinforced toe cap protects the shoe and your toes.

Athletic socks absorb sweat and give extra cushioning.

Perforations in the shoe allow air to circulate and keep your foot cool!

A lightweight but sturdy rubber sole is designed to provide maximum grip.

Shoe size
Make sure you buy shoes that are the right size or you may get blisters.

A thermal racket carrier protects your rackets when you're not using them. The shoulder strap makes it easy to carry and there is also a compartment for balls.

Girls' clothes
The same mainly white clothing rule applies to girls as well as boys. Most girls wear either a tennis dress or a skirt with a shirt, but you can wear a pair of shorts if you prefer. Do not wear jewelry as it can catch in your clothing.

Sweatbands
Wear elastic terry cloth wrist-bands to absorb perspiration while you are playing tennis.

Skincare
Use a hat and sun-block to protect your skin from the sun when playing outside.

Racket strings
Most rackets are now strung with synthetic strings rather than gut strings, which tend to be affected by temperature.

The racket head
The bigger the racket head, the better the hitting area on the strings. This area is called the "sweet spot." However, an oversized head can be difficult to control.

Your tracksuit can be any color or material. Natural fabrics, like cotton, are better than synthetic ones.

When buying a tracksuit, make sure it is big enough to allow plenty of movement.

The strings are woven over each other and are threaded through the holes in the racket frame.

The racket handle
The racket handle is usually covered in a grip of leather or synthetic rubber. After a lot of use, you may need to replace the grip with either an overgrip (shown below) or a padded grip.

Elastic wrist- and waistbands are more comfortable and let you stretch farther.

The sweet spot is located just below the center of the strings.

An overgrip will give you a better "feel" for the racket.

The butt is the very end of the handle.

Tennis balls
Once you are playing regularly it is important to use good quality balls. Pressurized balls are best, but soon lose their bounce. Keep a good supply of new balls on hand. It can damage your game to play with "dead" balls.

A ball clip is useful if you have no pockets.

Make sure you can slip your tracksuit off over your shoes.

A large bag will carry your clothes, a towel, and anything else you may need.

Ball covering
The rubber inner of a tennis ball is covered with a mixture of wool and artificial fibers.

Tracksuit
It is important to wear a tracksuit before, as you begin, and after playing tennis. This will warm up and cool down your body temperature slowly, preventing pulled muscles and other injuries.

The court and game

WHEN YOU STEP OUT on the court to play a match, you will need to understand some basic rules of tennis. Try to learn what all the court markings are for – these are the boundaries that limit your drives, volleys, and serves. Decide who will serve first by tossing a coin or spinning a racket. Then know when and where to return the ball to score. Also observe the unwritten rules about behavior and etiquette. Most importantly, be fair and honest at all times, especially when calling the score after a point.

Court surfaces

Tennis can be played on a variety of court surfaces, each of which affect the bounce of the ball in a different way. A slow court is one with a rough surface, such as clay. This makes the ball bounce higher and more slowly. A fast court surface, such as grass, is one that causes the ball to skid quickly as it bounces.

Singles sideline, 39 ft (11.89 m) long

Baseline center mark, small T

Short tennis

If you find full-sized tennis difficult at first, you could learn to play short tennis. This will help you develop your tennis strokes and teach you how to move and position yourself on the court. Short tennis is played using lightweight rackets and sponge balls. It is played on a badminton court, which is considerably smaller than a full-sized tennis court, with a baseline of only 20 ft (6.1 m) and a sideline of 44 ft (13.4 m). There are only 11 points in a game, but the game must be won by two clear points after the score reaches 10-10. Once you have mastered short tennis, you can move on to play transition tennis (see opposite page).

SHORT TENNIS

For short tennis, the badminton net is lowered to 2 ft 7 in (78 cm).

The short tennis court has no alleys or service boxes.

Tennis scoring system

Game Starting at 0, or "love," one player must win four points, called 15, 30, 40, and game.

Deuce If the score is deuce (40-40), the game continues until one player wins by two clear points: the advantage point, then the game point. If you lose the advantage point, the score returns to deuce.

Set The first player to win six games wins the set, but the winner must be at least two clear games in front. If the score in a set reaches 5-5, play seven games. If it is 6-6, play the first to seven points (a tiebreak), and whichever player wins the tiebreak wins the game and set.

Match A match is usually the best of three sets (five sets in men's professional matches).

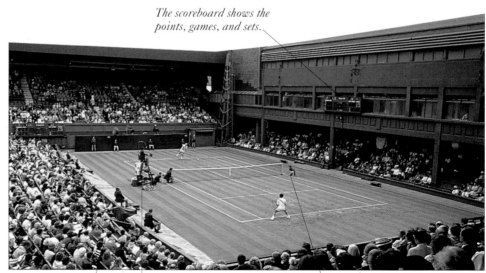

The scoreboard shows the points, games, and sets.

The linesmen and lineswomen are positioned around the court to call faults.

The umpire has a good view of the court from a high chair next to the net. The umpire's decision is final, and he or she announces the score after every point.

The ball boys and girls pick up every loose ball.

Left, or second, service court, 21 ft (6.4 m) x 13.5 ft (4.11 m)

Center service line, 21 ft (6.4 m)

Net, 3 ft (0.91 m) high in the center

Net post, 3 ft 6 in (1.07 m) high

Right, or first, service court

Service line, 27 ft (8.23 m) long

Baseline for transition tennis would lie across the middle of the court here.

Baseline, 36 ft (10.97 m) long

Alley, 4.5 ft (1.37 m) wide

Doubles sideline 78 ft (23.77 m) long

Transition tennis

As its name suggests, this is a step between short tennis and standard tennis. It is played on a full-sized singles tennis court with temporary baselines midway between the service line and baseline, making the court only 60 ft (18.29 m) long. Matches can be played to short tennis or standard tennis rules.

Line calling

When you play friendly or junior tournament matches, you usually make your own line calls. Judge as best as you can if the ball lands out and call it right away. If any part of the ball lands on the line, it is in, and you must play on. If there is a line call disagreement, then play the point again. This is called a let (a second chance).

Only this ball is out because all the others are touching the line.

Serving rules

The first serve of every game is taken from the right-hand side of the court. Stand behind the baseline and serve diagonally so that the ball bounces into your opponent's right service box. Alternate from right to left courts to serve for every new point. Each player serves for a full game, swapping ends after every other game. If the serve hits the top of the net and lands in, then a let is called, and the serve is taken again.

Positive thinking

When I am on the court I try to concentrate completely on my game and put my determination into every shot in order to win. If I lose a point, I try to put it out of my mind immediately. Thinking too much about a mistake can cause you to play another point badly. Keep calm, take each point as it comes, and play it as best you can. All professionals learn to think like this, and if you want to do well, so should you.

Court etiquette

Tennis is a very competitive sport and sometimes players find it difficult to control their behavior on the court. Never argue over a line call. Settle for a let if you disagree with your opponent and play the point again. Although it is important to be friendly, don't let your opponent walk all over you. Try to be fair and play your best game. Whether you win or lose, thank your opponent for playing.

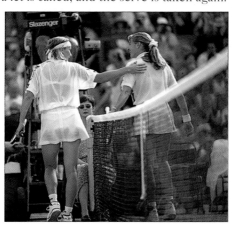

Preparing to play

BEFORE YOU START playing tennis, you should go through a stretching and movement routine to warm up. Warming up will loosen your muscles and joints, making you more flexible, which can help prevent injury. It will also make your heart beat faster, which will prepare you to move more quickly and stretch farther on the court. Going through a warm-up routine before a match can help you concentrate. There are also exercises you can practice at the side of the court to test your reactions and speed – footwork and timing are essential skills!

Groin stretch

This exercise will stretch your inner leg and groin area. Sit on the ground, bring the soles of your shoes together, and pull your ankles toward your body. To increase the stretch try pushing down slowly and gently on your knees with your elbows. Hold the position for 20 seconds, then relax. Repeat three times.

Keep your back straight.

Keep your ankles on the floor.

Leg stretch

This exercise stretches your hamstrings at the back of your legs. Sit on the ground with your legs stretched out in front of you. With the backs of your knees on the floor, reach for your toes. If you cannot touch your toes, then reach as far as you can. Hold the position for 20 seconds, then relax. Repeat three times.

Keep your feet together and the backs of your knees against the floor.

Shoulder stretch

Warm up your upper arm and shoulder area with this exercise. Stand upright and, using one arm, try to touch the bottom of your shoulder blade. Use the other hand to pull back gently on the elbow of your bent arm. Keep your head up and hold the position for 20 seconds. Repeat three times with each arm.

Keep your back straight throughout this exercise.

Figure eights

Improve your footwork and agility with this exercise. Place two tennis balls on the floor 3 ft (1 m) apart. Move as quickly as you can in a figure-eight pattern around the balls. Take small steps and stay low to help you keep your balance. Count how many times you can complete the figure eight in a minute, then change direction and do the same exercise the other way.

Face forward while moving.

Move smoothly
When stretching it is important never to bounce or jerk the movement.

Use your hands for balance.

Keep your knees bent.

Keeping your steps small, run as close to the tennis balls as you can.

Try not to lean forward.

Side stretch

To stretch your waist and stomach muscles, stand upright with your feet shoulder-width apart. Place your right hand on your hip and lean to your right, keeping your feet on the floor. Bring your left arm over to increase the stretch. Hold for 20 seconds, then do the same exercise on your left side. Repeat three times.

Quick reactions

To develop fast reactions you need to do exercises that test the speed at which you can move to the ball. Try the following game with a friend. Take turns catching the ball.

1 Your partner holds the ball out in front of her body while you rest your hand lightly on top of her hand.

Make sure the ball is facing the ground.

Stay on your toes.

2 At any time, your partner can drop the ball. You have to try to catch the ball before it bounces. If you find this difficult at first, ask your partner to hold the ball up higher.

Bring your hand under the ball as it drops.

Keep your feet apart to help you balance.

Watch the ball closely.

Both balls should be in the air at the same time.

Basic ball sense

Develop your hand-eye coordination with a partner by standing about 6 ft (2 m) apart and throwing each other a ball at the same time. Aim the ball carefully and throw underarm. To make it more difficult, clap or turn around before catching the ball.

Keep your knees bent.

Keep your feet shoulder-width apart for balance.

Ball control

To help your hitting coordination, bounce a ball up off your racket strings. Count how many times in a row you can hit the ball. To make it more difficult, try the same exercise without moving your feet. Hit the ball higher if you need more time.

Try to keep the racket between shoulder and knee height.

Crossover steps

In tennis, it is important to move quickly and with good footwork while keeping your balance at all times. To test your footwork and coordination, practice side-stepping along the baseline. Continue until you reach the end of the line, then do the opposite to travel back. Repeat three times.

1 From a standing position, travel to your left by bringing your right leg over in front of your left leg.

Leg tension
Try to bend your knees when you cross your legs and straighten them when you sidestep.

2 Bring your left leg across and into a wide sidestep.

Always face forward and keep your head still while you are moving.

Stay on your toes.

3 Bring your right leg across behind your left leg. Take another wide side-step with your left leg.

Use your hands for balance.

Try to step lightly.

Handling the racket

WHEN YOU START PLAYING tennis, it is important that you learn how to handle your racket properly. Try to choose a racket that is suitable for your age and size; it should feel like a natural extension of your arm and hand. Junior rackets come pre-strung and measure from 21 to 26 in (52 to 64 cm) in length. They also vary in frame thickness, or width, from narrow- to wide-bodied and tend to be very light. When you hold the handle, there should be a small gap between the top of your little finger and the heel of your hand. The more comfortable the racket feels, the better you will hit the ball. The action of hitting the ball is called a stroke, and has three main stages: the preparation or take-back, the hit, and the follow-through.

Lightweight wide-bodied junior racket

Wide-bodied rackets are currently the lightest and most powerful type of racket. The broad side-on width makes them stronger than slimmer models.

Racket frame

Cross strings run across the racket.

The grommet strip protects the strings.

Top plane, or top edge

There should be a small space between the little finger and the palm of your hand.

Racket shoulder

Left edge

Butt end

Right edge

Racket head

Main strings run lengthwise.

The middle main strings are threaded through the bridge of the racket.

The throat of the racket affects the flexibility in the frame.

Forehand grips

The way a stroke feels when you hit the ball, and the effect that the stroke has on the ball, largely depends on how you are holding the racket. This is called your racket grip. There are three main forehand grips: eastern, continental, and western. Each grip can be changed slightly for comfort. Hold the racket with your hand toward the butt end of the handle. This will give you room to add your other hand for two-handed grips. All grips are the same for left-handed players; follow these instructions using your left hand, remembering that the right edge of the racket becomes the left edge, and vice versa.

Eastern forehand grip

This is a very natural grip used to hit the ball at any height flat, or with topspin or slice. Simply shake hands with the racket. The "V" between your index finger and thumb should be on the right edge of the racket handle. Spread your index finger up the racket handle for more support.

Keep the heel of your hand at the butt end of the racket. Place your palm behind the handle for extra support.

Continental grip

Use this grip to tackle low balls. Place the "V" made by your thumb and index finger so that it is slightly to the left of center on the top edge of the handle. You may find it difficult to hit topspin with this grip.

Note the "V" between index finger and thumb.

Western forehand grip

This grip was developed in California, where cement courts make the ball bounce high. Use a western forehand grip for heavy topspin and to hit high-bouncing balls. Move the "V" toward the right edge of the handle. Place the knuckle of your index finger so that it is underneath the handle and wrap your thumb around the top.

Your wrist will be naturally bent backward by this grip.

Semi-western forehand grip

This grip is a modified western grip in which your wrist position is less exaggerated. Use this grip for extra topspin and to hit high-bouncing balls. The "V" between your finger and thumb should sit on the right edge of the handle. The knuckle of your index finger should be on the lower right edge, and your thumb should wrap around the handle.

It is difficult to hit low, wide balls using the semi-western forehand grip.

Backhand grips

There are two ways of holding the racket for a backhand stroke: one-handed or two-handed. Most players use a two-handed grip for extra support and power on their backhand. This also avoids making a grip change after playing a forehand shot. If you do find that you prefer to use one hand, always try to change your grip so you don't bend your wrist awkwardly when adding topspin to a stroke. If you are playing a sliced backhand, try to use a continental or an eastern backhand grip.

Eastern backhand grip

Eastern backhand is used for topspin and slice. Place the "V" on the left edge of the handle and the knuckle of your index finger on the upper left edge of the racket. Wrap your thumb around the handle.

Spread your index finger slightly up the handle for extra strength and flexibility.

Strong eastern backhand grip

Use this grip for heavy topspin. Place the knuckle of your index finger on the top edge of the handle and the "V" at the bottom left. If you use a strong eastern backhand grip, be aware that you need time for a greater change of grip (see page 21) between strokes.

Two-handed grip without change

This can only be done if you use an eastern grip for your forehand drive. With your playing hand in an eastern forehand grip at the butt end of the handle, simply add the other hand, also using eastern forehand. Be aware that a two-handed grip limits your reach for wide balls, and in those cases it is best to play a one-handed shot. If you usually play with a western or semi-western forehand grip, then you will need to change your grip for a two-handed backhand.

Two-handed grip with change

This grip change is especially useful for hitting heavy topspin on your backhand and can be effective when receiving a high-bouncing ball. With your playing hand in either an eastern backhand or strong eastern backhand grip, place your other hand higher on the handle in an eastern forehand or semi-western forehand grip.

Mirror image
Try holding a mirror alongside these pictures to see the left-handed positions on the handle.

Modified continental grip

This grip is ideal for volleying because you won't have time to change your grip between backhand and forehand shots. It is the best grip for serving because it allows for plenty of wrist action. However, you will need a strong wrist. Place the "V" between your finger and thumb in the center of the top edge of the handle. This is also known as the "chopper" grip because if you imagine you are chopping wood with the racket edge, your hand will naturally grip the handle correctly.

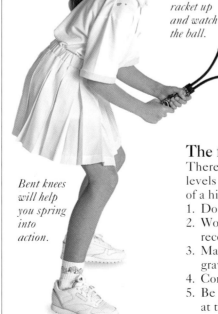

Hold your racket up and watch the ball.

Bent knees will help you spring into action.

Ready position

Once you have mastered how to hold your racket, you are ready to start playing. One of the most basic positions in tennis is the ready position. It is used to receive the serve and as a "home base" position between shots. Your ready position should be relaxed and focused, with knees bent and toes prepared to push off the ground in reaction to your opponent's shot. Keep your racket central so that you can prepare it quickly on either side.

The five fundamental skills

There are five basic skills that players of all ages and levels should try to develop in order to produce strokes of a high standard.
1. Do not take your eyes off the ball.
2. Work for speedy footwork to the ball and a quick recovery for the next shot.
3. Maintain good balance, keeping a low center of gravity and a still head.
4. Control your racket swing, throw, or punch.
5. Be aware of the height and angle of your racket face at the point of contact with the ball.

Forehand drive

THERE ARE TWO TYPES of ground strokes: forehand drive and backhand drive. Ground strokes are played after the ball has bounced once. For most players, the forehand drive is the strongest stroke. It is probably the stroke you will learn first. Try to develop this stroke so that you can rely on it for rallying and attacking. Aim for a relaxed and well-timed swinging action that feels natural, not forced.

Positioning your feet
If you are right-handed, step forward with your left foot (shown as violet); if you are left-handed, step with your right foot. This is called your front foot, and you use it to position yourself sideways-on to the ball. If you use a more open stance, step behind with your front foot (shown as blue).

Your forehand
Concentrate on each stage of your stroke: the take-back, hit, and follow-through. Remember the five basic skills (see page 17) to produce a smooth, controlled action.

Turn your shoulders as you bring your racket back.

Cocked wrist
Keep your wrist cocked back and lead with the butt end of the racket as you start to swing forward.

Try using an eastern forehand grip.

1 Stand in the ready position with your knees bent. Watch the ball and prepare your forehand grip as you move to make your shot.

2 In a low, compact position, start to take your racket back early. Guide it with your free hand to help turn your shoulders.

3 Take your racket back above shoulder height. The racket should form a natural loop as you bring it through to hit the ball.

Keep your knees bent.

Open stance forehand drive
When reaching for a wide forehand, many players like to hit the ball in less of a side-on position. This stance is useful for hitting a high-bouncing ball with a western or semi-western grip, but it is difficult to use for low shots. Open stance also helps disguise the direction of your shot. Step forward slightly with your front foot, but keep the weight on your back foot. As you swing through with your racket, push with your back leg so you "throw" your weight forward into the ball.

Turn your shoulders and take your racket back fully.

Step forward with your front foot.

Push with your back leg.

Quickly rotate your shoulders for extra power.

Step forward with your front foot.

Topspin

Hitting a ball with topspin causes the ball to kick up after it bounces. A forehand drive with topspin can make the ball rise high over the net and deep into your opponent's court. Take the racket back as normal, but this time drop it into a deep loop so it is below the height of the approaching ball. Swing the racket upward, brushing up behind the back of the ball, and follow through over the other shoulder.

Keep the racket head low and aim to hit the ball in front of your leading hip.

Bend your knees.

Turn your shoulders quickly to hit the ball harder.

Mastering topspin

Use the top edge of the racket to brush upward behind the back of the ball. The faster the racket moves, the more spin it will generate.

Turn your shoulders

Point toward the ball with your free hand. This keeps your shoulders turned and will help with your balance.

Talking tactics

A forehand ground stroke can be played from anywhere on the court. Aim your shots deep down the line or diagonally across the court. Draw your opponent wide occasionally with short, angled shots.

Topspin shot aimed deep cross court.

Keep your head still throughout the stroke.

5 Keep rotating your shoulders as you swing the racket through the hitting area (the area where you make your stroke).

Rotate your free arm along with your shoulders.

Point your elbow in the direction of the ball.

Your racket should meet the ball in front of your body.

As you hit through the ball, straighten up with your front leg.

6 With your body facing forward, follow through with the racket over your other shoulder. Move your back foot forward to keep your balance. This will also help you recover for the next shot.

4 Drop the racket head a little and then drive it up into the ball to give the shot some lift. Rotate your shoulders and hit the ball between knee and shoulder height in front of your body.

Keep your weight on your front foot.

Bend your back leg as you bring it forward so you can push off and recover quickly.

Ready position

After you have made your stroke, move back to a ready position behind the small T on the baseline.

Backhand drive

MOST PLAYERS BEGIN by using two hands on their backhand drive. You can progress to a one-handed stroke when you feel more confident, or continue to use two hands to give your stroke extra strength. Like the forehand drive, the backhand drive is a swinging action and you can use it to hit a ball flat, with topspin, or with slice. The backhand drive is often a harder stroke to master than the forehand, but with practice you can develop it into a very powerful shot.

Positioning your feet
If you are right-handed, step forward with your right foot as you hit your backhand drive (shown as violet). If you are left-handed, your left foot is your front foot. As with a forehand drive, you can hit a backhand with an open stance (shown as blue).

Use either of the two-handed grips (see page 17).

1 Stand in the ready position. Watch the ball come off your opponent's racket so that you can respond as quickly as possible to their shot.

Keep your eyes focused on the ball.

2 Turn your shoulders and bring your racket straight back with your wrists cocked. Support your weight on your back foot.

Keep the racket head just above wrist height.

Two-handed backhand

Using two hands on your backhand will make you feel more confident. A two-handed backhand can also make your shot more powerful and will give you better control of both the racket and the ball.

Your feet should be shoulder-width apart.

3 Step into the ball as it comes toward you. Keep your knees bent and your shoulders turned.

Follow through with your racket face open.

Sliced backhand
A sliced ball will skid and bounce lower than normal. Try using a one-handed backhand to slice, even if you usually use two hands. This will allow you to reach farther for wide balls. Turn your shoulders and take the racket back high. Swing from high to low, hitting the ball slightly more to the side of your body than you would with a flat driven shot. Follow through sideways-on, and keep your racket head high.

Slicing the ball
Cutting from high to low behind the ball with your racket makes the ball float low over the net.

Use a modified continental or eastern grip and support the racket head with your free hand.

Lead with the bottom edge of the racket, keeping the racket head slightly open.

One-handed backhand

This stroke allows you to reach farther for wide balls than you could with a two-handed backhand. A one-handed backhand can, with practice, be as powerful as a two-handed backhand. Take the racket back by turning your shoulders. Keep sideways-on as you swing through and hit the ball, then follow through with the racket high.

Point your front shoulder toward the ball.

Hit the ball in front of your body.

Keep your shoulder back for a bridged follow-through.

Keep your racket arm straight and support the racket head with your free hand.

Bend your knees as you step toward the ball.

Grip change

As you take the racket back on a one-handed backhand, use your free hand to turn the racket. Hold the throat of the racket with your free hand and change your grip to eastern backhand (see page 17).

Launch your body into the ball.

Keep your wrists cocked to help control the flight of the ball.

Keep your head still.

5 Still rotating your shoulders, swing the racket head out through the hitting area.

Stretch your arms so the contact point with the ball is in front of your body.

Push forward with your back foot.

4 Rotate your shoulders quickly and thrust your weight forward.

Arched follow-through

To generate more topspin or to hit a high-bouncing ball, use an arched follow-through. Let the racket travel from low to high in an arch in front of your body. Unlike in the bridged follow-through above, let your other shoulder come around. Your racket will brush up behind the back of the ball.

Point your elbow in the direction you want the ball to travel.

Shoulders are fully rotated and facing forward.

Bring this foot around to help you recover for the next shot.

Talking tactics

A backhand drive can be played from anywhere on the court, depending on where the ball lands. Keep your shots deep down the line or cross court. Try to make your opponent run wide with short, angled shots.

Down-the-line topspin shot

6 Follow through over your other shoulder with both hands still holding your racket. Bring your back foot forward for balance and to help you recover quickly.

The serve

IN A TENNIS MATCH, the serve, or service, is the most important stroke. It is the first shot of every point and, if played well, can give you an immediate advantage over your opponent. It is vital to develop a serve that you can repeat precisely over and over again. Try to make your serve as difficult as possible for your opponent to return. Decide on the direction and length of each serve before you begin and concentrate on accuracy rather than power. If you make a mistake, called a fault, you are allowed a second serve.

Throwing the ball
Practice your ball toss by standing in your serving position with your racket by your front foot. Toss the ball up in front of your body, slightly over to your racket side, and aim to bounce the ball off the racket face.

Holding the ball
Hold the ball lightly in your fingers. Have another ball in your pocket or ball clip, ready for a second serve.

Preparing to serve

The serving action is a fluid movement that should feel as if you are "throwing" your racket at the ball. Try counting "one, two, three, and hit" to help your timing. "One" as you prepare your racket, "two" as your arms pass down by your legs, "three" as your racket goes back and you toss the ball up, "and hit" as you bring your racket through behind your head and hit the ball.

Positioning your feet
A foot fault (shown as red) is declared if you touch the baseline, step on the extension of the center mark, or step on the sideline with either foot before hitting the ball. If you fault on your second serve (a double fault), then you lose the point.

1 Stand behind the baseline with your body sideways-on to the court. Try to hold the racket with a modified continental grip (see page 17). This will make it easier to put spin on the ball.

Keep both arms straight.

Rest the ball against the racket strings.

Before you serve
Wait until your opponent is in the ready position.

Let the racket drop naturally.

Make sure that your front foot is behind the baseline.

Feet shoulder-width apart

Place your weight on your back foot.

2 Bring both arms down slowly so that the ball hand touches your front leg and your racket hand brushes past your back leg.

Keep your racket shoulder back.

Bend your elbow.

3 Keep your racket arm away from the side of your body as you take your racket back. Your ball arm should be straight as you extend it above your head. Release the ball when your arm is fully stretched.

Begin to transfer your weight onto your front foot.

Topspin serve

Using topspin will make the ball arc over the net and kick up after the bounce. Throw the ball up toward your non-racket side. Turn your racket shoulder well back as you release the ball. As the ball starts to fall, spring up using your legs and bring your racket up almost edge-on to the ball. Take your racket up behind the back of the ball to create the topspin.

Slice serve

This spin will make the ball curve sideways. Throw the ball up farther over to your racket side. Use a modified continental grip to bring the bottom edge of your racket around the ball. If you are right-handed, slice your racket from right to left around the back of the ball. If you are left-handed, slice your racket from left to right. Follow through across your body as usual.

Open stance service

When serving, it is not always necessary to bring your back foot forward before hitting the ball. Pete Sampras of America, above, keeps his back foot behind because he feels more balanced in this position.

 Aim for accuracy
Do not try to make every first serve an ace. If you try to serve too hard, you will make mistakes.

Talking tactics

When playing singles, serve from near the center mark. Either hit diagonally into the service box down the center of the court, into your opponent's body, or wide.

Wide topspin serve

4 Bend your racket arm, ready to hit the ball. Point with your ball arm to keep your back shoulder lower than your front.

Imagine you are throwing overhand with your racket arm.

Throw the ball slightly higher than you can reach with your racket.

Push your front hip into the court.

5 Rotate your shoulders until they are parallel with the net. Straighten your legs and reach up to hit the ball just as it begins to fall.

6 Feel the speed of the racket head overtake your wrist after you have hit the ball. Use your ball arm to keep your balance as your body twists.

Bend your knees.

Push up from your knees.

Bring your ball arm down.

7 On the follow-through, let the racket come around your waist. Watch to see where your opponent is going to hit the return.

Bend at the waist.

Bring this leg around to help you recover for your next shot.

Drag your back foot forward.

The serve return

AFTER THE SERVE, the serve return is the most important shot. Not only do you have to keep the ball in the court, but you also have to make it difficult for your opponent to play his or her next shot. The moment the server throws the ball up, you will get an idea of the shot he or she has planned. If you are receiving a fast serve, stand about 3 ft (1 m) behind the baseline (it is easier to run forward than backward). If the serve is slower, then move forward into the court and aim to hit the ball at the top of the bounce. Try using your basic ground strokes, then adapt them in ways that add power, direction, and consistency to the stroke. Remember, the server's aim is to win the point right away. You must react quickly to stay in the game.

Take a guess
If you know your opponent well, you may be able to predict how he or she will serve.

Ready position
Stand 3 ft (1 m) behind where you imagine you will be hitting the ball. As soon as the server throws the ball up, move forward into a split-step (see page 38). This will help you stay on your toes and will force your weight forward so that you are ready to move quickly.

If your opponent's first serve is a fault, try standing just inside the baseline to show that you are ready to attack.

Two-handed backhand return
A two-handed backhand will give you extra strength to return a fast serve. Try to keep your racket between waist and shoulder height and lean into the ball. If your opponent knows that you have a strong two-handed backhand, it is very unlikely that he or she will serve the ball straight to your favorite stroke. If the serve is wide, you may need to use a one-handed backhand to reach farther.

The take-back
The speed of your opponent's serve will determine how much time you have for your take-back. A soft serve gives you time to take your racket back fully and add power to your shot, whereas a fast serve will require a short take-back. Whichever you use, make sure that you follow through properly.

On a long take-back, bring your racket right back.

Turn your body sideways-on to the court.

Stand with your feet apart and your knees bent to help keep your balance.

If you only have time for a short take-back, use your weight to put extra power behind the shot.

Keep your wrists firm.

Take control
If your opponent runs to the net after serving, try to return the ball low so that your shot lands at his or her feet.

Hit the ball in front of your body.

Don't let your racket head drop.

Deep topspin shot down the middle of the court

Keep your feet shoulder-width apart.

Talking tactics
The safest direction in which to return serve is deep across the court or down the middle. If you are hitting a more attacking shot, aim down the line or hit a short, angled shot cross court.

High-driven forehand return

With this stroke you are counterattacking the ball, sending it back to the server with equal or greater speed. From the ready position, take your racket back and quickly turn sideways-on to the court. If you are playing a forehand shot, rotate your shoulders and bring your weight onto your front foot as you drive your racket through. Keep your balance after the shot by bringing your racket leg forward, then recover to the baseline for your next shot.

Keep your head still.

Your racket should be between waist and shoulder height.

Your racket travels over your opposite shoulder as you follow through.

Hit the ball in front of your body.

Semi-western forehand grip

Use your free arm for balance.

Topspin tip

Use topspin on your high-driven return to keep your opponent in a defensive position on their baseline.

Step forward as you make your stroke.

Keep watching the ball.

To open the angle of your racket face, tilt it backward.

Low-driven backhand return

To return a low-bouncing ball on your backhand side, bend your knees and keep your body low as you step into the shot. Hit the ball in front of your body, with your racket head at a slightly open angle. This will lift the ball over the net.

Eastern backhand grip

Blocked forehand return

This is a very effective shot against a fast server. With a firm grip on your racket, use a short take-back and a volleylike punching action (see pages 26-27). Even though you may feel you are doing little to hit the ball, the speed of your opponent's serve and the correct angle of your racket face will combine to produce a deep return.

Slice it

Try using slice on the low backhand to give the shot lift and depth.

Aim to hit the ball on your racket's sweet spot.

Keep your wrist firm.

Chipped backhand return

To chip your serve return, you need to use a short take-back and lean into the ball. Here, Steffi Graf of Germany shows the similarity between the chipped backhand return and the backhand volley. Notice how Graf turns her shoulders, taking the ball to the side of her while keeping her racket arm straight. If the server runs in to the net, a chipped return will keep the ball low as it travels over the net and will make it land at the server's feet.

Step forward into the ball.

Forehand volley

A VOLLEY IS A SHOT played when the ball is in its first flight, before it bounces. Stand in an attacking position about 6 ft (2 m) away from the net. Your volley action should be a short, sharp punch that has very little take-back or follow-through. Concentrate on the angle of the racket face so that the ball goes in the right direction. To begin with, use any forehand grip as this will give extra support to your wrist. When you become stronger, try to use a modified continental grip for your volleys.

Use your free arm for balance.

Keep your head still and rotate your shoulders.

Drive volley

If your opponent consistently hits the ball high and deep but without any pace, then surprise him or her occasionally by adapting your ground stroke into a volley. The drive volley requires practice because your take-back must be speedy. Try to return the ball before it bounces to disrupt your opponent's rhythm.

Move your weight from your back foot to your front foot.

1 Move forward, turn your shoulders sideways, and take your racket back.

2 Move your weight forward as you hit the ball in front of your body.

Double pressure
Playing doubles is a good way to improve your volleying skills because you are forced to move forward more often.

Start to turn your shoulders.

Watch the ball.

Modified continental grip

Keep your knees bent.

Keep your feet shoulder-width apart and stay on your toes.

Your weight should be on this leg.

Keep a low center of gravity as you step forward.

Step forward and move your weight onto your front foot.

Practicing your volley

1 Stand in a ready position at the center line. Your position near the net means there is less distance between you and your opponent. Your reactions therefore have to be quicker than at any other time during a rally.

2 As you see the ball coming toward you, start to take your racket back. The racket head should be slightly above the height at which you will hit the ball. Use a short take-back (see page 24) and keep your wrist firm.

3 Turn your shoulders and step forward so that your weight is on your front foot. Hold the racket head high so that it forms a "V" shape with your forearm. Keep the racket face open (tilted backward) and punch the racket forward.

Swing your racket from low to high to generate topspin.

Bring your back foot around to help you recover for your next shot.

3 Bring your racket over your other shoulder as you follow through. Let your back foot come around.

High volley

Take your racket back high and position yourself sideways-on to the court. Rotate your shoulders slightly and punch down through the ball with your racket. Freeze your arm and keep the racket head up after you have hit the ball to avoid dragging the ball down into the net.

Lift your back heel to give you extra height.

Low volley

Step forward with your front foot and open your racket face more than normal to lift the ball up and over the net. Make sure that you get right under the ball by keeping your knees bent and your body low throughout the stroke. Stay in this position for a split second after you have hit the ball.

Watch the ball carefully, but do not lift your head.

Talking tactics

Try to keep your volleys deep cross court or down the line. Use a short, angled volley to hit the ball beyond your opponent's reach.

Short, angled shot

Squeeze hard

Give the racket handle an extra squeeze as you hit the ball. The power injected into the ball by your opponent will be reflected back by your volley.

Punch forward from your shoulder, not your elbow.

Lean into the shot and hit the ball in front of your body.

Use your free arm for balance.

Keep your grip as firm as possible.

Control the angle of the racket head.

Watch the ball after it leaves your racket.

Make a short, sharp follow-through, then hold your racket still momentarily.

Keep your balance and stay low.

4 Move forward to meet the ball in front of your body. Guide the bottom edge of your racket in a slight downward path behind the back of the ball. This will put slice on the ball, helping you aim your shot deep into your opponent's court.

5 The punching action of your shot will make the racket follow through slightly. As soon as this happens, freeze the racket face in the angle and the direction that you have hit the ball. This will help you control the flight of the ball.

Win the point

Do not stay too close to the net after your volley or your opponent may hit a lob (see pages 30-31) to the back of your court.

Backhand volley

MANY PLAYERS FIND the backhand volley easier to play than the forehand. Exactly the same principles apply for both shots, but the backhand volley often feels more natural because it is played from a sideways-on position. As well as an attacking stroke, the backhand volley can be used as a defensive shot if the ball is directed straight at your body. You must be decisive and have quick reflexes to reach the ball in a split second. Try to use a continental grip, but if your wrist is weak, change to a backhand grip or use a two-handed grip.

High backhand volley

For this stroke you will need to have a strong wrist and a firm grip to control the racket head. Don't let your racket drop or shake when it hits the ball.

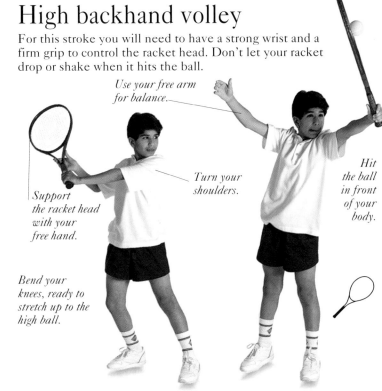

Use your free arm for balance.

Support the racket head with your free hand.

Turn your shoulders.

Hit the ball in front of your body.

Bend your knees, ready to stretch up to the high ball.

1 When you see a high ball approaching, turn sideways-on to the court and take your racket back high.

2 Punch through the ball with your racket. Do not reach over the net as you hit the ball or you will lose the point.

Low backhand volley

A low volley is very difficult to turn into an attacking stroke because it is below net height. As long as you get your body down underneath the ball, your shot need not be a defensive one.

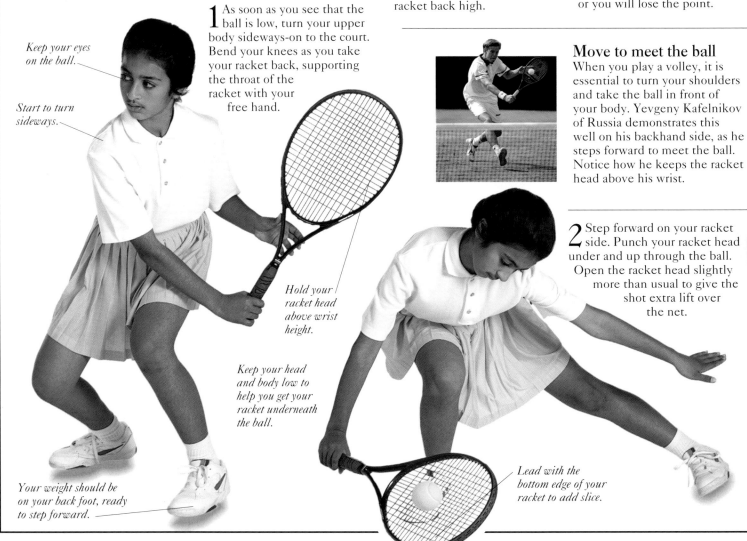

Keep your eyes on the ball.

Start to turn sideways.

1 As soon as you see that the ball is low, turn your upper body sideways-on to the court. Bend your knees as you take your racket back, supporting the throat of the racket with your free hand.

Hold your racket head above wrist height.

Keep your head and body low to help you get your racket underneath the ball.

Your weight should be on your back foot, ready to step forward.

Move to meet the ball

When you play a volley, it is essential to turn your shoulders and take the ball in front of your body. Yevgeny Kafelnikov of Russia demonstrates this well on his backhand side, as he steps forward to meet the ball. Notice how he keeps the racket head above his wrist.

2 Step forward on your racket side. Punch your racket head under and up through the ball. Open the racket head slightly more than usual to give the shot extra lift over the net.

Lead with the bottom edge of your racket to add slice.

Try not to take your eyes off the ball as your arm moves across your view.

Two-handed drive volley with topspin

Try using a two-handed backhand drive action to volley a high, slow ball. This sometimes feels like swinging a baseball bat, but your wrists must stay firm. With a controlled take-back, move forward and swing through the ball. To generate topspin on the ball, swing your racket up from low to high. Adding spin will control and guide the ball in the court. If you prefer to hit on your forehand, you may have time on some shots to run around the backhand and play a forehand shot.

Keep your head still.

Hit the ball in front of your body.

Follow through with the racket over your other shoulder.

Stay sideways-on to the court with your racket arm outstretched.

3 Use a short follow-through and hold the racket head high and slightly open.

Watch the ball leave your opponent's racket.

Make sure the action is from your racket shoulder and not your elbow.

Keep your head still and don't take your eyes off the ball.

Attacking backhand volley

If the ball is at or above net level, try playing a more attacking backhand volley. From the ready position, take your racket back slightly. Step forward on your racket foot and strike the ball with a firm punching action. Aim to hit the ball just over the top of the net and deep into your opponent's court. Keep the racket head above your wrist and follow through slightly. Briefly hold the racket head still before recovering.

Step forward.

Hit down through the back of the ball to generate slice.

Keep your racket head still for a moment.

Turn your upper body sideways-on to the court.

3 Freeze your racket head as you hit the ball. Keep your body low for a split second, then return to the ready position for your next shot. Keep watching the ball all the time.

Stay compact and low.

Keep your knees bent or the ball will go into the net.

Your weight should be on your front foot.

On the rebound

When volleying off a fast ball, imagine your racket is a wall and let the ball simply rebound from it.

Use your free arm for balance.

Deep attacking shot

Talking tactics

An effective low volley can win the point. Try taking speed off the ball by loosening your grip on the racket slightly and playing a short, angled shot. If your shot rises too high over the net, your opponent will have a chance to hit the ball past you.

The lob

A LOB SHOULD PASS HIGH over the top of your opponent's racket, otherwise he or she may take the opportunity to smash the ball back over the net. The flight of the ball must also be low enough that your opponent won't have time to recover the shot. A high, deep lob is extremely useful in a variety of situations. It is most often used as a defensive shot, or instead of a ground stroke to counterattack when your opponent has approached the net and played a volley.

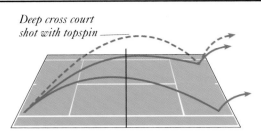

Deep cross court shot with topspin

Talking tactics

Aim your lob deep over your opponent's backhand side. Hit cross court if the extra distance will help you control the shot. The flight of the ball should be at its highest as it passes over your opponent's head. Remember that the wind will affect the flight of a high lob.

Flat backhand lob

If your opponent forces you out wide, or drives you back with a deep volley, then you are in a defensive position. Hit up a lob and force your opponent back to play the ball on their backhand side.

Watch the ball approaching.

Continental grip

Keep your head still.

Bend your knees.

Your follow-through is high with your racket out in front.

Use your free arm for balance.

Straighten up your body.

1 Take your racket back early and support it with your free hand.

2 Keep the racket face open as you bring your racket underneath the ball.

3 Swing the racket upward through the ball. Push up with your knees to give the shot extra lift.

2 As the ball starts to fall, step into it, rotate your shoulders, and swing the racket forward in a steep upward path. Make sure the racket face is open to help the ball rise over your opponent's head. Hit the ball in front of your body and continue bringing your racket through in a smooth, rising action.

Take your racket back early.

Low forehand lob

Your opponent does not have to be at the net in order for you to lob. If you are driven out wide by an attacking shot, use a lob to give yourself time to prepare for your next shot. If your opponent has hit a smash over the net, use a lob with a short take-back. However, if you fail to put enough strength into your lob, the ball could fall short and give your opponent the chance to smash a winner.

1 Take an early back swing and turn your shoulders. Use either an eastern forehand grip or a continental grip so that you can hit underneath the ball effectively. If the ball is low, move forward and bend your knees so that your preparation is low.

Keep your feet shoulder-width apart to help you balance.

Take control
If your lob is successful, try to take an attacking position at the net and win the point with an attacking volley or a smash.

3 Straighten your legs as the racket continues upward. Use your other arm for balance. The stroke finishes with a high follow-through. The better your follow-through, the less likely it is that your lob will be short. After playing a lob, make sure you recover to a good position.

Keep your racket face open.

Keep your head still.

Your racket should make contact with the ball out in front of your body.

Rotate your shoulders.

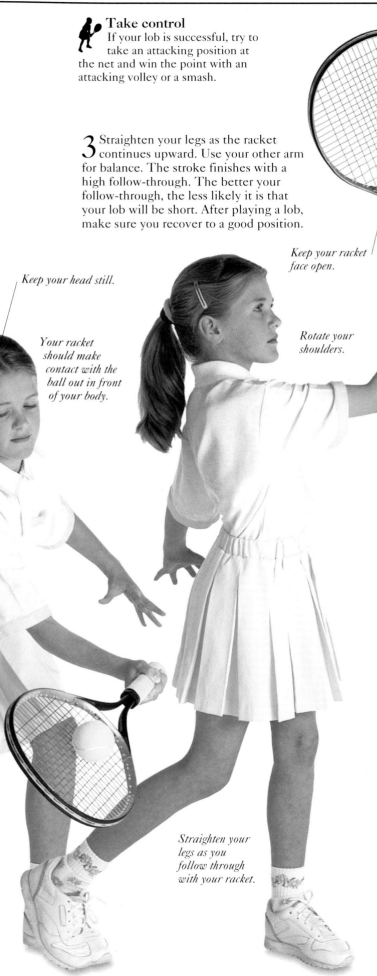

Straighten your legs as you follow through with your racket.

Careful aim
Here, Michael Chang of America has run fast and kept low to get his racket underneath the ball and lift it up over his opponent's head. Chang's lob is high and deep enough to give him time to get in a strong attacking position for his next shot.

Fool your opponent
Try to disguise your lob by preparing it with a ground stroke back swing.

Two-handed backhand lob with topspin

If played successfully, this type of shot can win the point outright. An attacking lob is best played with topspin. This will make the ball loop over your opponent's head, drop rapidly, and kick up and away from your opponent.

Make your follow-through long and high.

Keep watching the ball.

1 Use either two-handed grip. Turn your shoulders and take your racket back early, as if you are preparing to hit a ground stroke.

2 Lower your racket with a looping action, and brush up behind the back of the ball from low to high. Keep the racket face open slightly.

3 Rotate your shoulders and straighten your body, pushing up with your knees. Follow through with the racket over your other shoulder.

The smash

THIS CAN BE THE MOST powerful tennis stroke, but it requires extra confidence and concentration to hit successfully. A smash is best played at the net to return a short lob, or off a high, weak ball after it has bounced. Use a similar action to that of your serving stroke. Take care not to try to put too much power into the shot, but concentrate on your aim and timing. Place the ball deep and to your opponent's weaker side. Your opponent has very little chance of returning a smash and, with practice, your smash could win the point outright.

Airborne attack

In order to reach a high lob, Pete Sampras of America leaps in the air to reach the ball before it passes over his head. At the same time, Sampras produces a winning smash that is aggressive and controlled. The camera has caught the snapping action of his wrist as the racket head travels over the ball. Athletic Sampras doesn't take his eyes off the ball even when his feet are 3 ft (1 m) off the ground!

Practicing your jump smash

A jumping smash will enable you to reach a ball that you could not otherwise return. This stroke needs fine coordination in order to move into position and hit the ball while you are in midair. Make sure you prepare quickly and move sideways-on to a position where you can "snap" your wrist over the ball and direct your shot down into your opponent's court.

Preparing to smash

Use the same throwing action with your racket arm as you do when serving (see pages 22-23). Point at the approaching ball with your free arm for balance and to help you guide your stroke.

Look up along your free arm at the ball.

Keep your racket shoulder lower than your ball shoulder to ensure a good throwing action.

Use your cross-over steps (see page 15) to move across the court.

Lead with the butt of the racket handle.

Take the racket behind your shoulders, keeping your elbow high.

Start to bring your racket back.

1 Turn sideways-on to the court. Bend your elbow as you start to lift your racket up. Point to the ball with your other hand and follow it as you move into position.

2 If the lob is deep, start to move back by crossing your front leg over your back leg.

3 Take a large final step with your back foot and bend your knees, ready to jump. Move quickly, but don't rush into your jump.

Jump up with your racket leg.

Angled smash

If you can't get enough power into your smash to hit the ball past your opponent, use an angled smash. Move toward the ball and get into the ready position quickly. Stretch your body and reach up to the ball. Imagine you are playing a second serve with spin, and use the bottom edge of the racket to brush around the ball and send it back with slice. Follow through with your racket around your waist.

Cut around the ball with the bottom edge of the racket.

Catch your body weight by bringing your back foot forward.

Stand in a sideways-on position.

Backhand smash

If properly timed, it is possible to hit this shot with power. Always try to place your backhand smash deep to your opponent's weaker side, never straight down the middle of the court.

Support the racket head with your free hand.

Stand sideways-on to the court.

Run around

If the ball is coming to your backhand side, try and run around it to hit a more powerful smash on your forehand side.

Reach up to the ball with the contact point out in front of your body.

Follow through with the racket low in front of you.

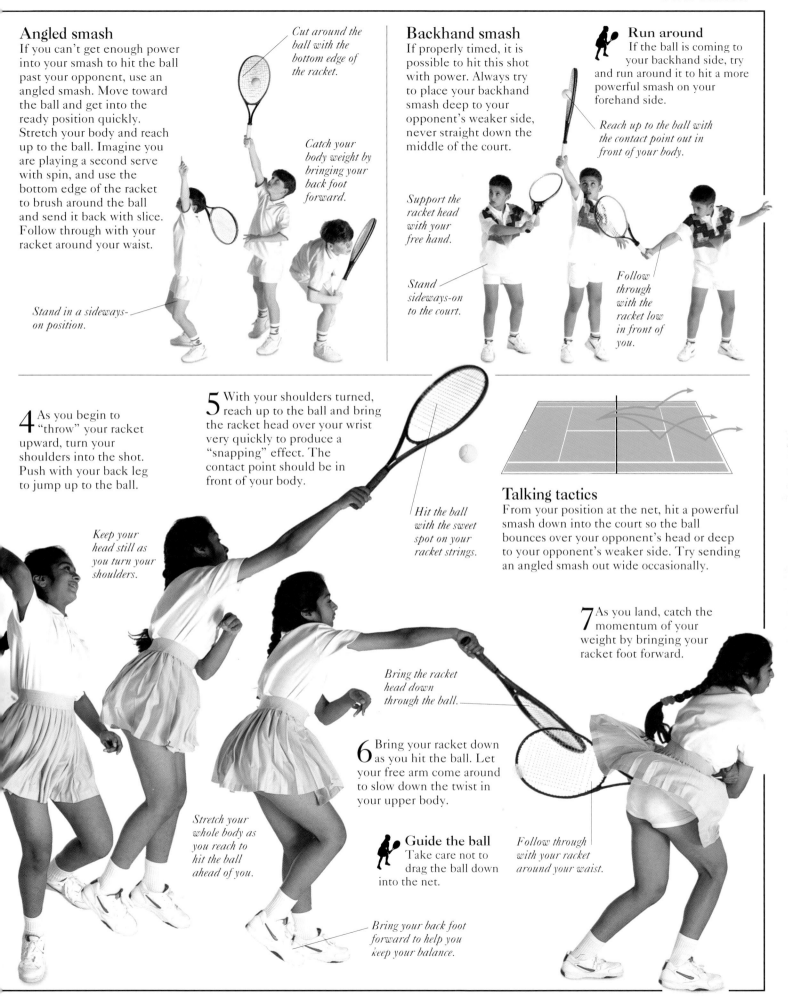

4 As you begin to "throw" your racket upward, turn your shoulders into the shot. Push with your back leg to jump up to the ball.

Keep your head still as you turn your shoulders.

5 With your shoulders turned, reach up to the ball and bring the racket head over your wrist very quickly to produce a "snapping" effect. The contact point should be in front of your body.

Hit the ball with the sweet spot on your racket strings.

Talking tactics

From your position at the net, hit a powerful smash down into the court so the ball bounces over your opponent's head or deep to your opponent's weaker side. Try sending an angled smash out wide occasionally.

7 As you land, catch the momentum of your weight by bringing your racket foot forward.

Bring the racket head down through the ball.

6 Bring your racket down as you hit the ball. Let your free arm come around to slow down the twist in your upper body.

Guide the ball
Take care not to drag the ball down into the net.

Stretch your whole body as you reach to hit the ball ahead of you.

Follow through with your racket around your waist.

Bring your back foot forward to help you keep your balance.

The drop shot

A WINNING GAME is not just about hitting as many powerful shots as possible. It is also about moving your opponent around, making spaces on the court into which you can attack. The drop shot will improve your ability to explore the size of the court. The drop shot is an example of a "touch" shot used to catch an overly defensive baseline player. It will force your opponent up to the net, where you can then hit a passing drive or a lob. Taking the pace off the ball and directing it with an accurate drop shot is typical of a "touch" game. This is a soft stroke that will not necessarily win you the point immediately, but will move your opponent out of position.

Backhand drop shot

Some players find it easier to play a drop shot on their backhand side. The backhand slicing action can feel more natural because of the side-on position. If you normally use a two-handed backhand, try to play with one hand for this soft stroke.

Rotate your shoulders.

Keep your racket face open. This will lift the ball just over the net.

Move your weight onto your front foot.

1 Use a high take-back and hold the racket with the grip you normally use for backhand slice.

2 Cut down behind the ball with the edge of your racket, then up through the hitting area.

Forehand drop shot

Try playing a drop shot from a short mid-court ball after you have pushed your opponent back with several deep shots. If you do not play an effective drop shot, then move back into a defensive position. If you play it well, move slightly forward so you can reach a counter drop shot from your opponent.

Turn sideways-on to the court and follow the ball carefully with your free arm.

1 Use your usual grip for playing ground strokes, or a continental grip to add more slice to your drop shot. Take your racket back higher and slightly farther than you would for a volley.

Start to turn your shoulders.

2 With a relaxed grip, start to bring your racket forward, leading with the bottom edge. There should be a slight downward path to your swing.

Keep your knees bent.

Talking tactics

Try not to play a drop shot from too far back on the court as the ball is less likely to clear the net. Wait for a shorter mid-court ball. Hit the ball softly, with slice, into an open space away from your opponent. The ball should already be dropping as it crosses the net and then will bounce very little.

Step forward with your weight on your front foot.

Keep your head still and your free shoulder back.

3 Follow through slightly up beyond the point of contact, with the racket facing in the direction you have hit the ball.

Disguised drop shot

An excellent way to catch your opponent off guard is to play a disguised drop shot. Take your racket back early as you would for a normal ground stroke and look as if you intend to hit a drive. At the last minute, slow down the racket to play your drop shot.

Use a full take-back of the racket.

Cut underneath the ball at the last minute.

Step forward to the ball.

Drop volley

1 While a drop shot is played as a ground stroke after the bounce, a drop volley is played at the net before the bounce. Prepare as you would to play a normal volley, stepping forward with a short take-back, and hitting the ball in front of your body.

2 Keep a very relaxed grip and, as the ball hits your racket strings, allow the racket head to move back and absorb the force of the shot. This deadens the speed of the ball and allows you to just clear the net with your shot.

Practice makes perfect
While practicing your drop shot, see how many bounces it takes for the ball to travel to your opponent's service line. More than three and it is a good, soft drop shot.

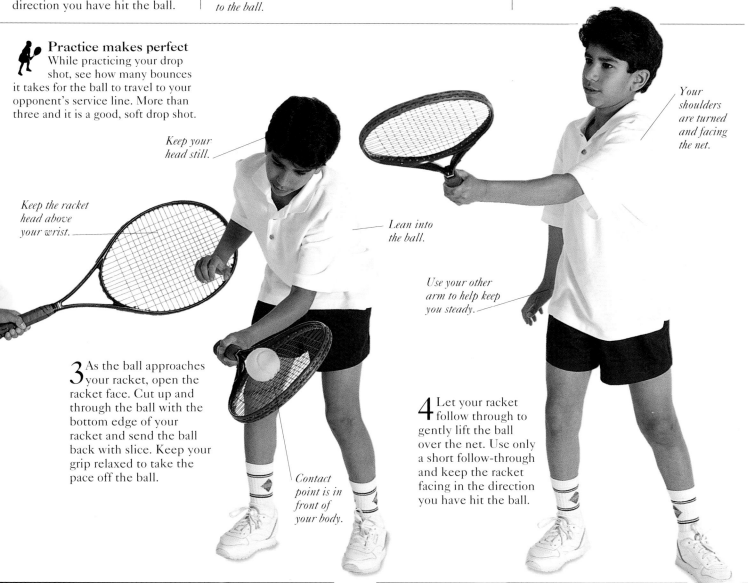

Keep your head still.

Keep the racket head above your wrist.

Lean into the ball.

Your shoulders are turned and facing the net.

Use your other arm to help keep you steady.

3 As the ball approaches your racket, open the racket face. Cut up and through the ball with the bottom edge of your racket and send the ball back with slice. Keep your grip relaxed to take the pace off the ball.

Contact point is in front of your body.

4 Let your racket follow through to gently lift the ball over the net. Use only a short follow-through and keep the racket facing in the direction you have hit the ball.

Playing at the baseline

Stand in the ready position on the T of the service line and keep your eyes on the ball as it leaves your partner's racket.

ALL TENNIS PLAYERS, from beginners to more advanced players, use the five fundamental skills (see page 17). These are especially important when rallying with an opponent from the back of the court. The level at which you play at the baseline depends on your ability and tactical awareness. As this improves, you should become familiar with the kind of decisions you need to make: where to move in order to play a good shot, and how or when to make your stroke. At first your decisions will be conscious ones, but with more practice, you will start to make decisions automatically, without actually thinking about them.

Step with your racket leg for a backhand shot.

Level one

To get an idea of what baseline play is like, begin by rallying with your opponent from service line to service line. At this stage, the first major decision is whether your shot will be a forehand or backhand (see above). The quicker you can decide, the quicker you can react to the approaching ball. After hitting the ball, recover to your home base at the T of the service line (see page 38).

Level two

When you start rallying from the baseline, you will notice how much ground you have to cover (see below). You will move farther and will receive a greater variety of shots at the baseline than from farther forward in the court. This leads you to the next major decision: where to move to. Movement from side to side is linked to the first level and depends on whether the shot is forehand or backhand. Now you also have to move forward if the ball lands short, or backward if the ball is traveling high and deep.

 Be ready
Concentrate on the ball so that you can anticipate how high and fast it is traveling over the net toward you.

As you move forward to a short ball, turn sideways-on and take your racket back early.

After each shot, try to recover to your home base position on the baseline (see page 38). From here, watch your opponent return the ball.

Move back quickly for a high ball to allow it to drop to a comfortable height before hitting it.

Quickly move sideways to a wide ball with your racket ready.

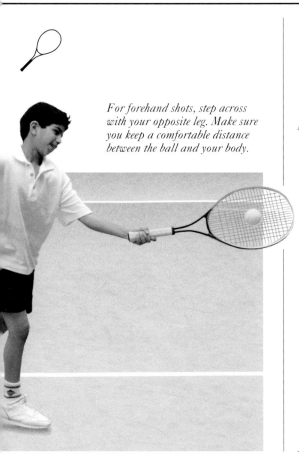

For forehand shots, step across with your opposite leg. Make sure you keep a comfortable distance between the ball and your body.

Level three

Once you feel comfortable moving to the ball and hitting it anywhere in the court, you can begin to decide how you are going to play the shot. Start by trying to direct the ball diagonally across the court or down the sideline. Vary the height at which you hit the ball over the net and experiment with your spins. Also try changing the direction of the ball. Hitting from down the line to cross court is easier than changing from cross court to down the line, because you are less likely to hit the ball out.

Level four

By this stage, you should be considering what you intend to do with the shot. Three options apply to every shot: rally, attack, or defend. These choices relate to your position on the court. From the defensive rally zone (red), you should hit deep rally shots consistently into your opponent's rally zone. Defensive shots are also played when you are scrambling the ball back into play. From the setting up zone (yellow), you can start to hit harder rally shots and sometimes go for a deep or angled attacking shot. From the attacking zone (green), you attack the ball with both ground strokes and volleys, and when you have the opening, hit a winner!

1 If you are drawn to one side with a high deep ball, take a short back swing and try to hit the ball as it rises.

Move without stepping back from the baseline.

Level five

At this stage, you should aim to hit the ball early, when it is rising or at the top of the bounce, brake after the shot (see below), and use a different type of recovery, called "center point" recovery. The center point is halfway between the two extreme possibilities of your opponent's return. For example, if you send a rally shot deep cross court, the center point would be on the near side of the small T on the baseline. The ball is likely to come back cross court, but you must be prepared to cover the other area of the court.

Center point

2 When rallying at the baseline, you should try to hit more cross court shots. After playing the stroke, brake your movement by bringing your back foot across.

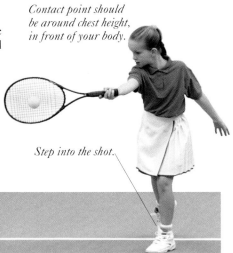

Contact point should be around chest height, in front of your body.

Step into the shot.

3 With your braking foot, push yourself back into the court and recover to a center point position, just to one side of the small T on the baseline. From there you should be ready to reach anywhere on the court to return the next shot.

Braking foot

Playing at the net

WHEN YOU START PLAYING tennis, you will hit ground strokes from the baseline most of the time. You may move forward to return a short ball when necessary, but recover back to the baseline. There is another option, however, and that is to move closer to the net to play volleys. The two strongest positions on the court are "home base" behind the center of the baseline, and "home base" 6 ft (2 m) back from the middle of the net. Your home bases are linked by two types of attacking shots: the approach shot (see below) and the serve.

Serve and volley

This tactic (right) is often used to pressure the opponent's return of serve and is most effective when playing doubles, or singles on a fast surface like grass.

1 Throw the ball up in front of you so your body weight is moving forward.

2 As you move forward after the serve, look up to see how your opponent is going to play the return.

3 Split-step as your opponent returns the ball.

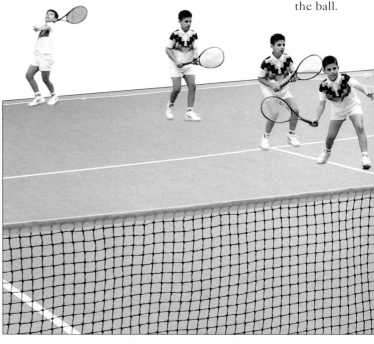

Approach and volley

An approach shot is played from a ball that has landed short, making you move forward to reach it. Use your approach shot to put your opponent under pressure. Hit the ball deep to your opponent's weaker side, using topspin to make the ball bounce away from him or her, or slice to keep the ball low. The lower and deeper you keep your approach shots, the more chance you will have of an easy return that you can put away. Alternatively, if you hit the ball down the middle of the court, you will limit the angle your opponent can use to hit an attacking return.

Practicing your split-step

Use a split-step as your opponent plays their shot. It will help equalize your balance and will prepare you to spring to one side for your volley. After recovering to either home base position, perform a split-step before playing your next shot. Simply plant your feet parallel to each other, shoulder-width apart, and bend your knees.

Let your body weight carry you forward through the shot and toward the net.

1 You must be prepared at all times to move forward for a short ball. This will be an ideal chance to attack your opponent from the net position. Stay on your toes in the ready position. Watch the ball as it leaves your opponent's racket and quickly decide on your next move.

2 If the ball is short, move forward to take it early when it is at the top of the bounce. The quicker you play the shot, the less time your opponent will have to recover and prepare for their next shot. However, it is important not to rush the stroke or get too close to the ball.

3 Move forward, bringing your body weight through the approach shot. As you see your opponent hit the ball back, perform a split-step. How close you get to the net will depend on how fast the ball is traveling toward you. Try to move inside the service line.

4 Step forward to meet the volley in front of your body.

5 Move in again to home base position and split-step for your next volley.

6 When you are in home base at the net, keep your body low and your knees bent, and do not move forward again. Hit an attacking volley if your opponent's shot is high; place the volley when the ball is below net height. You can also play a drop volley from here (see page 35).

Forehand step

When you volley, it is important that your contact point with the ball is in front of your body. To help play a volley correctly, step forward to meet the ball rather than waiting for it to come to you. After split-stepping, keep your knees bent and your weight moving forward in a continuous motion. Step forward with your racket foot for a backhand shot, and your other foot for a forehand shot. To reach for a wider ball, step farther across the court.

Hold your racket up ready to move to a forehand or backhand shot.

Talking tactics

When you serve and volley, be aware that a wide serve will give your opponent more angle to use for a passing return. Aim down the middle of the service box most of the time, and only occasionally serve out wide to your opponent's weaker side.

Net profit
Taking position at the net will intimidate your opponent and make it more difficult for him or her to hit past you.

Talking tactics

When you hit a wide approach shot or volley, position yourself off-center to the side that you have hit the ball. This will enable you to cover a down-the-line passing shot. When you are at the net, you can already intercept the cross court shot.

Attack or defend?
Successful net play is a combination of knowing when to attack or defend. In both cases, keep your volley action short and sharp.

4 Step forward from your split-step to play your first volley. Aim your volley deep into your opponent's back court, or place it at an angle to put pressure on your opponent. Think of your first volley as a set-up shot to get yourself into a good position for your second volley.

5 If you are not in a good home base position after hitting your first volley, move forward again and perform a split-step. It is important not to get too close to the net or you may touch it with your racket. Your opponent may easily lob the ball over your head, too.

6 Step forward from your split-step for your second volley. If your earlier shots went well, it is likely that you can use this shot to win the point. If the ball is high, attack the volley without swinging your racket. If the ball is below net height, think carefully where you want to place the ball.

Doubles

P LAYING DOUBLES is all about teamwork. You and your partner should understand each others' strengths and weaknesses so that you can play well together. The doubles court includes the alley area, so there is a larger court area in which to aim, but a smaller court area for each player to cover. When you first start to play doubles, you may feel safer staying back on the baseline and hitting ground strokes. Once you feel more confident as a doubles pair, try to play volleys from an attacking position at the net as much as possible.

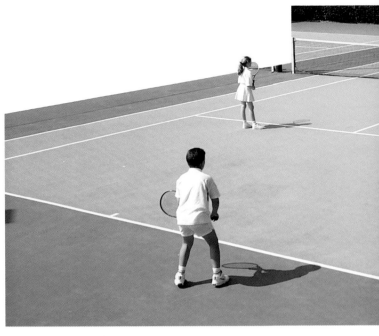

Covering the court
If you and your partner both cover the middle of the court, your opponents will be forced to aim their shots wide. This increases their chances of hitting the ball out.

When serving, try to serve deep so you have more time to prepare for your next shot.

Doubles service rules
If you and your partner have won first serve, tactically it is best for the stronger server to serve for the first game. If you serve first, your partner will be the third person to serve. All four players take turns serving; your opponents serve second and fourth. Players also take turns receiving serves. The scoring and rules are the same as in the singles game (see pages 12-13 and 44).

Serving
If you and your partner are serving, you automatically have the advantage of being able to claim the net position first by serving and volleying. As you serve, your partner should be in an attacking position close to the net. From there, he or she should be able to reach a down-the-middle or down-the-alley ball, depending on how the return of serve is played. When serving, stand at the baseline farther toward the alley than when playing singles in order to cover a possible angled return. At the beginning of each new point, swap sides with your partner.

Your partner must try not to let a gap open up or leave any part of the court out of reach.

Return of serve
With two people on the other side of the net, it is more important to return accurately than powerfully. If, after serving, your opponent comes straight in to a net position, then aim the ball at his or her feet as he or she is moving forward. Alternatively, make them stretch for a short, angled shot. If the server stays back, then return the ball deep to the baseline and claim the net position yourself. At the start of each new point, the player who was receiving at the baseline for the previous point moves forward, and their partner moves back, ready to return the next serve.

Move forward to meet the ball.

Your partner stands on the service line ready to move in to volley.

A problem shared

Here, Martina Navratilova of America has managed to jump up with enough height to reach a lob. However, notice her partner, Jon Stark. Throughout the shot, he is ready to move back to retrieve the ball just in case Martina doesn't reach it. If Martina had missed her lob, she would have moved to the left court to cover Stark's side. Good doubles partners must be prepared to cover for each other like this.

On the court

When serving and receiving, it is normal for each pair to have one player at the baseline and one near the net. Generally the server and receiver play the point out between them. Both baseline players rally until they get a chance to move forward and join their partners in an attacking position at the net. Meanwhile, the net players are covering their own side of the court, waiting for an opportunity to intercept the ball.

Decision making

Discuss tactics before and during the game. Try to make sure that your partner always knows your next move.

Your partner should keep an equal distance away from you – as if attached by a piece of string.

Volleying

If you and your partner are both at the net, keep an equal distance apart. Move sideways, backward, and forward together. As you retrieve the ball, your partner must stop any large spaces from opening up. Your opponents may try to hit attacking shots down the middle of the court in order to confuse you, so it is best if you decide before the match which one of you will cover this type of shot. When you are both positioned at the net, there is a chance that you will be lobbed. Call to your partner to decide who will return each ball.

Intercepting the ball

At any time during a rally, the players positioned at the net should be ready to intercept. This is a quick and easy way to win a point from a high, slow ground stroke. Even if your interception doesn't win the point, it is a good opportunity to attack. Start to move across to your partner's side of the court once your opponent has begun to take their shot. Do not move across too early or your opponent may change their plans and hit the ball past you down the alley. Your partner at the baseline should cover the side that you have just left.

You should try to move across and intercept any shot that is within reach.

Your partner moves over to cover the side that you have just left and stays there.

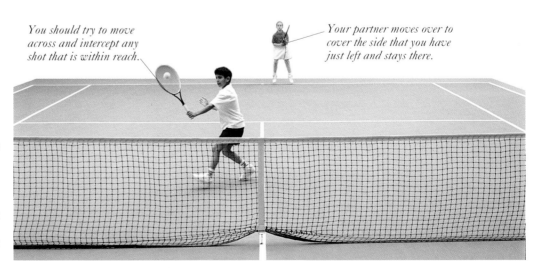

Coaching and tournaments

TENNIS IS A GAME of wits as much as it is an athletic challenge. Once you have started training, your mental game should begin to improve along with your technique. You may enjoy taking part in competitions arranged by your school or club. As you progress, you will compete against more experienced players and you will need commitment and determination in order to succeed. Very few players reach world class level, and even the best players always hope to improve their game. But whether you play or watch, tennis is one of the most popular and dramatic sports you can be a part of.

Wheelchair tennis
The International Wheelchair Tennis Federation (IWTF) rules are basically the same as regular tennis rules. Players have specially designed sports wheelchairs that are easy to maneuver around the court. The ball is allowed to bounce twice – the second bounce can land outside the court boundaries.

Lessons and coaching
Group lessons are fun for beginners. However, one-to-one coaching will give you a greater understanding of your own abilities and can help you concentrate and develop your own technique. Find a coach who is enthusiastic, knowledgeable, and supportive. A good coach should be capable of teaching tennis to people of all abilities. Ask at your school or local tennis club for information. Alternatively, contact one of the professional associations listed on page 45.

International competition
Playing professional tennis requires absolute dedication, long hours of traveling, and intense training. At tournaments such as the Monte Carlo Open, in France (above), temperatures can soar – players must learn not to let the weather affect their game.

Keeping watch
The International Tennis Federation (ITF) is the overall governing body of the game worldwide. Most countries have their own tennis associations to ensure standard rules are kept and to organize national leagues and tournaments. Some events are so large that many matches are played simultaneously. Sites need to be vast to accommodate the games and crowds. For instance, Wimbledon, London (above), has 14 courts.

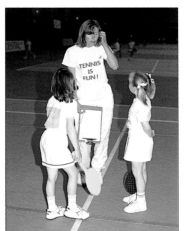

World ranking
Professional players are ranked, or "seeded," by their number of wins. The more wins, the better the seed. Boris Becker of Germany (above) is currently ranked the world men's Number Three seed. Ranking can help the better players make it to the final stages of tournaments.

Major international tournaments

The Grand Slam
This consists of four annual International Open Championships:
The Australian Open in January
The French Open in May/June
The British Open (Wimbledon) in June/July
The US Open in August/September
At each of these four tournaments there is a men's singles winner, a women's singles winner, men's doubles, women's doubles, and mixed doubles winners, and junior winners.

The Davis Cup
Four groups made up of more than 100 nations compete for this trophy throughout the year.

The Federation Cup
The premier team competition in women's tennis. From April to November every year, more than 80 nations battle for promotion within the three groups in the Fed Cup, as it is now known.

Glossary

During your tennis lessons, or when watching tennis, you may find it helpful to understand some of the following terms and phrases.

A

Ace A serve that lands out of reach of the receiver.

Advantage The next point to be won after deuce; advantage server or advantage receiver.

Alley The name given to the space between the parallel lines running down both sides of the tennis court. The outer is the boundary of the doubles court, the inner is the boundary of the singles court.

Approach shot A ground stroke made when running toward the net in expectation of playing a volley.

B

Back court The area behind the baseline.

Backspin See Slice.

Baseline game A method of play in which the player remains at the back of the court.

Block A short, punched ground stroke used to return a quickly traveling ball.

C

Cannonball serve An extremely fast serve of 100 mph (161 kph) or more.

Center mark The 4 in (10.16 cm) line in the middle of the baseline at each end of the court. Also called the "small T."

Center service line Divides the service area into two halves – left and right courts. Also called first and second courts.

Chip A short, sometimes angled, return; usually hit with slice.

Cross court A stroke played diagonally across the court.

D

Default A match is won by default if the opponent is absent or stops play before the match finishes.

Deuce The score whenever players are at 40-40, or have an even score after six points of a game.

Double fault Two successive serving faults, causing the server to lose the point.

Down the line A shot played parallel to the sidelines.

Drive A ground stroke played between waist and shoulder height, in which the ball is driven deep into the opponent's court.

Drop shot A ball hit lightly with underspin that lands just over the other side of the net.

F

Fault A ball that fails to land in the correct court.

Fifteen all The score when each player has scored one point. The word "all" is used instead of "each."

First flight The flight of the ball after it has been struck and before it bounces.

Flat stroke A ball hit without spin.

Follow-through The continuation of the racket after the ball has been struck.

Forecourt The area between the service line and the net.

H

Half volley A stroke where the racket meets the ball at the moment the ball bounces.

L

Let A ball that touches the net after it is served but still falls into the correct area of the opponent's court. The serve is taken again.

Love The tennis term for zero when scoring. Believed to have come from the French *l'oeuf*, meaning egg. It was joked that the zero looked like an egg on the scoreboard.

M

Match point The score when one player needs only one more point to win the match.

N

Net ball A ball that touches the net but remains in play so a rally continues. Also called net cord.

Net game Playing all your shots in an attacking position at the net in order to hurry your opponent and force them to make mistakes.

No man's land The area between the service line and the baseline.

P

Passing shot A shot that sends the ball beyond the reach of an opponent who is attacking from the net.

R

Rally A prolonged series of strokes played back from one player to another.

Retire When a player concedes victory before the completion of a match.

Retrieve To return a ball that is difficult to reach or handle.

Return The stroke that returns the serve. Can also describe any shot during a rally.

S

Second flight The flight of the ball after it has bounced once.

Set There are six games in a set and three sets in a match (five sets for professional male players).

Set up An easy return from which the opponent can hit a winner.

Slice Also called sidespin or backspin. The ball is "sliced" with the racket to spin it sideways and backward. The ball veers slightly in the direction of the spin in flight and more significantly after the bounce. Usually imparted during serve.

Stop volley A volley that absorbs the velocity of the ball and drops it just over the net.

T

Take-back The back swing in preparation for the stroke.

Tiebreak Comes into operation at six games all. The winner is the first to reach seven points (or the first to gain a two-point lead if the tiebreak score reaches six all). A tiebreak is not played in the final set, which must be won by two clear games.

Topspin A forward spin that makes the ball dip in flight and then bounce higher than normal. The top of the ball spins forward in the direction of its flight. Achieved by stroking the racket up behind the back of the ball.

Touch game Tactical play using soft strokes at the net.

More Tennis Rules

When to serve: The server must not serve until the receiver is ready. If the receiver attempts to return the serve, they shall be deemed ready.

Player loses the point:
a. if, in playing the ball, they deliberately carry or catch it on their racket or deliberately touch it with their racket more than once.
b. if the player, their racket, clothing, or anything they are carrying touches the net, the posts, or their opponent's court while the ball is in play.
c. if the player volleys the ball before it has passed the net.
d. if the ball in play touches a player or anything that they are wearing or carrying, except their racket or hands.
e. if they throw their racket and it hits the ball.
f. if they deliberately and materially change the shape of their racket during the playing of the point.

Player hinders opponent: If a player deliberately commits any act that hinders their opponent in making a stroke, then they lose the point. If the act was involuntary, the point should be replayed.

Changing ends: When changing ends, a maximum of one minute 30 seconds shall pass from the moment the ball goes out of play at the end of one game to the time the first ball is struck for the next game.

Time between points: Must not exceed 25 seconds.

Coaching: A player must not receive coaching during a match unless in a team competition.

It is a good return if:
a. the ball is returned outside the posts, provided that it hits the ground within the proper court.
b. a player's racket passes over the net after they have returned the ball, provided the ball passes the net before being played and is properly returned.
c. a player succeeds in returning the ball in play after it has hit another ball lying in the court.

Order of serve: If a player serves out of turn, the player who should have served shall serve as soon as the mistake is discovered. All points scored before such a discovery still stand. If a game is completed before such a discovery, the order of serve shall remain as altered.

Scoring: If there is a disagreement in scores, then both players shall return to the last agreed score.

Index

Useful addresses

These tennis organizations may be able to help you find a local club or coach. Ask at your school as well – it may have its own tennis program.

International Tennis Federation
Bank Lane
Roehampton
London SW15 5XZ
UK
(44) 181-878-6464

Intercollegiate Tennis Association
PO Box 71
Princeton University
Princeton, New Jersey 08544
(609) 258-1686

International Wheelchair Tennis Association
Rue de Talus 112
F92500 Rueil
Malmaison France
(331) 475-20108

Tennis Canada
3111 Steeles Avenue West
Downsview
Ontario M3J 3H2 Canada
(416) 665-9777

National Federation of State High School Associations
11724 N.W. Plaza Circle
Kansas City, Missouri 64195-0626
(816) 464-5400

United States Tennis Association
70 West Red Oak Lane
White Plains, New York 10604-3602
(914) 696-7000

National Foundation of Wheelchair Tennis
940 Calle Amanecer
Ste. B
San Clemente, California 92673
(949) 361-3663

National Junior College Athletic Association/NJCAA
1825 Austin Bluffs Pkwy
Ste. 100
Colorado Springs, Colorado 80918
(719) 590-9788

Steven Vance   Jessica London   Vishal Nayyar   Faye Mason   Nick Hamnabard   Namita Shah   Nick Çava Day

Acknowledgments

DK would like to thank the following people for their kind help in the production of this book:

Kester Jackson, tennis coach, who has been invaluable at every stage of this book's production; All the Young Tennis Players for their skill and enthusiasm during the photographic sessions, also their families; The Parklangley Tennis and Squash Club, Beckenham, Kent, for their help, patience, and hospitality; The Lawn Tennis Association, Wimbledon, London, for providing useful information; Bromley Lawn Tennis and Squash Club, Bromley, Kent, for allowing us the use of their indoor court; Carole Orbell for help during photography sessions; Jason Page for his editorial advice; Chetan Joshi and Floyd Sayers for their design assistance.

Picture credits
Key: c=center; b=bottom; r=right; l=left; t=top.
All Action/ Cholet: back cover
Russ Adams Productions Inc.: 8bc, 8br, 13bl;

Action Plus/Chris Barry: 12b, Mike Hewitt: 42cl; **Allsport UK Ltd.:** 28cr/ Clive Brunskill: 25bc, 32tr, Neale Haynes: 42t, Gray Mortimore: 42cr, Gary M. Prior: 13br, 23tl, 42bc, Chris Raphael: 12c, endpapers; **Colorsport:** 41tr; **Robert Harding Picture Library**/ Adam Woolfitt: 42bl; **Hulton-Deutsch Collection:** 9tl, 9c, 9cr; **Carol L. Newsom:** 8tl, 9br; **Sporting Pictures (UK) Ltd.:** 9bl, 31tr; **Wimbledon Tennis Museum:** 9bc.